# TWO WYCLIFFITE TEXTS

EARLY ENGLISH TEXT SOCIETY
O.S. 301
1993

Capitulum .j. questioun

Knowe be it to alle men þat
reden or heeren þis writinge
byneþe forþ. þat on þe sondai
next aftir þe feste of seint petir
þat we clepen lammasse in þe zeer
of oure lord a þousand foure hun 1407.
drid and seuene. I william of thorp
beynge in þe prisoun in þe castel of sa William of Thorp
ltwode. was brouzt bifore Tom
as of arundel. archebischop of
cauntirburie and chaunceler þanne of Arundel Archbish
ynglond. And whanne I cam
to him. he stood in a greet chaum
bre. and myche peple aboute him.
And whanne he siz me. he wente
in to a pryuy closet. comaundinge alle
seculer men þat sueden him in þidir.
For to goon forþ þennis from him
anoon. so þat no man lefte þanne in
closet no but þe archebischop
him silf and a phisician þat is clepid mal
uerne. persoun of seint dunstane

Oxford, Bodleian Library, MS Rawlinson C.208, f. 8r

# TWO WYCLIFFITE TEXTS

## The Sermon of William Taylor 1406
## The Testimony of William Thorpe 1407

EDITED BY

ANNE HUDSON

*Published for*

THE EARLY ENGLISH TEXT SOCIETY

*by the*

OXFORD UNIVERSITY PRESS

1993

*Oxford University Press, Walton Street, Oxford* OX2 6DP

*Oxford New York Toronto*
*Delhi Bombay Calcutta Madras Karachi*
*Kuala Lumpur Singapore Hong Kong Tokyo*
*Nairobi Dar es Salaam Cape Town*
*Melbourne Auckland Madrid*

*and associated companies in*
*Berlin Ibadan*

*Oxford is a trade mark of Oxford University Press*

*Published in the United States*
*by Oxford University Press Inc., New York*



*British Library Cataloguing in Publication Data*
*Data available*

*ISBN 0 19 722303 6*

*1 3 5 7 9 10 8 6 4 2*

*Typeset by Joshua Associates Ltd, Oxford*
*Printed in Great Britain*
*on acid-free paper by*
*Ipswich Book Company Ltd*

# PREFACE

The present edition represents the first half of work that has been long in progress. The Early English Text Society first accepted a proposal for an edition of Taylor's sermon and of Thorpe's testimony together with two anonymous texts by the same author (a long sermon found in BL Egerton 2820 and three other manuscripts, and the tract in BL Cotton Titus D.v); it became clear, however, that an edition of all four would be unreasonably bulky for a single book. This part is therefore the first installment; the second will appear separately.

I am glad to acknowledge permission to print the two texts here, and to include plates, from manuscripts in the Bodleian Library Oxford. I am also grateful to the authorities of the Prague Metropolitan Chapter Library and of the Österreichische Nationalbibliothek Vienna for access to the manuscripts of the Latin version of Thorpe's testimony; in particular I should like to thank the assistant in the former who facilitated my work in difficult times. I am indebted to the librarians at Brasenose College Oxford and at the Hunterian Library Glasgow who allowed me to consult the copies of the [1530] edition of Thorpe; I was also greatly helped by the temporary deposit of the Blickling Hall copy of the same edition in the Bodleian Library, and for this thanks are due to Mr.John Fuggles, of the National Trust. More generally I wish to express my continuing gratitude to the assistants in the Bodleian Library.

Personal debts for discussion and encouragement are more difficult to enumerate, not least because this edition is part of a longterm interest in Wyclif and his influence. In the last stages of this edition I am indebted to Dr. Marilyn Deegan of the Oxford Computing Service and to the Society's editorial secretary, Professor Malcolm Godden. I am grateful to Dr. Colin Tite for information about the early modern history of the Rawlinson manuscript. To Dr. Ian Doyle I am constantly indebted, for his help both generally and especially on paleographical matters; to Pamela Gradon I am, as always, grateful for her patient interest and encouragement to finish this edition. If this edition had a dedication it would, however, be to the memory of two scholars recently eminent in the Early English Text Society: Norman Davis, who for long guided its path as Director and who also supported my endeavours from my first graduate research, and Eric

Dobson, editor of three volumes in its series and for long a member of the Council, in the hope that he would have considered my editorial policy here at last properly stringent.

# LIST OF CONTENTS

# ABBREVIATIONS

References to unprinted sources, and to printed primary sources, are explained in sections 1–2 of the bibliography. The normal form of reference to printed secondary materials is by author's name, followed in brackets by date of publication, and by page or column numbers; these references are expanded in section 3 of the bibliography.

The main manuscripts and early printed text edited here are referred to under the following sigla:

A: the [1530] edition of Thorpe's testimony
D: Oxford, Bodleian Library MS Douce 53, Taylor's sermon
P: Prague, Metropolitan Chapter Library O.29, Latin text of Thorpe's testimony
R: Oxford, Bodleian Library MS Rawlinson C.208, English text of Thorpe's testimony
V: Vienna, Österreichische Nationalbibliothek MS 3936, Latin text of Thorpe's testimony

Throughout the edition line numbers prefixed by T refer to Taylor's sermon, those prefixed by H refer to the Sermon of the Horsedoun in Appendix I; line numbers without prefix refer to Thorpe's testimony.

The following abbreviations, and abbreviated titles of frequently cited works (details of which appear in the bibliography) have been used:

| | |
|---|---|
| *ALD* | See *An Apology for Lollard Doctrines* |
| *BIHR* | *Bulletin of the Institute of Historical Research* (London, 1923–) |
| *BJRL* | *Bulletin of the John Rylands Library* (Manchester, 1903–) |
| BL | British Library London |
| *Cal. Pap. Letters* | *Calendar of Papal Letters* |
| *CCCM* | *Corpus Christianorum, Continuatio Medievalis* (Turnholt, 1952–) |
| *CCR* | *Calendar of Close Rolls* |
| *CPR* | *Calendar of Patent Rolls* |
| CS | Camden Series (London, 1838–) |
| *CT* | Chaucer's *Canterbury Tales* |

| | |
|---|---|
| CUL | Cambridge University Library |
| CYS | Canterbury and York Society (London, 1907–) |
| *Doct.* | *Doctrinale* . . . by Netter of Walden, Thomas |
| EETS | Early English Text Society (London, 1864–); OS Original Series; ES Extra Series; SS Supplementary Series; where no indication of series is given, the Original Series is implied. |
| *EHR* | *English Historical Review* (London, 1886–) |
| Emden *Cambridge* | See Emden (1963) |
| Emden *Oxford* | See Emden (1957–9) |
| EV | Early Version of the Wycliffite bible |
| *EWS* | *English Wycliffite Sermons* |
| FM | See Forshall and Madden |
| *FZ* | *Fasciculi Zizaniorum* |
| *Gl.G.* | *Glossed Gospels* |
| *GO* | *Glossa Ordinaria* (Antwerp, 1617) |
| GP | General Prologue to the Wycliffite bible |
| *HBC* | *Handbook of British Chronology*, ed. E. B. Fryde *et al.* (London, 3rd ed., 1986). |
| *HF* | Chaucer's *House of Fame* |
| *JEH* | *Journal of Ecclesiastical History* (London, 1950–) |
| *LL* | *Lanterne of Li3t* |
| *LP* | *Letters and Papers, Foreign and Domestic, Henry VIII*, ed. J. S. Brewer *et al.* (21 vols. and Addenda, London, 1862–1932). |
| LV | Later Version of the Wycliffite bible |
| *MC* | *Of Mynystris in þe Chirche*, ed. *EWS* ii.328–65. |
| MED | *Middle English Dictionary*, ed. H. Kurath, S. M. Kuhn *et al.* (Ann Arbor, 1952–) |
| More *CW* | *The Complete Works of St Thomas More* |
| ns | new series |
| *ODCC* | *The Oxford Dictionary of the Christian Church*, ed. F. L. Cross (Oxford, 2nd edition, 1974). |
| *OED* | *Oxford English Dictionary* (13 vols., Oxford, reissued 1933). |
| *Op. Ard.* | *Opus Arduum*, see Brno University Library MS Mk 28 |
| *PG* | *Patrologia Graeca*, ed. J. P. Migne (Paris, 1857–66) |
| *PL* | *Patrologia Latina*, ed. J. P. Migne (Paris, 1841–) |
| *PPl* | *Piers Plowman* |

| | |
|---|---|
| *PPl. Crede* | *Pierce the Ploughman's Crede* |
| *PR* | See Hudson (1988) |
| Ps. Bodley 288, Ps. Bodley 877, Ps. Lambeth, Ps. Royal | Wycliffite revisions of Rolle's English Psalter commentary, found respectively in MSS Bodley 288, Bodley 877, Lambeth Palace 34, BL Royal 18 C.xxvi |
| *Rot.Parl.* | *Rotuli Parliamentorum* (7 vols., London, 1832) |
| RS | Rolls Series (London, 1858–1911) |
| *SC* | *A Summary Catalogue of Western Manuscripts in the Bodleian Library at Oxford* (Oxford, 1895–1953) |
| *SCH* | *Studies in Church History* (London, 1964–) |
| *SEWW* | *Selections from English Wycliffite Writings* |
| STC | *A Short-Title Catalogue of Books printed in England, Scotland and Ireland and of English Books printed abroad 1475–1640*, ed. A. W. Pollard and G. R. Redgrave, revised W. A. Jackson, F. S. Ferguson and K. F. Pantzer (2 vols., I-Z London, 1976, A-H London, 1986) |
| TCC | Trinity College Cambridge |
| TCD | Trinity College Dublin |
| Thomson (with page) | See Thomson, J. A. F. (1965) |
| Thomson (with no.) | See Thomson, W. R. (1983) |
| *VO* | *Vae Octuplex*, ed. *EWS* ii.366–78. |
| Walsingham, *Chron. Angl.* | Walsingham, *Chronicon Anglie* |
| Walsingham, *Hist. Angl.* | Walsingham, *Historia Anglicana* |
| WB | Wycliffite Bible |
| Wilkins | *Concilia Magnae Britanniae et Hiberniae A. D. 446–1717*, ed. D. Wilkins (4 vols., London, 1737) |

Wyclif works:

| | |
|---|---|
| *De apos.* | *De apostasia* |
| *De civ. dom.* | *De civili dominio* (3 vols.) |
| *De eccl.* | *De ecclesia* |
| *De euch.* | *De eucharistia* |
| *De man.* | *De mandatis* |
| *De pot. pap.* | *De potestate pape* |
| *Opus evan.* | *Opus evangelicum* (2 vols.) |
| *Pol. wks.* | *Polemical Works* (2 vols.) |
| *Serm.* | *Sermones* (4 vols.) |

# INTRODUCTION

## 1. THE SERMON OF WILLIAM TAYLOR

### MANUSCRIPT

The sermon survives in a single manuscript only.

*Bodleian Library MS Douce 53 (SC 21627)* s.xv[1]

32 parchment leaves, size 148mm by 105mm; ruled in two columns of 21 lines each; written space 100mm by 71mm. Collation: ii paper flyleaves, 1–4[8], ii paper flyleaves; medieval quire signatures b–c survive on some leaves of the third and fourth gatherings; catchwords survive.

1. ff. 1–30 inc. *Here bigynneþ a sermoun of maistir Wiliam Taylour Unde ememus* . . .; ends two-thirds of the way down second column on f. 30.

2. ff. 30–32ᵛ straight on from the last *Here eendiþ þis sermoun and bigynneþ þe sermoun of þe horsedoun Omnis arbor* . . .; ends incomplete on f. 32ᵛ *now in heerynge now* (catchwords) *in talkinge*.

The modern pencil foliation is followed here. An earlier foliation in ink starts on f. 1 at '44' and continues to '75' on f. 32. The quire signatures suggest that nothing has been lost at the beginning of the manuscript as that was originally designed; if the ink foliation was ever correct (and there seems no reason to doubt this), it must have been appropriate when another manuscript was bound before this.

The manuscript has suffered badly from damp at its outer edges and, to judge by the discolouration on ff. 1 and 32ᵛ, from being unbound for some time. Parts of col. 2 on f. 1 and col. 1 of f. 32ᵛ are virtually illegible without ultra-violet light. The manuscript was well written, with headings in red, red underlining of biblical quotations, red touching of capitals and some other letters and blue paraph marks. The initial of the Latin text for each sermon is in blue with red flourishing.

There are no marks of medieval or later ownership save the note on the first paper flyleaf in Douce's handwriting 'F. Douce 1827 The gift of Mʳ. Laing.' Madan in *SC* 21627 suggested that Mʳ Laing was Robert

Lang, but E. W. B. Nicholson in an added note preferred David Laing who corresponded with Douce at least as early as 1830.[1]

There is a transcript of considerable extracts from the manuscript in archbishop Ussher's collections in Trinity College Dublin MS 775 (olim D.3.4), ff. 128$^{v}$–129$^{v}$. That it was the manuscript now Douce 53, and not another copy of Taylor's sermon, is clear from the fact that the extracts continue into the sermon of the *Horsedoun* and end at line 28 of that sermon, just before the badly damaged final leaf of the book.[2] Equally, medieval spellings preserved in Ussher's transcript correspond with spellings in Douce 53. This makes it clear that the book was mutilated and in its present state by the end of the seventeenth century. Unfortunately, Ussher's notes do not reveal where the manuscript was at the time he saw it. Two other manuscripts from which extracts are transcribed into the same notebook were in London: the Alnwick courtbook (now Westminster Cathedral Diocesan Archives B.2) is said to have been in *Bibliotheca Lambethana* (f. 119),[3] and a copy of Pecock's *Poore Mennis Myrrour* (f. 126$^{v}$)[4] was in the possession of *Mr.Smith of Lincolns inne*. It may be reasonable to think that Douce 53 was also in London, but this hardly elucidates much.

The second item in MS Douce 53, the *Sermoun of þe Horsedoun*, is the only surviving part of this sermon. It seems likely, however, that the sermon is identifiable with a text owned by the heretic John Claydon, and mentioned in the material concerning his trial in 1415 found in archbishop Chichele's episcopal register.[5] Claydon is said to have valued a book he owned *propter unum sermonem alias predicatum apud Horsaldowne qui erat scriptus in libro illo*.[6] This book seems to have been the same as that which contained the *Lanterne of Liȝt*, whose heretical content formed the case against Claydon and which is described therefore in much greater detail, and also a commentary on the ten commandments. It is said that the book had been brought to Claydon

[1] For Laing's career as a bookseller and editor of Scottish texts see D. Murray, *David Laing Antiquary and Bibliographer* (Glasgow, 1915); note p. 16 where Laing's activities as a bookseller until 1837 are noted. See also A. N. L. Munby, *Connoisseurs and Medieval Miniatures 1750—1850* (Oxford, 1972), pp. 35–56 and esp. p. 51 for Douce's collection.

[2] Marks in Douce 53 were the indications to Ussher's amanuensis of the extracts to be copied.

[3] See Tanner (1977), especially pp. 5–6.

[4] The text survives now in only one copy, BL Additional 37788; it has not been edited in this form, but is related to the first part of the *Donet*, for which see the edition by E. V. Hitchcock (EETS 156, 1921), p. xxi.

[5] Chichele reg. iv.132–8; for comments on Claydon, his earlier career and his trial, see *PR* pp. 211–14.

[6] Quotation at p. 133.

in unbound quires by one John Gryme, who had written it at Claydon's expense; Claydon had then had it bound in red leather. Claydon admitted that he could not himself read, but that another had read the material to him. The surviving manuscript is not part of that volume, since Claydon's books were burnt with their owner on 10 September 1415 at Smithfield. The date at which the *Horsedoun* sermon was preached is uncertain, save that it must have been prior to Claydon's trial in 1415. The text with which it begins is part of the gospel for the 8th Sunday after Trinity; the sermon was almost certainly intended for that occasion. The sermon takes its name from the place where it was preached, now Horsleydown in the parish of St.Olave's Southwark.[1] The fragment is edited in appendix I.

### THE OCCASION OF TAYLOR'S SERMON

The text of Taylor's sermon derives from John 6:5, the beginning of the gospel used in the Sarum liturgy for the 25th Sunday after Trinity, a gospel used whatever the number of Sundays after Trinity for the Sunday next before Advent. It is plain from line 2 that the sermon was preached on such a Sunday. Lines 719ff make it clear that 1405 years had passed before the preaching of the sermon (see note to that line for the computation); this would suggest that the sermon was preached on the Sunday next before Advent in the year 1406, namely 21 November.

In the *St.Alban's Chronicle* it is recorded that during the parliament of 1406 William Taylor, a master of arts from Oxford, preached *apud Crucem* in London the opinions and conclusions of Wyclif; Taylor is described as *quidam adulator Londoniis*.[2] Parliament sat in 1406 at various sessions between 1 March and 22 December.[3] The 'Cross' mentioned is (as will be confirmed below) fairly certainly the celebrated St.Paul's Cross.[4] Taylor is said by the chronicler to have preached against clerical possessions and in favour of temporal lords; he urged that the religious should not own worldly possessions and that in certain circumstances these may be removed by temporal lords and, adds the writer, *plura deliramenta alia*. Lines 98ff, 221ff and 234ff of the sermon printed here attest the detailed charges of the chronicler. There seems no reason to doubt that the sermon preserved in Douce 53 is a copy of the sermon described by the *Chronicle*.

[1] See Stow, *Survey of London* ii.52.

[2] *St.Alban's Chron*. pp. 1–2.

[3] See *HBC* p. 566.

[4] For the later history of this site, see M. MacLure, *The Paul's Cross Sermons 1534–1642* (Toronto, 1958).

It is clear that Taylor's sermon on 21 November 1406 caused a considerable stir. The *St.Alban's Chronicle* continues to describe how the following day master Alkerton preached in the same place, refuted all of Taylor's arguments and showed all plunderers of church property to be anathema.[1] Whilst Alkerton's answer pleased the Benedictine of St.Alban's, it met with less favour from some of the assembled laity. One Robert Waterton sent his servant to Alkerton to offer him a curry comb as a flatterer of prelates. News of this insult reached archbishop Arundel, who swore that Waterton should pay for this shame to the preacher. The King heard of the archbishop's wrath; he allowed that the prelate should do his duty, but urged him to curb his temper. Arundel demanded that Waterton should seek pardon in the publicity of parliament, and should swear there to stand by the claims of the church. The King pleaded for Waterton, and persuaded Arundel to commute the penance to one less public: Waterton was to do private penance, and his servant was to carry a curry comb in one hand and a candle in the other, and to precede the procession on certain days. In this colourful story it should be remembered that Waterton was one of Henry IV's lifelong friends: he had landed with Henry Bolingbroke in 1399, in 1405 raised troops with Westmoreland for Henry and acted as one of the King's executors at his death.[2] He was a member of the 1406 parliament, but he did not appear at the session on 26 November.[3]

There are two other pieces of evidence which bear out the truth of the chronicler's narrative. The first is the allusion to the events of the sermon in Thorpe's autobiography, lines 1961ff. Taylor is not there mentioned by name. But it is made plain that Alkerton at St.Paul's Cross was preaching in answer to an unnamed Lollard speaker, a *clerk of Oxenford*. It appears that Waterton was not the only one to object to Alkerton's reply: Thorpe too seems after the sermon to have accosted Alkerton and called him *fals flaterer and ypocrite*. Interestingly, Thorpe alleged that the Lollard's sermon was known in both Latin and English form, and was possessed by many; this suggests that Taylor's

[1] The *Chronicle* gives Alkerton's first name as *Thomas* (p. 2/2), but this is a mistake for *Richard*; see below p. xvi. For Alkerton see Emden *Oxford* i.25, and below.

[2] See Jacob (1961), pp. 2, 53, 63 and cf. McNiven (1987), pp. 77, 102; Waterton is named as executor in Chichele reg. iv.128. For his offices held in the Duchy of Lancaster from Richard II's reign through to his death on 17 January 1425 see R. Somerville, *History of the Duchy of Lancaster* i (London, 1953), 137, 174, 176, 378–9, 417–19, 515, 528–9, 533, 563, 573.

[3] Jacob (1961), p. 100.

opening sermon had made as much impact as Alkerton's reply. Thorpe also alludes to an appearance of the Lollard before Arundel to answer for his sermon (1985–9). This allusion is partially borne out by Arundel's register: a citation there, dated 9 March 1409/10, calls for Taylor to appear before the archbishop within fifteen days and notes that Taylor is under penalty for contumacy for failing to appear *per triennium* on a similar charge.[1] Reference is made within the citation to a sermon preached by Taylor at St.Paul's Cross *non* ... *diu* to the people, in which, amongst other *grauia et enormia*, Taylor had urged, and had supported his opinion by scriptural citations, that the possessions of the church might be forcibly removed from it *quasi per violentam cedicionem populi*.[2] Whether this sermon is one and the same as that in November 1406, or a later repeat performance when Taylor expressed the same opinions, it is clear that from 1406 onwards Arundel had attempted to bring him to book for his Wycliffism. Arundel's clerk in Thorpe's account implies (1979–80) that Taylor had been too frightened to defend his sermon. Thorpe suggests that Taylor had defended his views before Arundel;[3] but all the other available evidence indicates that Taylor never appeared. In 1420 at his first investigation before Chichele, it is reported that Taylor had been excommunicated by Arundel for his failure to answer the archbishop's summons, and that Taylor had been under sentence of excommunication for fourteen years—a time that would take the sentence back to 1406 or 1407.[4] The probability would seem to be that Taylor preached only the one sermon at St.Paul's Cross, on 21 November 1406, that Arundel soon after called him to account, but that either Taylor did not respond at all (Thorpe's assertion that he did being due to either wishful thinking or confusion), or that he appeared once but failed to reappear when cited again.[5] Having excommunicated Taylor for his non-appearance in the early months of 1407, Arundel tried again to bring him to trial in March 1410; this attempt once more failed.

It is unfortunate that we do not have the reply of Alkerton which obviously contributed to the popular outcry after Taylor's sermon, and doubtless contributed to that sermon's repute. Tantalisingly,

[1] Lambeth reg. Arundel ii, ff. 118v-119.

[2] The renewed interest in Taylor's case in 1410, and the specification of this particular view, was perhaps the result of the presentation of the Lollard Disendowment Bill in that year (see *SEWW* no. 27 and notes, *PR* pp. 114–15).

[3] See lines 1985–9.

[4] Chichele reg. iii.157–8, and below p. xvii.

[5] Kightly (1975), p. 251 suggests the second.

there is in BL MS Additional 37677, ff.57–61 the end of a sermon said to have been preached by *Maistir Richard Alkarton* at St.Mary Spitel in Easter week 1406[1]; a Latin version of the entire sermon is found in Trinity College Oxford MS 42, ff.56–9.[2] If *Eestir woke* has its proper meaning, this dates the sermon between 12 and 17 April 1406; in fact, the text, preserved only in the Latin version but clear from a reference in the English, was Luke 24:18, and this identifies the occasion as Monday 12 April 1406. This means that the reference within the English sermon to a discussion of treachery to God *as I seide late in a sermoun at Poules Cros* must be to an earlier appearance of Alkerton there and not to the sermon that angered Waterton and Thorpe.[3] Alkerton was, like Taylor, an Oxford graduate. Indeed, in that he was a member of Merton College between 1373 and 1387 and subsequently rented a room in Queen's College from 1398 to 1400, he followed to some extent the steps of Wyclif twenty years previously. His preaching against Taylor may well have gained in ferocity precisely because of his experiences in Oxford: Merton men continued to show sympathy towards their old alumnus long after his condemnation in 1382.[4] By the time of his sermon in November 1407 Alkerton held the living of Hartfield in Sussex, was a canon of Chichester cathedral and held the prebendary of Wightring. Though by contemporary standards not an

[1] St.Mary Spitel was in Bishopsgate ward, at the north east extremity of the city of London. Stow i.167 noted that a 'Pulpit Crosse ... somewhat like to that in *Paules* Church yard' still survived to his day in the churchyard, and reports how an old custom also survived for 'some especiall learned man, by appoyntment of the Prelats' to preach on Good Friday, and three similar clerics preached on Monday, Tuesday and Wednesday of the week following, whilst another learned man gave a review of these four sermons at St.Paul's Cross on Low Sunday; at all of these five sermons the mayor of London and aldermen were accustomed to be present.

[2] Dr. Veronica O'Mara is preparing an edition of both English and Latin texts, to be published in the series *Leeds Texts and Monographs*. Owst (1926), p. 24 n. 1 notes the Latin version. A brief account of the manuscript is given in H. O. Coxe, *Catalogus Codicum MSS. qui in Collegiis Aulisque Oxoniensibus hodie adservantur* (Oxford, 1862), ii. Trinity 16–17. Ff. 1–89[v] contain a collection of sermons in Latin, of varying lengths and occasions (though the first group covers with some regularity the Sundays between 1 Advent and Easter). Immediately before the Alkerton sermon is a copy of Thomas of Wimbledon's *Redde racionem villicacionis tue* sermon in Latin (not recorded in I. K. Knight's edition (Pittsburgh, 1967), pp. 18–20). The collection of sermons is headed with a dedication of the work by 'dominus W. de O[.]kston sacri Collegii Cicestrie canonice siue sacris religionis professor', where the name is defaced by a small hole. I have not been able to trace a canon of Chichester in the fifteenth century whose name could be assimilated to any possible reconstruction of this.

[3] For the quotation see f. 59. The Latin version, f. 57[v], gives a slightly less specific reference *sicut tarde dixi et semper crescunt proditores*, perhaps because the copy was made later.

[4] See *PR* pp. 88–92.

outrageous pluralist, Alkerton would not be likely to sympathise with the more radical ideas of Taylor for disendowment.

### TAYLOR'S CAREER

In 1406 William Taylor was only at the beginning of a long struggle with the contemporary hierarchy of the church. He seems to have been a Worcestershire man, but he first appears in a rental of 1405–6 named as the Principal of St.Edmund Hall Oxford.[1] How long he held this position is uncertain, but another is named in 1408.[2] It might be thought that he could hardly have escaped Arundel so long had he returned to the university after his sermon, but it should be remembered that the period 1406–11 saw the university's attempts to resist the visitations of both the bishop of Lincoln and of Arundel himself,[3] and that one of Taylor's successors as principal of St.Edmund Hall was Peter Payne, an equally ardent and outspoken Lollard.[4] Oxford might at that time have been one of the safer resorts for Wycliffites. Certainly Taylor seems to have escaped further notice for more than ten years, even though he apparently never recanted.[5] Perhaps strangely in view of his earlier opinions, he is not recorded amongst the investigations into the Oldcastle revolt.

Taylor next appeared before archbishop Chichele on 12 February 1420. To judge by the record, Chichele's main legal accusation against him at that point was his longstanding status as an excommunicate for fourteen years. By 1420 suspicions about his orthodoxy were rife: 'pro tali lollardo apud clerum et populum erat et est publice diffamatus et reputatus'.[6] Taylor showed himself suitably contrite and willing to do penance for his contumacy; on 14 February he was absolved from his excommunication, and told to reappear at the next convocation to receive penance; if he were prevented from appearing personally, he should send a deputy.[7] The description of the abasement required of

[1] A number of clerics of this name appear in the register of bishop Wakefield of Worcester (1375–95), but none can certainly be identified with the man here in question.

[2] See Emden *Oxford* iii.1852 and in more detail Emden (1968), pp. 125–35, 143, 271.

[3] See *PR* pp. 82–5, 99–103 and references there given, especially Snappe pp. 95–115.

[4] Emden (1968), pp. 133–54 and *PR* pp. 99–102.

[5] See the statement (mentioned above p. xv) in Chichele's register iii.158 that in 1420 Taylor had been excommunicate for fourteen years.

[6] Chichele reg. iii.158. Variants from a second copy of the material is printed from ff. $335^{v}$–7 at iv.203.

[7] Chichele reg. iii.157–9.

Taylor before his conditional release is long and elaborate: in the course of it Taylor had to swear not to hold, preach, teach or maintain anything contrary to the determination of the church, and 'omnemque errorem et heresim abjuravit et anathematizavit.'[1] No list of the tenets that Taylor had held is, however, given. The procedure was notwithstanding regarded by Chichele as a full legal abjuration, and is so described by the archbishop on Taylor's subsequent appearance before him.[2]

Specific charges against Taylor do emerge from a letter of purgation granted to him only four months later by the prior of Worcester, John de Fordham, acting for bishop Morgan of Worcester on 20 June 1420.[3] There it is stated that Taylor, of Aston Somerfeld, or later Somervyle (i.e. Aston Summerville, Glos.) in the Worcester diocese, had preached on Whitsunday 1417 (30 May 1417) at Norton Underhill in the same diocese and county[4] and elsewhere various erroneous and heretical opinions: notably, that images in the churches are not to be honoured by the people, that if people fast on bread and water on the vigils of Sts. Peter and Paul and of St.John the Baptist they have no need of other confession, and that Taylor held such opinions and encouraged others to do so against the dignity of the king and the statute ordained at Leicester. Taylor, it is said, had been accused by twelve men in the secular court; subsequently he had been captured and imprisoned in Worcester castle by a justice of the king, and had been handed over to the clerical authorities for investigation. Taylor denied all the charges.

The sequence of events both between Taylor's sermon in May 1417 and his appearance before Chichele in February 1420, and between his release by Chichele and subsequent presence before Morgan's officials in June 1420, is far from clear. Chichele's enquiries do not mention a prior investigation by Morgan, though one would be expected if Taylor's activities in Worcestershire were the reason for his arrest; it is surprising also that the process does not mention the specific allegations of doctrinal irregularity. Equally, the letter of purgation issued by Morgan's deputy does not refer to any investigation

[1] Chichele reg. iii.159.

[2] Chichele reg. iii.68.

[3] Worcester reg. Morgan p. 27.

[4] The identification of this place is uncertain: Kightly (1975) p. 252 suggests it might be Bredons Norton, just north of Bredon, where there was certainly a chapel in medieval times. Alternatively, it might have been Norton Subedge, currently just over the border in Gloucestershire. Either hamlet is within ten miles of Aston Summerville.

by Chichele, nor to the longstanding sentence of excommunication against Taylor with which the archbishop was apparently so concerned. The Worcester document appears to imply that Taylor was released following his production of compurgators, and that the letter was issued in response to that.[1]

For the moment, in any event, Taylor in June 1420 was freed. On 7 August 1420, however, bishop Morgan received letters from the mayor and sheriffs of Bristol complaining that Thomas Drayton, rector of Holy Trinity, in a sermon in the cemetery of St.Augustine's monastery in the city, and William Taylor in sermons at Holy Trinity itself, had both preached heresy; according to the current legislation, Taylor and Drayton had been sought out and had been arrested. The bishop's investigation of the case extended through August and September.[2]

The association with Drayton reveals clearly that Taylor was by no means an isolated preacher in the west. Drayton's career in Lollardy goes back at least to the Oldcastle revolt.[3] At that point he was rector of Drayton Beauchamp in Buckinghamshire, a living in the patronage of the Cheyne family; three of the Cheyne family partipated in the revolt, Roger the father who probably died in the Tower awaiting sentence, the sons John and Thomas, both excluded from the first pardon but eventually pardoned.[4] Drayton was evidently heavily implicated in gaining support for the revolt by his preaching in the Buckinghamshire area; he eventually appeared before bishop Repingdon on 27 May 1415, but was pardoned and resumed his benefice.[5] In January 1416, however, he exchanged it for the parish of Holy Trinity in Bristol.[6] Drayton's activities there make it plain that the move was intended to give him more freedom for maneouvre—he was leaving an area where his sympathies were too well-known to the authorities for another where he would be less familiar, but where his views would meet ready ears.

[1] Thomson (pp. 24–5) implies that Taylor was investigated for his 1417 sermon that same year, but that he was probably in hiding and was arrested in 1420 and taken straight to Chichele. This, however, does not seem consonant with the statement in the Morgan register that Taylor was brought from Worcester castle to the bishop.

[2] Worcester reg. Morgan pp. 33–8; at p. 36 it emerges that Drayton had been questioned on 13 August.

[3] PRO Pardon Roll C.67 no.37, m.59; KB 9/209 no.45.

[4] See Thomson pp. 53–4; the family was also related to that of Sir John Cheyne, added by Walsingham to his list of Lollard knights (see McFarlane (1972), esp. pp. 148–9, 163; and Aston (1984[1]), p. 47).

[5] No record of this appearance is found in Repingdon's Lincoln register; it emerges during Drayton's later trial before Chichele (his reg. iii.107).

[6] Worcester reg. Peverell pp. 152–3.

In the course of bishop Morgan's enquiries in August 1420 it emerged that Drayton had used Taylor virtually as a curate. Drayton denied the charges that he had allowed Taylor to deputise for him and had effectually given the cure into Taylor's hands; he likewise denied that he himself had preached against the adoration of images, vocal prayer and the prayers of religious. He admitted, however, that he had 'diverted the church' to Taylor, though he had known Taylor to be a heretic and Lollard of long standing (*ab antiquo*). Drayton's pleas seem to have been credited, since he was allowed to purge himself. That the bishop should not have believed Drayton's specious reasoning (the difference between the charge, which Drayton admitted, that he had 'diverted the church' to Taylor, and those which he denied, that he had allowed Taylor to deputise for him and had 'given his cure into Taylor's keeping' is surely a hair-splitting one)[1] is evident both from Drayton's later career and more immediately from the questionable nature of at least one of his compurgators, John Mybbes—Mybbes's arrest in Oxford had been ordered in 1414 for his suspected incitement of support for the Oldcastle revolt.[2] At this point, however, Drayton seems to have escaped by feigning penitence. At the same time it was objected against Taylor that he had participated in the diversion of Drayton's cure to himself; his sermons are described as 'plebem et populum quasi ad insurrectiones periculosius incitant'. No further details are given of Morgan's investigation of Taylor.[3] Doubtless because of Taylor's recent record, Morgan decided to follow the provisions of the 1416 provincial constitution, and remit the case to convocation.[4]

At this point of necessity Drayton and Taylor parted, Drayton apparently to return, albeit briefly, to his cure at Holy Trinity Bristol,[5] Taylor to committal to the bishop's prison. Morgan, even if he

[1] Though it may have prevented Drayton from necessarily incurring condemnation under the terms of the 1408 Constitutions (the *statuta regia contra predicatores* is mentioned p. 35).

[2] For Mybbes see Emden *Oxford* ii.1332; the other compurgators were nine laymen of Bristol, John Wylle clerk of St. John and St. Laurence Bristol, and John Bele rector of St. Helen's Worcester.

[3] Worcester reg. Morgan p. 37.

[4] Chichele reg. iii.18–19 and cf. i.cxxxii.

[5] Drayton left Bristol soon in February 1422 for Staines (Worcester reg. Morgan p. 91), and by December 1422 he was exchanging the benefice of Staines for the rectory of Snave, near Tenterden in Kent (Chichele reg. i.207). In June 1425 Drayton was again in trouble for heresy; despite convocation's knowledge of his longstanding commitment, he was allowed to abjure once more, found security for his good behaviour, and was released (Chichele reg. iii.107–9). Five weeks after this trial, Drayton moved cure again, this time to Herne, a benefice in the archbishop's gift (i.227).

had been fooled by Drayton, was evidently now better informed about Taylor. He produced him during the meeting of the Canterbury convocation the following year, on 24 May 1421, and with him a list of three errors : that Taylor had preached in Bristol that whoever hangs anything written around his neck takes away the honour due to God alone and submits to the devil, that Christ is not to be prayed to in his humanity but only in his divinity, and that the saints in heaven are not to be invoked by the people.[1] Confronted with this evidence, Taylor denied that he had preached and defended them, but agreed that he had written and communicated the second and third; he then 'extraxit de sinu suo quasdam auctoritates et dicta doctorum in quadam papiri cedula scripta'.[2] The matter was referred to three clerks, who were to consider the views and report back the following Monday. The clerks duly reported that they considered the views heretical, and Taylor agreed with them.[3] Chichele reminded Taylor and convocation that Taylor had only recently been absolved from the excommunication incurred under Arundel, and produced the process of abjuration. Perpetual imprisonment was considered a suitable punishment in the light of this further evidence of heresy. But, because Taylor showed some signs of penitence, and subject to the production of security *in cancellaria regia* with which the royal chancellor should be satisfied, he might be released from Morgan's prison. Taylor was returned to Morgan, *nisi securitatem invenire posset coram Cancellario Anglie*.[4] Apparently he did find security, since on 2 June 1421 sureties were given by four men, on pain of a fine of £100, that Taylor would appear within fifteen days before the council if summoned, and that 'he would henceforth preach or teach no error or heresy'.[5]

On 11 February 1423 Taylor was once more produced before Chichele and other bishops and clerics. It seems that he must have been released after the investigation of May 1421, since he is described as *iterum arrestatus propter heresim*. This time the evidence against him was *certa folia papiri scripta*, which Taylor agreed to be in his handwriting and to have been communicated by him to a priest, Thomas

[1] Chichele reg. iii.67–8 and again 160–61.

[2] Loc. cit. p. 67.

[3] Loc. cit. p. 68.

[4] Loc. cit. pp. 68–9, 160–1. The Chancellor at this date was Thomas Langley, bishop of Durham (*HBC* p. 87).

[5] *CCR 1419—22*, p. 199; the sureties were John Sengelton 'gentilman' of Chart (Kent), and three artisans from the London area.

Smith, in Bristol.[1] The paper is reproduced *de verbo ad verbum* in the register. It consists of a reply to Smith's refutation of an argument in favour of the proposition that all prayer is to be directed to God alone, adducing many biblical quotations and passages from Augustine and Bernard in support.[2] The paper was copied and sent to representatives of the four orders of friars. On 20 February five Dominican, three Franciscan and six Carmelite friars (amongst them Thomas Netter) agreed that the document was heretical; Peter Partrich, canon of Lincoln, agreed on behalf of the secular clergy. Four articles were extracted from the text : that all prayer for any supernatural gift was to be directed to God alone; that all prayer was to be to God only; that to pray to any creature is idolatry; that the faithful should never direct prayer to Christ in his humanity, only in his divinity.[3] To make doubly sure, Chichele sent these four summary articles to the doctors of divinity of the four orders of friars, who on 25 February again stated them heretical.[4] Chichele then turned to the jurists and asked them about Taylor's position with regard to relapse. Lyndwood gave his view that one who had failed to answer a charge of heresy must be deeply suspect, and that one who stood under sentence of excommunication for a year must be regarded as condemned as a heretic; if such a person appeared and was prepared to abjure, he should be given mercy to the extent of not being handed over to the secular arm, though he might be punished by the bishop; such a person, having abjured heresy, if he fell again into heresy must be adjudged a relapse and handed over to the secular arm without hope of mercy and without hearing by the secular power. The other jurists present agreed with this view.[5] From this it would appear that Taylor could hardly hope to escape the fire—and, indeed, that he had been lucky to have escaped it in 1421.[6]

[1] Loc. cit. pp. 161–2. Kightly (1975), p. 258 suggests he is to be identified with the man of the same name who was chaplain at a chantry in St. Nicholas's church, near that of Holy Trinity, Broad Street Bristol (see *Notes on the Wills in the Great Orphan Book and Book of Wills in the Council House at Bristol*, ed. T. P. Wadley (Bristol, 1886), pp. 69, 71, 73). It should be noted, however, that the dates of the documents in which he is mentioned are 1404 and 1405, substantially earlier than Taylor's communication.

[2] Loc. cit. pp. 162–6; the patristic quotations are identified in the notes.

[3] Loc. cit. pp. 166–8.

[4] Loc. cit. p. 168.

[5] Loc. cit. pp. 168–9.

[6] For Jacob's comments, see Chichele reg. i.cxxxiv-cxxxv. Jacob takes Lyndwood's point concerning the implications of a year's excommunication to indicate that Taylor had been excommunicated following his paper to Thomas Smith; it seems more likely, and more in accord with the chronology suggested by the sequence of Lyndwood's comments, that the point goes right back to Taylor's excommunication under Arundel.

At this stage, on 26 February, yet more evidence was produced against Taylor. Richard Flemyng, bishop of Lincoln, read in public a list of five articles which Taylor was said to hold and to defend, articles that are clearly much more incriminating than views about prayer to saints: that civil dominion was identical with secular, and as such so imperfect that it was not legitimate to combine with a priest's perfection; that the common method of begging used by the friars was damnable; that anyone making offerings to the cross or to any saint commits idolatry; that even though such opinions may be condemned by the Council of Constance, they are catholic and approved by Christ; that God does not actively but only permissively wish kings and princes, even if they are good men, to rule over his subjects and their realms and temporal domains. Taylor agreed that he held, and continued to hold, the first four, but denied the fifth.[1] Chichele then summoned Partriche, and in his presence, asked Flemyng if he had ever heard Taylor affirm the last article; Flemyng replied that he had done so on 11 February in the chapel of the bishop's inn *apud vetus templum*, and that he had written it down with his own hand; Partriche concurred in all this.[2] It is tempting to think that Taylor's indiscretion before Flemyng and Partriche was the result of their Oxford acquaintance: both Flemyng and Partriche flirted briefly with Wycliffite views in their early careers there.[3]

Taylor was given time for consideration, but the following day after further consultations was sentenced as an obdurate and relapsed heretic. On 1 March at St.Paul's he was degraded, handed over to the secular arm and the following day burnt at Smithfield.[4]

The case is recorded with notable amplitude in Chichele's register, and the account can be filled out a little more from comments in Netter's *Doctrinale*. In the sixth book, especially in chapter 108, is found some of the discussion between Taylor and his investigators.[5] The discussion apparently relates to the views discussed from the schedule produced on 11 February 1423, though the first biblical passage cited by Netter is not quoted there. This was Romans 15:30

[1] Loc. cit. pp. 169–70.

[2] Loc. cit. p. 170.

[3] See *PR* pp. 99–100, 102 and references there.

[4] *CCR 1422–9*, p. 28, Chichele reg. pp. 170–73 dates the degradation as 27 February; cf. Netter *Doct*. ii.33–4. A document copied into St.John's College Cambridge MS H.7, f. 340v, lists Taylor's chief heretical views, combining the four articles on prayer with those produced by Flemyng.

[5] Taylor's case is mentioned in VI.108, 109, 117, 119, 121 (iii.687–9, 692, 729–36, 743, 755); in V.doct.11 (ii.33–4) mention is made of Taylor and his degradation.

*obsecro vos fratres per Dominum nostrum Jesum Christum, et charitatem Spiritus sancti, . . . ut sollicitudinem impertiamini in orationibus pro me ad Deum*, a passage which Taylor's opponents suggested must reveal Paul to be a heretic since it appealed for prayers through Christ and the Spirit and not to God alone, and since it asked for individual advantage. Taylor apparently equivocated by claiming that the use of the word *obsecro* rather than *oro* was acceptable, and did not imply the inferior status of the suppliant.[1] A host of biblical and patristic citations was produced to refute this distinction. Discussion continued on the issue of whether prayer should be directed towards God alone. Later in chapter 117 Netter quotes part of the schedule transcribed in Chichele's register, describing it as a *libellus De orandis sanctis*.[2]

Taylor thus emerges as a persistent and, in the end at least, fearless follower of Lollard views. In some respects, notably in his views about prayer, he was more extreme in his formulations than Wyclif;[3] in others it may be that Taylor was misreported.[4] But in the final list of five articles produced by Flemyng appear two opinions that are traceable in the 1406 sermon here edited: on the incompatibility of civil dominion with clerical status (see lines 75–269, 473–97), and on the culpability of fraternal begging (601–709). Since, apart from this sermon, evidence concerning Taylor's views are for the most part from hostile reports (the exception of Taylor's reply to the Bristol priest is only partial, as it was provoked by a hostile response), it must be recognized that we only have partial access to Taylor's thought. It remains noteworthy, however, that at no point in the various accusations against him is heresy concerning the eucharist mentioned. Taylor in the sermon here rather ostentatiously avoids the subject.[5] Since this was the central topic on which Lollards were normally questioned, it would seem possible that Taylor's views on the issue were not overtly heterodox. Taylor's career superficially traces the course usually ascribed by modern observers to second-generation Lollards: from the academic world of Oxford, through London to the

[1] Quoted by Netter *Doct.* VI.108 (iii.687).

[2] *Doct.* VI.117 (iii.729), quoting Chichele reg. iii.162/26–31 and 164/18–27.

[3] Netter observed this *Doct.* VI.13 (iii.111), though not specifically in regard to Taylor.

[4] For instance in the accusation regarding fasting on certain vigils as a substitute for confession, reported from the May 1417 sermon (above p. xviii).

[5] See lines 340–1; if this avoidance were merely in the written form of the sermon, and not in the sermon as delivered, it would be expected that some allusion to it would be found in the extensive documentation about its reception.

rural backwoods of Worcestershire. But such a view ignores complexities visible even from the partial evidence that survives. Taylor's most 'academic' surviving text is his reply to the Bristol priest concerning prayer, dating presumably from some ten years after his departure from Oxford. From the obscurity of Norton Underhill Taylor went to Bristol, a large town with a longstanding connection with Lollardy.[1] To judge by the testimony of John Walcote in 1425, a humble shepherd but known for heresy not only in his native village of Hasleton just north of Bristol but also in Bristol itself, in London and Northampton, Taylor was ranked along with William Swinderby, John Purvey, Sir John Oldcastle and the Londoner John Claydon, burnt in 1415.[2] This may indicate a linking in repute only. William Thorpe also, despite his claims to personal knowledge, may not have been a close associate of Taylor. But Taylor's connection with Drayton implies more substantial links with the Lollard movement outside the west country: Drayton's early career was protected by sympathetic gentry, his final benefices were in an area of Kent notable for its ardour in Lollard causes, and the juxtaposition of Drayton's case in 1425 with that of Robert Hoke of Braybrooke, even though no explicit connection between the two men is asserted, may indicate some link between the two notorious and longstanding disseminators of heresy.[3] At least during Taylor's lifetime, and arguably for some years after it, any simple line of social or intellectual marginalization in the development of Wycliffism is not to be discerned. The limited information available for Taylor's career and thought contributes to the picture of a more complex and shifting development.

## LANGUAGE OF DOUCE 53

The laborious analysis of scribal features in later medieval manuscripts has become redundant following the publication of *A Linguistic Atlas of Late Medieval English*. The ensuing brief account relies heavily upon that work as indicated. The general character of the language as central east Midland can be established on the following, limited, features: third person plural personal pronoun forms *þei*, *hem*, *her* (*Atlas* i maps 30, 40, 52); present indicative endings of verbs, 3sg. *-eþ*,

[1] See Thomson pp. 20–37, *PR* p. 78.
[2] Worcester reg. Morgan pp. 168–9.
[3] Chichele reg. iii.105–12.

pl. *-en* (maps 646, 652).[1] That the northern boundary is unlikely to be north of the Wash, given the easterly nature of the language, is shown by the invariable *ȝ-* forms of the verb 'give' (map 425). More precise location may be deduced from the forms *moche* 'much' (map 103), *whanne* (map 337), *ony* 12 times against *any* three (maps 99, 97 respectively), *eche* (map 86), *whiche* (map 79), *sich* 10 times against *siche* six times and *suche* once (map 68), and the preterite forms *siȝ* and *siȝen* of the verb 'to see' (map 514). This last is especially limited, virtually excludes East Anglia (of whose characteristic idiosyncracies there is anyway no sign), and, in conjunction with the other forms, points towards south-east Huntingdonshire or Cambridgeshire. The spelling *þurȝ* for 'through' suggests the latter (*Atlas* ii map 54(6)).

Comparing the language of Douce 53 with the localized texts used by the *Atlas*, there is a very close similarity between it and the analysis given of Huntington HM 134 (LP 753, *Atlas* iii.28), a copy of the Wycliffite Bible New Testament in the Later Version. The range of linguistic material offered by this longer text is inevitably greater, but there are few significant discrepancies.[2] The *Atlas* gives a grid reference of 528 255 for the Huntington scribe, in Cambridgeshire just over the border from Huntingdonshire in the area of Caxton or Bourne. The close similarity shown by Douce 53 would indicate a similar place of origin.

## 2. THE TESTIMONY OF WILLIAM THORPE

### MANUSCRIPTS AND PRINTED VERSIONS

There are four primary witnesses to the text of Thorpe's autobiographical account of his trial: one medieval manuscript in English, two medieval manuscripts in Latin and one early printed version in

[1] There is only one dubious trace of the plural ending *-eþ* that appears in limited areas of the east Midlands (see A. McIntosh, 'Present Indicative Plural Forms in the Later Middle English of the North Midlands', in *Middle English Studies presented to Norman Davis*, ed. D. Gray and E. G. Stanley (Oxford, 1983), pp. 235–44. The single case is *vnabliþ* T456, where the subject is plural but the verb may have been attracted into the singular by the main verb in the sentence.

[2] Douce has three times *any* against twelve times *ony*, whereas only the latter is recorded for Huntington; Douce has *-yng* for the present participle against Huntington forms with final *-e* (*-ynge*, *inge*); Douce has *þouȝ* for 'though' against Huntington *þoȝ*; Douce has medial *-sk-* as well as medial *-x-* forms in the verb 'ask', Huntington only the latter.

English. One further medieval Latin copy is known to have existed but the material no longer survives.[1]

i) *Bodleian Library MS Rawlinson C.208* (R) s.xv[1]

91 parchment leaves, size 149mm by 103mm; ruled in a single column of 22 lines; written space 108 mm by 68 mm. Collation: vii paper flyleaves, 1–9$^{8}$, 10$^{6}$, 11$^{8}$, 12$^{8}$ lacks leaves 6–8 cut out, v paper flyleaves; medieval quire signatures b–d survive on quires 2–4, and quires 5–12 are so numbered in a medieval hand; catchwords do not usually survive. It should be noted that ff. 73–74 are numbered 10.i and 10.ii but f. 75 is numbered 10.iiij, though nothing is lost between f. 74$^{v}$ and f. 75; f. 75 is conjugate with f. 76 and f. 74 with f. 77. Also f. 18 is marked as c and is the first leaf of quire 3, but the catchword appears on f. 18$^{v}$, f. 79 is marked 11.i and is the first leaf of quire 11, though the catchword appears on f. 79$^{v}$.

1. ff. 1–91$^{v}$ inc. *A prolog The lord god þat knowiþ* . . .; ends part way down f. 91$^{v}$ *in stidefast hope and in parfiȝt charite. Amen Amen Amen.*

The whole manuscript is written in a somewhat ungainly though practised textura hand of the early fifteenth century.[2] There are red paraph marks; red underlining of the names of authorities and of some translated quotations in the text is not carried through entirely consistently. In the margins the original scribe entered some side headings and the names of authorities mentioned within the text; these are often enclosed in red boxes of varied geometrical shape (often almost a Greek cross). Some sections have headings in red, and there are usually running titles also in red. There are strips of rough ornamentation of amateur kind in red and black on ff. 1 and 8, the latter the beginning of the text proper.

There is no sign of medieval ownership. At the foot of f. 1 the name of *Robertus Cotton Bruceus 1599* has been partially erased.[3] The

[1] See *Katalogý Knihoven Kolejí Karlovy University*, ed. J. Bečka and E. Urbánková (Prague, 1948), p. 162: item P22 includes 'Tractatulus Wilhelmi Anglici Torp*er* de responsionibus ad doctorem', the manuscript is now Prague University Library IV.H.17 (see J. Truhlář, *Catalogus Codicum Manu Scriptorum Latinorum . . . in Bibliotheca Publica atque Universitatis Pragensis* (Prague, 1905–6), i.317), but ff. 122–144, on which, according to the medieval list of contents, Thorpe's text should have occurred, are now missing.

[2] Dr. Ian Doyle observes that the hand is probably of the first quarter of the fifteenth century.

[3] This form of signature Cotton used from his knighting by James I in 1603, but he

manuscript seems to have been given by Cotton to James Ussher, archbishop of Armagh, at the latter's request in 1606 for the library at Trinity College Dublin. It is not clear when, between 1606 and Rawlinson's death in 1755, it left that collection.[1] There is some marginal annotation in a seventeenth-century hand.

ii) *Vienna Österreichische Nationalbibliothek MS 3936* (V) s.xv[1]

128 paper leaves; size 305mm by 210mm; ruled for a single column of writing 208mm by 127mm. Collation: i strip parchment, 1 paper flyleaf, 1–10[12], 11[12] leaves 8–12 cut away, 12[6] leaves 1–5 cut away, i strip parchment; the centres of all quires and the outside of some are strengthened with tiny strips of paper or, in the case of quire 12, of parchment. Quire numbers 2–5 appearing in red on the last leaves of the present quires 4–7 show that item 2 was originally intended as a separate book. The parchment strips at the beginning and end of the manuscript are a bifolium from a small volume in Latin used sideways, but have a German note at the top

1. ff. 1–22[v] [Thorpe's trial] inc. *[N]otum sit vniuersis legentibus* . . .; lacking the *prolog* of the English manuscript; in the present text corresponding to lines 166–2255.

2. ff. 23–24[v] blank; ff. 25–92 Hus's *De Ecclesia*, preceded by an index.[2]

3. ff. 92[v]–93[v] excerpts from the gloss of Innocent III on the mass; ff. 94–128 blank save for a single note on f. 128; f. 128[v] some further notes on the mass.

The entire manuscript is written in Bohemian hands of c.1420: two are involved in the Thorpe trial, the first from ff. 1–12[v] and the second, slightly more compressed and considerably more abbreviated, from f. 13 to the end of the item. Space was left for large capitals in the

sometimes modified inscriptions written earlier (see C. E. Wright, 'The Elizabethan Society of Antiquaries and the Formation of the Cottonian Library' in F. Wormald and C. E. Wright, *The English Library before 1700* (London, 1958), pp. 192 and 200). It is not clear when the manuscript left the Cotton collection.

[1] I owe the information about Cotton's gift to Ussher to the kindness of Dr. Colin Tite; he pointed out Ussher's letter, mentioning 'the examination of Thorpe' as one of the manuscripts he hoped Cotton would donate, dated 30 October 1606 printed in T. Smith, *V. Cl. Gulielmi Camdeni et Illustrium Virorum ad G. Camdenum Epistolae* (London, 1691), p. 86.

[2] *Magistri Johannis Hus Tractatus de Ecclesia*, ed. S. Harrison Thomson (Cambridge, 1956), pp. xxvi–xxvii.

Thorpe text, but these were never supplied; there is no ornamentation in the item; on f.1 some underlining and punctuation in red appears, but this is not continued beyond the leaf. A contemporary hand, probably not that of either scribe, has added some marginal side-notes drawing attention to matter in the text especially at the beginning. The text is divided in this copy into chapters of uneven length, for which numbers (or indeed any marking beyond a new line and space for a capital) are often not provided; assuming that all the breaks indicate the start of a new chapter, there are thirteen chapters. Some speech indications are underlined by the scribe, but this is not done consistently.

A post-medieval hand has added a note at the head of f. 1 explaining the nature of the following text. There is no indication in the volume that it has ever been outside the old Bohemian area.

iii) *Prague Metropolitan Chapter Library MS O.29* (P) s.xv mid

317 paper leaves, size 213mm by 150mm. Collation: $1–5^{12}$, single leaf (f. 61), $6–9^{12}$, $10^{8}$, $11–15^{12}$, $16^{10}$, $17–20^{12}$, $21^{10}$, $22–27^{12}$. The manuscript is a collection of texts, extracts and notes on matters of Wycliffite and Hussite interest. The most important items are listed in the published catalogue of the library;[1] they include extracts from a number of Wyclif's own writings, six brief texts by Wyclif and Peter Payne's *Propositiones contra M.Johannes de Pribram*.[2] The section of concern here is:

ff. 188–209 (using the stamped foliation, first leaf of quire 17–leaf 6 of quire 18)[3] headed *M.Wilhelmi Torpe*, text inc. *Notum sit vniuersis legentibus*; lacking the prologue of the English manuscript; in the present text corresponding to lines 166–2255. Ends at the foot of f. 209 *Explicit responsio Wylhelmi Thorpt*.

The manuscript is written in a variety of Bohemian hands of c.1430; that which wrote the Thorpe trial seems to have begun work at f. 184 and to have continued to f. 211$^{v}$. Space was left for large capitals, but these, apart from the first, were never supplied; there is no ornamentation in

[1] *Soupis Rukopisů Knihovny Metropolitní Kapitoly Pražské*, ed.A. Podlaha (Prague, 1910–22), ii.492–5, no.1613.

[2] For the Wyclif texts see Thomson nos.28–31, 34–8, 47, 52, 395–6, 404, 414, 417; for Payne's text see F. M. Bartoš, 'Literární Činnost M. Jana Rokycany, M. Jana Přibrama, M. Petra Payna', *Sbirka Pramenů k Poznání Literárního Života Československého Skupina* iii *Číslo* 9 (Prague, 1928), pp. 103–4 no.13.

[3] The quire is completed with two anonymous sermons.

the item. There are a few side-notes, probably in the hand of the scribe. The material is divided into the same thirteen sections as in V; none of these has any heading, or indication that there is a change of chapter.

The paste-down at the front has a list of contents, without folio references, in a medieval hand; this includes *Item omelie Torp* at the right place. It is not known how the manuscript came into its present keeping, but there is no indication in the volume that it has ever been outside the old Bohemian area.

iv) *STC 24045* (A) [1530?]

An octavo volume of 68 unnumbered leaves; collation A–H$^8$, I$^4$. The title page reads: The examinaci/on of Master William Thorpe preste accused / of heresye before Thomas Arundell Archebis/hop of Canturbury the yere of ower Lorde .M./CCCC. and seuen. / The examinacion of the honorable knight syr / Jhon Oldcastell Lorde Cobham burnt bi the / said Archebisshop in the fyrste yere of Kynge / Henry the fyfth. / Be no more ashamed to heare it then ye were / and be to do it.

1. sigs.A.1$^v$–A.2$^v$ [preface] *Vnto the Christen Reader*

2. sigs.A.3–G.6 [the trial, including the *prolog* of the manuscript]; in the present edition corresponding to lines 1–2255.

3. sigs.G.6–H.2$^v$ straight on from last, *Thus endeth the examynacion of Master / Wyllyam Thorpe. And here after foloweth / hys testamente*. There is no parallel to this section in the manuscript; it is printed in appendix III.

4. sigs.H.3–I.4$^v$ [the Examination of Oldcastle].

The book has no imprint or date. But the reference in the preface, sig.A.2, to *that good preaste and holye martyr Syr Thomas hitton was brente now thys yere at maydstone yn Kent* makes a date in 1530 or 1531 certain.[1] From the typeface and the initials it has been argued that the book was printed in Antwerp, one of a series of English works produced by the reformers on presses there that sometimes carry the name of Hans Luft.[2] For a discussion of the responsibility for printing the book see below pp. xxxiii–xxxvii.

[1] Hitton was burnt for heresy in February 1530; see More *CW* 8. 13–17, 1207–8.

[2] See Hume in More *CW* 8.1077–8, no.18 and references there given; *PR* pp. 492–4. For the typeface and initials see M. E. Kronenberg, 'De geheimzinnige Drukkers Adan Anonymus te Bazel en Hans Luft te Marburg ontmaskerd', *Het Boek* 8 (1919), 240–79; the Thorpe edition is no. 23 on p. 272. STC 24045 has three decorated initials, all of which have similarities to those illustrated on pp. 244, 248.

There are four copies of the book known to survive. I have used primarily the facsimile of the British Library copy (shelfmark G.12012) produced in 1975, checking any obscurities against the book itself.[1] I have also checked the other three copies in Brasenose College Oxford, in the University of Glasgow Library, and in the library of Blickling Hall; these are identical, though all are in better condition than the British Library copy, with less cropping.[2]

Before considering the relation of these four primary witnesses to each other, a brief account must be given of a number of sixteenth-century secondary witnesses. The first of these is a Latin version of the trial written in to Bodleian MS e Musaeo 86, f. 105ᵛ and five inserted unnumbered leaves, by John Bale; the manuscript is the sole surviving copy of the compilation known as *Fasciculi Zizaniorum*.[3] This version, compared with the four described so far, is abbreviated, and is now incomplete because of the loss of one leaf after f. 105ᵛ and of final leaves; the text ends at material corresponding to line 1389 here.[4] Bale's heading to the text makes it clear that he was translating the work himself from English, and that the version was made in 1543.[5] This makes it possible that Bale was working from the [1530] print. Bale's text as it survives corresponds, with abbreviation, to lines 166–1389 of the present edition; it therefore has no version of the opening material or *prolog* of the [1530] print, and loss of leaves conceals whether it contained any version of the *testamente*. Further

[1] Facsimile produced by Theatrum Orbis Terrarum Ltd. and Walter J. Johnson Inc. (Amsterdam and Norwood N.J., 1975).

[2] Brasenose UB/S.III.14, where STC 24045 is bound as the first item with three Latin texts, the first STC 17040, the others published abroad, W. Ames and N. Eaton, *Inquisitio in variantes Theologorum* (1633) and P. Molina, *Anatome Missae* (1637). Glasgow Hunterian Library Cm 2.13, in which STC 24045 is preceded by a copy of STC 1303 and followed by copies of STC 14828 and 19902; Blickling I.e.17, where it is bound with an unrecorded copy of STC 1462.3 otherwise only known from a copy in the Bodleian Library, Wood 774. From the condition of the type at the beginning of lines 1–2 of sig.A.7ᵛ it seems that the Blickling copy may have been printed before the other three, since the initial *t-* of *thyng* is slipping but not lost.

[3] For the manuscript see J. Crompton, '*Fasciculi Zizaniorum*', *JEH* 12 (1961), 35–45, 155–66. Parts of the opening section were printed by W. W. Shirley (RS 1858). None of the foliations in the manuscript are either correct or consistent; I have used that in black pencil.

[4] Explicit . . . *an licite possint sacerdotes a*.

[5] The heading reads 'Examinacio magistri guilhelmi thorpe sacerdotis hereseos accusati coram Thoma Arundell archiepiscopo cantuariensi anno domini M.CCCC.VII per Joannam Baleum anglum sudo volgum in latinum versa. 1543'. Bale owned the manuscript between c.1540 and 1552, and copiously annotated it. But it seems likely that Bale knew the text, and in all probability this manuscript, before the dissolution of the monasteries and before his own defection from the Carmelite order.

examination reveals that there is nothing within the text to contradict derivation from the print.[1] It should be noted that, where in lines 499–507 the print uses initials rather than the full names of Wyclif's early followers, Bale supplies them: he expands *H* correctly as Nicholas Hereford, *J/P* as John Purvey, but *B* as Thomas Britwell. The first two Bale could have found in full in the print a little later, at lines 573–4, and were in any case well known; the print never gives anything beyond the initial for the last, and Bowland (as the name appears in RVP) was apparently unknown to Bale.[2] But at 570–4 Bale follows the print exactly: most notable here is the name *Dauid gotray e pakrynge*, and consequently Bale's list of early Lollards in the manuscript (ff. 61ᵛ–63ᵛ) does not include Geoffrey of Pickering but has the fictional *Dauy Gotray*.[3] It may safely be concluded that he made his translation from that source. Consequently, Bale's version is of no independent textual value.

Bale's friend John Foxe used the trial of Thorpe first in the *Commentarii Rerum in Ecclesia Gestarum* (Strasbourg, 1554), ff. 118–157. With some verbal alterations, abbreviations and embellishments, this is the Latin translation made by Bale, and is by a side-note (f. 117ᵛ *Ex Ioan. Baleo & aliis*) acknowledged to be so. The text is complete, as it must have been before the loss of leaves from the single manuscript; it covers the *testamente* as well as 166 onwards of the text proper. Foxe has all the expansions given by Bale, and produces these again at 2086–7; he substitutes *homines quatuor* for the abbreviation of the print at 2104, but gives surnames at 2167.[4]

All of this was reprinted in Foxe's *Rerum in Ecclesia Gestarum* (Basel, 1559), pp. 79–96 without significant alteration, though with some abbreviation especially of the *testamente*. But in this later work the source is said to be *ex uerissima Gulielmi Tyndalli & historicorum narratione*.[5] This reflects not a new source for the material, but Foxe's

[1] Bale's text agrees with both English versions in lines 875, 1147 against VP; it agrees with A rather than R in lines 413–15, 1015, 1181, 1193–4, 1226, 1359 and 1370.

[2] MS f. 105aᵛ col.2; Bale's text is not, of course, available for the later instances in RVP at 2087, 2105. For Bowland's identity see note to line 500; Britwell appears f.62 amongst Bale's biographical sketches of Lollards.

[3] MS f. 105b col.1; Bale also only describes the man as *monachus de bylande*, not, as VP have it, *abbas*. The details about *Dauy Gotray* (ff. 61ᵛ–62) correspond exactly to Thorpe's on Geoffrey of Pickering.

[4] Fols. 122, 124, 152ᵛ, 153, 154; the relevance of the last point will appear below in discussion of Foxe's 1563 print.

[5] For these two works, in which Foxe prepared the way for his major production, see J. F. Mozley, *John Foxe and His Book* (London, 1940), pp. 118–28, W. Haller, *Foxe's Book of Martyrs and the Elect Nation* (London, 1963), pp. 70–2, F. J. Levy, *Tudor Historical Thought* (San Marino, 1967), pp. 98–105, and Aston (1964), pp. 237–8.

acceptance by 1559 that the [1530] print had been put out by Tyndale; this claim will be discussed below pp. xxxiii–xxxvii.

When Foxe issued the first edition of his *Actes and Monuments* (London, 1563), he substituted for the Latin version a straight reprint of the [1530] English edition, including the prefatory material of that work.[1] All the abbreviations of the print are reproduced, but the most conclusive proof of the origins of Foxe's text comes at line 2167 where Foxe reproduced the erroneous christian name for Purvey, *Thom*, found at that point in the [1530] print.[2]

Foxe's change of exemplar in 1563 was not just because the language of Foxe's own work had changed, but as the result of a letter from the outspoken puritan William Turner written to Foxe in 1561 or 1562: Turner had urged that, since Thorpe's account had originally been composed in English, it would be more likely to be an accurate version if Foxe could print the trial in that language.[3] Though the source of Foxe's text is undoubtedly the [1530] print, he prefaced it with a long and confusing account of its origin from which the reader might well get the impression that Foxe's source was a manuscript.[4] This impression would be confirmed by the note added between the trial and the *testamente*, where Foxe observes, apparently implying its separation from the rest:

> Besides this examination here aboue described, came an other treatise also to oure handes of the same William Thorpe, vnder the name and title of his testament . . .[5]

But, even if Foxe had a handwritten copy of the [1530] print rather than an ordinary copy, his text has no value independent of that print.

The question remains of the responsibility for the issue of the edition of [1530]. It is clear that by 1547 Bale thought that the man responsible for the [1530] edition was William Tyndale. This is shown

[1] STC 11222, pp. 144–72; the note was slightly changed in the second edition of 1570 (STC 11223) i.629, but thereafter remained the same through the subsequent editions (STC 11224–8).

[2] STC 24045, sig.G.3$^{v}$, where it appears in all copies as *tom*.

[3] Turner's letter survives in BL Harley 416, comment on f. 132 verso. It is undated, but Turner signed himself as dean of Wells, a post he held from 1551–4 and, after deprivation under Mary, again from 1561 until he was suspended for nonconformity in 1564. The letter is not mentioned in the recent biography by W. R. D. Jones, *William Turner, Tudor Naturalist, Physician and Divine* (London, 1988).

[4] Agreement of Foxe's text with A is seen in numerous cases, for instance lines 715, 803, 831, 863, 888 etc.

[5] 1563 edition p. 170; 1570 edition i.647.

by his entry in *Illustrium majoris Britanniae Scriptorum Summarium* (Ipswich, 1548, STC 1295), f. 221 under Tyndale's name: 'In lucem emisit quoque examinationes Thorpii & Cobhami, cum Agricolae preaecatione, ac similibus'. A similar entry appears in Bale's later, amplified *Scriptorum Illustrium Maioris Brytanniae Catalogus* (Basel, 1557–9), i.659 'Praelo etiam dedit examinationes Guilhemi Thorpi & Ioannis Oldcastelli, & alia, additis suis praefationibus.' The grouping of Thorpe with Oldcastle and the reference to prefatory material, the *Vnto the Christen Reader* of A, makes it plain that it is the edition we know that is in question. In the *Catalogus* Bale lists the trial also under Thorpe's name (i.538), immediately followed by 'Testamentum uitae ultimum Lib.1 Matthaeus Apostolus Christi'. Unfortunately what led Bale to his ascription to Tyndale is not clear; it would seem to have been some information which reached him between 1543, when he translated the text but made no comment about its origin, and 1548.[1] The other text which Bale associated with Tyndale, *The praier and complaynte of the ploweman vnto Christe* ([Antwerp], 1531; STC 20036), is a Lollard text now not extant in manuscript; it shares with the Thorpe volume a reference to Thomas Hitton.[2] The first edition, like the Thorpe book, gives no indication of its originator; but the second (STC 20036.5), perhaps of [1532] and probably printed by Thomas Godfrey, headed the preface, otherwise reprinted without change, 'W.T. to the reder'.[3] Such a heading appears in the authentic Tyndale *The prophete Ionas*.[4] The Thorpe edition contains no such initials and, though the sentiments of its 'Vnto the Christen Reader' are comparable, they are hardly identical in wording or sufficiently distinctive to require common authorship. Tyndale, if he were responsible for the print, seems to have avoided making changes to the text as he received it: the translation of Matt. 4:17 at 230 is unaltered from R's 'Do ȝe penaunce'.[5]

[1] None of Bale's surviving notebooks seems to date from this period: see Fairfield (1976), pp. 157–64. It should be noted that the [1530] print does not seem to be listed anywhere in Bale's *Index Britanniae Scriptorum*, ed. R. L. Poole and M. Bateson (Oxford, 1902).

[2] STC 20036, sig.A.2$^{v}$.

[3] STC 200236.5, sig.A.2. The edition has a different collation, and omits the glossary. Mozley (1937), p. 346 accepted Tyndale's responsibility for the Antwerp edition, Hume in More *CW* 8.1078–9 doubted it; it emerges, however, that Mozley only knew the single surviving copy of STC 20036.5, whereas Hume (in her unpublished 1961 London Ph.D. thesis 'A Study of the Writings of the English Protestant Exiles 1525–35', pp. 315–16) worked from a copy of STC 20036. Cf. *PR* pp. 493–4.

[4] STC 2788, probably May 1531, sig.A.2.

[5] Cf. Tyndale's translation *repent*, and the arguments between Tyndale and More on this and similar instances.

Foxe's first attribution to Tyndale is thus credibly dependent upon Bale, just as was his text in both his Latin volumes. But the prefatory note in the first edition of the *Actes* appears to offer more information and deserves to be quoted in full:

To the text of the story we haue neither added nor diminished: But as we haue receiued it copied out and corrected, by Maister William Tindall (who had his owne hande writing) so we haue here sent it and set it out abroade. The english though the saide Maister Tindall did somwhat amend, and frame it after our manner: yet not fully in all wordes, but that some thing dooth remaine, sauering the old speache of that time. What y[e] causes were, why this good man and seruaunt of Christe, did write it and pen it out him selfe, it is sufficiently declared in his owne preface, set before his boke. Which here is prefixed in manner as foloweth.

The 1570 edition omits the second and third sentences of this, but adds instead:

Although for the more credite of the matter, I rather wished it in his own naturall speache, wherin it was first writen. Notwithstandyng, to put away all doubt and scruple herein, this I thought before to premonishe and testifie to the reader touchyng the certeintie hereof: that they bee yet a lyve, which haue seen the selfe same copy in his own old Englishe, resemblyng the true antiquitie both of the speache and of the tyme: The name of whom as for record of the same to auouche, is maister Whithead, who, as he hath seen the true auncient copy in the hands of George Constantine, so hath he geuen credible relation of the same, both to the printer and to me. Furthermore, the sayd maister Tyndall (albeit he did somwhat alter and amend the English therof, and frame it after our maner) yet not fully in all wordes, but that some thing doth remaine, saueryng of the old speach of y[e] tyme.[1]

The passage is not without its obscurities, but would seem to imply that Tyndale had made his own handwritten copy in somewhat modernized language, and this was distinct from the *true auncient copy* which had been in the hands of George Constantine. The last sentence seems to go back to the same copy as that referred to in the first. But Foxe's print undoubtedly derives from the [1530] print. It seems perhaps possible, however, that Tyndale's name should not appear in this note at all. Mention was made above (p. xxxv) of the letter to Foxe from William Turner, urging Foxe to produce an English version of the trial. Turner's initials are the same as Tyndale's, and it seems credible that Foxe first wrote this note using just the initials

[1] *Actes* (1563), p. 143; in the 1570 edition i.629.

'W.T.'; either he or more probably his printer subsequently expanded these to the better-known name, possible in the light of Foxe's side-note in his second Latin work. Turner's anxiety about authenticity of language, expressed in the letter, would explain Foxe's rather laborious and repetitious excuses.[1] Foxe may well have turned back the request for the English version on its maker with a demand for a copy. That Turner should then copy out the [1530] print and supply it to Foxe seems entirely credible—and much more likely that Foxe should have it than a copy written by Tyndale.

The other puzzle of this note is, of course, the copy that George Constantine had once owned. Even before Bale, Sir Thomas More had reported the opinion that Constantine had in fact issued the printed version of Thorpe: in the preface to his *Confutation of Tyndale's Answer*, published in 1532, he mentioned in a review of recently published heretical books 'the examynacyon of Thorpe put forth as it is sayd by George Constantine (by whom there hath ben I wote well of y^t^ sorte grete plentye sent into this realme)'.[2] Foxe's report that Constantine had owned a manuscript copy of the Thorpe trial is entirely credible: by 1528 Constantine was in touch with purveyors of heretical books in London, and with believers in the ideas they purveyed as far afield as Shropshire.[3] By the same date Francis Denham reported that he had spent ten months with Constantine in Paris, and that Constantine had there acquired many reforming books and transported them back to England.[4] Constantine fell into More's hands in 1532, and was induced by More to betray many of his former friends.[5] It might be expected that More would have obtained certain information then about his prisoner's relationship with the Thorpe print; the wording 'put forth as it is sayd' suggests that More derived the notion from popular rumour rather than from the man himself.

The [1530] print, whoever its instigator may have been, ensured Thorpe's position in the later sixteenth-century history of the antecedents to reformation. But, despite the fact that only a single English

[1] Note especially in Turner's letter 'Recte igitur me iudice facturus es si alicundi thorpij autographum nancissi possis, ea lingua edas qua ille conscripserit. Expende queso in quorum potissimum gratiam librum conscripseris. Quo facto non dubito licet typographus insaniat, quin sis librum ad verae ecclesiae vtilitatem, maiorem sis editurus.'

[2] More *CW* 8.8/25; More refers to the Thorpe trial again 301/26 where he compares Thorpe's view on the eucharist with that of Tyndale.

[3] See Strype I.ii.63–5 and Lichfield reg. Blythe, ff. 51–2; *PR* pp. 481–2.

[4] *LP* 4(2).4396 dated 19 June 1528.

[5] More *CW* 8.18/5–20/36 and see comment pp. 1247–8; also the note in *CW* 9.366–8.

manuscript survives from the medieval period, Thorpe's text was apparently known to Lollards in the early years of the century. John Edmunds of Burford during the enquiries by bishop Longland's officials between 1518 and 1521 owned 'a book named William Thorpe', and had discussed it with his friends.[1] The printed version reinforced the popularity and notoriety of the text: it appears in two early lists of prohibited books, both of which seem to have been put out in 1531.[2] The linking of Thorpe with Oldcastle in that printed version, whether coincidentally or deliberately, carried forward the hagiographic tone of Thorpe's text. Foxe described Thorpe as 'that constant servant of God', and, whilst acknowledging that no mention is found of Thorpe's burning, nonetheless evidently regarded him as one of the pre-eminent witnesses to earlier fidelity.[3]

## THE RELATIONSHIP OF THE VERSIONS AND MANUSCRIPTS

From the preceding sections it will be plain that the editor of Thorpe's text has to consider only four sources: R and A in English, V and P in Latin; all other texts are derivative from A and have no independent value. Of these four, A is distant from the occasion narrated by over a hundred years; P and V were copied in areas geographically remote from the original events described. It is hardly surprising, therefore, that all these three texts contain extraneous elements that are unlikely to have been part of the original work; indeed, the more surprising fact is that they do not contain more such elements.

The relationship between the four witnesses can be expressed by the following diagram:

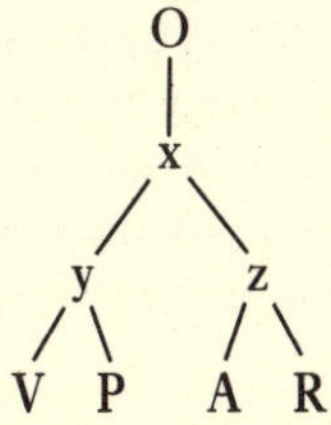


[1] Foxe iv.235 and 238; the latter seems to imply that Edmunds had talked of the work with the group centred on Richard Colins of Ginge in the north Berkshire downs (for this group see *PR* pp. 462–5).

[2] See respectively *LP* 5 app. no. 18, and More *CW* 8.7–11; see further *PR* pp. 490–1 and, for the background to these lists, Brigden (1989), pp. 179–87.

[3] Foxe iii.249, 285; for the hagiographic element in Thorpe's text see below pp. lvi–lviii.

This may be supported as follows:

a) V cannot be the source of P, nor P the source of V, since each contains errors not found in the other.[1] Each must be an independent copy of y.

b) The common descent of V and P from an exemplar y, and the Hussite origins of that exemplar are seen from the addition, in keeping with Hussite concern about utraquism, of the words *et calix* and *et calix sanguis eius* at 1008–9 to a quotation from Augustine concerning the eucharist; these words are not in the English version, nor in the source, nor in that source as it was incorporated into canon law.[2] At 573 the heretic Nicholas Hereford appears as *archidiaconus Herford* (V *Herforo*), a mistake that doubtless arose through ignorance of Hereford and by association with the position of Repingdon, repeatedly stated to have been bishop of Lincoln after his recantation.[3] There are a number of other cases where VP also share a reading that seems erroneous.[4] VP lack the opening section of the text as that appears in both R and A, lines 1–164; there seems no reason to doubt the authenticity of this section, a section which explains how the text came to be written. It was presumably lacking in y, either because of accidental loss in that or its exemplar, or because the material was thought inappropriate to an audience separated in time and place from the author. Peculiar to VP contrariwise is the inclusion of two long passages near the end of the text, the shorter after 2151 and the longer after 2221; neither of these passages contains anything that would be impossible from an English Wycliffite context, but neither adds anything to the shorter version as that appears in RA. The second especially, which provides Thorpe with a speech longer than almost any other in the conversation, seems out of place so late: by that stage of affairs the discussion between Thorpe and Arundel was over, and Thorpe was apparently at 2213–15 being given a last chance to renounce his errors in summary terms.[5]

[1] See, for instance, variants for V at lines 188, 201, 206, 341, 411 etc., and for P at 189, 318, 342, 417, 428 etc.

[2] Augustine (PL 38.1246), in canon law *De cons.* dist.II c.58 (Friedberg i.1336).

[3] Hereford held a canonry and prebend at Hereford for some years after 1394, and was treasurer there from 1397 to 1417, but there is no evidence that he was archdeacon there or anywhere else; see Emden *Oxford* ii.914, and note to 499.

[4] See variants to lines 482, 490–1, 494–6, 506–7, 875, 1111, 1524–5, 1722–4.

[5] These two passages are edited in appendix II.

c) On grounds of date alone, A cannot have been the exemplar of R. R, however, cannot have been the printer's copy for A, since R has numerous errors not shared by A.[1] It is hard to disentangle the linguistic changes made in A from erroneous readings that A inherited from its exemplar; some mistakes in A itself may reflect the printer's unfamiliarity with the earlier language of his copy.[2] But there are some cases where it is tempting to suggest that the line of descent between z and A must have included at least one stage.[3] A alone has the *testamente* appended at the end of the text (sigs. G.6–H.2$^v$). It seems unlikely that this was ever present in R. The text in R ends twelve lines down f.91$^v$, that leaf being the fifth of an eight leaf quire; leaves 6–8 have been cut out, but there is no indication that anything was intended to follow. The three leaves excised would not have sufficed for the *testamente*: for that a further six leaves beyond the quire would have been needed.[4] The only other break in the text that might indicate whether R's scribe might leave a gap before the *testamente* is that between the *prolog* (lines 1–164) and the remainder; unfortunately, the *prolog* ends at the foot of a verso leaf, so that no guidance is afforded. But the content of the *testamente* is, as will be described below (pp. 143–6) highly dubious in its association with Thorpe.[5] It seems fairly certain that this appendix, whether introduced by the printer of A or by another further back in the tradition, was not an original part of the text and was not in z, let alone in x or O.

d) The common descent of R and A from z is shown by a number of cases where the English manuscripts share an error not found in either Latin text. Most notable are a couple of cases where VP preserve, sometimes in corrupted form, proper names not found in

[1] See, for instance, variants to lines 305, 340, 374, 427, 490–1, 511, 726, 732 etc. Further evidence for the independence of R will be discussed below at pp. xl–xli.

[2] Most notably the avoidance in A of the word *sowde* at lines 1494 and 1501, but see also variants at lines 543, 1047, 1179, 1219, 1296, 1306, 1777, 1922, 1962, 2003, 2044.

[3] Possible errors of that exemplar can be seen in the variants to lines 269, 499, 509, 525, 560–1, 573, 576, 641–2 etc.

[4] The *testamente* occupies nine sides of the print's small format; the first nine sides of the print cover lines 1–202, which in R extends almost exactly to the end of f. 9.

[5] It is interesting that Foxe, although he had included a summary of the *testamente* in his 1554 and 1559 works, goes some way to acknowledge the independence of the text when he came to print it in full in 1563. He introduces it: (p.170) 'Besides this examination here aboue described came an other treatise also to oure handes of the same William Thorpe, vnder the name and title of his testament, *which rather by the matter and handlyng thereof myght seame to be counted a complaynte of vicious Priestes*, whiche treatise or testament in this place we thought not to be left out' (my italics). The *testamente* is printed in smaller type than the preceding item.

RA; since English proper names naturally gave the continental scribes some trouble, it seems inconceivable that VP should have introduced them without warranty. At 417 VP add *in Smethfel(d)* as the place of Sautry's burning for heresy; at 1971–2 both attempt to locate the dispute between Alkerton and the clerk in Watling Street (V *in Watlyngsarte*, P *in Watlingvsterwe*), a credible location since a street of that name led east from the east end of St. Paul's, at whose cross Alkerton had preached his sermon.[1] There are other cases where VP on balance seem to offer a better reading than RA, or have convincing repetitions of idioms found elsewhere in the text; these suggest that y's text was better than z's.[2]

e) That x was not itself the original is suggested by 2156, where V alone has a possible reading; the problem was the repetitive phrasing at this point, but the remainder of Arundel's speech makes it clear that the young follower of Thorpe *had* agreed to conform, as only V's reading allows. AP share the same error, and R omits the phrase. It seems likely that V corrected an error in his exemplar, that error being the reading found in AP; it would be entirely characteristic of R, faced with a senseless phrase, to leave it out. Another case where z and y may both have been incorrect is at line 1442, where the origin of personal tithes is attributed to pope Gregory X by both RA and V; only P has the correct *Gregorius nonus*.[3] If this hypothesis is correct, x was probably not the original.[4]

Though this formally establishes the stemma, it does not indicate the chief usefulness of it. Because the modernization of language found in A results in a constant minor rewording, the texts of R and of VP usually stand together in contrast to A: looking at cases where no claim concerning originality can reasonably be advanced, R agrees with VP against A in over 300 readings, A agrees with VP against R in only 80.[5] But there is a considerable number of places where A agrees

[1] See notes to lines 409, 1965 for further evidence that VP are correct.

[2] See variants at lines 702, 1381, 1719–20, 1957, 2090–1, 2092–3, 2117–20; at 1676–7 both R and A seem to be independent attempts to gloss over a difficulty, whilst the Latin is clear.

[3] The source is given as Higden's *Polychronicon*, which has the correct name; but see further the note to this line.

[4] There are four instances of agreement between P and R against AV (441, 1045, 1286, 1842), one of P and A against VR (1786); in none of these can originality of reading be firmly established, and it seems likely that these are coincidental convergences.

[5] For examples of the latter see variants to lines 228, 598, 906, 914, 942 etc.; for examples of the former 236, 271, 293, 318 etc.

with VP in material readings against R. This can only imply that R is corrupt, and that the reading of AVP must have stood in x, y and z. That this is correct is confirmed by the fact that many of the errors in R are of simple homeoteleuton.[1] These cases reveal the inaccuracy of the scribe of R (or of a scribe between R and z), and suggest that in a variety of other instances where R makes possible sense but AVP concur in another reading, R should be emended.[2] Were it not for A's rewording, it would, of course, be necessary to assume that any agreement between A and VP must require the emendation of R; but the possibility of coincidental concurrence between A and VP, a possibility the more difficult to evaluate because of the difference of language, has led to the retention of R at some possible places for emendation.[3]

Any edition of the English text must be based on R, since this is the only version in that language which represents the orthography of the first half of the fifteenth century. But, unlike many Wycliffite texts where frequent and careful correction makes it plain that considerable control was exercised over the activities of the scribes,[4] R's work needs extensive emendation. Since that emendation derives from the evidence of the other versions, the variants give fairly full citation of VP as well as of A. Because of differences of language, however, the citation of these variants is not complete, and is subject to unavoidable constraints; an account of the method used is given below pp. lxi–lxii. The emendations made in R are based on the readings of AVP, but they have been rewritten in R's language. This was done with the help of a computer-generated complete verbal index of R, which facilitated the choice of forms used elsewhere in R or, where two variant forms existed in the same context, selection of the commonest form. There remained a few words necessitated by the emendations which were not recorded elsewhere in R; these have been assimilated to R's spelling system, but are marked with a dagger in the glossary.

The establishment of the stemma so far did not require the resolution of the question of the original language of the text. It seems safe to assume that, in the diagram on p. xxxvii, z was an English version, y a

[1] See lines 491–2, 781–2, 1193–4, 1263, 1359–61, 1490–1, 1517–19, 1522, 1622–3, 1779–80, 1881, 2049, 2156.

[2] Cases where such readings have been emended may be seen at 187, 249, 293, 374, 427, 662, 704, 732 etc.

[3] See, for instance, variants at lines 336, 598, 867.

[4] See particularly the case of the English Wycliffite sermons described in *EWS* i.138–51, ii.lxxi–lxxxii, iii.lix–lxiii.

Latin one. But what was the language of x or, more importantly, of O? The question is surprisingly difficult to answer with any certainty. In the first place, the note prefacing A's text, commenting on how the printer has modernized 'for ower sothern men' and announcing his intention of putting the text out again 'in his owne olde english . . . for the northern men and the faythfull brothern of scotlande', is of no significance for the original; all it shows is that the printer had no knowledge of a Latin version.[1] Equally, the later sixteenth-century comments by William Turner and Foxe, noted above pp. xxxiii, xxxv–xxxvi, throw no light on the problem; in particular, nothing in their writing, or in that of John Bale earlier, reveals any awareness of the existence of a fifteenth-century Latin text.

The normal direction of translation in the medieval period is, of course, out of Latin and into the vernacular. Leaving aside the familiar instance of the bible translation, this is the case even with newly composed Wycliffite texts, where the early academic compilation of the *Rosarium*, itself an abbreviation of the longer and more overtly radical *Floretum*, was subsequently translated into English.[2] Equally, were the account of Thorpe's conversations an official one, there could be no doubt that at this date the Latin version would have been the original. From his account of himself as a student at Oxford, it must be supposed that Thorpe knew Latin and could have conducted his defence in that language; consequently, there is no reason why any official record should have diverged from the usual language of such documents.[3]

The use of the vernacular, however, was one of the most important elements in Lollard belief, and there is every reason to think that Thorpe shared this view.[4] As early as 1382 Repingdon, Hereford and Aston had used English as a means of defence against the accusations of archbishop Courtenay and the Blackfriars Council, a gesture made as defiance and understood as such.[5] In the *prolog* to his account of the conversation with Arundel, Thorpe explains how he was prevailed

[1] [1530] print 'Vnto the Christen Reader', sig. A.2v.

[2] For this work see *PR* pp. 106–8 and references there given; extracts from the English *Rosarium* are edited by von Nolcken (1979).

[3] Vernacular material concerning heresy in episcopal registers in the late fourteenth or early fifteenth centuries, such as that concerning Swinderby in 1390 in Trefnant's Hereford register (pp. 236–51) is limited to evidence from the suspect, whilst the official side of the case is in Latin.

[4] See the material collected by Aston (1977) and (1987), Hudson (1982) and (1986), pp. 85–103.

[5] For the episode see *FZ* pp. 290, 329–31, Knighton ii.170–2, and Aston (1987), pp. 297–300, 328–30.

upon to write it, and mentions the exhortations of his friends *to go as nyȝ þe sentence and þe wordis as I can* (36–7). That this accuracy might extend to the language of the conversation may be suggested by a later observation (1018–19), where Thorpe impudently demands that the Archbishop should *declare here opinli in Ynglische* the meaning of certain sentences in the liturgy; the specification of language remains in the Latin version. It seems not impossible, given Thorpe's disclaimer of *scole-mater* as *sofestrie* (1030–3), that he might, as a matter of Lollard principle, have affected such inadequacy in Latin that the conversation had to be conducted in English.[1]

Evidence from within the textual tradition of Thorpe's work reveals very little of use. The major features of the four copies offer no guidance: R's haplographies are peculiar to that manuscript and cannot be held to go back to x, and in any case could have happened with equal ease in either language. Arguments from idiom or vocabulary are circular: if apparent 'anglicisms' appear in the Latin, this could arise from an Englishman's importation of the oddities of his native language into his Latin writing as much as by translation from the vernacular; conversely, if 'latinisms' appear in the English version, this could merely reflect the usage of a man accustomed to think about theological matters in Latin and to use such idioms in his vernacular.[2] Quotations, especially of biblical material, might seem to offer firmer ground: were the original Latin, precise verbal adherence to the Vulgate might be expected in that language with perhaps more frequent paraphrase in the vernacular; were the original English, the paraphrases or double renderings of the biblical translation might be found reflected in the Latin text. The theoretical problem here is that, whatever the original language, Thorpe may not have quoted the bible precisely in the Vulgate words; in the circumstances of the conversation described by him, he evidently could not have checked his citations even had he wished to do so.[3] The practical difficulty is that

[1] This would offer the opposite of the situation with Walter Brut, *laycus literatus*, where Latin was used despite the status of the suspect (Hereford reg. Trefnant pp. 278–394). Equally Oldcastle in 1413 was sent a statement 'in scriptis terminis Latinis, pro leviori intellectu ejusdem in Anglicum translatis' (*FZ* 441), a phrase which, though revealing the secondary nature of the English version, derives from an official source.

[2] A possible instance of the former is at 2139 *ad standum firmius* for *stonde þe more styflier*, of the latter at 908 *þe fend forsakinge* for *dyaboli renunccians*.

[3] The situation, at least in Thorpe's account of it, is thus very different from that of Brut who was, to judge by the multiplicity of quotations from that source alone, in possession of a copy of the bible when he was writing his response (Hereford reg. Trefnant pp. 285–358).

the actual evidence seems inconclusive. There are a handful of cases where the Latin and English texts of Thorpe present mirror images of each other, both departing from the Vulgate text. Thus at 2186 both texts incorporate a gloss and a double rendering in Jeremiah 28:9: R (with which A agrees) *whanne þe word, þat is þe prophecie of a profet, is knowen or fulfillid, þanne it schal be knowen þat þe Lord sente þat prophete in treuþe*, VP *quando verbum quod est prophetia prophete est notum uel impletum, tunc scietur quod Dominus misit prophetam illum in veritate* as against the Vulgate *cum venerit verbum eius, scietur propheta quem misit Dominus in veritate*.[1] Here it may seem more probable that the Latin version is a literal rendering of the English, that English deriving by paraphrase, or memorial reconstruction, of the Vulgate. There are other cases which seem to point in the opposite direction, but all are complicated by divergence between the two English texts. Double renderings in R's English are not always found in the Latin: thus at 803–4, dependent upon Hebrews 13:7, the English in R reads *haue ȝe mynde, or be ȝe myndeful* but the Latin agrees precisely with the Vulgate in having simply *mementote*, and A omits *haue ȝe mynde*. Similarly, at 978 R's *þis þing fele ȝe in ȝou or vndirstonde* is simplified in A by the omission of *or vndirstonde* to bring the text into line with VP and the Vulgate *hoc sentite in vobis*. But at 1206–7 R's *sechiþ or coueitiþ toknes or miraclis and wondris* is only partially simplified to A's *requireth tokyns miracles and wonders* as against VP *signum* (P *signa*) *querit*, Vulgate *signum quaerit*. This last may suggest that the changes in the English text reflect A's simplification rather than R's elaboration. Equally, the Latin is sometimes very close to the Vulgate in a reading that is paraphrased in the English: so the second half of the quotation of Heb. 13:7 reads both R and A *and sue ȝe þe feiþ of hem whos conuersacioun ȝe knowen to be vertuous*, whilst the Latin has *quorum intuentes conuersacioni imitamini et fidem*, an expansion of the Vulgate *quorum intuentes exitum conversationis imitamini fidem*, but nonetheless one that keeps roughly to its syntax. Such conflicting evidence could be explained in either of two ways: that a Latin translator of an original English text had on occasion reverted to the Vulgate, working either from memory or from reference to that text, or that an English translator of an original Latin account had sometimes paraphrased or expanded his exemplar.[2] The first of these two hypo-

[1] Comparable examples may be seen at 188, 222, 702, 1779–80.

[2] For cases where strict adherence to the Vulgate text may not be a sure guide to originality of reading, despite Wycliffite stress on the precise wording of scripture, see *EWS* i.181–6 discussion of 2/26, 15/62, 21/23, 38/63–4, 44/26, 49/15, E26/3–4, E39/41, E49/38–9.

theses could perhaps more securely be ruled out if evidence were available of mirror translation in quotations from the fathers—checking back against a patristic source would be less credible. Mirror translation is indeed the norm in regard to such quotations in Thorpe's text. But, given the presentation of Thorpe's case, the departures from the original authority could be explained as Thorpe's lapses of memory—in either language.[1]

The case seems to come back to external probabilities. Here it would seem to me that the balance must rest in favour of the originality of the English version, given the date and Thorpe's declarations concerning the intended audience in his *prolog*. What remains to be explained, if this is correct, is the reason for the Latin translation. Thorpe himself declares (1983–4) that William Taylor's sermon at St. Paul's Cross *is writun boþe in Latyn and in Engelisch*, though no trace of the Latin version has been found. Had Thorpe made two versions of his own autobiography, it might have been expected that he would have claimed so. It is tempting to suggest that the Latin version was made for the Bohemian market and in that area. As will be described below (pp. lii–liii), no trace appears of Thorpe in England after the events narrated in this conversation, despite Thorpe's evident intention at the end of that interchange to remain steadfast in his faith; but Thorpe is one of the very few English Wycliffites whose name is found in Bohemian sources, apart from Peter Payne. But the translation of *Yngelond* at 1182 as *istius regni* in VP indicates that, despite the provenance of the two surviving manuscripts, the Latin version is likely to have been made in England.[2] Given the dating of V as c.1420, the translation and, equally, its transmission to Bohemia must have been early.

## THE HISTORICITY OF THORPE'S TEXT

There is no trace of any investigation of William Thorpe in archbishop Arundel's archiepiscopal register.[3] Of itself this does not disprove the accuracy of Thorpe's account. The meeting that Thorpe

[1] Examples may be seen at 877 from Grosseteste, at 1381 from Gregory; for the inaccuracies in quotation see the notes to these lines. VP have a Hussite expansion in 1008–9 (see above p. xxxviii).

[2] Though compare 486, 606, 2181 where RA *þis londe* is transferred to VP as *Anglie* or *ad Angliam*.

[3] Lambeth Palace Library, two volumes; for a brief account of the contents see Smith (1981), pp. 10–12.

records was not a formal process for heresy, but an informal conversation: though Arundel had the list of five accusations from the men of Shrewsbury (618–32 and frequent allusions to the list thereafter), the archbishop was not accompanied by the trained legal advisers that would be expected in a formal trial,[1] and the process ends not with formal sentence or even referral to further enquiry but with Thorpe being sent to cool his heels in prison with no indication of the procedure next to be followed. Whilst it is reasonable to think that Thorpe's account of the archbishop's discomfiture, and his frequent outwitting by the heretic, may be fictional, there seems no reason for Thorpe's falsification of these details. But although the informality of the conversation recorded in the present text may explain why no mention of it appears in Arundel's register, this does not explain why there is no trace of a subsequent legal process against Thorpe. Thorpe obviously wished his account here to give the impression that he would never waver in his allegiance to Lollardy; were this the case, his trial as a heretic would seem inevitable. It is possible that such a trial was recorded not in Arundel's register but in a separate quire for heresy; that main register, however, does contain the processes for Sawtry, Purvey, Badby and the incipient legal process against Taylor.[2] Alternatively, and perhaps more probably, the absence may result from the fact that Thorpe never came to formal trial. As will be seen below, it is tempting to think that Thorpe escaped from the archbishop's hands at some time between the conversation recorded in the present text and that formal investigation.

An obvious objection to the historicity of Thorpe's account is the improbability of its survival and dissemination if Thorpe's claims in it are to be believed. If Thorpe adhered to his views, as he wished the readers to believe he intended, how could he have penned such a damaging document, and how could he have passed it out of prison to his friends? The archbishop's alleged use of an *agent provocateur* (see lines 1827–39) might explain the first, but it can hardly account for the second. Equally, if Thorpe recanted to obtain his release, he would not have wished to put out such a narrative: if his recantation were genuine, he would have wished to suppress his former follies; if it were a time-serving gesture, he would hardly have advertized his claims of

[1] See, for instance, the large number of advisers present at the trial of John Badby before Arundel in 1409, Wilkins iii.326–7.

[2] The first three are printed from the register in Wilkins iii.254–63, 325–9; for the last see above p. xv.

steadfastness. Thorpe claims (31) that he had been visited by friends in the archbishop's prison, friends who could apparently speak freely to him. There is one close parallel to Thorpe's text, a parallel written in a situation similar to that in which Thorpe seems to have been. This is the letter of Richard Wyche written some time between 1401 and 1403, giving an account of his investigation by Walter Skirlawe, bishop of Durham.[1] The letter presents a number of parallels to Thorpe's account: Wyche wrote from prison, and his letter was evidently smuggled out to friends; Skirlawe conducted a number of conversations with Wyche, and his deputies did likewise, all apparently informal; Skirlawe's main aim appears to have been to gain Wyche's oath of submission, and he was prepared to use an *agent provocateur* to persuade Wyche to take the oath though with mental reservations. Like Thorpe's text, Wyche's letter was apparently written when the eventual outcome of his investigation remained unclear. Wyche's letter reinforces the claims for the historicity of Thorpe's text.[2]

Any assertion of its veracity, however, must depend upon the credibility of the detail within it—and Thorpe provided a fair amount of detail whose accuracy can to a large extent be checked. Arundel claims (180–5) that Thorpe had *þis twenti wyntir and more traueilid aboute bisili in þe norþ lond and in oþir diuerse contrees of Ynglond*. Dependent upon this is Aston's suggestion that Thorpe should be identified with a man of the same name who was instituted to the vicarage of Marske, Cleveland, in March 1395.[3] The living was in the hands of the Augustinian canons of Guisborough (N.Yorks.). If the identification is correct, Thorpe must have been non-resident for much of the time according to the next detail to be considered.

Arundel reminds Thorpe that he had previously been investigated by bishop Braybrooke of London for heresy, and that he had gained his release as a result of Arundel's own exile at the end of Richard II's reign. Thorpe accepts the major part of this account, though alleges that Braybrooke had released him after Arundel's departure abroad without submission, since he could find no valid charge against him (see lines 2169–80). Part of this story finds verification in two documents found in the notebook of John Lydford, though no mention of

[1] Preserved only in Prague University Library III.G.11, ff. 89$^{v}$–99$^{v}$; printed by F. D. Matthew, 'The Trial of Richard Wyche', *EHR* 5 (1890), 530–44.

[2] For further parallels between Thorpe's text and Wyche's letter see below pp. lvii–lix.

[3] Aston (1967), p. 326 n.2, citing York reg.Arundel f. 49; there are two villages named *Marske* in the York diocese, one near Richmond and the other near Guisborough, but the register specifies the second here as *Mersk in Clyueland*.

Thorpe occurs in Braybrooke's London register. The first of these documents records a list of articles drawn up against William Thorpe for presentation to Robert Braybrooke, bishop of London; the second purports to be a reply by Thorpe to those articles.[1] At the end of the second is appended a note, in a different hand from that of the rest of the material, noting Braybrooke's excommunication of Thorpe on the grounds of his failure to recant. The six charges against Thorpe recorded in the Lydford notebook overlap only to a very limited extent with the issues in debate with Arundel, though the outlook they reflect is not incompatible with them. Thorpe was charged on the following points: he had preached that a priest in mortal sin did not consecrate the host any more than a layman; that a priest had no obligation to say the canonical hours, but only to say the Lord's prayer and to preach; that likewise at mass the priest was obliged only to say the Lord's prayer and to preach; that it was right for the laity to have legal jurisdiction over priests, to withdraw tithes and that those giving to churches or to ecclesiastics sin mortally; that bishops serve no useful purpose, but only advance dandies and rascals; that the form of baptism should be simple. Thorpe in the present text certainly places great emphasis on the clerical duty of preaching (lines 707–886), and also argues the legitimacy of withdrawing tithes (the fourth charge of the men of Shrewsbury, lines 1390–1631). But the other accusations from Shrewsbury concentrate on issues more central to the Wycliffite creed than the earlier charges. The mode of argument in Thorpe's reply to the charges in the Lydford notebook is very similar to that used in the text here edited: citation of biblical, patristic and canonistic support, quibbling about the precise wording of the complaints and assertion of compliance in the unlikely event that legitimate cause for condemnation be found.[2]

The documents in the Lydford notebook are not dated. The editor of the notebook suggested that the events they narrate should be dated between 1393–97. But references within the documents to the persons on whose information the charges against Thorpe were brought make such a late date impossible. The document was drawn up for Robert

[1] See *John Lydford's Book*, ed. D. M. Owen (Devon and Cornwall Record Society ns xix, 1974), nos. 206, 209. Since the transcription here is in a number of points so inaccurate as to be unintelligible, I have checked and corrected the text against the original in Devon Record Office pp. 141, 143–4; I am indebted to the Office for sending me photographic copies of these pages.

[2] See for examples of each of these respectively Lydford p. 110/2, 5, 7 etc., 28, pp. 110/20, 28, 111/39; p. 111/7ff, 61ff; pp. 110/29ff, 112/2ff.

Braybrooke, bishop of London from January 1382. Thorpe in his reply refers to William Cheser, rector of St. Martin Orgar, to one Richard, rector of St. Benedict's *iuxta Pauliswarf*, and to *dominus W.Stapelford*.[1] The most helpful of these references is the first.[2] A William de Chestre is recorded as rector of St. Martin's Orgar in 1382,[3] but by 24 January 1387 he had been replaced by Henry Churchehull.[4] Since the sermon from which Chester derived his testimony against Thorpe occurred on Corpus Christi day, that sermon must have been delivered between 1382 when Braybrooke became bishop of London and 1386.

The problem of reconciling the Lydford evidence with that in Thorpe's own text comes with the end of Thorpe's story: Arundel alleges, and Thorpe accepts the allegation, that Thorpe escaped from Braybrooke's hands just after Arundel's departure into exile, hence soon after 11 January 1397. If this is to be accepted, then the Lydford evidence could be integrated by assuming that Thorpe had remained in Braybrooke's prison from 1386 at the latest until early 1397. This would seem to preclude the identification with the William Thorpe instituted to Marske in 1395; since the name is not particularly unusual this may have to be accepted. More difficult is the reconciliation of the final note in the Lydford notebook, asserting that Thorpe had been excommunicated because of his failure to recant, with the outcome in Thorpe's account that he had been released by Braybrooke because the bishop *fond in me no cause for to holden me no lengir in prisoun* (2176). Arundel, in Thorpe's account, does not challenge this part of the story, and throughout Thorpe is never treated as a relapse. This clash of evidence is only unsatisfactorily and partially possible to explain. It is possible that the appended note in Lydford concerning the excommunication is not authoritative: the book was evidently intended to provide model documents, and it may be that a user of it, realising that no form for excommunication is to be found in the book, added one as a model to Thorpe's evidently incomplete case. More difficult is the question of date, 1386 at the latest for the events in the

[1] Lydford p. 111/7, 27, 34.

[2] Unfortunately, the absence of surname in the second case precludes identification since Richard Euerdon, rector of St. Benedict's, exchanged the living with Richard Mokynton in August 1385 (London reg. Braybrooke f. 98v); Mokynton's relinquishment of the living is not recorded in that register before a date precluded by evidence concerning Cheser. The last can presumably not be the William Stapelford included by Emden *Oxford* iii.1765, not ordained until 1406.

[3] G. Hennessy, *Novum Repertorium . . . Londinense* (London, 1898), p. 130 citing Hustings Rolls London 111 (6), (88), a reference provided by Kightly (1975), p. 438.

[4] *CCR 1392–6* p. 524, also in Kightly (1975), p. 438.

notebook, 1397 for the events as retailed by Thorpe. Imprisonment over such a long period would seem to require the appearance of some formal procedure in Braybrooke's episcopal register. It should, however, be observed that the Lydford documents do not precisely state that Thorpe was already in the bishop's care, though that would be the natural interpretation. It is perhaps possible that the accusations retailed in the first of Lydford's documents were answered by Thorpe in the second whilst the heretic was still at liberty, and that Thorpe, whether by lying low or by retreat to some other part of the country, escaped arrest until nearer 1397. The escape that Thorpe himself describes would then be the result of a second attempt in London to bring him to justice; a second attempt (if we are to believe Thorpe's own words) may have been instigated by Arundel rather than by Braybrooke. If so, then even the identification with the vicar of Marske in 1395 is feasible: Arundel, who instituted the man to that living, may well have become aware of his heterodoxy soon after and, finding Thorpe once again in London after his own translation from York to Canterbury in September 1396, urged Braybrooke once more into action. The long delay in bringing a suspect to book is paralleled in the case of Taylor (above pp. xv–xvii).

Leaving aside for the moment the details in Thorpe's account that relate to its author's life, there remain other points that can be checked. The only opponent apart from Arundel whom Thorpe names is John Malvern, described as *phisician* and as *persoun of seint Dunstane in þe eest in Londoun* (176–7). Both details are correct: Malvern was physician to Henry IV, and held, amongst other benefices, the living of St. Dunstan's in the East, London, from 1402 to his death in 1422.[1] It is entirely credible that Malvern should have been present in the course of heresy investigations: he had been a witness at the trial of Walter Brut before bishop Trefnant of Hereford in 1393 and later acted at the trial of John Badby before Arundel in 1410.[2] Yet, though a credible participant, Malvern can hardly have been the most obvious candidate for a fictional projection—in such a case, a canon lawyer would be a more likely invention. A fuller discussion of the fracas that accompanied Alkerton's sermon at St. Paul's Cross, a fracas described here at lines 1961–93, has already been given in relation to Taylor's sermon (pp. xiii–xvi above); as was seen there, almost everything that Thorpe says is reconcilable with the other evidence.

[1] See Emden *Oxford* ii.1211.

[2] Hereford reg.Trefnant p. 360; Wilkins iii.326.

Thorpe mentions six men as special followers of Wyclif: Nicholas Hereford, Philip Repingdon, John Purvey, John Aston, Robert Bowland and Geoffrey of Pickering (see especially lines 499–516, 570–7 and 2085–9). The first four of these are well enough known from other sources. Nothing that Thorpe says about them is incompatible with what is known from elsewhere; equally, if the account here is not what it purports to be, its author could have found the details about them quite easily. This is particularly true of Hereford and Repingdon, and Thorpe's anger against them is paralleled elsewhere.[1] Thorpe's assertions about Aston (570–2) are not an entirely candid presentation of Aston's career, since he recanted in 1382; but his reversion to Wycliffite causes was complete by 1387 and at least partial by 1383.[2] Thorpe gives a little more detail about Purvey than appears in other sources: Thorpe's observation that *he schewiþ now himsilf to be neiþir hoot ne coold* (547–8), and the tense in which Arundel refers to Purvey's alleged avarice for tithes (*I herde moore compleynt . . . þan I dide* 541–4), would coincide with the fact that Purvey vacated in 1403 the benefice that Arundel had given him at West Hythe on his recantation in 1401, and that his movements after that are obscure until his re-emergence as a supporter of Oldcastle in 1414.[3]

A more crucial test of Thorpe's historical credibility are the other two mentioned: Robert Bowland and Geoffrey of Pickering. As the note concerning the first to line 500 argues, Bowland seems a reasonable addition to the list of early Wycliffite supporters: he certainly was in trouble with the ecclesiastical authorities in 1401, though for immorality rather than heresy, apparently knew Repingdon and thought he would be a favourable judge of his case then, and was pardoned for further unspecified crimes, this time probably involving civil insubordination, in 1410. Geoffrey of Pickering is the only case where Thorpe's allegation seems perhaps improbable.[4] However, the amount of information about his early career is very slight. It may be assumed from the absence of any mention of him in sources such as

[1] For other sources concerning Hereford, Repingdon, Purvey and Aston see notes to 499–501, 570. For the hatred of Lollards against Hereford see Hereford reg.Trefnant pp. 394–6, a letter of a Lollard in 1393 upbraiding the renegade; for that of the Lollard John Belgrave of Leicester against Repingdon in 1413 see Lincoln Vj/O, f. 10 printed Crompton (1968–9), p. 40.

[2] See note to 570 for evidence.

[3] See Hudson (1981), pp. 88–9.

[4] The identity of the man Thorpe named is hardly questionable: VP describe him as *abbas* of Byland, a post he held by 1397, whereas RA call him simply *monke*. The latter was obviously correct for the period, if any, at which Geoffrey held Wycliffite views.

Knighton, Walsingham or the *Fasciculi Zizaniorum*, that Geoffrey was never as ardent a proponent of Wycliffite causes as Repingdon and Hereford, but their later promotions within the established church should make one pause before dismissing the charge against Geoffrey solely on the grounds that he subsequently became abbot of Byland.[1]

On almost every issue where Thorpe can be checked, therefore, he can be shown to be reasonably reliable. The exception is his comments on Taylor's response to Arundel's challenge to his sermon (see above p. xv), where Thorpe's anxiety to clear his fellow Lollard seems to have led to inaccuracy or, perhaps, wishful thinking. Thorpe ends his testimony with his own assignment to gaol by Arundel: the impression that his final sentences seem intended to purvey is that the text was composed on or very soon after 7 August 1407, the date of the archbishop's conversation with him (lines 166–9). But the colophon that follows the prologue speaks of 'Arnedel, Archebischop *sumtyme* of Cauntirbirie' (lines 161–2), indicating a date not earlier than late February 1414. The colophon may well, however, be an addition on the part of the scribe of R and not original: VP lack the whole prologue and therefore naturally do not contain the colophon, but A presents the prologue but lacks just the colophon (lines 160–4). Whilst the colophon provides a *terminus post quem* for R itself, it need not indicate the date of the composition of the text itself. Certainly, there is nothing within the text that appears to refer to events after 1407—and some of those events, such as the publication of Arundel's *Constitutions* in 1409, the presentation of the Lollard Disendowment Bill in 1410, or the Oldcastle rising of 1413–14, were of a significance to both sides in the case that would make allusion probable.[2]

What happened to Thorpe after his assignment to Arundel's gaol in Saltwood? We do not know: at this point Thorpe disappears entirely from English records. The only hint, and it is one that is infuriatingly vague, comes from Bohemian sources. Thorpe is one of the very few English Wycliffites whose name is found in Bohemian sources, other than Peter Payne (Peter Engliš normally in continental texts); Payne's flight to Prague, and his participation in Hussite activities from 1415,

[1] Stronger objection might perhaps be made because of his membership of the Cistercian order: it is certainly difficult to find a parallel, though it might be permissible to wonder whether the anxiety of William of Rymington O.Cist. concerning Wycliffism, an anxiety that issued in two texts between 1383 and c. 1385 (see *PR* pp. 45–6 and references there given), could have been encouraged by his knowledge of a disciple within his own order.

[2] For the events see *PR* pp. 15, 114–17 and references there given.

is sufficient explanation for his exception.[1] Richard Wyche wrote to Hus in 1410, and it is thus not altogether surprising that the only copy of the letter he wrote whilst imprisoned by bishop Skirlawe of Durham in 1401–3 should appear in a Bohemian manuscript.[2] Apart from the three copies (one now lost) of Thorpe's conversations, conversations which, however wide the doctrinal issues covered, are nonetheless couched in strongly personal terms, there is a list of beliefs in Prague Metropolitan Chapter Library MS D.49, ff.179$^{v}$–181$^{v}$ headed *Opiniones Wylhelmi Torp* (or *Corp*), *cuius librum ego habeo*.[3] The beliefs concern the eucharist, and are certainly Wycliffite; there is nothing in them that would compel an identification with the author of the present text, but equally there is nothing in them that would preclude such identification. Although Thorpe has not so far been identified in records of Hussite affairs, this interest in an English Wycliffite seems unparalleled unless he had had some contact with Bohemia. Though it must, until further evidence is found, remain conjecture, Thorpe may well have decided, on his escape or release from Arundel's keeping, to seek refuge in Bohemia. In the same year as Thorpe's arrest two Czechs, Mikuláš Faulfiš and Jiří Kněhnic, were copying works by Wyclif in Braybrooke (Northants.), Kemerton (Glos.) and Oxford; along with these, a fragment of Wyclif's tomb, and a testimonial in favour of Wyclif purporting to be endorsed by the Oxford congregation supplied through the agency of Peter Payne, they returned to Prague.[4] It seems not inconceivable that Thorpe accompanied them, or at least followed the same route shortly after them.

## THE GENRE OF THORPE'S TEXT

Thorpe's text printed here is in some respects atypical of Lollard writing. Whilst many tracts or sermons that were produced by the sect are unremittingly serious-minded, grimly polemical with the message impersonally and sometimes censoriously purveyed, Thorpe's account

[1] See Emden *Oxford* iii.1441–3 and references there given, and in more detail W. R. Cook, *Peter Payne, Theologian and Diplomat of the Hussite Revolution* (unpub. Ph.D. thesis, Cornell, 1971).

[2] For the letter to Hus see *Geschichtschreiber der husitischen Bewegung in Böhmen*, ed. K. Höfler (Fontes Rerum Austriacarum . . . Scriptores VI, Vienna, 1865), pp. 210–12 from Prague University XI.E.3, ff. 112$^{v}$–113; for the earlier letter see Matthew (1890), 530–44 from Prague University Library III.G.11, ff. 89$^{v}$–99$^{v}$.

[3] The manuscript is an anthology of Wycliffite and Hussite materials; capital *T* and *C* are usually indistinguishable in Bohemian hands.

[4] For these events see *PR* pp. 90–91.

of his conversation with Arundel is witty and often personal. Though texts such as *Jack Upland* may show some humour at the expense of the friars, the points are to the modern reader repetitive and too predictable. Very rarely the English sermons have a sly, and perhaps to a contemporary audience pointed, dig at individual targets, but they use no friars' fables nor any exemplary tales to forward their message. Thorpe's text has a strong narrative line, and its traditional targets are individualized: names are named, including that of archbishop Arundel.

However, despite its presentation within a lively frame, it is clear that Thorpe's text at heart purveys the same doctrine that is to be found in the more usual defences of Wycliffite tenets. The central issues discussed are those of the list sent by the men of Shrewsbury, the eucharist, images, pilgrimages, tithes and oaths, all, with the possible exception of the last, the usual central issues of both Wycliffite defence and orthodox attack.[1] To these Thorpe ingeniously adds at the start the questions of the nature of the church and the freedom of preaching, both issues that affect all the charges that follow. Towards the close one of Arundel's clerks introduces the issue of oral confession, and this, together with Thorpe's prevarications, opens the debate to a more general argument on the sources of authority for the christian.[2] Thus the main central tenets of Lollardy are displayed.

Equally, the mode of argument used by Thorpe is conventional in Lollard texts. In particular it can be paralleled in texts that more schematically present the opposing views of the orthodox to be countered by those of the Lollard *true men*, texts such as *Sixteen Points on which the Bishops accuse Lollards*, *Twenty-Five Articles* or *Thirty-Seven Conclusions*.[3] In all these, as in Thorpe's presentation, the defence of Lollard standpoints and the attack on the views of the establishment proceed by the citation of biblical texts, and the addition of supporting evidence from canon law, the liturgy, the fathers of the church and, less frequently, more recent acceptable writers such as Bernard, Grosseteste or FitzRalph. All these latter are subordinated to the authority of the bible, and are of value only in so far as they ground themselves upon biblical testimony. This primacy of biblical wording is emphasised by Thorpe as he wryly questions or reproaches Arundel for his use of terms such as *material bred*, *accidents* and *substance*, insists

[1] See the notes for detailed analysis; for the issues more widely in Wycliffite history see *PR* pp. 281–90, 301–9, 334–46, 371–4.

[2] Again see the notes; the clerk's intrusion begins line 1827.

[3] See, respectively, *SEWW* no. 2, Arnold iii.454–96 and Forshall (1851).

on a scriptural understanding of the words *in forme of*, or provides biblical opposition to Arundel's praise for music.[1]

But this last example also demonstrates how far Thorpe's presentation departs from the earnest argument familiar from Lollard texts. In a long description of a contemporary pilgrimage to Canterbury, one whose wording hardly allows it to be viewed as a reflection of Chaucer's account but which does much to support that as based in observation of contemporary fact, Thorpe particularly condemns the music with which pilgrims help pass the way. Imprudently Arundel attempts to justify the playing of bagpipes (1334ff) as encouragement along a hard road. Thorpe retorts that Paul teaches not to laugh but to weep with men in affliction (1342–3). Undeterred by this warning, Arundel goes on to argue in favour of music in church by the example of David's praise of various instruments in the Psalms (1350–1). Thorpe counters that this must be taken figuratively, as is shown by Christ's expulsion of the minstrels from the house before he would heal Jairus's daughter (1361–2). To hear a sermon is better than any *fleischli solas* (1372–82). Arundel,outraged by Thorpe's audacity, moves on. But, though Thorpe has rejected music, he has not eschewed humour: not only is Arundel faulted in his perception of scripture, but he is shown as constantly outwitted by the suspect he is supposed to be questioning.

It is quite clear that Thorpe's text is not a dispassionate account of a legal process. Arundel is repeatedly shown as angry, as switching the attack because he cannot answer Thorpe's points, and as outmanœuvred by Thorpe's tactics. In realistic terms it is incredible that Arundel should have allowed Thorpe to continue his disquisitions or argue his views with so little and so ineffective opposition without, at least, abrupt silencing. At times Thorpe effectively takes over the conduct of the debate, questioning the archbishop and demanding an explanation from him.[2] Certainly, in the early trials of William Swinderby or Walter Brut, the suspect was given the opportunity to set out his arguments in full; but this in those cases was done by inviting them to set down their ideas in writing.[3] These were answered by a number of written orthodox tracts.[4]

[1] See, respectively, lines 951f, 1032ff, 977ff, 1342ff.

[2] For instance, at lines 845, 1745, 2025–58.

[3] See Hereford reg. Trefnant pp. 237–51, 252–3, 257–61, 262–70, 271–8 for various documents written by Swinderby in his own defence, pp. 285–358 for the long submission of Brut.

[4] For these see Hereford reg. Trefnant pp. 368–94 and also Woodford's tract in Paris BN lat.3381, ff. 115–124$^{v}$.

It is equally improbable that, even if argument with a heretic were allowed to proceed, Arundel should personally have undertaken the opposition without expert theological assistance. At other trials (though it must be remembered that Thorpe's conversation is plainly not a trial) of heretics as learned and sophisticated as Thorpe shows himself to be, the ecclesiastical officials brought forward a team of opponents fully capable of answering biblical text with biblical text and one patristic authority with another. The archbishops' support at the trials of, for instance, Badby, Oldcastle, or of William Taylor make this quite clear.[1]

More unusually, Thorpe's text appears to be in some senses a substitute saint's life—substitute, that is, for the hagiography of which the Lollards generally thoroughly disapproved.[2] But, just as they were not wholly consistent in their rejection of respect for those who excelled in devotion to their own cause,[3] so the Lollards were not absolute in their avoidance of the literary form that resulted from that respect. Certainly, Thorpe's account lacks two essential elements in the normal saint's life: death and authenticating miracles after death.[4] But, though the first is only feebly matched by Thorpe's unremitting insistence upon his determination not to compromise with Arundel's demands, compensation for the second might in sympathetic eyes be afforded by the wondrous way in which Thorpe manages to turn the tables on his opponent. Like a good saint's life, Thorpe's account has a moral and didactic content; but it also has a story line, an element of excitement—how will our man win against such odds? Equally, like any good old-fashioned saint's life, it does as much to establish the devilish nature of the opponent as to prove the sanctity of the hero. Only here, of course, the devil's surrogate is the primate of England,

[1] See Netter *Doctrinale* V.63 (ii.386–7), *FZ* 442–3 and Chichele reg. iii.167 respectively.

[2] For Lollard views on saints see *PR* pp. 197, 302–3; the vernacular sermon-cycle provides only a brief number of sermons for specified saints' days, almost all of them biblical figures, and achieves the remarkable feat of not mentioning the ostensible dedicatee in those provided for the feasts of St. Martin or the Seven Sleepers (see *EWS* ii.108, 110).

[3] See *PR* pp. 171–2 and von Nolcken (1987), 429–43.

[4] For the form, with particular reference to examples known in medieval England, see G. H. Gerould, *Saints' Legends* (Boston, 1916), R. Kieckhefer, *Unquiet Souls: Fourteenth Century Saints and their Religious Milieu* (Chicago, 1984) and T. J .Heffernan, *Sacred Biography: Saints and their Biographers in the Middle Ages* (New York, 1988). The discussion of Thorpe's text as 'dramatic' in R. D. Kendall, *The Drama of Dissent: The Radical Poetics of Nonconformity, 1380–1590* (Chapel Hill and London, 1986), pp. 58–67 does not seem to me particularly illuminating.

and the fiendish practices are those of the established hierarchy of the church. A slightly later Lollard text may describe Arundel as *þe grettist enmy þat Crist haþ in Ynglond*, but it is Thorpe's portrayal that demonstrates and dramatizes that claim.[1] The continuing popularity of the text into the early Reformation period demonstrates also that, even if an audience before Arundel's death in 1414 might have gained particular pleasure from the portrayal, the continuing oppression of Lollards meant that the hagiographical presentation retained its interest. John Bale is often credited with initiating the cults of 'protestant saints', but his work followed a pattern already provided by Thorpe and publicized in the [1530] print of his text.[2] The combination of Thorpe's text with an account of Oldcastle's trial, itself apparently of composite origin, in the [1530] print makes it clear that their adherence to a common genre was understood; that that genre was hagiography is revealed by the editorial material attached to each text.[3] Bale's own productions are later than the [1530] print, and, to judge by Bale's Latin translation of it, could well have been based on that model.[4] Certainly, Foxe regarded Thorpe's history as having all the force of a saint's example: he concluded the encomium of Thorpe which prefaces his reprint of the print 'thou shalt behold here in this man, the marvellous force and strength of the Lord's might, spirit and grace, working and fighting in his soldiers, and also speaking in their mouths, according to the word of his promise.'[5]

Foxe, however, correctly apprehended that Thorpe's example was cause for the reader 'both to learn and to marvel'. The instructional element would probably have gained stronger support from its author. In this regard, as in some parallel details between their accounts, it is worth comparing Thorpe's text with the letter of Richard Wyche, written probably in 1402–3 and thus only a few years before Thorpe's.[6] Wyche's letter, as it stands in the single surviving copy,

[1] BL Cotton Titus D.v, f. 13$^{v}$.

[2] See especially L. P. Fairfield, 'John Bale and the Development of Protestant Hagiography in England', *JEH* 24 (1973), 145–60.

[3] For the first see appendix III, for the second the [1530] print sig.I.4$^{v}$.

[4] See above pp. xxxi–xxxii; Bale's first printed hagiography was *A brefe chronycle concernynge the examinaciyon and death of the martyr syr J. Oldcastell* ([Antwerp], 1544; STC 1276), though, as Fairfield shows from Bale's surviving notebooks, his interest in the form goes back to his Carmelite days in the early 1520s. *Kynge Johan* seems to have been put together in the 1530s but revised later; see the details given by P. Happé, *The Complete Plays on John Bale* (2 vols., Cambridge, 1985), i.4, 9–11.

[5] *Actes and Monuments* (1563), p. 144; (1570), i.629.

[6] Transcribed from Prague University Library MS III.G.11, ff.89$^{v}$–99$^{v}$ by F. D. Matthew, *EHR* 5 (1890), 531–44; for the events surrounding Wyche's arrest and trial see

purports to be a personal document, naming some individual friends and conveying requests for materials to be brought to him in prison. Though some of these individual details are found in a final section, following on from a doxology, and could have been added to a letter intended for wider circulation, others are more firmly embedded.[1] Despite this, the tone of the letter is obviously imitated from the more personal letters of St. Paul, combining salutations to named adherents with more general exhortations.[2] Wyche's account certainly appears to describe a more credible sequence of events and investigations than Thorpe's narrative, though details of both men's experienes are parallel.[3] If difficulties arise in explaining how Thorpe's was conveyed to followers outside Saltwood, the same problem exists with Wyche's letter, even though Wyche's certainly did not gain the circulation of Thorpe's. There remain two tantalising hints, which, in default of more evidence, can hardly be amplified. First that both texts gained circulation, and in the case of Wyche's sole preservation, in Bohemia. Secondly, that Thorpe may have been known to Wyche and consequently that Thorpe's own text may have been modelled on Wyche's letter. Wyche, as one who will help fulfil his specific requests, mentions 'Henricus dc Topcliff, quia ipse habet fratrem in Topcliff qui desponsatur sorori domini Wilhelmi Corpp' (p.543).[4] There is no doubt that the manuscript reads *corpp* and not *torpp*, but the two letters, *c* and *t*, are readily confused in English or continental script of the time, and the spelling of English proper names in Bohemian copies is understandably unpredictable.[5] The list of beliefs, perhaps attributable to Thorpe, found in another Bohemian manuscript has a similar form.[6] Thorpe possibly derived from the north, and had, according to Arundel's claim, preached for twenty years in that area.[7] Acquaintance with Wyche is thus entirely credible. It is therefore

M. G. Snape, 'Some Evidence of Lollard Activity in the Diocese of Durham in the early fifteenth century', *Archaeologia Aeliana*, 4th series, 39 (1961), 355–61.

[1] See text pp. 543–4 for the requests for books, but compare p.541 for other personal greetings.

[2] Compare, for instance, Col. 4:1–18 with Wyche's final paragraphs.

[3] See comparisons above pp. xlvi–xlvii.

[4] Henricus de Topcliff was ordained subdeacon and subsequently deacon by Arundel when archbishop of York in 1392 (York reg. Arundel f. $64^{r-v}$) on the sponsorship of the Benedictine nuns of Arden, N. Yorks.

[5] See the variants from the Latin copies of Thorpe's text, lines 417, 499–501, 572–3 and elsewhere. Compare the comments of Snape (1961), p. 357.

[6] See above p. liii; Prague Metropolitan Chapter Library MS D.49, f. $179^{v}$ 'Wylhelmi Torp (or Corp), cuius librum ego habeo'.

[7] See pp. xlvii, xlix–l and lines 180–3.

possible that it was Wyche's example that led Thorpe to compose his witness, and to choose the form he did. As in Wyche's letter, the end of the story is not revealed by its teller.

## THE DIALECT OF THORPE'S TEXT

The general features of the language of Rawlinson C.208 are remarkably similar to those of Douce 53. Thus third person plural personal pronoun forms *þei*, *hem*, *her* (*Atlas* i maps 30, 40, 52); present indicative endings of verbs, 3sg. *-eþ*, pl. *-en*, *-e* (maps 646, 652). Again the northern boundary is unlikely to be north of the Wash, given the easterly nature of the language, shown by the invariable *ȝ-* forms of the verb 'give' (map 425). More precise location may be deduced from the forms *myche* twelve times beside *moche* three times for 'much' (maps 102–103), *whanne* (46 times beside *whan* three, map 337), *ony* 110 times against *eny* twice (maps 99, 98 respectively), *ech(e* (map 86), *which(e* (map 79), *sich(e* 43 times against *such(e* 39 times (maps 68 and 70), the past participle form *ȝouun* 'given' (map 432), and the preterite form *siȝ* of the verb 'to see' (map 514). Rawlinson differs from Douce in having *þoruȝ* for 'through', a form which, together with the other features, suggests Huntingdonshire.

The language of Rawlinson is similar to a number of Wycliffite orthographies localized in Huntingdonshire, as these are analysed in the *Atlas* (iii.181–94); but it seems to be identical in almost every particular with that in Lambeth Palace Library 369 (LP 427, *Atlas* iii.183–4), a copy of the Later Version of the Wycliffite New Testament.[1] The grid reference for Lambeth is given as 533 272, that is in east central Huntingdonshire, near to St. Ives and the border with Cambridgeshire and the Isle of Ely.

The language presented by A can for the most part not be localized, since it uses the standard printed orthography of its period. There is, however, a possibility that the exemplar for A was a manuscript in northern Middle English, distinctively more northern than the extant

[1] The only discrepancies are the minority forms *eny* (*ony* with very unusual *any* in Lambeth, *ony* as majority form in Rawlinson), and *moche* (only *myche* in Lambeth, as majority form in Rawlinson); Rawlinson has regular *þoruȝ*, but variation between *þenke* and *þinke* (against more variety in the former, but invariable *þenke* in the latter in Lambeth); Rawlinson uses forms in medial *-i-* for both verb and adj./adv. 'busy' whereas Lambeth has *-e-* invariably for the verb but forms in *-i-* for the adj./adv. The hands of these two manuscripts are similar but, unless the scribe's habits had in some degree changed, they are not the same.

R. This may be indicated by the appearance in A of *there* at 416 and *their* at 90, both in place of R's *þese*, implying an exemplar with the northern plural demonstrative *þir* (map 4); the isolated *tauchte* in the variant to R's *prechid* at line 1639 may originate from a northern, usually Scottish, spelling with *ch* for OE *h* (cf. ii.map 53(1)); also the nonsensical reading *seide* for R's *sad* at 520 may have been caused by a northern spelling ⟨ai⟩ for ⟨a⟩ (recorded by MED for the adjective; cf. map 637 and see Jordan §196). The concluding note of the prologue to A certainly implies the writer's awareness of linguistic differences between the north and south, and indicates also his confidence that he can supply a text for the former 'in his owne olde english'. The only trace in R of such northernism is the contracted form *tanne* for 'taken' at 468. The evidence, however, even for A's exemplar is slight.

## 3. EDITORIAL PROCEDURES

### i. *Text*

The edition of Taylor's sermon is necessarily based upon the single surviving manuscript, Bodleian MS Douce 53, ff.1–30; that of Thorpe's text on the only medieval English manuscript, Bodleian MS Rawlinson C.208, ff.1–91$^{v}$. Modern punctuation and capitalization have been substituted for that in the manuscripts, modern paragraph division has been introduced and modern word division used. Marginal or interlinear additions are shown by half brackets; responsibility for these is not specified if they were made by the original scribe, but otherwise they are designated in the variants *corr*. Letters or words that are now obscured in the manuscript (especially common on the first leaf of Taylor's text) are enclosed in angle brackets ⟨. . .⟩. Modifications in the manuscript are recorded in the variants. Emendations that consist in the addition to, or alteration of, what is written in the manuscript are shown by square brackets [ . . . ]; those emendations that consist in the suppression of words or letters in the manuscript are recorded in the variants. The beginning of a new folio in the manuscript is marked by a line | in the text, and by the details in the margin; the start of a new column is not noted. Marginal material written by the original scribe is recorded in the variants.

All abbreviations, whether in the main English text or in occasional Latin quotations, are expanded without notice. The abbreviations in both manuscripts are in the main standard, and give rise to no doubts of interpretation. Expansion of ꝑ to *per* or *par* in English follows the modern spelling of the word in question; *iħu(s)* is expanded *Iesu(s)*, *an̄crist* transcribed as *anticrist*, *g'g'* is expanded as *Gregor*. There are a few less common abbrevations and inconsistencies in both scribes' use :

i) in Douce 53 superscript *u* is used for ⟨a⟩ in 80, 745 *day*, 188 *was*, 491 *Abrahams* (second *a*), but, judging by the normal unabbreviated spelling, for ⟨an⟩ in 138, 258 etc. *þanne*, 55, 185 etc. *whanne*; crossed *l* represent ⟨ul⟩ in 386 *multiplieþ*, 474 *multiplyen*.

ii) in Rawlinson C.208 superscript *u* is used for ⟨a⟩ in 694 *was* but for ⟨u⟩ in 1229 *ȝou*; superscript *s* is used for ⟨is⟩ in 965, 2002 *þis* but for ⟨s⟩ in 900 *þis*; superscript *t* is used for ⟨ot⟩ in 57, 614 etc. *not*, but for ⟨ut⟩ in 2043 *but*; *c̄chirche* is expanded as *Cristis chirche* at 1928, *arch'* as *archebischop* 2189 etc., *q^s* as *question* 1390, 1632.

The scribe of neither manuscript is consistent in the rubrication of biblical and other quotations: some are underlined, others not. Since in some cases quotation merges imperceptibly with comment, or snatches of quotation are worked into the fabric of the writer's own material, it has been decided to reserve italicization (the modern equivalent of rubrication) for any material in Latin. Extensive precise quotation in English is enclosed in single quotation marks. In Thorpe's work biblical references by book and chapter are often given within the main text column as well as in the margin; these have been retained within round brackets, but have not been completed by the addition of verse numbers (which can be found in the notes).

## ii. *Apparatus*

In the case of Taylor's sermon the apparatus consists solely of a record of scribal corrections and of editorial emendations. The same information is recorded in the apparatus to Thorpe's text, the manuscript to which the information refers being the base, Bodleian MS Rawlinson C.208. But the apparatus for Thorpe's text is complicated by the existence of A, distant in time from the composition and subject to constant minor linguistic variation, and of VP in Latin. The justification for the treatment of these manuscripts is provided in chapter 2.b above; the following notes detail the presentation simply:

a) A. No purely linguistic divergence of any sort, orthographic, morphological, syntactic or lexical, is recorded unless it makes a clear difference to the sense. The only exceptions made to this are in the few cases where A's form might throw light on the textual history of the work. In addition minor rewording, or changes in word order, that make no difference to the meaning of the sentence are generally ignored; again the few cases where this rule is broken are where A's reading, because of its similarity to the Latin of VP, might be of interest for textual history.

b) VP. Since the language of these two manuscripts is Latin, only those readings which depart in sense from R are recorded. Readings are given in Latin, in the orthography of the manuscript cited immediately after the variant (V in the case of readings found in both VP).

In both cases, a and b, complete consistency is impossible to achieve, but I have attempted to be generous in my record. Especially in the case of proper names I have given variants wherever they might throw light on identification, even though one may suspect that VP's forms are unreliable attempts at rendering forms bizarre to the scribes. Variants from the three manuscripts, AVP, have normally been given in that order, though if V or P preserves a reading closer to the text, that is advanced. The spelling of the variant is always that of the manuscript named first; where V or P has an isolative minor variant, that is given in brackets immediately following the word in question. Where R has been emended on the basis of readings in AVP, or one or two of these, the justification for the reading of the text is given first, followed by any variant and the reading of R. These procedures produce one oddity: VP may be cited as justification for, or in support of, a reading in English, e.g. 187 my] AVP, *om.*R; obviously, VP actually have the word in Latin (here *mea*). In those cases where R would need emendation even if AVP did not exist, the full readings of AVP are (for the sake of brevity, especially given the complications of the two languages involved) not set out; but where R makes sense as it stands though is held to be defective in comparison with AVP, or where RA are both considered inferior to VP, the full justification from the other manuscripts is set out.

The following conventions are used in the variants:

] a single square bracket separates lemma from variant.
, comma separates variants to the same lemma.
*om*. omitted.
*rev*. order of two words reversed.
*marked for rev*. words written in order stated but marked for reversal
*canc*. cancelled, either by subpunction or crossing through.
*eras*. erased.
*corr*. corrected.
*on eras. corr*. written over an erasure by a corrector.
/ change of line.
// change of folio or column. These last two sometimes account for otherwise incomprehensible errors.
⌜. . .⌝ insertion above the line or in the margin.
⟨. . .⟩ letters now illegible and restored in editing.
[. . .] editorial addition to, or alteration of, the base text.
[ following word, usually in the margin, to indicate that something may have been lost by cropping.

60 17

þle of god sū men
also taugt ī mēnys
lawis recken not
how ofte þei serue͞
þe deuel : ȝhe & bico
mē his soudeouris
aȝēs god · & receyue͞
wagis wrongly for
to oppresse truþe ne
þeles in a riȝtful &
cause bisily trauayl
ned for to receyue
of a myȝty man cō
petently & mesura
bly : I trowe be no
synne    And amō
ge marchauntis is
a newe deuelrie ·
þurȝ sliȝte of þe de
uel newely brouȝt
yn : þat is callid þe

newe cheuyschaūce
so how þe deuel bap ./.
tisiþ synnes vndir
þe names of hones
tee : þ^t þei be þe lasse
orrible to men / þus
is now pride callid
honestee / demaūce :
manhood glotenye :
good felouship lec
cherie : kyndely so
lace / coueitise : wys
dom / symonye : cou
good turne for ano ./.
þer & vsurie : cheuy
schaūce þis vsurie
þanne þat I now
speke of : shulde
not be callid þe ne
we cheuyschaunce :
but þe newe vsurie

Oxford, Bodleian Library, MS Douce 53, f. 17r

# TEXTS

# THE SERMON OF WILLIAM TAYLOR

Here bigynneþ a sermoun of maistir Wiliam Taylour

*Unde ememus panes ut manducent hii. Johannis vi$^{o}$ c$^{o}$.*

þouȝ þat dyuerse doctours moralizen on dyuerse wise þese fyue louys of þe whiche is maad mencioun in þe gospel of þis day, I purpose now for shortnesse of tyme to speke to ȝow of þre maner breed of þe whiche spekiþ þe scripture. And þe firste of þese is breed of doctryne of þe word of God; þe secunde is breed of Cristis body, and þe þridde is breed of almes. As for þe firste it is writun (⟨Matt.⟩ iiii$^{o}$) 'Man lyueþ not oonly by breed but by euery word þat comeþ of þe mouþ of God.' As for þe secunde Crist seiþ (Io.vi$^{o}$) 'þe breed þat I ȝyue to ⟨ȝou is⟩ my b⟨ody⟩ for þe liif of ⟨þe world⟩.' And ⟨for⟩ þe þriide maner of breed it is writun (Isaie lviii$^{o}$) 'Breke þi breed to þe hungri' etc.

Now þanne for þe proces in þis sermoun ȝe shal | vndirstonde þat, f. 1$^{v}$ for þe puple of God shulde not perisshe bi þe hungir of breed of þe word of God, Crist whanne he shulde go up into heuene diligently comaundid his disciplis, and in hem alle disciplis of office þat weren to comynge aftir þat tyme, to breke þis breed to þe puple of God; and, in þe maner of a wiis husbonde man þat is to go from his meynee þat he mo⟨st⟩ chargide, last bi⟨hiȝt⟩ to hem seiynge 'Go ȝe and prechiþ þe gospel to euery creature.' þis þerfore is a werk of greet charge and of passyng merite if it be weel parfourmed. þerfore seiþ þe apostle (1 Thimo.v$^{o}$) 'þo prestis þat ben wel bisi, þat is to seie upon þe puple, be þei had worþi double worship, moost þei þat laboren in word and doctryn', þat is to seie goostly obedience and mynystracioun of þat þat is needeful to hem. As for þe firste seiþ Poul (to Ebrewis þe laste c$^{o}$) 'Be ȝe obedient to ȝoure curatis; þei forso|þe waken as þo þat shulen f. 2 ȝyue rekenyng for ȝoure soulis.' And for þe secunde Crist seiþ 'þe werkman is worþi his meede.' And, as þis ocupacioun diligently perfourmed is of passyng meriit, so þe necligence of þis axiþ deep dampnacioun. Herfore seiþ seint Austyn in a sermoun þat bigynneþ

1–43 ff.1–2 have been damaged by damp, especially in their outer columns; letters lost which have been supplied in the printed text are enclosed in angle brackets.
3 shortnesse] þe *canc.* shortnesse 12 shulde] shul *canc.*/ shulde 27 necligence] n *canc.*/ necligence

þus *Si diligenter attenditis fratres* 'Mi breþeren, if ȝe taken bisily entent,
alle þe preestis of þe Lord, not oonly bisshopis but also preestis and
mynystris of chirchis, ȝe knowen to be in greet perel; for to hem
witnessiþ þe Hooly Goost seyinge "Crye and cece þou not, as a
trumpe enhaunce þi voys and shewe þou to my puple þe synnes of
hem"; and also "If þou haue not shewid þe wickid man his wickidnes I
shal seke his blood of þyn hond." And if for himsilf, my moost dere
breþeren, euery man vnneþe at þe day of doom shal mow ȝyue ⟨a⟩
f. 2v rekenyng, what shal bitide þan ⟨to⟩ preestis of ⟨whom⟩ | þe soulis of
alle shal be axid?' And for to conseyue more openly þis perel Lyncolne
in þe nynteneþe dicte puttiþ þis caas, þat if a nedy man þat vnneþe
haþ plente of oo loof bynde streitly himsilf to feede plenteuously and
gloriously a ful greet puple perisshinge for hungre, and he puttiþ herto
also þat he þus boundun be necgligent to seke mete notwiþstondinge
þat he haþ but ful litil, and ⟨it⟩ [b]e litil what [he] haue [ʒit he] castiþ it
awey folily, is not sich oon gilty of þe deeþ of hem þat perisshen for
hungir, whom bi his boond he is hooldun to feede? Siche ben today
many heerdis, whanne, þe puple beynge in perel þurʒ hungir of þe
word of God, þei taken upon hem þe office of an heerde, upon peyne
of dampnacioun to feede wiþ breed of þe word of God, of verry feiþ
and moral preceptis, in þe whiche stondiþ heelþe and wiþoute whom
f. 3 heelþe is not. Þei ben also nedy of mete, for þei mown treuly | seie þe
wordis of Isaie þe profete (iii° c°) 'In myn hous is no breed.' For manye
of hem can not expowne to þe puple oon article of þe feiþ, ne oon of
þe ten heestis; and of so manye loouys ben þei nedy how manye
articlis ben of þe feiþ and of moral preceptis needeful to heelþe, þe
whiche þei can not expowne. And, whanne þei han not þese louys and
ben boundun to fede þe puple soget to hem wiþ þese louys, ʒit þat þat
þei can not þei ben recheles to lerne, ʒhe, manye of hem dispisen
wiisdom and doctrin. And, moreouer, if þei ouʒt haue of kunnyng,
encumbr[i]n[ge] hemsilf in worldly ocupaciouns and ʒyuyng entent to
lustis, þei forʒeten þat litil kunnyng so ferforþ þat þei han no sauour,
and also kunnen not comyne of heuenly and goostly þingis.' For, as þe
gospel seiþ, 'He þat is of þe erþe spekiþ of þe erþe.'

f. 3v And certeyn þurʒ malice of þe deuel, bi whos enuye deeþ | haþ
entrid into al þe world, al þis is wrouʒt þat preestis ben þus drawun fro
goostly lyuyng and prestly ocupacioun and ben acumbrid in worldly

43 be] he   56 ʒit] and ʒit   59 encumbringe] encumbren   60 þei[1]] þat þei   64 wrouʒt] wro *canc./* wrouʒt

nedis. Herfore in þe Apocalips xiiº cº, it is writun þat 'þe wrooþ serpent, knowinge þat he shulde haue but a litil tyme, sente out a greet flood out of his mouþ aftir þe womman fleynge into desert, þer to make hir be drawun of þe flood.' þis serpent is þe deuel, as we reden in Genesis iiiº cº. þis serpent is wrooþ for he knowiþ þat þe tyme bi þe which he shal tempte man is but short, in þe which tyme he haþ a delectacioun in temptinge of men, and woot weel þat aftir þat tyme he shal haue ful peyne wiþouten any liking. And herfore he is more cruel aȝens þe chirche of hem þat shulen be saued for to tarie it and þe day of doome. And, bicause þat he siȝ þat, if þe chirche and þe spouse of Crist and specialy þe spiritual part þerof | (þat is to seie þe clergie) f. 4 were so feruent in preestly office as it was in þe bigynnynge, fleynge into desert of contemplacioun, of studie and trewe and hooly preching, disseuered from þe noyse of temporal þingis, þe noumbre of hem þat shulden be saued [shulde be] fulfillid [and] þe day of doom shulde anoon be present, þerfore þe wrooþ deuel sente a greet flood aftir þis womman, þat is to seie to greet habundaunce of temporal goodis as Parisience seiþ on þe same text. And þis dide þe deuel for to make þe womman to be drawun of þe flood. And so he haþ his purpos and haþ wiþdrawun þe clergie from preestly office and brouȝt it into so greet worldlynesse as we now seen, þat vnneþe reckiþ now ony man of þe office of preesthood to þe puple. Wel woot þe malicious deuel bi oold experience þat if he myȝte acumbre ony of þe clergie in þis flood þat he shulde spedily fulfille his office. | Herfore þe fool deuel, seynge f. 4v Iesu, an innocent man, trewe and leuyng þe world, dredinge lest Crist shulde strongly wiþstonde him, wolde haue cumbrid him in þis flood. Herfore, as we may rede in þe iiijº cº of Mt., 'þe deuel took up Iesu into a ful hiȝ hille, and shewide him alle þe kingdomes of þe world and þe glorie of hem, and seide to Iesu "Alle þese þingis I shal ȝyue to þee, if þou fallinge doun shalt worshipe me." And Iesu seide to him "Go, Sathan! It is writun 'þe Lord þi God þou shalt worshipe, and to him aloone þou shalt serue.'"'

Neþeles for þis temporal lordship þat Crist, in ensaumple of þo þat shulden be hise foleweris, fully refuside, sum men, pretendinge or shewinge hemsilf to ocupie Cristis stide and his apostlis, goen ful lowe not oonly to men, leuynge þe fredom of þe gospel wherbi a spiritual man deemeþ alle þingis, but also falliþ doun bi symonye to þe deuel bi

87 woot] w *canc.*/ woot    89 shulde] shulde not    93 world] a *canc.*/ world

f. 5 vsurie, | flateringe and lesynge and oþere hidouse synnes. And þat is ful hiȝ merueyle to þenke on þo þat in þe bigynnynge of þe chirche at þe ensaumple of Crist and his apostlis dredden worldly lordship, and leften hous and feeldis, londis and rentis, as a þing wiþdrawing men fro plentee of perfeccioun of þe gospel and fro þe maner of lyuyng in þe staat of innocence, þe which lyuyng parfiit men aftir her power shulden desire, ben so fer fallun þat vnneþe þe more part of temporaltees and fatte beneficis may fulfille her appetiit. So ferforþ þei ben bisottid bi vnordynat loue to þe world þat þei reioycen hem to be callid lordis and kingis in her owne. And certeyn in þis þei ben ful contrarious to Crist, for, as þe gospel of þis day wiþ þat þat sueþ folewinge telliþ þat, aftir tyme þat Crist had merueylously fed þe puple, f. 5v and þei wolden | haue takun him for to haue made him seculer king upon hem, he fledde into þe hil, vttirly refusynge seculer lordship, confermynge þat to seculer lordis, seyinge on þis wise 'Ȝeldiþ to Cesar þat bilongiþ to Cesar.' Lo! Crist, notwiþstondynge þat Cesar was no riȝtful man but a mawmetrer, confermyde to him his seculer lordship raþere þan he wolde receyue it himsilf. And Petir, wiþoute meene tauȝt of Crist, seiþ þus 'þer shulde be no lordis in þe clergie, but þat þei shulden be maad ensaumple of þe flok of wille,' þat is to seie of meekenes and of forsaking of þe world. And Petir, conformynge his speche to Cristis wordis, seiþ in his firste epistle þe secunde chapitir 'Seruauntis, be ȝe sugetis to lordis in al drede, not oonly to goode and mesurable but also to trewauntis.' þe same techiþ Poul bi word and ensaumple: in word in þat þat he techiþ in þe firste pistle to f. 6 Thimo[the] vi$^{o}$ c$^{o}$ 'Seruaun|tis be ȝe obedient, not oonly to feiþful but also to vnfeiþful lordis'; in dede techiþ he þis, for he dredde so moche for to be acumbrid wiþ þis flood and for to ȝyue oþere men occasioun or ensaumple of couetise, þat he lefte for to receyue þat þing þat was grauntid to him bi autoritee of þe gospel, and wiþ his owne hondis gat þat him nedide.

And as longe as it stood þus in þe chirche, and þe apostlis wiþ þo þat ocupieden her stides fledden worldlynesse and weren war þat þei weren not encumbrid in seculer nedis, fleynge þe occasioun þerof (þat is to seie seculer lordship), þe chirche encrecide in noumbre of verry cristen men in name and dede. And þanne was þe puple as þe preestis ful feruent in þe loue of God and keping of his lawe, where now as þe puple so þe prestis ben fallun into obstynat and customable breking of

113 gospel] g *canc.*/ gospel 134 chirche] a *canc.*/ chirche

þe comaundementis of God. And þus, as þe Iewis in tyme of Crist boostiden and magnifie|den hemsilf of þe bodily circumcisioun, not f. 6v charginge þe circumcisioun of þe herte þat God cheefly sou3t, so now cristen ypocritis, defoulid or infect wiþ þe sourdow of fariseis þat is ypocrisie, wherof Crist comaundid his disciplis to be war, boosten of her bodily baptym, not chargynge þe baptym of soule from al vnclennesse. A3ens suche puple spekiþ seint Petir in his firste pistle iii° c° 'Cristenyng makeþ us saaf, not þe puttinge awey of þe vnclennesse of þe fleish but þe examynyng of a good conscience to God.'

And of þis blynd ypocrisie, in þe which restiþ þe chirche boþe of lerid and of lewde, sorwfully pleyneþ seint Bernard (*super Cantica omelia* xxix[a]) where he techiþ þat on þre maners þe deuel antecrist pursueþ Cristis chirche, first bi tirauntrie in tyme of martris, aftir bi heresie in tyme of doctouris and now bi ypocrisie. And þis per-secucioun is moost | perelous, as Bernard seiþ, for 'If þer roos up an f. 7 opyn eretiik he shulde be cast out and wexe drye, and if þer roos up a violent enemy a man my3te hide him fro him. But now whom shal a man caste out, or fro whom shal a man hide him? For alle ben frendis and alle ben enemyes, alle nedeful and alle aduersaries, alle of houshoold and noon pesible, alle nei3eboris and alle seken þat þat is hers, mynystris of Crist and seruen antecrist. Woo to þis generacioun for þe sourdow of farisees þat is ypocrisie! And it shulde be seid ypocrisie, þat now hidiþ him not, and for aboundaunce may not, and for defaute of shame it desiriþ not to be hid. Þis rootid scabbe crepiþ aboute bi al þe body of þe chirche, and þe bradder þe lesse hope of amendement, and þe ynnere it goiþ þe more perelous it is. Sumtyme it was seid, and tyme of fulfillinge is come, "Lo in pees my | bittirnesse is f. 7v moost bittir". Þis is þe vois of þe chirche: it was bittir in þe tyme of martris, bitterere aftirward in þe confluct or striif of eretikis, but now moost bittir in maners of þo þat ben of houshold. Now a man may not chace hem awey, neþir fle hem, so stronge þei ben woxun and multiplied aboue noumbre; ingrowun and vncurable is þe wounde or þe myscheef of þe chirche. And þerfore in pees is þe bittirnesse þerof moost bittir. But in what pees? Þer is pees and þer is no pees: pees fro paynyms, pees fro eretikis, but not pees from þe sones. Þis is þe voys of þe weylynge chirche in þis tyme: "Sones haue I norischid and

142 not] and not may] a *canc.*/ may 158 but] bi *canc.*/ but 171 moost] n *canc.*/ moost

enhaunsid, þei forsoþe han forsake me.” þei han forsake me and defoulid me bi foul liif, foul wynnyng and foul marchaundise’, as is symonye and oþir marchaundise in þe chirche, and also bi ypocrisie.
f. 8 And certis, if we taken bisily heede of þe | staat of þe chirche, resonably shulde it stonde wiþ us as sumtyme it stood wiþ þe children of Irael, as it is writun in þe [firste] book of Esdras þe iii$^{o}$ c$^{o}$ where þe book seiþ þat ful many of þe preestis and dekenes and eldre men, þat siȝen þe temple of God first whanne it was foundid and þe [secunde] temple, in her iȝen þanne wepten wiþ a greet vois, hauynge mynde of þe noblete and glorie of þe raþere temple, in reward of which þe secunde was nouȝt. Certeyn, so haue we greet mater of weping, if we biholden þe nobletee, glorie and clennesse of þe raþere chirche in Cristis tyme and his apostlis and þo þat sueden hem vnto þe tyme þat þe serpent (as I seide bifore) had cast þe greet flood aftir þis womman. For in þat tyme þe puple feruently louede God and his lawe, and weren diligent in þe kepynge þerof, and dredden synnes and specialy
f. 8$^{v}$ summe to hidouse, as vsurie, | symonye, auoutrie, forswering, manslauȝtir and þe vnmesurable filþehede of leccherie, þe which of oolde rootid custom so fer ben brouȝt into wone þat vnneþe now þei moun be repreued, but raþer (as in tyme of distruccioun of Sodom and Gomor) is blamed þe repreuer of synne þan þe doer of synne. And so wondirful is þe chirche in comparisoun of þe tyme herbifore. Neþeles summe now as in þat tyme, not seynge þe abhomynacioun of þe desolacioun stondinge in þe hooly place, shynyngly arayed and delicatly fed wiþ poore mennys goodis, criynge areren up her vois in gladnesse—and summe wepen; and so þe vois of hem þat maken mirþe and þe vois of þe wepyng of þe puple ben medlid togidere. But þe vois of þe wepers, takynge heede to her owne wrecchidnesse bodily and goostly, desirynge for to be releued fro bodily myseese and to be
f. 9 liȝtned in soule bi þe word of | God, weilen her owne mysese and oþeris boþe. But þat vois is so þinne and so lowe þat it may not be herd among þe vois of hem þat maken ioye, þe whiche, not reckinge of þe heelþe of her owne soule neþir of oþeris þat ben bitakun to her cure, seien in effect þat word of Zacharie xi$^{o}$ c$^{o}$ ‘Blessid be God we ben maad riche,’ and lyuen as delicatly and rechelesly as þouȝ þat þei weren in dispeir of liif to comynge.

Lord! wher þer be ony hope of amendement of þe myscheef þat þe

183 firste] secunde 185 secunde] *om.* 187 which] o *canc./* which 196 custom] and custom 200 now] no *canc./* now 209 vois] vo *canc./* vois whiche] w *canc./* whiche 214 wher] se *canc./* wher

chirche stondiþ ynne, and of þe wiþdrawing of þe clergie from her office and fro þe maner of lyuyng of Crist and his apostlis? Certeyn, me leeueþ þat þer shal be remedye, for þe text of þe Apocalips seiþ þus suynge þat 'þe erþe halp þe womman, and openede his mouþ and swolewide þe flood þat þe dragun sente out of his mouþ, and | þus f. 9v delyuerede þe womman fro þe flood þat she myȝte freely flee into desert.' So it is to hope. And to þat sowneþ þe profecie of Hildegar þat temporal lordis wiþ þe comuntee, þe whiche lyuen actiifly and sumtyme weren but as erþe in comparisoun of þe clergie, whos lyuyng or conuersacioun shulde be in heuene (as þe Apostle seiþ), of wilful, free and meek delyueraunce of þe clergie shal take in greet partie þis flood fro þe clergie, and shal helpe it þat it be not drawun of þe flood of temporaltees fro his office, but þat it may freely flee into desert of contemplacioun and take entent to preestly ocupacioun. And to þis shulde þe clergie be redy and wel willid. For, if Crist and his apostlis, exempt fro payinge of heed money bicause þat þei vsiden no marchaundise or craft neþer hadden londis ne rentis seculerly, ȝit payede tribute þat þei wolden not | offende þe lordis and þe puple (as f. 10 seint Austyn seiþ in þe *Book of Questiouns of þe Oolde and þe Newe Lawe* þe lxxixº cº), how moche raþir oure clerkis, and specialy þo þat ben deed to þe world, in so greet a neede of þe rewme shulden be redy to delyuere up into þe hondis of seculer men alle her poscessiouns and tresours euene to þe reule of þe apostle, þat is to seie þat 'þei holde hem apayd wiþ necessarie liiflode and hilyng'; and on þis wise releeue þe chirche of Engelond and peese it and specialy þe comyntee, at þe ensaumple of Crist and his apostlis þat releuede þe nedy puple as þe gospel of þis day telliþ. Þus seynt Austyn, as Possedony telliþ, preiede þe citeseyns þat þei shulden take þe possessiouns þat þei hadden ȝoue to him and his felowis.

And Hildegar in hir profecie seiþ þat boþe þe more and þe | lesse of f. 10v eiþir puple shulden so ordeyne for þe clergie, and so dispose þo þingis þat ben nedeful vnto hem, þat neþer in liiflode ne cloþing shulden þei haue defaute. And þis profecie is þe more to be bileeued þat she seiþ þat antecrist shal bisie him to wiþstonde þis purpos of God wiþ bynding and vnbynding, wiþ flatering and wiþ þretenyng, wiþ noyse of armure and closing of heuene. And summe of þese we han seyn bitidde: closing of heuene is no þing ellis þan hidyng of þe lawe of

233 austyn] a *canc.*/ austyn 234 how] ho *canc.*/ how 235 greet] m *canc.*/ greet 243 him] him *canc.*/ him

God and of Cristis lyuyng fro þe puple, as Crisostom seiþ upon þat word of þe gospel 'Woo to ȝow scribis and farisees þat closen þe kingdom of heuenes bifore men.' Wel woot þe deuel antecrist, wiþ þo þat cleuen to him, þat he shal be killid wiþ þe spiriit of Cristis mouþ, as seint Poul techiþ in þe secunde pistle to Tessalonycences ii$^{o}$ c$^{o}$; and þe spiriit of Goddis mouþ is Cristis lawe, as he seiþ himsilf 'þe wordis
f. 11 þat I haue spoke to | ȝow ben spiriit and liif.' þanne bi þis spiriit shal antecrist be killid, acordinge to seint Ion in his pistle and seint Austyn upon þe same pistle and in a book þat is clepid Austyn *Of þe Wordis of þe Lord* þe xlvi$^{o}$ c$^{o}$, and Lyncolne in partie acordiþ to þis in a sermoun þat bigynneþ *Natis educatis et assuefactis*. Acordinge þanne wiþ þese I calle antecrist al þe confederacie of hem þat aȝens Crist and aboue his gospel magnyfien mennys tradiciouns and lawis for wynnyng and delicat liif, and bisily doen execucioun of her owne wille and comaunding, not reckinge of þe heestis of God and his lawe. And how shal God slee þis antecrist? Truly I hope neþir bodily ne goostly, but as þe postle spekiþ to þe Romains þe vi$^{o}$ c$^{o}$, þat is to seie þat þis antecrist 'Be deed toward synne and quyk in Iesu Crist.'

And truly God haþ blowun a blast of þe spiriit of his mouþ upon þis
f. 11$^{v}$ antecrist, for to slee him bi preching of his gos|pel. And þe mynystris of antecrist bisien hem for to quenche þis spiriit. But þe vnauysi deuel wiþ his lymes, euere enforsinge aȝens himsilf, shal not haue þe maistri aȝens þe truþe and trewe men þe whiche, þe more þat þei ben oppressid, þe more encreecen wiþ þe children of Irael. And to þis purpos spekiþ also Crist in Mathew xvii$^{o}$ c$^{o}$, seiynge þat 'Helie shal come and restore alle þingis,' declaringe þe gilis of antecrist and his ypocrisie, and as Abraham, Moyses and Crist shal renewe þe lawe of God in þe puple and bringe þe puple to þe knowing of God. But wheþir þis shal be Helye in persoone, as it semeþ to manye men, or ellis wiþ Ion Helye in condicioun, or wheþer he be now comun longiþ not to me for to seie, for I kan not. But þis knowe I weel, into þe tyme þat þe clergie þat, as Crisostom seiþ, is þe stomak of þe chirche, be
f. 12 clensid of þat þat is cause of al þe discrasyng | and siknesse in þe body of þe chirche, shal þer be no stidefast and long heelþe in þe chirche, þouȝ medicyn of sorewe, shrift and penaunce doyng aswagiþ þe sorewe and aking for a tyme in þe sike lymes. But as men weren wont aftir feyned turnyng in lente turne aȝen to her synne, so shal þei

259 acordinge] whom acordinge 264 wynnyng] *above first* y *otiose nasal mark*
273 not] a *canc./* not 275 oppressid] op *canc./* oppressid

hereaftir,—and þat for defaute of þe breed of Goddis lawe mynystrid to hem in ensaumple and word.

For if þe clergie, þat shulde be þe liȝt of þe worlde, is turned into derknesse, how shal þe puple conteyne hem in þe weie þat lediþ to heuene, 'Whanne he þat walkiþ in derknesse woot not whidir he goiþ,' as þe gospel seiþ. Also þe clergie shulde be þe salt of þe erþe as Crist seiþ, wherbi þe puple shulde be kept fro corrupcioun of synne; and if þis salt bi yuel ensaumple be turned into corrupcioun, what shal be in þe chirche but corrupcioun? Also þe clergie shulde be a citee | sett on (f. 12v) an hil wherynne þe puple shulde fynde plenteuous vitailis of trewe doctryne and hooly ensaumple; and if þis citee be turned into an vplondish þroop, nakid of vitailis how shulde þe puple be fed? And if þe clergie, þat shulde be þe aungel of God of oostis, ledinge þe puple fro Egipt into þe lond of biheeste, be an aungel of Sathanas transfigurid into an aungel of liȝt, how shulde þe puple walke sikirly to þe place purposid, while þe leder techiþ aweyward? And if þe clergie, þat shulde be þe spiritual part of þe chirche, quykenynge þe body of þe chirche as þe soule doiþ mannys body, be turned into deeþ no wondir þouȝ þe body of þe chirche ligge deed. And on þis wise shal it stonde into þe tyme þat þer be a contrarie turnyng, þat is to meene þat derknesse be maad liȝt, corrupcioun be maad salt, þat þe vplondish þroop be | maad a citee, (f. 13) þat þe aungel transfigurid into an aungel of liȝt be maad in deede an aungel of liȝt, and deeþ be maad liif, þat of þe same come liif of whom came deeþ. Certeyn, ellis wole not þe puple be fed wiþ þe touȝ breed of þe gospel.

And herfore Crist in þe gospel of þis day comaundide his disciplis þat þei shulden make men to sitte doun. So, certeyn, mosten þe disciplis of office þat ben preestis make men to sitte doun, þat is to seie bi good ensaumple þei make men obedient to God and his lawe, and redy to ete of þis breed, etinge wiþ hem of þe same, ȝyuynge to hem appetiit. Ellis forsoþe þe puple shulen refuse þis breed, seiynge wiþ þe children of Irael 'Oure liif wlatiþ on þis mete moost liȝt'; and þei shulen feede hem wiþ þe fleish of Egipt, þat is to meene wiþ lustis of þis world, þe whiche þei seen her dukis gladly ete. Þis is shewid bi comun | (f. 13v) experience þat we seen þe vntauȝt puple excuse her synne bi her autours of synne. And, if ony man wolde dele amonge hem þe breed of þe gospel, þei refusen it and asken breed þat þei seen oþir ete

289 mynystrid] mynystri/trid 300 shulde] sh *canc.*/ shulde 310 þat] sett on an hil *canc.* þat 316 doun] a *canc.*// doun 325 þei[2]] þ *canc.*/ þei

lustily, and seien 'Whi repreuest þou me of my synne?'; and leyen for hem, and seien 'Seest þou not þis bisshop, þis persoun and þis preest, how þei doen?' þanne at þis siik stomak moste we bigynne if we wolen heele þe siik body of þe chirche.

Herfore seiþ God to hem þat shulden clense þe citee from synne, as we reden in Ezechiel þe ix° c° 'Bigynne ȝe at my seintuarie.' Herfore also Crist, comynge to purge þe chirche of his Fadir, he bigan at þe temple and castide out alle þe abhomynaciouns þerof, and chacide awey out of þe temple biggeris and silleris, þe whiche, as Parisiense [f. 14] seiþ in þe *Book of Vicis* figuriþ symonyentis. þese symonyentis | shenden al þat þer is, and bicause þei han sold grace þei han no grace to profite in þe chirche; and also þei ben acursid of Crist and of seint Petir and of al Cristis chirche, and ben brouȝt yn bi þe deuel her patroun, and his desiris þei wolen fulfille.

Leuynge at þis tyme for defaute of space to speke of þe secunde breed, I go to þe þridde breed þe which as I seide is breed of almes. Almesdede is a werk of greet charge. For, certeyn, for þat duly fulfillid or þurȝ necgligence left, Crist bihotiþ us blisse or peyne euerlastinge, as it is writun in þe gospel of Matheu xxv° c°. And bicause þat we shulden be war þat we be not vnmerciful, Crist techiþ us in Luc þe xvi° c° what bitidde of an vnmerciful man, riche and glotoun, þat delicatly and shynyngly fedde himsilf wiþ his owne goodis, not [f. 14v] reckynge of þe wrecchid Lazar | ligginge at his ȝatis; and so þe riche man diede and was biried in helle. Upon þis axiþ seint Austyn þe cause of þe dampnyng of þis riche man, namely siþen þer is no mencioun maad in þe gospel þat he was a raueynour, wrongful chalenger and extorcioner, ne oppresser of fadirles and modirles children or of widowis, but he was riche. Wherof was he riche?—of his owne. What þanne was þe cause of þe dampnyng of hym? Certeyn, bicause þat he was vnmerciful, seynge þe mysese of his broþir and hauynge no mercy on him: for þis vnmanheed was he dampned. And if þis, seiþ seint Austyn, be þe peyne of auarous men, what is þe peyne of raueynours? If he is sent into helle þat ȝaf not of his owne goodis, whidir shal he be sente þat bi raueyne takiþ oþere mennys goodis? If he brennyþ wiþ þe deuel þat cloþide not, whidir shal he be sent þat [f. 15] spoylide | men? Also in Luc þe xii° c° Crist telliþ how 'þe feeld of a riche man brouȝt forþ plenteuous fruytis, and he seide wiþynne himsilf "What shal I do þat I haue not whidir to gedre my fruytis?"

336 sold] le *canc.*/ sold 338 þe] þe *canc.*/ þe 342 of] of gr/ werk *canc.* of

And he seide “þis shal I do: I shal stroye my bernes and I shal make grettere, and þidir shal I gedere alle þingis þat ben growun to me and my goodis. And I shal seie to my soule ‘Soule, þou hast manye goodis putt up into ful manye ȝeeris; reste, ete, drinke and make feeste.’” Forsoþe, God seide to him “Fool! In þis nyȝt þei shulen take þi soule fro þee”’, þat is to seie þe deuel. ‘“þo þingis þat þou hast arayed, whos shulen þei be?”’ Lo, what bitidde of þis riche man! Certeyn, I doute me not, manye men ben in þe caas of þis riche man or ellis in worse, þat laboren to encreece her poscesciouns and richessis, and to fulfille bernes and shoppis and gedren bisily, and holden hem no⟨ȝt⟩ | f. 15v apayed wiþ her owne goodis, but bi extorcioun, wilis of þe lawe and ouerledyng of poore men, bi false and gileful weiȝtis, wily wordis, vnriȝtwise mesuris, vsurie, symonye and ypocrisie and oþere vnleeful meenys wiþoute noumbre geten hem goodis. And þei maken noon eende of her hertily bisynesse aboute þe world, seiynge wiþ þis riche man ‘Soule, reste þou’.

But if a clerk haue getun him a benefice þat is worþ þe rule of þe apostle, þat is to seie liiflode and cloþing, þanne getiþ he him a pluralitee and traueliþ day and nyȝt bi flateringe, presentis and ȝiftis and aȝens þe lawe of God acumbriþ him⌜silf⌝ in seculer ocupacioun to plese men and to encreece his goodis. Notwiþstondinge þat he woot weel þat he shal be dampned for necligence aboute þat litil cure þat he haþ, but if he do betere his diligence, ȝit he multiplieþ him cure upon cure as he wolde | haue depper dampnacioun. f. 16 And sich oon may not glose himsilf wenynge þat he be excusid bi his viker. For as Lyncolne seiþ in a sermoun þat bigynneþ þus *Scriptum est de leuitis*, þouȝ sugetis of sich a recheles curat be saued bi oþere, ȝit for he doiþ not his bisynesse he is gilty. And þerfore he puttiþ sich an ensaumple: if ony man ouȝte for to mynystre to anoþer man bodily liiflode and he wiþdrawiþ it fro hym, þouȝ he dye not but lyueþ bi þat liiflode þat he getiþ elliswhere, ȝit he sleeþ him in as moche as in hym is. Herfore also seiþ Gregori þat so manye deþis ben þei worþi to how manye þei myȝten haue profitid if þei hadden come forþ into an opyn place. And Lyncolne seiþ also, in a sermoun þat bigynneþ þus *Natis educatis etc.*, þat he þat on þis wise haþ a vikery in cure shal haue a vikeri in þe laste rewardynge. And | wher þou þat aȝens þe lawe of God stondist f. 16v acoumbrid in worldly nedis art bettir þan Moyses whos glorie of contemplacioun was shewid out of his face? Or art þou bettir ocupied

400 worldly] la *canc.*/ worldly

þan was he þat in þe hille of contemplacioun talkide wiþ God as a freend is wont to speke wiþ his freend? þe which Moyses also lefte in his absence two wise vikeris, Aaron and Vr, þat kouden answere to þe questiouns of þe puple as Moyses seiþ. And ȝit God comaundid him for to go doun for þe puple had synned, bicause þat Moyses himsilf shulde refourme þe puple to þe lawe of God. How moche raþere þou þat vnneþe hast oon fool preest, also vnkunnyng as is þe puple þat is sogett to þee, shuldist go doun, leuynge þi worldly ocupacioun þat þou ocupiest aȝens þe lawe of God, so þat þou boþe bi ensaumple and
f. 17 word brynge aȝen þe pu|ple of God.

Sum men also, tauȝt in mennys lawis, recken not how ofte þei seruen þe deuel, ȝhe, and bicomen his soudeouris aȝens God and receyuen wagis witingly for to oppresse truþe; neþeles in a riȝtful cause bisily examyned for to receyue of a myȝty man competently and mesurably I trowe be no synne. And amonge marchauntis is a newe deuelrie, þurȝ sliȝte of þe deuel newely brouȝt yn, þat is callid þe newe cheuyshaunce. Lo! how þe deuel baptisiþ synnes vndir þe names of honestee þat þei be þe lasse orrible to men. þus is now pride callid honestee, veniaunce manhood, glotenye good felouship, leccherie kyndely solace, couetise wiisdom, symonye oon good turne for anoþir, and vsurie cheuyshaunce. þis vsurie þanne þat I now speke of shulde
f. 17v not be callid þe newe cheuyshaunce but þe newe vsurie. | But certis Crist, willynge to putte awey al maner of vsurie boþe opyn and colourid, þe which is more perelous þat it liȝtloker drawiþ a man þerto, seiþ þus 'Ȝyueþ ȝoure loone, hopynge no þing aȝen þerof', so þat þe leenyng shulde be ȝouun and not solde. And if up hap þou þenkist 'My goodis in þe meene tyme myȝten haue encree⟨cid⟩ my poscescioun', so certeyn þei myȝten þe meene while haue be etun wiþ wormes and stolun of þeues or haue ben stried wiþ rust. Ȝhe, more it is þat God ȝyueþ to þee for þi charitable loone, þat is to meene a gree of meriit wiþ þe meede suynge, þan alle þe goodis þat þou hast or maist haue. Ȝhe, it is licly þat þi goodis ben encreecid bi þi charitable loone, for þe Wise Man seiþ in þe Prouerbis xiº cº. 'Sum men departen her owne goodis and ben maad þe ricchere, and summe bi raueyne taken
f. 18 oþere mennys goodis and euere | ben in neede.' Herfore þe Iewis þat, aȝens þe lawe of Crist and his gospel, wolden be maad riche bi vsurie ben maad so poore þat þei ne haue lond ne citee to dwelle ynne but bi

404 kouden] ko *canc.*/ kouden    410 so] and so    415 cause] n *canc.*/ cause
430 wormes] a *canc.*/ wormes    438 dwelle] dw *canc.*/ dwelle

greet daunger. And certeyn ofte tyme we seen þis bityde þat aftir tyme þat men bi vnleeful meenes ben maad riche and enhauncid in þe world, and han shoppis, bernes and shelues fulle of goodis, faire wyues, children and meyne, and wolden wiþ þese þingis lyue a longe lusty liif and reste þerynne, þanne sodeynly in effect God seiþ to hem þat 'in þis ny3t', þat is to seie in derknesse of vnkunnyngnesse and faute of puruyaunce for liif to comynge, þat 'þei shulden dye'; manye siche in a short tyme shulden we haue seyn dye. Neþeles what bitidde aftir of siche men bilongiþ not us to deeme. And of euery sich chynche, and specialy of a clerk, may it be askid 'þo þat þou hast | arayed, whos [f. 18v] shal þei be?' þerfore, enauntir lest it bitide þee, as it bitidde þat riche chynche, bi tyme breke þi breed of almes amonge þi nedy breþeren.

And aftir þe biddyng of Crist in þe gospel of Luk þe xiiii$^{o}$ c$^{o}$ 'Whanne þou makist þi feest of pitee calle poore feble, lame and blynde and þou shalt be blessid; for þei han not wherwiþ for to rewarde þee, it shal be rewardid þee in þe rewardyng of ri3twise men.' For þe vndirstondyng of þis text Crist techiþ and specifieþ here þre bodily mysesis þat vnabliþ a man to gete his liiflode bi his labour, þat is to seie feblenesse bi age or siiknesse, lamenesse þat is depryuyng of mannys lymes bi birþe, hap or violence as bi prysonyng, and þe þridde is blyndnesse. Euery of þese bi himsilf vndisposiþ a man to labore. þanne whanne it is so þat a man haþ ony of þese mysesis wiþ pouert, þat is | wantyng of goodis of þis world, he shulde be callid to þis feeste; [f. 19] and riche men shulden make a puruyaunce for siche men þat þei shulden not bi neede be constreyned to go aboute as we now seen. And þat meeneþ Crist whanne he seiþ in þe text þat I aleyde bifore 'Calle poore' etc. What shulde greue þee, þat of mouable þingis art worþ two or foure hundrid pound, and wiþ þat maist spende of 3eeris rente twenty pound, for to fynde two or þre þat on þis wise ben at nownpower to laboure? And what shulde greue a clerk seculer or religious, þat may spende bi 3eer foure or fyue þousand pound of almes of poore men to þis eende bitakun to her disposicioun, to fynde two hundrid or þre hundrid on þat wise as I tolde bifore vnable to gete her liiflode?

But what doen þei nowadayes? Certeyn, as we seen aftir þe quantite of almes of poore men, | þei multiplyen hem meynee as worldly as a [f. 19v] temporal lord, and alle þe my3tye of þe cuntree þei confederen to hem

446 what] w *canc./* what 449 lest] lest if 459 blyndnesse] bl *canc./* blyndnesse 461 shulde] sh *canc./* shulde 466 maist] ia *canc./* maist

for to putte doun vndir foot þe poore, alwey bringing yn, in as moche
as in hem is, newe bondage as Farao dide on þe children of Israel. And
whanne þei han waastid þe bodyes of her sogetis, vsynge hem as
beestis, and bi extorcioun haue take of her goodis and trauelis as
moche as þei may, þanne þei suffren hem for to go whidir þat þei
wolen abeggid. Oo! how fer ben þese vnmerciful fro þe condiciouns of
merciful Iesu and his apostlis, þat alle her vitaylis, fyue looues and
twey fisshis, ful gladly and diligently delyden in releeuynge of nedy
men? And summe of þese han in her ordynaunce of poore mennys
almes, what in moeblis and vnmoeblis, twenty þousand pound,
waastynge þat in worldly vanytees, suffren poore men þat owen þese
f. 20 goodis to peris|she in body as we seen, and also in soule as it is to
drede. Wher we moun þanne leeue þat God, þat is a riȝtful iuge and
indifferent, þat biriede in helle þese two riche chynchis of þe whiche
we han spoke bifore, shal birie siche vnmerciful boþe clerkis and
vnlettrid in Abrahams bosum? It is no doute stondynge oure feiþ, but
if þei do fruytful penaunce, þei shulen haue sorewe up hepid. For if
þes sueris of Iudas, vndir colour of releeuynge þe nedy puple,
heepynge and encreecynge to hem þe patrymonye of Crist, þat is þe
almesse goodis, not reckynge of þe nedye as þe dede shewiþ, shulden
ascape wiþoute ful greuous peyne, it nedide not a man to charge of þe
getyng and spendyng of worldly goodis.

Þanne bi her couetise þei constreynen þe nedy puple to begge
f. 20v aȝeen þe lawe of God. For in tyme of lawe of kynde I am not | avisid
þat ony man beggide; and in tyme of lawe ȝouun to Moyses
begging was ful streitly forbodun in Deutronomy xvº cº. And in tyme
of lawe ȝouun bi Crist, Crist ordeynede sufficiently for his chirche:
for temporal lordis, confermynge to hem her worldly lordship,
seiynge 'Ȝeldiþ to Cesar þat longiþ to Cesar', þe same dide Petir and
Poul as it is writun bifore. For þe clerkis Crist also ordeynede,
ensaumplynge hem and techynge hem to receyue þat þat was
nedeful to liiflode bi title of þe gospel and not of beggyng, seiynge on
þis wise 'Þe werkman is worþi his meede'; and þerfore he took þat
hym nedide of hem þat he dide to a preestis office. And for þe
comyntee he ordeynede, confermynge her iust labour, partynge wiþ
hem of her goodis. And wiþ þo þat myȝten not laboure he chargide
f. 21 þese þre par|tis of þe chirche, so þat þe clergie procure to hem þat þat

478 han] se *canc.*/ han 483 gladly] n *canc.*/ gladly 486 waastynge] and waastynge 488 wher] o *canc.*/ wher 501 ful] fu *canc.*/ ful

hem nediþ, as seint Poul dide, as it is writun in þe firste pistle to Corinthis þe xvi$^{o}$ c$^{o}$, where he comaundide a colect to be maad for þo þat hadden no fredom of labour. And how þat oþere shulden calle sich puple to þe feeste of pitee, makynge a puruyaunce for her nedis, techiþ Crist as it is writun bifore, and bihotiþ for þat mercyful dede euerlastinge liif, as it is writun in Mathew xxv$^{o}$ c$^{o}$ where Crist seiþ þat he shal rewarde wiþ þe kingdom of heuenes þo þat releeuen men in prisoun, or ellis siik wiþ ony of þese þre maner siiknessis specified bifore, wheþir it be mete or drinke, cloþing or housyng, þe whiche foure ben nedeful to euery man. Poul also in þe firste pistle to Tymothe þe v$^{o}$ c$^{o}$ techiþ þat a widewe shulde not be chosun to lyue on þe almes | of þe chirche bifore sixty wyntir, but þat she shulde laboure f. 21$^{v}$ in trewe mennys housis, getynge her owne lyuyng, þat þe chirche shulde not be ouerchargid and vnsufficient for verry widowis. Also Petir, as it is writun in þe storie of seint Clement, blamyde Clementis modir for hir begging and seide þat she shulde traueile wiþ hir hondis. Þe apostlis also, in whom was þe plente of perfeccioun of þe gospel, whiche also hadden þe firste fruytis of þe Hooly Goost, wiþ a comyn asent ordeyneden þat þer shulde be no needy man or womman amonge hem, for it was departid to euery as it was neede. Þus also Clement, as we may rede in his storie, ordeynede þat þer shulde be no nedy man and begger amonge þe puple.

Of þis processe þanne it semeþ þat it was of þe purpos of Crist, Petir and Poul, Clement, ȝhe and alle þe apostlis, þat þer shul|de no f. 22 nedy man and begger be amonge þe puple. But 'Poore men', Crist seiþ 'alwey shulen we haue wiþ us,' for ellis riche men shulden be bareyn, as Crisostom seiþ, not hauynge whom þei shulde releeue wiþ to moche abundaunce and superfluytee of her goodis. And if þis blessid rule, ordynaunce or pollicie of Crist and his apostlis had be kept for to now, we shulden not haue fallun into so manye inconuenyentis as we ben now, ne þer shulde not haue be sich a grucching and rumour for vitaylis amonge þe puple vnpayed, and gaderingis or quyletis maad as we now heeren. For temporal lordis shulden haue be sufficient in rentis and possessiouns for to defende hemsilf and þe rewme, and for to auaunce her children, where now, as Bede techiþ in a pistle *Ad Egbertum episcopum Eboracencem*, so manye temporaltees bi þe foly ȝyuyng of | temporal lordis ben ȝouun to vnprofitable puple to God f. 22$^{v}$

513 seint] se *canc.*/ seint   516 makynge] m *canc.*/ makynge   525 housis] ho *canc.*/ housis   530 fruytis] fr *canc.*/ fruytis

and man þat vnneþe is lefte wherwiþ þat fortraueilid kny3tis sones may be releeued. And þe cause whi þat þis puple is vnprofitable and first to God is for þei lyuen vnreligiously to Godward and as to her nei3heboris. For two causis þei ben vnprofitable: first for þei prechen not, defendinge þe puple from goostly enemyes; þe secunde for þei fi3ten not bodily, defendynge þe puple from bodily enemyes. And certis þe wagis ordeyned of Crist hadden be ynow3 to susteyne þe clergie nedeful to þe puple to mynystre hem lore and doctryn and sacramentis.

But whanne ony man spekiþ of þis mater sum men anoon caren for susteynynge of greet bildyngis of tree and stoon, and recken not of þe susteynynge of þe hooly temple of God þat is man, þe which, glorified
f. 23 in body and soule, shal be euerlas|tynge tabernacle of God, for þe which to be repareilid Crist fro þe myddis of his herte shedde out his precious blood endelesly, lasse reckinge of sich costlew bilding. Herfore whanne þe apostlis of a maner worldly curiouste shewiden Crist þe bildyng of þe temple, he seide ‘Not a stoon shal abide upon anoþir but þat it be distryed.’ But 3it meene I not oþerwise but þat cristen men shulden haue an honest hous, not ful costlew, neþer abiect, for to come togidere þere to preye God, heere his lawe and to receyue her sacramentis. And certis, if þis ordynaunce of Crist and his apostlis hadde be kept, þe comyntee of þe puple shulde haue be my3ty and sufficient in husbondderie and marchaundise to susteyne hemsilf, to paye þe lordis her rentis and oþere þingis þat ben due to hem, and
f. 23v to susteyne þe clergie in her office, and wiþ two oþere partis | of þe chirche to bere þe charge of fyndyng of þo þat moun no lengere traueile; where now, for þe wiþdrawing of þe ordynaunce and þe pollicie of Crist and his apostlis, we ben fallun into so greet a defaute and into a maner wrecchidnesse þat euery astaat pleyneþ of pouerte and defaute. And no wondir þou3 men, presumynge to amende þe ordynaunce and þe pollicie of Crist, fallen into inconuenyentis vnsuffrable, þo3 it seme hem to be spedy for a tyme. Þe cause whi þat Crist and his apostlis wolde no beggeris be may resonably be þe greuouse synnes þat comunly suen customable beggeris, as ypocrisie, flateringe, lyinge, enuye, drunkenesse and leccherie. Neþeles þis yuel þus is brou3t yn, as in þe eelde testament, aftir tyme þat bisshopis dignytees weren bou3t and soold, as Ierom seiþ upon Mathew. And
f. 24 biside þe lawe of God weren brou3t yn coueitou|se sectis as farisees,

572 husbondderie] husbond/derie

gaderinge to hemsilf wiþ her ypocrisie þe substaunce of þe almes aȝens þe lawe of God. Clamerous beggeris weren nedid to sitte at ȝatis ⌜and⌝ biside weies, and crye and begge. And in tokenynge þat Crist loþide sich begging, he heelide siche men not oonly in soule but also in body, þat þei myȝten gete þat hem nedide bi her bodily labour. Þus in þe newe testament aftir þe chargeous noumbre of sectis brouȝt yn biside þe lawe or ensaumple of Crist þat as farisees bi ypocrisie, flateringe and fals suggestioun appropren to hem þe goodis of hooly chirche, swolewinge up þe substaunce of almes due bi Cristis wille to poore men þat I haue specified bifore, and aftir þe fal of þe clergie into þis wondirful worldlynesse, ben wrecchid cristen men as we seen for to gete hem goodis constreyned for to grope aboute from dore to dore and crye and begge.

And ouer þis, þe | more sorewe is, þer growiþ up a newe vnfoundid f. 24v sect of beggeris, walkinge in greete noumbre in habiite of seculer preestis, þat prechen for wynnyng, and merueilously wiþ her fablis bimadden þe puple, and so sclaundren Crist and his chirche, and specialy oþere honest preestis of good lyuyng and competent lettrure þat freeliche at þe ensaumple of Crist and his apostlis prechen to þe puple þe truþe of þe gospel. And for to coloure her vngroundid beggyng þei putten upon Crist þat he shulde haue beggid of þe womman of Samarie, whanne he seide to hir 'Womman, ȝyue me drinke'. But, and her malice had not ablyndid hem, þei myȝten se þere how Crist had sente his disciplis into þe toun for to araye hem mete not beggid but bouȝt. For þe text seiþ þus 'Disciplis of Iesu weren goon into þe citee for to bie mete'—and þat was no tokene of a begger. Þei myȝten ferþermore perceyue if þei wolden þat Crist, | innocent f. 25 man, whos ben alle þe goodis of þe world bi title of innocence, seide not in begginge maner but on comaundinge maner 'Womman, ȝyue me drynke'. Þei myȝten also se bi þe dede or effect suynge þat it was not bodily watir þat Crist principaly axide of þe womman, but watir of sorewe for synne and of feiþ, not oonly of þat womman but of manye oþere Samaritans. Herfore Crist, verri man, so moche enioyede himsilf in spiriit of þe turnyng of þe Samaritans þat him lust not ete of þe mete þat was arayed for him, but seide 'I haue mete for to ete þat ȝe knowen not', þat is, as þe glose seiþ, þe turnyng of þe Samaritans to þe bileeue. And bicause Crist was a Iew of nacioun and tunge, and þe womman was a Samaritan, and Samaritans and Iewis comynen not

599 goodis] -is *partially eras.*

togidere, herfore Crist, for to bringe yn comynyng wiþ þe womman of
f. 25v þe watir of liif, seide 'Wom|man, ȝyue me drinke', for it is þe maner of a
discreet man, if he haue ony greete þing to be sped aȝens ony þat he is
not homely wiþ, for to bringe yn his cheef entent bi meenys. þus bi
meenes he brouȝt yn more comunyng wiþ þe womman, for to repreue
hir of hir auoutrie, and seide 'Go and calle þyn husbonde, and come
hidir.' And þe womman seide 'I haue noon husbonde.' And Iesu seide
to hir 'Wel hast þou seid þou hast noon husbonde, for þou hast had
fyue husbondis, and he þat þou hast is not þyn husbonde.' Wiste not
Crist as weel þat þis womman had noon husbonde as he wiste þat she
hadde fyue afore, and þat he þat hadde hir at þat tyme was not hir
husbonde? But, for to bringe yn his cheef entent for to speke to þis
womman of hir auoutrie, he seide 'Go and clepe þin husbonde, and
come hidir', as to þe same entent he seide 'Womman, ȝyue me drinke.'
f. 26 | And þurȝ þe wiisdom of þe Hooly Goost ben þese two clausis set
togidere in þe gospel: ' "Womman, ȝyue me drynke." And his disciplis
weren goon into þe citee to bye hem mete', þat enemyes of Crist þat of
þe firste wolden bilyȝe Crist, seiynge þat he beggide whanne he seide
'Womman, ȝyue me drinke', bi þe nexte clause suynge aftir þei shulden
perceyue þat he had no neede, and þus þei shulden be takun in her
owne falsnesse.

þese enemyes of God seien ferþermore þat oure Iesu shulde haue
beggid an hous of Zachee, whanne Crist, seynge Zachee upon þe tree,
seide to him 'Zachee, hastynge come doun, for þis day I moste dwelle
in þyn hous', where Crist spekiþ as a lord comaundynge and not as a
nedy man begginge. And Crist þat tyme hadde aboute hym a greet
noumbre of puple, as þe gospel seiþ, and eche of hem desiride þe
f. 26v presence of Crist as Zachee dide; and þei þat weren | myȝty wolden
haue had him to her placis, and þerfore þei grucchiden þat Crist ȝede
forþ wiþ Zachee. þanne nedide not Crist for to begge an hous. For
Zachees profiit þanne, for to turne him to þe feiþ, and not for his owne
neede, maistirfully he lymytide to himsilf Zacheis hous, and
comaundide him to go doun for to receyue him into his hous.

And ouer þis þese lyeris colouren þer beggyng, seiynge þat Crist
shulde haue beggid þo þre dayes þat Marie and Ioseph hadden left
hym in Ierusalem and þei weren turned hoom toward Nazareth. But
certis þis is not licly, for it was writun in þe lawe þat Crist came not to
distruye but for to fulfille þat 'On no wise shulde a nedy man and a
begger be amonge þe puple'. And þouȝ it so be þat Crist, þat is truþe
and eende of figuris of þe oolde lawe, breeke summe serimonyes þat

weren figuris, in tokenynge þat, comynge þe | f. 27 truþe, figuris shulden ceesse, ȝit am I not auysid þat he brak ony moral precept, but raþere confermyde hem and declaride hem as we reden in Mathew þe v° c°. And þouȝ Crist at nownpower to laboure þanne, but a child and fer from hoome, hadde beggid þilke þre dayes, as Bernard or Alred his clerke meueþ (as it semeþ uppon þat word of þe gospel *Cum factus esset Iesus annorum duodecim*), ȝit shulde not þis be clepid strong, wilful, clamerous and customable begging þat I inpugne now but begging constreyned. Þus knyȝtis, as we weenen, spuylid in fer cuntrees, haastynge to her owne, beggen for þe tyme leeffully. And also aftir þo þre dayes bi þe whiche, as Cristis aduersaries seyen, he shulde haue beggid, Crist ȝede doun wiþ Marie and Ioseph into Nazareth and was sogete to hem, and vside, as summe doctouris seien, Iosephis craft—and þis is ful licly, for þe Iewis calliden him not oonly carpenteris sone, but also þei cal| f. 27v liden hym Iesu þe carpenter, as it is writun in Markis gospel—and þat shulde not Crist haue doon if it hadde be so greet of perfeccioun to lyue bi customable begging as summe ypocritis boosten now, namely siþ þe gospel seiþ þat fro þis tyme forþ 'Iesu wexide in wiisdom, age and grace bifore God and al þe puple.' Þanne, if þei wolen take a ground of perfeccioun and perfiit lyuyng of Crist, þei shulden raþer take it from þat tyme forþward þan fro þat tyme bifore, and aftirward he beggide not as I suppose now. And as to Bernard or Alrede his clerk answeriþ Ardmakan and seiþ þat it is seid bi maner of meuyng and not bi maner of affermyng.

Herfore also Fraunceis, as it is writun in his *Rule* and *Testament*, wolde not his breþeren begge, as he neuere beggide but trauelide wiþ his hondis, and wolde þat alle his breþeren traueliden and gaten her liiflode wiþ ho| f. 28 nest labour, and not receyue money bi hemsilf, neþir bi meene persoones; and wolde also þat þis *Rule* shulde be vndirstonde wiþouten any glose aftir þe witt of grammer, and þat þei shulde not seie þis is not þe *Rule* but anoþir. Þanne good were it for to wiþstonde þis errour in þe bigynnyng, for a litil errour in þe bigynnyng wiþouten wiþstonding bringiþ in a ful greete. And lete us not paciently heere so greete a blasfemye falsly put upon Crist, þat is to seie þat he, as þe bigylid puple weeneþ, hadde beggide, for þat myȝte not he do for þre causis. First for Crist is God, wherfore he hadde ful lordship uppon alle creaturis bi title of creacioun. Bi title also of innocense he hadde as Adam ful lordship of alle þingis þat nediden to mannys vse. And þe

696 wiþstonde] w *canc.*/ wiþstonde

þridde skile is for he was a trewe preest and bisshop to þe Iewis, doynge duly his office to þe puple, þerfore he my3te, as he dide bi title f. 28v of þe | gospel, receyue þat þat was needeful to hym in execucioun of his office.

Lete us not þerfore li3tly leeue to hem þat so vngroundly putten begging upon Crist. And, 'While we han tyme, lete us do good', for anoon we shal go and stonde bifore þe iugement of Crist to resceyue þere aftir oure werkis. For vnneþe suffisiþ any of us to lyue fourty wyntir, and what is þat, siþen þat a þousand 3eer bifore þe i3en of God ben but as 3istirday þat is passid, and ofte tyme we seen weel þat þe 3ongeste sonnest dyen. And ouer þis, as it semeþ to seint Austyn in þe *Book of Questiouns of þe Oolde and þe Newe Lawe* in þe C and vi° c°, þat þe day of doome is uppon us, where seynt Austyn seiþ þat, as in þe sixte day God made man and in þe seuenþe day he restide from alle his werkis, so in þe sixte þousand of 3eeris God bou3te man, and in þe f. 29 seuenþe þousand of 3eeris þe world shal cece. And bi þe cronyclis of | þe world þer ben passid of þe seuenþe þousand sixe hundrid and fyue. And up hap, as Crist bood not vnto þe eende of þe sixte þousand for to bigge man, but bou3te man in þe eende of þe secunde hundrid of þe sixte þousand, so li3tly shal he not abide into þe eende of þe seuenþe þousand for to deeme þe world. And þis seiyng of Austyn is þe more euydent þat we seen signes ben verified þat Crist spekiþ of, 'Of erþequakis and hungir bi placis, of batels and opynyouns of batels, of þe bitrayyng of þe fadris and eldris bi her sones and ny3 kyn' and oþere moo, and specialy of þe tribulacioun which oon was not fro þe bigynnyng, of þe which it semeþ of þe dede is now present. For in þe tyme of þe lawe of innocence þe deuel pursuede Adam and Eue; and no wondir for þei weren þat tyme of contrariouse lawes. In tyme also f. 29v of þe lawe of kynde mawmetreris and oþere þat kepten it not | pursueden hem þat kepten it, as we may rede in processe of scripture. In tyme of lawe 3ouun bi Moyses paynyms þat receyueden it not pursueden Iewis þat bileeueden þerupon. And in tyme of lawe 3ouun bi Crist and his apostlis Iewis and paynymys out of þe bileeue pursueden feiþful men þat bileeueden it and kepten it. But now is þer a tribulacioun—was þer neuer noon sich—for he þat pretendiþ himsilf moost parfiit cristen man, boþe bicause of staat and of ordre, pursueþ anoþir cristen man þat to þis eende comyneþ in þe lawe of God for to

712 wyntir] u *canc.*/ wyntir    722 man[1]] n *canc.*/ man    man[2]] re *canc.*/ man
732 not] not i, i *canc.*    733 scripture] scrip/scripture

lerne it and enfourme, as he is holdun, his sogetis and for to be saued bi it. And certeyn to deuely a dede is it for to chace men fro knowyng of þe lawe of God. For, þouȝ it be not spedy to boistous puple in manye sotiltees to curiously ocupie her wittis, in tokenynge wherof Crist in þe gospel of þis day comaundide not þe | puple but his f. 30
disciplis to gadere þe relifs of ⟨þe fe⟩este, ȝit for to werne þe puple þe greete and historial mater of þe gospel were noon oþir but to kille hem. Wiþdrawe þee þerfore from yuel and do good, brekynge þe breed of almes amonge þe nedy, as it is seid bifore. And, as þou releeuest a man wiþ þi worldly goodis, so do wiþ þi goodis of kynde and of grace, þat wiþ þi strengþe þou defende hem, if neede be, and wiþ þi kunnyng and discrescioun þou gouerne hem and enfourme hem. And so in alle wise letiþ ȝoure plentee, as Poul biddiþ, fulfille oþere mennys defautis. And if ȝe do þus God shal dwelle wiþ ȝow, here bi grace, and in liif to come bi ioye; and þat graunte ȝow God. Amen.

Here eendiþ þis sermoun and bigynneþ þe sermoun of þe Horsedoun.

742 knowyng] kn *canc.*/ knowyng

# THE TESTIMONY OF WILLIAM THORPE

## A Prolog

The lord God þat knowiþ alle þingis woot þat I am riȝt sorwful for to write or to make knowe þis sentence bineþeforþ, forþi þat of myn euencristen sett in hiȝe staate and in dignite so greete blyndenesse and malice mai be knowen þat þei, þat presumen of hemsilf for to distroien vicis and to plant in men vertues, neiþir dreden to offende God ne louen to plesen hym, as her werkis schewen. For, certis, þe heestis of God and his lawe, whiche into þe preisynge of his moost holy name he comaundiþ to be knowen and kept of alle men and wymmen, ȝonge and olde, aftir þe kunnynge and power þat he haþ ȝouen to hem, pr[e]latis of þis londe and her mynystris, wiþ þe comente of prestis chefly consentynge to hem, enforsen hem moost bisili to wiþstoonde, f. 1v settyn[g] | at nouȝt þis holi ordinaunce of God. And hereþoruȝ þe Lord is wraþþid greetli and moued to take hard veniaunce, not oonli on hem þat doon þis yuel, but also vpon alle hem þat consenten to þese antecristis lymes, whiche knowen eiþir miȝte knowen her malice and her tirauntrie, and ouȝten to wiþstonde her viciousnesse and wol not.

Naþeles foure þingis mouen me for to write þis sentence bineþeforþ. þe firste þing þat moueþ me hereto is þis: whanne it was knowen to diuerse freendis þat I cam from þe prisoun of Schrouesbori, gessynge, as it bifelle in dede, þat I schulde go into þe Erchebischopis prisoun of Cauntirbirie, þanne dyuerse freendis in sunder placis spaken to me ful herteli. And þei diden to me ful f. 2 freendli, comaundinge to me | þat if it bifel þat I schulde be examyned bifore þe Erchebischop, þat I schulde, if I miȝte in ony wise, write to hem boþe myn aposynge and myn answeringe. And I behiȝt to þese

a prolog . . . on erþe (164)] *om.* VP  a prolog] *om.* A  2 bineþeforþ] beneth written A  forþi] where A  6 heestis] biddinge A  10 prelatis] pr/latis R  12 settyng . . . þis] and destroye the A  settyng] settyn R  16 tirauntrie] falshode A  ouȝten] dresse them not A  viciousnesse . . . not (17)] malice and their greate pryde A  19 whanne] wher as A  *margin* 1 R  20 diuerse] certeyn A  21 gessynge] and A  go] *om.* A  22 erchebischopis] *om.* A  23 þei . . . me[2]] *om.* A  24 freendli] tenderly A  25 to hem boþe] *om.* A my special frendis, if I myȝte and whanne I miȝte, þat I wolde ful gladli as I miȝte do her biddinge.

þe secunde þing þat moueþ me for to write þis sentence is þis: diuerse frendis, whiche haue herde þat I haue ben examyned bifore þe Erchebischop, haue come to me into prisoun, counseilinge me bisili, and coueitynge greetli þat I schulde do þis same þing. And oþere special frendis haue sent to me, requyringe me on Goddis bihalue þat I schulde write oute and make knowen boþe myn apposynge and myn answring, for þe profit þat þei seyen ouer my knowyng may | come f. 2v
þerof. But þis þei bidden me: þat I bisie me wiþ alle my wittis to go as nyȝ þe sentence and þe wordis as I can, boþe þat weren þere spoken to me and þat I spak, enaunter þis my writynge come ony tyme bifore [þe] Erchebischop. And of þis counseile I am riȝt glad; for in my conscience I was moued to bisie me hereaboute, and to axe herto þe special help of God. And so þanne I, ymagynynge þe greet desire of þese sondir and diuerse frendis of sondri placis and cuntrees, acoordinge alle in oon, I occupiede me herwiþ diuerse tymes so bisili [in] my wittis þat þoruȝ Goddis grace I perseyued, bi her good mouynge and of her cheritable desir, sum profit þat myȝt come of þis writing. For truþe haþ þis condicioun: whereeuere it is enpugned, þer comeþ þerof odour of good smel, and þe more | violentli þat enemyes enforsen hem to f. 3
oppressen and to wiþstoonde þe truþe of Goddis word, þe ferþir þe swete smel þerof strecchiþ. And no doute, whanne þis heuenli smel is moued, it wol not as smoke passe awei wiþ þe wynde; but it wol descende and reste in summe clene soule þirstinge þeraftir.

And þus sumdel bi þis writyng mai be perseyued þoruȝ Goddis grace how þat enemyes of truþe, perseuerynge boldli in her malice, enforsen hem for to wiþstonde þe fredom of Cristis gospel, for which fredom Crist bicam man and schedde oute his hert blood. And herfore, þat is for pitee and sorowe þat many men and wymmen doon her owne weyward wille, and bisien hem not to knowen ne to don þe

27 and . . . miȝte] *om.* A 29 *margin* 2 R 33 special frendis] brethren A requyringe] and requyringe R, and required A 38 ony] another A þe erchebischop] erchebischop R, þe Archebishope and his counsell A 40 bisie . . . -aboute] do this thing A 42 and cuntrees] *om.* A 43 me . . . wittis] all my mynde and my writtes so besyly A in] *om.* R 44 good] *om.* A 45 of . . . writing] ther throwe A truþe] sothefastenesse and trouth A þis condicioun] these condicions A 46 odour . . . smel (47)] a swete smell and thereof comes a swete savoure A 47 enforsen] dressen A 48 of goddis word] *om.* A ferþir . . . strecchiþ (49)] þe greater and the sweter smell cometh therof A 49 no . . . whanne] therfore A is moued it] of goddes worde A 53 perseuerynge] standing A 56 for] great A

plesyng wille of God, þo men and wymmen þat louen truþe, and
f. 3v heeren or knowen of þis pursuyng þat now is in þe | chirche, owen
hereþoruȝ to be þe more moued in alle her wittis, to ablen hem to
grace, and to setten so litil pris bi hemsilf þat þei wiþouten tariinge
forsaken wilfuli and gladli al þe wrecchidnesse of þis liif, siþ þei
weten not how soone, neiþer whanne, ne where, ne how, ne bi whom
God wol visite hem and asaie her pacience. For no doute whoeuere
wolen lyue here piteousli, þat is cheritabli in Crist Iesu, schulen suffre
now heere in þis liif persecucioun in o wise or in oþere—þat is, [if] we
schulen be saued. We moten ymagyne ful bisili þe vilþe and þe
hideousnes of synne, and how þat þe lord God is displesid þerþoruȝ;
and so of þis vilþe and hideousnesse of synne we moten bisien vs in
alle oure wittis, for to cacchen and holden in oure mynde a greet
f. 4 schame of synnynge; and | so þanne we owen for to sorewen hertili
þerfore, and to haten it euermore, fleynge þe occasiouns þerof. And
þanne we moten taken vpon vs and vsen scharp penaunce contynuelli,
for to deseruen of þe Lord forȝeuenesse of oure forme-don synnes,
and grace to absteyne vs heraftirward fro synne. And, but we enforsen
vs to don þus wilfulli and in couenable tyme, þe Lord, if he wol not
lese vs, wol in dyuerse maneres moue tyrauntis aȝens vs, for to
constreynen vs violentli for to don penaunce, whiche we wolden not
don wilfulli. And, certis, þis doynge is a special grace of þe Lord, and
a greet tookne of loue and of merci. And no doute whoeuere wolen not
bisien hem, as it is seid bifore, for to ponyschen hemsilf wilfulli, neiþer
wolen suffre pacientli, mekli and gladli þe ȝerde of þe Lord, howeuere
| þat he wole ponysche hem, her weiward willis and her vnpacience
f. 4v ben to alle siche folkis erlis of euerlastinge dampnacioun. But, forþi
þat þer ben no but fewe in noumbre þat ablen hem þus feiþfulli to
grace, for to lyuen here sympli and poreli, and wiþouten galle of
malice and of grucchyng, herfore þe louers of þis world haten and
pursuen hem whom þei knowen pacient, meke and mylde, sobir, chast
and wilful pore, hating and fleyng alle worldli vanitees and fleischli

58 louen truþe] heare the truthe and sothefastenesse A 59 pursuyng þat] perceyuynge what A 61 so litil] lesser A 62 gladli] bodely A 64 visite] teache A 66 if we] A, we R 67 þe hideousnes] foulnesse A 69 and[2]] of A 70 cacchen] abhorre A 72 to haten it] *om.* A occasiouns] occasyon A 73 and vsen] *om.* A contynuelli] contynuynge therin A 76 in couenable] inconuenient A 77 lese vs] vtterly destroye and caste vs awaye A 80 loue] lyfe A 81 bisien hem] applye himselfe A hemsilf] hymselfe A 83 hem] hym A 86 poreli] purely A 88 mylde sobir] *om.* A

lustis—for, certis, þese vertuous condiciouns ben euene contrarie to þe maners of þis world.

Þe þridde þing þat moueþ me to write þis sentence is þis: I coueite, as I schulde bisie me mysilf to do feiþfulli, þat alle men and wymmen occupieden feiþfulli alle her wittis in knowynge and kepynge of Goddis heestis, ablynge hem so to grace þat | [f. 5] þei mi3ten vndirstonde truli þe truþe, and haue and vsen vertues prudence; and so to deseruen for to ben li3tned fro aboue wiþ heuenli wiisdom, so þat alle her wordis and her werkis ben herþoru3 maad plesynge sacrifise to þe lord God, and not oonli for þe helþe of her owne soulis but also for þe edificacioun of al holi chirche. For I doute not þat ne alle þei þat wolen ablen hem to haue þis forseide bisinesse schulen profite ful myche boþe to freendis and to enemyes. For summe enemyes of truþe þoru3 þe grace of God schulen bi siche charitable folkis ben maad astonyed in her concience, and in hap conuertid from her vicis to vertues. And also þei þat bisien hem feiþfuli to knowe and to kepe þe heestis of God, and to suffren pacientli alle aduersitees, schulen herþoru3 counforte manye freendis. | [f. 5v]

And þe fourþe þing þat moueþ me to write þis sentence is þis: I knowe, bi my sodeyne and vnwarned apposynge and answerynge, þat alle þei þat wolen of good herte wiþouten feynyng oblischen hemsilf wilfulli and gladli aftir her kunnyng and her powere to suen Crist pacientli, trauelyng bisili, priuili and apeertli in werk and in word to wiþdrawen whom þei mowen fro vicis, plantyng in hem vertues if þei mowen, comfortyng and ferþeryng alle hem þat stonden in grace, if herwiþ þei ben not enhauncid into veyn glorie þoru3 presumcioun of her wisdam neiþer englaymed wiþ ony worldli prosperite, but meke and pacient, purposyng to abide perceuerauntli þe wille of God, suffryng wilfulli and gladli wiþouten ony grucchynge whateuer 3erde þat þe Lord wole chastise hem wiþ, þis good Lord | [f. 6] wole not þanne faile for to counforte, and helpe alle siche men and wymmen in euery moment and at euery poynt of ech temptacioun þat euery enemye purposiþ a3ens hem. For to siche feiþful louers specialli, and pacient

90 þese] their A   92 coueite as] thought A   *margin* 3 R   94 occupieden] occupiyng A   wittis] besynes A   95 ablynge] able A   99 helþe] helpe A   105 bisien hem] laboure A   108 *margin* 4 R   109 bi] *om.* A   110 oblischen] able A   114 stonden] stondyeth A   if] so that A   116 englaymed] enflamyd A   120 and helpe] *om.* A   euery moment] all their tribulacyons A   121 ech] *om.* A   euery[2]] any A

suers of Crist, þis Lord sendiþ his wisdom fro aboue, which aduersariis of þe truþe moun not knowen neiþir vndirstonden.

But, þoruȝ her olde and her newe vnschamefast synnes, þese tirauntis and enemyes of truþe schullen be so blyndid and so obstinate in yuel þat þei schullen gessen hemsilf to don plesyng sacrifice to þe lord God in her malicious and wrongful pursuyng and destroiyng of innocent ⌜men⌝ and wymmens bodies, which men and wymmen for hei vertues lyuynge, and for her trewe knowlechyng of f. 6v truþe, and for her pacient, wilful and glad suffrynge | of persecucioun for riȝtwisnesse, deseruen þoruȝ þe grace of God to ben eiris of þe eendles blis of heuene. And for þe feruent desir and þe greet loue þat þese men and wymmen han to stonden hemsilf in truþe and to witnessen it, þouȝ þei ben sodeynli and vnwarned brouȝt forþ to ben apposid of aduersaries, þe Holi Goost, þat ruliþ hem and moueþ hem þoruȝ his charite, wole in þe our of her answeringe speke in hem and schewe sich wisdam, whiche alle her enemyes schulen neiþer aȝenseie neiþer aȝenstonde lawfulli. And herfore alle þei þat ben stidfast in þe feiþ of God, which þoruȝ þe ⌜bisie⌝ kepinge of his heestis, and for her pacient suffring of whateuere aduersite þat comeþ to hem, hopen tristili in his merci, purposynge to stonde continualli in þe f. 7 parfit | charite. For þese men and wymmen dreden not so þe aduersitees of þis liif þat ne þei wolen, aftir her kunnyng and her power, knowlechen prudentli þe truþe of Goddis word, whanne and where and to whom þat þei haue euydence þat her knowlechynge mai profite. And þouȝ herfor persecucioun come to hem in oo wyse or in oþere, certis, as alle þei knowen whos conuersacioun is in heuenes, it is a passinge rewarde and a special grace of God for to haue and to welde þe euerlastinge heritage of heuene, for þe suffringe of ony persecucioun in so schort tyme as is þe terme of þis liif. For lo! þis heuenli herritage and eendeles rewarde is þe lord God himsilf, whiche is þe beste þing þat mai be: þis sentence witnessiþ þe lord God himf. 7v silf, | seiinge to Abraham in Gen. 15° c°, 'I am þi meede.' And, as þe Lord seide he was and is þe meede of Abraham, so he is of alle his oþer seyntis. Þis mooste passynge and best meede he graunte to vs alle for his holy name þat made vs of nouȝt, and sente his oonli and moost

128 sacrifice] sacrifyces A 130 hei] their A 134 truþe] sothefastenesse A 142 tristili] surely A 144 aftir . . . knowlechen (145)] feare (after their connyng and their power) to knowlege A 146 haue . . . her] thynke A 148 as . . . whos] thei paciently take hit knowyng their A 149 passinge] hye A 150 welde] enioye A ony] one A 154 in Gen. 15° c°] *om.* A 156 passynge] blessyd A

dereworþe sone, oure lord Iesu Crist, for to aȝenbeie vs wiþ his moost prescious herte blood! Amen, Amen.

Here eendiþ þe prolog of þis book, and and bigynneþ a book of a clerke þat was apposid of fyue þingis of Arnedel, Archebischop sumtyme of Cauntirbirie; of þe whiche fyue questiouns þe clerk answeriþ bi holi scripture, of þe whiche scripture þis clerke makiþ knowen his bileue to Goddis chirche on erþe.| f. 8

þe I questioun

Knowen be it to alle men þat reden or heeren þis writinge byneþforþ þat, on þe Sondai next aftir þe feste of seint Petir þat we clepen Lammasse, in þe ȝeer of oure Lord a þousand foure hundrid and seuene, I, William of Thorp, beynge in þe prisoun in þe castel of Saltwode, was brouȝt bifore Tomas of Arnedel, Archebischop of Cauntirbirie and chaunceler þanne of Ynglond. And whanne I cam to him, he stood in a greet chaumbre and myche peple aboute him, and, whanne he siȝ me, he wente into a priuy closet, comaundinge alle seculer men þat suden him in þidir for to goon forþ þennis from him anoon, so þat no man lefte þanne ⌜in⟩ closet, no but þe Archebischop himsilf and a phisician þat is clepid Maluerne, persoun of seint Dunstane | in þe eest in Londoun, and oþer tw[o] persoones vnknowen to me whiche weren maistris of þe lawe, and I stondinge f. 8v þere bifore hem.

And anoon þanne þe Archebischop seide to me, 'William, I knowe wel þat þou hast þis twenti wyntir and more traueilid aboute bisili in þe norþ lond and in oþir diuerse contrees of Ynglond, sowynge aboute fals doctryne, havynge greet bisynesse and schrewid wille for to enfecte and poysoune al þis lond if þou myȝtist wiþ þin vntrwe techynge. But þoruȝ þe grace of God þou art wiþstonde and brouȝt into my warde, so þat I schal mow sequestre þee from þin yuel purpos and lette þee to enuenym þe scheep of [my] province. Naþeles seynt Poul seiþ "If it mai be, in þat þing þat in vs is, we owen to haue pees wiþ alle men." Forþi, William, if | þou wolt now mekeli and of good f. 9

160 here . . . erþe (164)] *in red* R, *om.* A bigynneþ] bigy/gynneþ R 165 þe I questioun] *om.* AVP 166 or heeren] *om.* VP 173 into] faste into A priuy] *om.* A 176 phisician] medicus doctor in theologya et medicinis VP 177 in þe eest] *om.* A two] tw R 178 maistris] minysterys A 184 and poysoune] *om.* VP if þou myȝtist] *om.* VP 186 mow] now A 187 my] AVP, *om.* R 188 we owen] *om.* V 189 if þou wolt] *om.* P

herte wiþouten ony feynynge knele doun and leie þin hond vpon a book and kisse it, bihotinge feiþfulli, as I schal here charge þee, þat þou wolt submytte þee to my correccioun and stonde to myn ordinaunce, and fulfille it dewli bi alle þi kunnynge and þi power, þou schalt fynde me gracious and frendli to þee.'

And I seide to þe Archebischop, 'Sir, siþ ȝe demen me an eretike out of bileue, wole ȝe ȝeue me audience to telle to ȝou here my bileue?'

And he seide, 'Ȝhe, telle on.'

And I seid 'þe first questioun of my bileue is þis: I bileue þat þere is no but o God almiȝti; and in þis godheed and of þis godheede ben þre persoones, þat is þe Fadir, þe Sone and þe sooþfast Holi Goost. And I
f. 9v bileue þat alle þese þre persoones ben euene in power, in kunnynge, |
and in wille, ful of grace and of alle goodnesse; for whateuer þing þe Fadir doiþ, eiþer can or wol, þat þing also þe Sone doiþ, and can and wol, and in al her power, kunnynge and wille þe Holi Goost is euene to þe Fadir and to þe Sone. Ouer þis I bileue þat þoruȝ counseil of þis moost blessid Trinite, in moost couenable tyme bifore ordeyned for þe saluacioun of mankynde, þe secunde persoone of þis Trinite was ordeyned to take þe foorme of man, þat is þe kynde of man. And I bileue þat þis secunde persoone, oure lord Iesu Crist, was conseyued of þe Holi Goost in þe wombe of þe most blessid virgyne Marie wiþouten mannis seed. And I bileue þat aftir nyne moneþis Crist was born of þis moost holi virgyne, and wiþouten ony peyne, eiþer
f. 10 þerbrekinge | of þe cloistre of hir wombe, and wiþouten wem of hir
virgynyte.

'And I bileue þat Crist oure sauyour was circumcidid in þe eiȝtþe dai aftir his birþe in fulfillinge of þe lawe; and his name was clepid Iesu, þat was clepid of þe aungel bifore þat he schulde be conseyued in þe wombe of Marie his modir. And I bileue þat Crist, whanne he was bigynnynge as of þritti ȝeer age, he was fullid in þe flood of Iordane of Ioon Baptist; and in þe liiknesse of a culuer þe Ho⌜ly⌝ Goost dissencide þer vpon Crist. "And a vois was herd þere fro heuene seiynge 'þou art my wel beloued Soone; in þe I am fulli plesid.'" And I bileue þat Crist was moued þanne bi þe Holi Goost for to goon into

191 as . . . þee] *om.* VP 194 and frendli] *om.* A 198 þe . . . þis] *in red* R, *om.* AVP 200 sooþfast] -st, *letter eras.after* R, *om.* VP 201 þre] *om.* V 202 and in wille] and in myght A, *om.* VP 206 in . . . ordeyned] *om.* V for . . . mankynde (207)] *om.* V 212 holi] blessyd A 216 of þe lawe] legis antiqui VP 218 whanne he was bigynnynge] *om.* A 220 holy] -ly *dh* R 222 wel beloued] dilectus benedictus P, dilectus V 223 þanne] *om.* A

deseert; and þere he fastid þanne fourti daies and | fourti niȝtis f. 10v wiþouten bodili mete and drynk. And I bileue þat anoon aftir þis fastynge, whanne þe manheede of Crist hungridde, þe fende neiȝide to him and temptide him, in glotonye, in veyn glorie, and in couetise; but in alle þese þre temptaciouns Crist concludid þe fende and wiþstood him. And þanne anoon Iesu bigan to preche and to seie to þe peple "Do ȝe penaunce, for þe rewme of heuenes haþ neiȝed." ([Mt.] þe 4 c.) And I bileue þat Crist in al his tyme here lyuede moost holili, and tauȝte þe wille of his Fadir most truli. And I bileue þat he suffride most wrongfulli grettist repreues and dispite[s].

'And aftir þis, whanne Crist wolde make an eende here of his temperal lyf, I bileue þat in þe dai next bifore þat he wolde suffre wilfulli passioun on þe morn, in | foorme of breed and of wyne he f. 11 ordeynede his fleisch and his blood þat is his owne moost precious bodi, and ȝaf it to hise apostlis for to eten, comaundinge hem and bi hem alle her aftir-comers þat þei schulden, in þis foorme þat he schewid to hem, vsen hemsilf and techen and comowne forþ to oþir men and wymmen þis moost worschipful and holiest sacrament, into myndefulnesse of his moost holiest lyuynge and moost trewe techyng, and of his wilful and pacient suffrynge of þe moost peyneful passioun.

'And I bileue þat þis Crist oure sauyour, aftir þat he had þus ordeined þis moost holi and worþi sacrament of his owne most precious bodi, he went forþ wilful aȝens his enemyes; and he suffride hem moost pacientli for to leyen ⌜her⌝ hondis moost violentli vpon him, and to | bynden him and to leden him forþ as a þeef, and to scorne him f. 11v and to buffeten him, and to al tobawme him wiþ her spittinge[s]. Ouer þis I bileue þat Crist suffride moost mekeli and pacientli hise enemyes for to beten out wiþ scharpe scorgis þe blood þat was betwexe his felle and his fleisch; ȝhe, wiþouten grucchynge Crist suffrid þe cruel Iewes to crowne him wiþ moost scharp þornes and to beten him wiþ a reed. And þereaftir Crist suffride þe felle Iewes for to drawen him out vpon þe cros, and for to naile him þervpon hoond and foot. And so þoruȝ

225 and[2] . . . Crist (226)] *om.* VP 228 þre] *om.* AVP 230 heuenes] heuen A haþ neiȝed] appropinquabit VP Mt. þe 4 c.] luk þe 4 c., *margin* Luk 4 c. R, *om.* AVP 231 here] peregrinacionis sue in terris VP 232 þat] pro hiis scilicet sanctitate uite et veritate doctrine VP 233 dispites] VP, despysynges A, dispite R 234 wolde] *om.* V 236 wilfulli] *om.* A 237 his[1]] þe sacramente of hys A moost] *om.* A 245 holi and] *om.* A 246 bodi] corporis et sanguinis V 249 spittinges] AVP, spittinge R 252 þe cruel Iewes] *om.* VP 253 him[2]] se in caput VP

þis dispiteous nailynge Crist schedde out wilfulli for mannes loue þe blood þat was in his veynes; and Crist ȝaf wilfulli his spirit into þe f. 12 hondis or power of his Fadir. And so, | whanne he wolde and as he wolde, Crist diede wilfulli for mannes sake vpon þe cros. And ȝit, forþi þat, whanne Crist was þus wilfulli, peynefulli and schamefulli deed as to þe world, þere was left blood and watir in his herte, he bifore ordeyned þat he wolde schede out þis blood and þis watir for mannes saluacioun: he suffride þe Iewes for to make a blynde kniȝt for to stike him to þe herte wiþ a scharp spere; and þus þe blood and þe watir þat was in his herte Crist wolde schede out for mannes loue. And aftir þis I bileue þat Crist was taken doun from þe crosse and biried. And I bileue þat in þe þridde dai bi power of his godheede Crist roos vp aȝen f. 12ᵛ from deeþ to liif. And fourti daies | þeraftir I bileue þat Crist stiede vp into heuenes, and þere he sittiþ on þe riȝt half of God, þe Fadir almiȝti. And þe tenþe dai aftir his vpstiinge he sente þe Holi Goost into his apostlis, as he bifore hiȝte to hem. And I bileue þat Crist is to come for to deme al mankynde, summe into euerlastynge blis and summe into euerlastynge peynes.

'And, as I bileue into þe Fadir and into þe Sone þat þei ben o God almiȝti, so I bileue into þe Holi Goost, þat he is also wiþ hem þe same God almiȝti. And I bileue holi chirche: þat is, I bileue þat þere haþ ben, and þat þer ȝit now is, and alwei to þe worldes eende schal be, a peple whiche schulen bisie hem for to knowe and to kepe þe heestis of God, dredinge ouer al þing to offende God, and louynge and sechynge f. 13 moost to plesen him. And I bileue þat alle þei þat | had, and ȝit haue, and alle þei þat ben to haue þese forseide vertues, stabli stondinge in þe bileue of God, hopinge stidefastli in his merciful doyngis, perseuerynge into her eende in perfit charite, wilfulli, pacientli and gladli suffringe persecuciouns bi ensaumple of Crist chefli and of his apostlis, alle þese haue her names writen in þe book of liif. Þerfore I bileue þat þe feiþful gederinge togidre of þis peple, lyuynge now here in þis liif, is þe holi chirch of God, fiȝtinge here in erþe aȝens þe fend and þe prosperite of þis world and her fleischli lustis. And forþi þat þe hool gederinge togidere of þis forseid chirche and euery part þerof

256, 257 wilfulli] *om.* VP 258 and[2] . . . loue (265)] et post sanguinem et aquam sui preciosi cordis pro redempcione humani generis preordinata effudit per manus militis excecati sicut est opinio in populo christiano VP 269 heuenes] heuen A 271 his] this A 272 al mankynde] viuos et mortuos VP 276 I[2] . . . haþ] all thei that haue A 278 schulen bisie] solicitat solicitauit et solicitabit VP 286 *margin* nota R

neiþir coueitiþ, ne wilneþ, ne loueþ, ne sechiþ ony þing, no but to eschewe þe offence of God, and to do his plesyng wille, mekeli, wilfulli and gladli of al myn herte I submitte me to þis | holi chirche of Crist, to f. 13v be [euer] buxum and obedient to þe ordinaunce and þe gouernaunce of it and of euery membre þerof aftir my kunnynge and my power bi þe help of God. Forþi I knowleche now, and eueremore schal if God wol, þat of al myn herte and of al my mi3t I wole submitte me oonli to þe rule and gouernaunce of hem aftir my knowynge whom, bi þe hauynge and vsynge of þe forseide vertues, I perceyue to ben þe membris of holi chirche. þerfore þese forseid articlis of bileue, and alle oþere boþe of þe olde lawe and of þe newe which aftir þe heest of God ony lyf owiþ to bileue, I bileue verily in my soule, as a synful deedli wrecche of my kunnynge and power owiþ to bileue, praiynge þe lord God for his moost holi name for to eche to my bileue and to helpe my mysbileue.

'And, forþi þat [to] | þe p[reis]ynge of Goddis name I coueite ouer al f. 14 þing for to be a feiþful membre of holi chirche, I make þis protestacioun bifore 3ou alle foure þat ben now here present, coueitynge þat alle men and wymmen, which now ben here absent, knowen þe same: þat, whateuer þing bifore þis tyme I haue þou3t or don or seide, eiþir what þat I schal now here do or seie eiþir ony tyme heraftir, I bileue þat al þe olde lawe and þe newe, 3ouen and ordeyned bi þe counseile of þre persoones of þe holi Trinite, weren 3ouen and writen to þe saluacioun of mankynde. And I bileue þat þese lawes suffisen to mannes saluacioun, and I bileue in euery article of þese lawes to þe entent þat þese articlis weren ordeyned and comaundid of þese persoones of þe moost blessid Trinite to ben bileued. And þerfore, to þe rule and to þe gouernaunce | of þese lawis of God, f. 14v mekeli, wilfulli and gladli I submitte me of al myn herte, so þat whoeuere can and wole bi auctorite of Goddis lawe eiþir bi open resoun telle to me þat I haue errid, eiþer now erre, or ony tyme herafter schal erre in ony article of bileue—fro which inconuenient God kepe me for his goodnesse!—I submitte me to be reconceilid and to be buxum and obedient to þees forseid lawes of God and to ech article of hem. For bi autorite speciali of þese lawes I wole þoru3 þe

293 euer] AVP, *om.* R and[2] . . . gouernaunce] *om.* A 296 submitte] sub-submitte R 300 of[1] . . . newe] tam noue quam veteris P 305 to þe preisynge] AVP, þe perseyuynge R 309 þou3t or] *om.* A 315 to] and to R 318 mekeli] *om.* P wilfulli and gladli] gladly and wilfully A 324 I . . . lawes (325)] *om.* VP

grace of God be ooned charitabli to þese lawes. Ʒhe, ser, and ouer al þis bileue, ȝit I admitte alle þe sentencis and þe autoritees and þe resouns of alle þe seintis and doctours, acordinge to holi writt and declaringe it truli, submyttinge me wilfuli and mekeli to be euer f. 15 obedient and buxum after | my kunnynge and my power to alle þese seintis and doctours, as þei ben obedient and buxum in work or in word to God and to his lawe—and firþer not to my knowynge, neiþer for ony erþeli power, dignite or staat þoruȝ þe helpe of God! But, ser, I praie ȝou þat ȝe wole telle me if aftir ȝoure biddyng I schal ley myn hond vpon þe book in entent to swere þerbi?'

And þe Archebischop seide to me, 'Ʒhe! wherto ellis?'

And I seide to him, 'Sir, I vndirstonde a book is no þing ellis, no but a þing compilid togidere of diuerse creaturis, and so to swere bi a book is to swere bi dyuerse craturis; and to swere bi ony creature boþe Goddis lawe and mannes lawe is þeraȝen. But, sir, þis þing I seie to ȝou bifore þese [ȝ]oure clerkis wiþ my forseid protestacioun þat how, f. 15v where and | whanne, and to whom me owiþ for to swere, eiþir to obeie, in ony wise as Goddis lawe and seintis, and trewe doctouris acordinge wiþ Goddis ordynaunce or word comaundid of God, I wole þoruȝ Goddis grace be euere redi to do wiþ al my kunnynge and power. But I praie ȝou, ser, for þe charite of God, þat ȝe wol, bifore þat I swere as I haue here rehersid to ȝou, telle me how and whereto I schal submitte me, and schewiþ to me whereof þat ȝe wol corecte me, and what is þe ordenaunce þat ȝe wol þus oblische me to fulfille.'

And þe Archabischop seide to me, 'I wole schortli þat þou swere now here to me þat þou schalt forsake alle þe opynynouns whiche þe sect of Lollers holdiþ and is sclaundrid wiþ, so þat aftir þis tyme f. 16 neiþir priuyli ne apeertli þou holde noon opynyoun whiche | I schal, aftir þat þou hast sworun, reherse here to þee. Neiþir þou schalt fauoure man ne womman, ȝong ne olde, þat holdiþ ony of þese forseide opynynouns, but aftir þi kunnynge and power þou schalt bisie þee to wiþstonde alle suche distroublers of holi chirche in euery diocise þat þou comest ynne; and hem þat wol not leue þees dampnable opinyouns þou schalt putten vp, pupblischinge her

326 bileue ȝit I] I beleue and A 327 alle] *om.* A 329 and buxum] *om.* A 330 and buxum] *om.* A 336 I vndirstonde] *om.* AVP 337 compilid] coupled A and . . . craturis (338)] *om.* VP a[2] . . . bi[2] (338)] *om.* A 340 ȝoure] A, foure (*margin* ȝ *with no indication of position*) R, tribus VP 341 where and whanne] quando vbi V me owiþ] men are bounden A 342 and seintis] *om.* P 343 ordynaunce . . . god] lawe A

names, and make hem knowen to þe bischop of þe diocise þat þese ben inne, eiþir to þe bischopis mynystris. And ouer þis I wole þat þou preche no more, to þe tyme þat I knowe bi good witnesse and trewe þat þi conuersacioun be suche þat þin herte and þi mouþ acorden trewli in oon, contrariing alle þe lore þat þou hast tauȝt herbifore.'

And I heerynge þese wordis þouȝte in myn herte þat þis was an vnleeful | [f. 16v] askynge, and I demed mysilf cursid of God if I consentid herto; and I þouȝte how Susanne seide 'Angwysschis ben to me on euery side', and forþi þat I stood stille musynge and spak not.

And þe Archebischop seide to me, 'Answere o wise or oþer.'

And I seide 'Sere, if I consentid to do þus as ȝe haue here rehersid to me, I schulde become apelour, eiþir euery bischopis aspie or sumnour of þis lond. For, if I schulde þus putt vp and publische þe names of men and of wymmen, I schulde hereinne diseese ful manye persoones—ȝhe, ser, as it is lickli bi þe dom of [my] conscience, I schulde hereinne be cause of þe deeþ boþe of men and of wymmen, ȝhe, boþe bodili and as I gesse goostli. For manye men and wymen þat stonden now in truþe and ben in wei of saluacioun, if I schulde for þe leernynge and redinge of her bileue pub|[f. 17]blischen hem and putten hem herfore vp to vnpiteous bischopis and mynystris, I knowe sumdel bi experience þat þei schulden be so troubld, and disesid wiþ o persecussioun and wiþ oþere þat manye of hem, I gesse, wolden raþer chese to forsake þe truþe þan to be trauailid, scorned, sclaundrid or ponyschid as bischopis and her mynystris now [vsen] for to constreynen men and wymmen to consenten to hem. But, sire, I fynde nouȝwhere in holi writ þat þis office þat ȝe wolden enfeffen me now herewiþ acordiþ to ony preest of Cristis sect, neiþir to ony oþer cristen man; þerfor to do þus it were to me a ful noyous bonde to be tied wiþ, an ouer greuous charge. For I gesse, sere, þat if I þus dide many men and wymmen wolden, ȝhe, ser, þei myȝten iustli into my confusioun seyen to me þat I were a traitour | [f. 17v] to God and to hem, siþ, as I gesse in myn herte, manye men and wymmen tristen so myche to me in þis caas þat I wolde not for sauynge of my liif do þus to hem. For if I þus schulde do, ful manye men and wymmen wolden, as þei miȝten truli,

367 angwysschis ben] anguyssch is A 368 musynge] *om.* A 372 þis lond] all Englonde A 373 diseese] deceive A 374 my] AVP, *om.* R 376 as I gesse] *om.* A 377 truþe] ueritate et firma fide VP 378 bileue] fidei et aliorum concurrencium salutem animarum suarum in materna lingwa uel aliena VP 383 vsen] AVP, *om.* R

seyen þat I hadde falsli and cowardli forsaken þe truþe and sclaundrid schamefuli þe word of God. Forþi, ser, if I consentid to ȝou to do hereinne ȝoure wille, eiþer for boncheef or myscheef þat mai falle to me in þis lyf, I deme in my consience þat I were worþi to be cursid of God and so of alle seyntis—fro whiche inconuenyent kepe me and alle cristin peple now and euere almiȝti God for his moost hiȝe and holi name!'

And þanne þe Archebischop seide to me, 'O, þin herte is ful hard f. 18 endured, | as was þe herte of Farao! And þe deuel haþ ouercome þee and cumbrid þee, and haþ so blyndid þee in alle þi wittis þat þou hast no grace to knowe þe trewþe, neiþir þe mesure of merci þat I haue profrid here to þee. For, as I parseyue now bi þi foli answer, þou hast no wille to leeue þin olde errours. But I seie to þee, lewid losel, eiþir now anoon consente to myn ordynaunce and submytte þee to stonde to myn decre, or bi seint Tomas þou schalt be schauen and sue þi felow into Smeþefelde!'

And at þis seiynge I stood stille and spak not. But in myn herte I þouȝte þat God dide to me a greet grace if he wolde of his greet mercy brynge me into suche an eende, and [in] myn herte I was no þing maad⌝ f. 18v agast wiþ þis manassynge of þe Archebischop. But | more herþoruȝ myn herte was confortid and stablischid in þe drede and loue of God. And I lokinge biheeld inwardli þe Archebischop, and I considride þese to þingis in him: oon þat he was not ȝit sorowful forþi þat he hadde maade Wiliam Sautri [at Smeþefelde] to be wrongfulli brent, and also I considride þat þe Archebischop þirstide ȝit aftir þe schedynge out of more innocent blood. And anoon herfore I was moued in alle my wittis for to holde þe Archebischop neiþir prelat ne preest of God; and, forþi þat myn inner man was altogidre þus departid from þe Archebischop, me þowȝte I schulde not haue ony drede of him. But I was riȝt heuy and sorowful forþi þat þere was noon audience þere of seculer men, but in myn herte I preiede þe lord God f. 19 for to conforte me and strengþe | me aȝens hem þat þere weren aȝens þe truþe. And I purposid to speke no more to þe Archebischop ne to þe clerkis þan me nede bihoue[d]. And also I preiede God for his goodnesse to ȝeue me þanne and alwei grace to speke wiþ a meke and

399 moost . . . and[2]] *om.* A    401 o] Wilhelme Thorpt P    408 decre] decrees A    411 greet[1]] *om.* V    412 in] AVP, *om.* R    413 but . . . archebischop (415)] *om.* A    416 þese] there A    417 Sautri] Dauir V, *om.* P    at Smeþefelde] in Smethfeld VP, *om.* RA    426 to þe clerkis] tribus clericis VP    427 bihoued] AVP, bihoueþ R    428 to ȝeue me] *om.* P

an esy spirit, and, whateuer þing þat I schulde speke, þat I mi3te haue þerto trewe autorite of scripture or open resoun. And forþi þat I stood þus stille and noþing spak, oon of þe Archebischopis clerkis seide to me 'What þing musist þou? Do þou anoon as my lord haþ comaundid to þee!'

And 3it I stood stille and answerid him not. And þanne soone aftir þe Archebischop seide to me 'Art þou not 3it biþou3t where þou wolt do as I haue here seide to þee?'

And I seide þanne þus to him 'Ser, my fadir and my modir, | whoos f. 19v
soulis God asoile if it be his wille, spendiden moche moneye in dyuerse placis aboute my lore, in entent to haue me a preest of God. But whanne I cam into 3eeris of discressioun I hadde no wille to be preest; and herfore my freendis weren ofte ri3t heuy towardis me. And þanne me þou3te her grucchynge a3ens me was so disesi to me þat I purposide herfore to haue laft her companye. And whanne þei perseyueden þis in me þei spaken sumtyme ful fair and plesyng wordis to me; but forþi þat þei my3ten not make me to consente of good herte for to be preest þei spaken to me feele tymes ful row3 wordis and greuous, þretynge and manassynge me in dyuerse maners, schewynge to me ofte ful heuy | cheere. And þus boþe in faire maner and in greete, f. 20
þei weren longe tyme as me þou3te ful bisie aboute me or þat I consentid to hem to be preest. But at þe laste whanne in þis mater þei wolden no longer suffre myn excusaciouns, but eiþir I schulde consente to hem eiþir I schulde bere euere her indignacioun, 3he, ser, her curse, as þei leten, I þanne, seynge þis, praieden hem þat þei wolden fouchesaaf for to 3eue me lycence for to gon to hem þat weren named wyse preestis and of vertues conuersacioun to haue her counseile, and to knowe of hem þe office and þe charge of preesthode. And herto my fadir and my modir consentiden ful gladli and þei 3auen to me her blessyng and good leue to go, and þei token me money to spende in þis iornay.

'And so þanne I wente to þo preestis | whom I herde to ben losid or f. 20v
named of moost holi lyuynge, and best tau3t and moost wyse of heuenly wysdom. And, ser, I comowned wiþ hem to þe tyme þat I perseyued, bi her vertues and contynuel occupacioun, þat her honest

430 autorite of scripture] authorites of scriptures A 438 asoile] haue mercy A 441 ofte] *om.* AV 444 ful] *om.* P 446 ful . . . cheere (448)] ostendebant voltum grauem V row3] *om.* A 447 þretynge] *om.* A 448 ofte] *om.* A 454 fouchesaaf for to] *om.* A 460 losid or named] herde to be of beste name and A 463 occupacioun] occupacions A

werkis and charitable passid her fame which I hadde herd biforehonde of hem. Wherefore, ser, bi ensaumple of þe doctryne of þese men and speciali for þe goodlich and innocent werkis whiche I perseyuede þanne of hem and in hem, after my kunnynge and my power I haue bisied me þan and tanne into þis tyme to knowe in partie Goddis lawe, hauynge a wille and a desyre to lyue þeraftir, willnynge þat alle men and wymmen bisieden hem feiþfulli heraboute. If þanne, ser, eiþer for
f. 21 plesynge or displesynge of hem þat ben neiþer so wise ne of so greet | vertuous conuersacioun in my knowynge, neiþer bi comoun fame in ony oþir mennes knowynge of þis londe, as þese men weren of which I tooke my counseile and myn enformacioun, I schulde now forsake þus sodeynli, schortli and vnwarned, al þe lore þat I haue bisied me fore þis þritti ȝeer and more, my conscience schulde euer be herwiþ ouer mesure vnquyetid. And also, ser, I knowe wel þat manye men and wymmen schulden ben herþoruȝ greetli troublid and sclaundrid; and, as I seide, ser, to ȝou bifore, [for] myn vntruþe and fals cowardise many oon schulde be putt into ful greet repreef. Ȝhe, ser, I dreede þat many oon, as þei myȝten þanne iustli, wolden curse me ful bittirli. And, ser, I drede not þat ⌜ne⌝ þe curs of God (which I schulde deserue
f. 21v herynne) wolde brynge me | into a ful yuel eende if I contynuede þus. And if, þoruȝ remorse of conscience, I repentide me ony tyme, turnynge aȝen into þe wei which ȝe bisien ȝou now to make me forsake, ȝe, ser, and alle þe bischopis of þis londe wiþ oþer ful many preestis, wolden defame me and pursuen me as a relapis. And þei þat now haue, þouȝ I vnworþi be, sum affiaunce in me heraftir wolden neuer tristen to me, þouȝ I cowde teche and lyue myche moore vertuousli þan euer I schal conne eiþir do. For, if aftir ȝoure counseile I lefte vttirli al my loore, I schulde herþoruȝ first [wounde and defyle myn owne soule, and also I schulde herþoruȝ] ȝeue occasioun to many men and wymmen of ful sore hurtynge; ȝhe, ser, as it is ful lickli to me, if I consentide þus to ȝoure wille, I schulde herynne bi myn yuel
f. 22 ensaumple in þat þat in me were sle so manye folkis goostli | þat I schulde neuere deserue to haue grace of God to edefien his chirche,

468 tanne] *om.* A in partie] perfectly A 471 greet] *om.* A 473 mennes] mannis A 479 for] AVP, *om.* R 482 which . . . herynne (483)] *om.* VP 486 of þis londe] Anglie VP 487 and pursuen me] *om.* VP relapis] relapsum statim morte dignum VP 489 neuer] nunquam amplius V 490 for . . . loore (491)] *om.* VP 491 wounde . . . herþoruȝ (492)] wounde and defyle myne owne soule and also I shulde herethrough A, et me ipsum spiritualiter macularem et VP, *om.* R 494 herynne . . . schulde (496)] *om.* VP

neiþir mysilf ne ony oþer lyf. And þanne I were moost wrecchidli ouercomen and vndon boþe bifore God and man.

'But, ser, bi ensaumple cheefli of Nycol Herforde, of Ioon Purueye, of Robert Bowland, and also bi þe present doynge of Filip Repingtoun, þat is now bicome bischop of Lyncolne, I am now lerned, as many oþer ben and manye mo heraftir þoruȝ Goddis grace schulen be lerned, to hate and to fleen al sich sclaundre þat þese forseid men cheefli haue defouliden wiþ principali hemsilf. And in þat þat in hem is þei haue enuenymed al þe chirche of God, for þe sclaundres reuokinge at þe cros of Poulis, of Hertforde, Purueye and ⌜of⌝ Bowland. And how Filip of Repintoun pursueþ now cristen peple, and þe feynynge þat þese dissimylen | now þoruȝ worldli prudence, kepynge so couertli in her prechinge, and comownynge wiþinne þe boondis and þe teermes whiche wiþouten blame mowen be spoken, and schewid out to þe moost worldeli l[y]uers, wolen not ben vnponyschid of God, for to þe poynt of truþe þat þese men schewiden out sumtyme, þese wolden not now strecche forþ her lyues, but bi ensaumple eche of hem of oþer, as her wordis and her werkis schewen, þei bisien hem þoruȝ her feynyng for to sclaundre and to pursue Crist in his membris raþer þan þei wolde be pursued.' f. 22v

And þe Archebischop seide to me, 'þese men of whom þou spekist now weren folis and eretikis whanne þat þei weren gessid wise men of þee and of sich oþir losels. But now þei ben wise men þouȝ þou and sich oþer demen hem vnwise. Naþeles I | wiste neuer noon riȝt sad man þat was ony while enuenymed wiþ ȝoure contagious doctrine.' f. 23v

And I seide to þe Archebischop, 'Ser, I gesse wel þat þese men and such oþere ben now wise men as to þis world, but as her wordis sowneden sumtyme, and her werkis schewiden outward, it was licly to many men þat þei hadden eer[n]is of þe wisdam of God, and þei schulden haue deserued myche grace of God to haue saued her owne

497 ne . . . lyf] *om.* VP and . . . ouercomen (498)] *om.* A 499 of[1]] of some whos names I will not now reherse A Nycol Herforde] H A Ioon Purueye] J/P A 500 of Robert Bowland] and B A, Roberti Bouland V, Roberti Rolant P 501 Repingtoun] of Rampenton A, Bepyngeoun V, depington P 502 oþer . . . manye] *om.* A heraftir] *om.* P 506 of[2] . . . peple (507)] istorum predictorum virorum persequitur nunc populum christianum VP Hertforde] H A Purueye] P A Bowland] B A 507 Repintoun] Rampentoun A 508 now] *om.* A 509 so couertli] them cowerdly A 511 lyuers] AVP, louers R 514 of oþer] *om.* A 518 wise men] *om.* P 520 riȝt sad man] that right seide A 521 contagious] contagiousnesse that is contaminate and spottid A 525 many men] moue me A eernis] eeris R of god] *om.* V

soulis and manye oþer mennes if þei hadden perseyuered feiþfulli in wilful pouert and in oþir symple and vertues lyuyng, and speciali if wiþ þese forseid vertues þei hadden contynewid in her bisie and frutuous sowinge of Goddis word, as to many mennes knowynge þei occupieden þanne alle her wittis ful bisily to knowe þe plesinge wille f. 23v of God, traueilynge alle her membris | ful blessidli for to doon þeraftir pureli and cheeffli to þe preisynge of þe moost holi name of God, and for grace of edificacioun and saluacioun of alle cristen peple. But wo worþ fals coueitise and yuel counseile and tirauntrie bi whiche þei and manye oþer men and wymmen ben lad blyndelyngis into an yuel eende!'

And þe Archebischop seide to me, 'þou and sich oþer losels of þi sect wolden schaue ȝoure beerdis ful nyȝ for to haue beneficis, for bi Iesu I knowe noon more coueitous schrewis þanne ȝe ben whanne þat ȝe haue benefices. For lo I ȝaf to him, Ioon Purueye, a benefice no but a myle out of þis castel, and I herde moore compleynt and wondir of f. 24 his coueitise aboute tiþis and oþer dewtees þan I dide of alle þe men | þat weren avaunsid wiþinne my diosyse.'

And I seide to þe Archebischop, 'Ser, Purueye is neyþir wiþ ȝou now here for þe benefice þat ȝe ȝaf to him, neiþir he holdiþ feiþfulli wiþ þe lore þat he tauȝte and wroot biforehonde, and þus he schewiþ now himsilf to be neiþir hoot ne coold. And herfore he and hise felowis mowen sore drede but if þei turnen hastili into þe weie þat þei haue forsaken, last þei ben sodeynli vomed out of þe noumbre of Goddis chosen peple.'

And þe Archebishop seide, 'þouȝ Purueie be now a fals harlot, I quitid me to him. But come he more for siche a cause bifore me, er þat we departen I schal wite wiþ whom he schal holde. But I seie to þee, f. 24v whiche ben þo holi men and wise | of whiche þou hast taken þin enformacioun?'

And I seide, 'Ser, in his tyme maister Ioon Wiclef was holden of ful many men þe grettist clerk þat þei knewen lyuynge vpon erþe. And þerwiþ he was named, as I gesse worþili, a passing reuli man and an innocent in al his lyuynge. And herfore grete men of kunnynge and oþer also drowen myche to him, and comownede ofte wiþ him. And

531 alle] a season in all A 532 blessidli] besily A 534 alle] *om.* A 539 beneficis] a benefice A 541 benefices] a benefice A 542 compleynt and wondir] compleintis A 543 dewtees] mysdoyngys A 557 in his tyme] *om.* A 559 as . . . worþili] *om.* A 560 of . . . and[1] (561)] *om.* A

þei sauouriden so his loore þat þei wroten it bisili and enforsiden hem to rulen hem þeraftir. And forþi, ser, þat þis forseid lore of maistir Ioon Wiclef is ȝit holden of ful manye men and wymmen þe moost acordinge lore to þe lyuynge and to þe techynge of Crist and his apostlis, and moost opinli schewynge and declarynge how þe chirche of Crist haþ be and ȝit schal be rulid and gouerned, herfore manye | f. 25 men and wymmen accepten þis lore and purposen þoruȝ Goddis help for to conferme her lyuynge like herto to þis lore of Ioon Wiclef. Maistir Ion Aston tauȝte and wroot acordingli and ful bisili, where and whanne and to whom he myȝte, and he vsid it himsilf, I gesse, riȝt perfyȝtli vnto his lyues eende. Also Filip of Repintoun whilis he was a chanoun of Leycetre, Nycol Herforde, dane Geffrey of Pikeringe, monke of Biland and a maistir of dyuynyte, and Ioon Purueye, and manye oþer whiche weren holden riȝtwise men and prudent, tauȝten and wroten bisili þis forseide lore of Wiclef, and conformeden hem þerto. And wiþ alle þese men I was ofte homli and I comownede wiþ hem long tyme and fele, and so bifore alle oþir men I chees wilfulli to be enformed bi hem and of hem, and speciali of Wiclef himsilf, as of þe | f. 25v moost vertuous and goodlich wise man þat I herde of owhere eiþer knew. And herfore of Wicleef speciali and of þese men I toke þe lore whiche I haue tauȝte and purpose to lyue aftir, if God wole, to my lyues ende. For now þouȝ summe of þese men ben contrarie to þe loore þat þei tauȝten biforehonde, I wot wel ȝit her loore was trewe whiche þei tauȝten and þerfore wiþ þe help of God I purpose for to holde and vse þe loore whiche I herde of hem whilis þat þei saten in Moysees chaire and speciali whilis þei saten on þe chaire of Crist. But aftir her werkis þat þei now schewen I wol not do wiþ Goddis help, for þei feynen, hiden and contrarien þe truþe which biforehonde þei tauȝten out pleynli and trewli. For as I knowe wel, whanne summe of þese men haue | f. 26 ben vndirnommyn for her sclaundrouus doynge, þei knowelich not þat þei tauȝten errour biforehonde, but þat þei weren constreyned bi peyne for to ȝeue to telle out þe truþe; and þus þei

568 accepten] acceptabant P help] grace A 569 Ioon] *om.* A 570 maistir] conformiter ad hanc doctrinam magister VP 571 I gesse] *om.* A 572 Repintoun] Rampenton A, Repingeon V 573 Nycol Herforde] archidiaconus Herford P, archidiaconus Herforo V dane Geffrey] Dauy Gotray A Pikeringe] Pykerig V, Pigerid P, Pakring A 574 monke] abbas VP a maistir] doctores VP 576 of Wiclef] *om.* A 577 homli] right homely A 578 wilfulli] volenter et gaudenter VP 581 Wicleef] hym A 583 now] *om.* A 589 feynen hiden] similatum ostendunt P

chesen now raþer to blasfemen God þan to suffre a while here bodili persecucioun for þe truþe þat Crist schedde out for his herte blood.'

And þe Archebischop seide to me, 'þat loore þat þou clepist truþe is opin sclaundre in holi chirche, as it is proued of holi chirche. For al be it þat Wiclef ȝoure maistir and auctour was a greet clerk, and þouȝ many men helden him a perfit lyuer, ȝit his doctryne is not apreued of holi chirche but many sentencis of his lore ben dampned as þei wel worþi ben. But, as touchinge Filip of R[e]pintoun, þat was first
f. 26v chanoun and aftirwarde abbot of Leycetre, | whiche is now bischop of Lyncolne, I telle to þee þat þe dai is comen for þe which he fastide þe euen, for he neiþir holdiþ now, neiþir wole holde, þe loore þat he tauȝte whanne he was no but chanoun of Leycetre, for noo bischop of þis londe pursueþ now scharplier hem þat holden þat wei þan he doiþ.'

And I seide, 'Ser, herfor ful many men and wymmen also wondren vpon him, and speken him myche schame and holden him Cristis enemye.'

And þe Archebischop seide to me, 'Wherto tariest þou me wiþ sich fablis? Wolt þou not schortli, as I haue seid to þee, submytte þee to me or nay?'

And I seide, 'Ser, I telle ȝou at oo word, I dar not for þe drede of God submitte me to ȝou aftir þe tenour of þe sentence þat ȝe haue aboue rehersid to me.'

f. 27 And þanne | as if he hadde ben wrooþ, þe Archebischop seide to oon of his clerkis, 'Take hidir anoon þe certificat þat cam to me from Schrouesbirie vndir þe bailyes seelis, witnessynge þe errours and þe eresies whiche þis losel haþ venymously sowen þere.'

And anoon þe clerke took out and leide forþ vpon a cupbord dyuerse rollis and oþer writingis, among which was a litil rolle which þe clerk toke to þe Erchebischop. And anoon þe Archebischop radde þis rolle conteynynge þis sentence: 'þe þridde Sonedai after Ester in þe ȝeer of oure Lord a þousand foure hundrid and seuene, William Thorp cam into þe toun of Schrouesbirie, and, þoruȝ leue grauntid to

594 now] *om.* V 596 truþe] trewthe and sothefastnesse A 597 as . . . chirche[2]] *om.* VP 598 maistir and] *om.* AVP 601 Repintoun] rpintoun R, of Rampeton A, Repingeon V, Depington P 602 Leycetre] *om.* P 606 þis londe] Anglie VP þat[2]] thy A 609 Cristis enemye] inimicum crucis Christi VP, for a cursid enemye of the treuthe A 612 not] *om.* A 615 of þe] and A 617 þe archebischop] he A 619 seelis] seale A 624 rolle] rotulam reuoluit eam V

him for to preche, he seide openli in seynt Chaddis chirche | in his sermoun þat þe sacrament of þe auter aftir þe consecracioun was material breed; and þat ymagis schulden in noo wyse be worschippid; and þat men schulden not goon in pilgrimage; and þat preestis haue now no titil to tiþis; and þat it is not leeful to swere in ony maner.' And whanne þe Archebischop hadde rad þis rolle he rollid it vp aȝen. f. 27v

A questioun

And þe Archebischop seide to me, 'Is þis holsum loore to teche among þe peple?'

And I seide to him, 'Ser, I am boþe aschamed on her bihalue and riȝt sorouful for hem þat haue certified to ȝou þese þingis þus vntruli, for I prechide neuer neiþir tauȝte þus priuyli ne apeertly.'

And þe Archebischop | seide to me. 'I wole ȝeue credence to þese worschipful men, which haue writun to me and witnessen vndir her seelis þat þou prechidest þus openli þese forseide errours and heresies þere among hem. Þouȝ þou denye now þis, gessist þou þat I wol ȝeue credence to þee, þou losel?—þat hast so troublid þe worschipful comounte of Schrouesbirie þat þe bailies and þe comouns of þat toun haue writun to me, prayngе me þat am Archebischop of Cauntirbirie, primate of al Yngelonde and chaunceler, þat I wolde vouchesaaf to graunte to hem þat, if þou schalt be deed, as þou art worþi, and suffre openli þi i⌜e⌝wise for þin eresies, þat þou maist haue þi iewise openli þere among hem, so þat alle þei, whom þou and oþer suche losels haue þere | peruertid, moun þoruȝ drede of þi deeþ ben reconseilid aȝen to þe vnyte of holi chirche, and also þei þat stoonden in trewe feiþ of holi chirche moun þoruȝ þi deeþ be þe moore stablischid þerinne.' f. 28 f. 28v

And, as if þis askinge hadde plesid þe Archebischop, he seide þanne þere, 'Bi my þrifte, þis hertli preier and feruent request schal be þouȝt on.'

But certis, neiþer þis preier of men of Schrouesbori neiþir þe manassynge of þe Archebischop ferede me ony þing. But in þe rehersynge of þis malice and in þe heringe of it, myn herte was greetly

628, 629, 630, 631 *margin* 1–5 R    630 pilgrimage] pilgremages A    631 now] *om.* A    633 a questioun] *om.* AVP, *margin* Argumentis/ ]pter predicare/ ]wangelium dei R    634 teche] be A    636 her] *twice* R    640 witnessen] witnessed A    641 þat . . . heresies (642)] *om.* A    646 of[2] . . . chaunceler (647)] and chaunceler of Englond A    648 deed] made A    openli] *om.* VP    650 peruertid moun] seduxerunt V

reioisid, and ȝit is, þankid be God, for þe grace þat I þanne gesse[d] and ȝit gesse schal come al to þe chirche of Crist herþoruȝ bi þe f. 29 special merci[ful doynge] of þis Lord. And, as hauynge no drede | of þe malice of tirauntis, but tristinge stidefastli in þe help of þe Lord, wiþ ful purpos for to knoweleche þe trewþe and to stonde þerbi perseuerauntli aftir my kunnynge and my power, I seide to þe Archebischop, 'Ser, if þe truþe of Goddis word miȝte now be accept of men as it schulde be, I doute not bi licli euydence þat ne þei þat ben seide out of þe feiþ of holi chirche in Schrouesbirie and elliswhere ben in trwe feiþ of Crist. For, as her wordes sownen and her werkis schewen to mannes doom, dredynge and louynge feiþfulli God, her wille, her desir, her loue, her bisinesse ben moost sett for to dreden to offenden God and to loue for to plesen him in trewe knowynge and in f. 29v feiþful kepynge of hise heestis. | And aȝenward þei þat ben seid to ben in þe feiþ of holy chirche in Schrouesbirie and elliswhere, bi open evedence of her prowde, enuyous, malicious, coueitous, leccherous and oþere ful vicious wordis and werkis, neiþer knowen, neiþer haue wille to knowe, neiþer to occupien her wittis to knowe truli and effectuelli þe feiþ of holi chirche; wherefore þese, ne noon þat suen her maners, schulen ony tyme comen verily to þe feiþ of holi chirche, no but þei bisien hem truli to come into þe wei whiche þei now dispisen. For þese men and wymmen þat ben now clepid feiþful, and ben holden iust, neiþer knowen, neiþer wolen bisien hem to knowe effectuely ony heeste of God. And þus ful manye men now, and specialli men þat ben named to ben principal lymes of þe chirche, f. 30 terren God to greet wraþþe and deseruen his curse, forþi | þat þei clepen or holden hem iust men whiche ben ful vniust, as her vicious wordis and her greet custumable sweringe and her sclaundrous and vnschamefast werkis openli witnessen. And herfore suche vicious men and vniust into her owne confusioun clepen hem vniust men and wymmen which, aftir her kunnyng and her power, bisien hem to lyue iustly after þe heestis of God. And where, ser, ȝe seie þat I haue

660 gessed] thought A, estimaui VP, gesse R 662 special] spirituale P merciful doynge] mercyfull doynge A, misericors factum VP, merci R 663 but] by A 665 perseuerauntli] *om.* A kunnynge. . . .power] potenciam . . . scienciam VP 666 of men] *om.* A 669 Crist] holy church A 672 knowynge and in] and A 675 malicious] *om.* VP 676 ful vicious] foule A 677 truli and] *om.* VP 681 and wymmen] *om.* VP 683 effectuely] of faythfulnesse A men] men and women A 684 þe] holy A 687 wordis] opera VP 688 werkis] uerba VP openli] shew openly and A 689 and wymmen] *om.* VP 691 heestis] commaundement A

troublid þe comounte of Schrouesbirie, and manye oþer men and wymmen, wiþ my techynge, þis doynge if it þus be is not to be wondrid of wiise men, siþen alle þe comountee of þe citee of Ierusalem was troublid wiþ þe techynge of Cristis owne persone, þat was veri God and man and þe moost prudente prechour þat euere was or schal be. Also, ser, al þe synagoge of Nazareth was so moued aȝens Crist, and so | fulfillid wiþ wraþþe towardis him for his prechinge þat þe men of þe f. 30v synagoge rison vp, and þei þresten Crist out of her citee, and þei ledden him vp vnto þe heiȝþe of a mounteyne for to haue þrowen him doun þere heedlyngis. Also acoordingli herto þe Lord witnessiþ bi Moysees þat he schal putte deuysioun bitwixe his peple and þe peple þat contrarieþ and pursueþ his peple. Who, ser, is he þanne þat schal preche þe trouþe of Goddis word to þe [vn]feiþful peple, and schal lette þe treuþe of þe gospel and þe profecie of God almyȝti to be fulfillid?'

And þe Archebischop seide to me, 'It sueþ of þese þi wordis þat þou and suche oþer deemen þat ȝe doon riȝt wel for to preche and to teche as ȝe doon wiþouten autorite of ony bischop. For ȝe presumen þat þe Lord haþ chosen ȝou oonli for to preche as feiþful dissciplis and special suers | of Crist.' f. 31

And I seide, 'Ser, bi autorite of Goddis lawe, and also of seinttis and doctours, I am lerned to deme þat it is euery preestis office and cheef dette for to preche bisili, frely and treuli þe word of God. For no doute euery prest scholde purpose first in his soule to coueite cheefli to take þe ordre of presthoode for to make knowen to þe peple þe word of God, aftir his kunnynge and his power, appreuynge his wordis euere to be trewe bi his vertues werkis. And for þis eende we gessen þat bischoppis and euery prelate of holi chirche schulde chefli take and vse his prelacie; and for þe same cause bischopis schulden ȝeue to prestis her ordres, for bischopis scholden accepten no man to presthoode, no but him þat hadde good wille and ful purpose, and were wel disposid for to preche. Wherefore, | ser, þouȝ bi þe heeste of f. 31v Crist and bi ensaumple of his moost holi lyuynge, and also bi witnesse of his holi apostlis and profetis, we ben endettid vpon ful greet peyne

695 wiþ þe techynge] *om.* A 700 mounteyne] montis super quem ciuitas eorum erat fundata VP 701 *margin* moysees witnessiþ in exodi þe 8 c° R 702 deuysioun] diuisionem VP, deuysiouns R, dissension A 704 vnfeiþful] vnfeithfull A, infideli VP, feiþful R 712 ser] *om.* P 713 cheef dette] deutie A 714 for² . . . power (717)] *om.* P 715 cheefli] *om.* A 718 eende] entent A 719 euery prelate] other prelates A 720 his] ther A 722 good] *om.* P 723 disposid] disposed and well learned A for to] to for to R

to bisien vs aftir oure kunnynge and oure power, as [eu]eri prest is chargid of God to fulfille duli þe office of presthod, we presumen not ⌜herfor⌝ of ouresilf for to be, neiþer in oure owne reputacioun, ne in ony oþer mannes, holden þe feiþful dissciplis of Crist neiþer his special suers. But, ser, as I seide to ȝou biforehonde, we deemen þis bi autorite cheefli of Goddis word þat it is þe cheef dette of euery prest to [bisien him feiþfulli to] make þe lawe of God knowen to his peple, and so to commoune þe heestis of God charitabli, how þat we mowen best, where and whanne and to whomeuere þat we schulen mow. And, for f. 32 þe wille and bisinesse þat we haue of dewe dette | to do iustli oure office þoruȝ þe mouynge, as we tristen, and þe special helpe of God, hopinge stidefastli in his mercy, we desiren to be þe feiþful disciplis of Crist. And we praien þis gracious Lord for his moost holi name, þat he make vs able so to plesen him wiþ deuout praiers and charitable prestli werkis þat we moun deseruen of him for to suen him þankfulli.'

And þe Archebischop seide to me, 'Lewed losel! whereto makist þou siche veyn resouns to me? Axiþ not seint Poul how preestis schulden preche no but þei were sente? But I sent þe neuere to preche, for þi venymous doctrine is so knowen þoruȝout al Yngelonde þat no bischop wol admitte or graunte þee for to preche bi witnesse of her f. 32v lettris. Whi þanne, lewid ydeot, wolt þou presume to preche | siþe þou art not sent neiþer licensid of þi souereyns to preche? Seiþ not seint Poul þat sogetis owe to be obedient to her souereyns, and not oonli sogettis owen to be obedient to good souereyns and vertues but also to trowantis þat ben vicious men?'

And I seide to þe Archebischop, 'Ser, as touchinge ȝoure letter and þe lettres of oþere bischopis, whiche ȝe seien we schulden haue to witnesse þat we weren able for to preche, we knowen wel, ser, þat neiþer ȝe ne ony oþer bischop of þis lond wol graunte to vs ony suche lettre of licence, but we schulden oblischen vs to ȝou and to oþer bischopis bi vnleeful ooþis, for to not passe þe bondis or termes which ȝe, ser, and oþer bischopis wolen lymyten to vs. And siþen in þese f. 33 maters ȝoure termes ben sumtyme to straite and sumtyme to large, we |

726 eueri] AP, solicitari se V, a verri R 729 special] spirituales P 732 bisien him feiþfulli to] besy them feithfully to A, solicitare se fideliter ad VP, *om.* R 733 heestis] commaundement A how . . . best] *om.* VP 738 moost] *om.* A 740 prestli] *om.* VP 742 *marginal box for reference not entered* R 745 or graunte] *om.* AVP 747 souereyns] souereyn A 749 sogettis . . . to[2]] *om.* A and vertues] *om.* VP 751 letter . . . of (752)] letter of licence or A 753 able] able to be sent A 755 lettre] letters A vs to ȝou] *om.* V and . . . bischopis (756)] *om.* VP 758 straite . . . large] large . . . streite A

dur not obleschen vs to ben þus bounden to ȝou for to kepe þe termes which ȝe wolden lymyte to vs, as ȝe don to freris and to suche oþer ȝoure proctours. And herfore, þouȝ we haue not ȝoure lettre neiþer lettris of oþir bischopis writun wiþ enke vpon parchemyne, we dur not herfore leeue þe office of prechynge, to whiche prechinge alle prestis aftir her kunnynge and her power ben bounden bi dyuerse witnessingis of Goddis lawe and of greet doctours, wiþouten ony mencioun makynge of bischopis lettres.

'Forþi, siþen we haue taken vpon vs þe office of presthood, þouȝ we ben vnworþi þerto, we coueiten and purposen to fulfille it wiþ þe helpe of God, bi autorite of his owne lawe and bi witnesse of seintis and of greete doctours acordinge þerto, | f. 33v tristinge stidefastli to þe merci of God þat he, forþi þat he comaundiþ vs to doon þe office of presthood, wol be oure sufficient witnesse, if we bi ensaumple of his holi lyuynge and techynge speciali bisien vs feiþfulli to do oure office iustli. Ȝhe, þe peple to whom we prechen, be þei feiþful eiþer vnfeiþful, schulen be oure lettris þat is oure witnesse-berers; for truþe whanne it is sowen may not ben vnwitnessid. For alle þei, þat ben conuertid or saued bi herynge of Goddis word and worchen þeraftir, ben witnesse-berers þat þe truþe þat þei herden and diden after is cause of her saluacioun. And aȝenward alle vnfeiþful men and wymmen, whiche herden þe truþe tolde out to hem and wolden not do þeraftir, [also alle þei þat myȝten haue herd þe truþe and wolden not heren it, forþi þat þei wolden not do þeraftir], alle þese schulen beren witnesse aȝens hemsilf | f. 34 þat þe truþe, whiche þei wolden not heeren, eiþer herden and dispiseden to do þeraftir, þis her vnfeiþfulnes is now and schal be cause of her dampnacioun.

'Wherfore, ser, siþe þis forseide witnessynge of God and of dyuerse seyntis and doctouris and of alle þe peple, good and yule, suffisiþ to alle trewe prechours, we demen þat we doon not þe office of presthood if we leeuen oure prechinge, forþi þat we haue not ne

761 ȝoure proctours] prechers A ȝoure¹] ȝu ȝoure R proctours] procuratoribus illegitimos terminos imponendo VP 765 greet] aliorum sanctorum et magnorum VP 768 coueiten] come A 769 seintis . . . doctours (770)] doctours . . . seintes A 772 witnesse] letters and witnesse A 776 whanne] where A 777 herynge] learninge A 778 and diden after] *om.* VP 781 also . . . þeraftir (782)] also all they that might haue herde the truthe and wold not heare it because that they wolde not do thereafter A, et similiter omnes qui potuerunt audiuisse veritatem et noluerunt operare secundum eam VP, *om.* R 784 eiþer] neiþer R, or els A þis] thorow A now] *om.* A, nunc testimonium contra eos VP 785 dampnacioun] dampnacionis nisi ante mortem peniteant fructuose VP

moun not haue deweli bischopis letters to witnessen þat we ben sent of hem to preche. þis sentence apreueþ seynt Poul, (in þe ii Cor. þe 3 c°) where he seiþ of himsilf and of oþere feiþful apostlis and dissciplis seiinge þus "We neden no lettris of comendacioun, as summe oþer prechours neden whiche prechen for couetise of temperal goodis eiþir for mannes presumynge." And where 3e seien,
f. 34v ser, þat Poul biddiþ sogettis | to obeien to her souereynes, þis mai not be denyed. But þer ben two manere souereynes: vertues souereynes and vicious tirauntis. And to þese souereynes men and wymmen þat ben sogettis owen to obeie in to maners. To vertuous souereynes and charitable sogettis owen to obeien wilfulli and gladly, in heeringe of her good counseilis, in consentynge to her charitable heestis and in worchinge after her [fructuouse] werkis. þis sentence apreueþ Poul, where he seiþ þus to sogettis, "Haue 3e mynde, or be 3e myndeful, of 3oure souereynes þat speken to 3ou þe word of God, and sue 3e þe feiþ of hem whos conuersacioun 3e knowen to be vertuous." For, as Poul seiþ anoon after, þe souereyns to whom sogettis owen to obeie in suynge of her maneres, þese souereynes
f. 35 waken bisili in holi | studiinge how þei mowen wiþstonde and distroyen vicis, in hemsilf first and siþ in alle her sogettis, and how þei moun best plante in hem vertues. Also þese souereynes waken in deuout and feruent praiers for to purchace grace of þe lord God, þat þei and her sogettis moun ouer alle þingis dreden to offenden him and louen him and to plesen him. Also þese souereynes, to whom Poul biddiþ vs to obeien as it is seide bifore, lyuen so vertuousli þat alle þei þat wolen lyue wel moun take of hem good ensaumple, to knowe and to kepe Goddis heestis. But in þis forseid wise sogettis owen not to be obedient to trowauntis, whiche ben vicious tirauntis, siþe her willes, her counseilis, her heestis and her werkis ben so vicious þat þei owen to be hatid and left. And þou3 siche tirauntis

791 *margin* poule in þe ij. cor. þe 3 c° R   in . . . 3 c°] *om.* AVP   794 couetise of temperal goodis] questum VP   795 mannes presumynge] mennes praising A   796 mai] is soth and may A   798 and[2]] therfore A   souereynes[2]] last souereyns nother A   801 in heeringe] obediendo V   counseilis] counsell A   802 fructuouse] frutefull A, fructuosa VP, charitable R   803 *margin* haue 3e mynde or be 3e myndeful of 3oure souereyns seiþ poul R   haue . . . or] *om.* AVP   805 and . . . vertuous (806)] quorum intuentes conuersacioni imitamini et fidem VP   806 anoon] *om.* A   808 waken] worke A   809 siþ] communiter VP   810 waken in] make A   813 and[2]] for to A   817 be] obeye nor to be A   whiche] while they A, quia P   818 willes] will A   counseilis] counsell A

ben maistirful and cruel in bostinge, in manassinge, in betinge | and f. 35v in diuerse ponyschinge, seint Peter biddiþ þe seruauntis of suche tirauntis to obeien mekeli to suche trowauntis, suffringe mekeli her malicious cruelte. [But Peter counseiliþ] not ony seruaunt or sogett to obeie to ony lord or souereyn in ony þing þat is not plesinge to God.'

And þe Archebischop seide to me, 'If a souereyne bidde his soget do þat þing þat is vicious, þis souereyn herinne is to blame, but þe soget for his obedience deserueþ mede of God, for obedience plesiþ more God þan ⌜ony⌝ sacrafice.'

And I seide, 'Ser, Samuel þe profite seide to Saul þe wickid king þat God was more plesid wiþ obedience to hise heestis þan wiþ ony sacrifice of beestis. But Dauiþ seiþ and seint Poul and seint Gregor acordingli alle togidere þa⌜t⌝ not oonli þei þat don yuele ben worþi | f. 36 deeþ or dampnacioun, but also þei þat consenten to yuele doeres. And, ser, þe lawe of holi chirche techeþ in decrees þat no seruaunt to his lord, neiþir child to his fadir ne to modir, neiþer wiif to her housebonde, ne monke to his abbot owiþ to obeie, no but in leeful þingis and lawful.'

And þe Archebischop seide to me, 'Alle þese aleggeaunces þat þou bryngist forþ ben not ellis no but prowde presumtousnessis. For herbi þou enforsist þee to preue þat þou and siche oþer ben so iust þat ȝe owen not to be obedient to prelatis. And þus, aȝen þe loore of seint Poul þat techiþ ȝou not to preche but if ȝe were sent, of ȝoure owne autorite ȝe wolen go forþ and preche and do what ȝou list.'

And I seide, 'Ser, presentiþ not euery preest þe office of þe apostlis of Crist, eiþer þe office of þe two and seuenti | disciplis of Crist?' f. 36v

And þe Archebischop seide, 'Ȝis.'

And I seide, 'Ser, as þe tenþe chapitre of Mathew and þe laste chapitre of Mark witnessen þat Crist sent hise apostlis for to preche, and also þe x. c. of Luk witnessiþ þat Crist sente his two and seuenti dissciplis for to preche into euery place þat he was to comen to, and

820 cruel] crudeles et feroces VP betinge] oppressions A 821 ponyschinge] punysshyngis A *margin* seint petir seiþ in þe ij c° R 822 mekeli] paciently A 823 but . . . counseiliþ] but Petyr counsellith A, sed Petrus . . . consulit (consuluit V) VP, *om.* R 824 or] or prince or A 830 *margin* samuel þe prophete R 831 heestis] commaundement A 832 Dauiþ] dicendum V 835 *margin* in þe decrees R 839 aleggeaunces] allegingis A presumtousnessis] presumptuousnes A 845 and I seide] *om.* P 846 of Crist[1]] *om.* A two and seuenti] *om.* A 848 *margin* crist seiþ in þe 10 c° of mt. and in þe last c° of mr. luk x c° R

seint Gregor in þe comoun lawe seiþ þat euery man þat neiȝiþ to presthood takiþ vpon him þe office of prechinge, for, as he seiþ, þat prest terriþ God to greet wraþþe of whoos mouþ is not herd þe vois of prechinge, and as þe interlynarie glose vpon Ezechiel witnessiþ þat prest þat prechiþ not to þe peple bisili schal be partyner of her dampnacioun whiche perischen in his defaute, ȝhe, þouȝ þe peple be f. 37 saued bi oþer special grace of God þan bi prestis | prechinge, ȝit prestis, forþi þat þei ben ordeyned of God to preche and prechen not, as bifore God þei ben mansleers. For in þat þing þat in hem is, preestis þat prechen not truli and bisili sleen alle þe peple goostly, in þat þat þei wiþholden fro hem þe word of God, þat is liif and sustynaunce of cristen soulis. And seint Isidre seiþ prestis schulen be dampned for wickidnesse of þe peple, if þei techen not hem þat ben vnkunnynge, eiþer blame not hem þat ben synners; for al þe werk ⌜or⌝ bisines þat stoondiþ in prestis stoondiþ in prechinge and in techinge, þat þei edefien alle men as wel bi þe kunnynge of feiþ as bi werkis of disciplyne þat is vertuous techinge. And þe gospel witnessiþ Crist seide "Into þis þing I am borun and came into þis world, þat I bere witnesse to truþe; he þat is of truþe heeriþ my vois." þanne, ser, siþen f. 37v bi þe | word of Crist speciali þat is his vois prestis ben comaundid to preche, whateuere prest þanne þat it be þat haþ not good wille and ful purpos to doon þus, and abliþ him not aftir his kunnynge and his power to doon his office, bi þe ensaumple of Crist and of hise apostlis, displesiþ God whateuere oþer þing he doiþ. For seint Gregor seiþ, þat þing leeft þat a man is holden to do chefly, whateuer þing þat man doiþ is vnþankful to þe Holi Goost. And herfore seiþ Lyncoln "þat prest þat prechi[þ] not þe word of God, þouȝ he be seen to haue noon oþer ⌜de⌝faute, he is antecrist and sathanas, a niȝt þeef and a dai þeef, a sleer of soulis and an aungel of liȝt turned into derknesse." Wherfore, ser, þese autoritees and oþer wel considerid, I deme mysilf dampnable if I, eiþer for plesaunce [or for displesaunce] of ony creature, bisie me f. 38 not to pre|che þe worde of God. And in þe same dampnacioun I

855 þe . . . glose] other more gloses A 858 ȝit] ȝht *canc.* ȝit R 859 of God] *om.* A prechen not] non predicant fideliter libere et solicite VP 861 truli and bisili] *om.* VP 863 cristen] mennis A *margin* Isidre R 867 werkis of disciplyne] discipline of workes AVP 868 *margin* þe 18 c° of Ioon R 869 þis þing] his teaching A þat I bere] to beare A 872 good wille] vocem bonam P 873 abliþ] humilitat VP 875 seint Gregor seiþ] ut dicitur in fide mea scripta archiepiscopo illo dimisso VP 877 *margin* lyncoln R 878 prechiþ] AVP, prechid R 880 *box in margin for reference not supplied* R 882 or for displesaunce] or displeasure A, aut displicenciam VP, *om.* R

deeme alle þo prestis, which of good purpos and wille enforsen hem not bisili to do þus, and also alle hem þat haue purpos or wille to lette ony preest of þis bisinesse.'

And þe Archebischop seide to þe þre clerkis þat stoden bifore him, 'Lo, seres, þis is þe bisinesse and þe maner of þis losel and siche oþer: to pike out scharpe sentencis of holy writ and of doctours for to maynteyne her sect and her loore aȝens þe ordenaunce of holi chirche. And herfore, losel, it is þat þou coueitist to haue aȝen þe Sauter þat I made to be taken fro þee at Cauntirbirie, forþi þat þou woldist gadere out þereof and recorde scharpe verses aȝens vs. But þou schalt neuere haue þat Sauter neiþir ony oþer book, til þat I wite þat þin hert | and þi f. 38v
mouþ acorden fulli to be gouerned bi holi chirche.'

And I seide, 'Ser, al my wille and purpos is and euer schal be, I triste to God, to be gouerned bi holi chirche.'

And þe Archebischop axid me what I clepid holi chirche.

And I seide, 'Ser, I toolde to ȝou bifore what was holi chirche. But siþ ȝe axen me ȝit þis demaunde, I clepe Crist and his seintis holi chirche.'

And þe Archebischop seide to me, 'I wot wel Crist and his seyntis ben holi chirche in heuene. But what is holi chirche here in erþe?'

And I seide, 'Ser, þouȝ holi chirche be euere oon in charite, ȝit it haþ two parties: þe firste and þe principal haþ ouercomen perfitli al þe wickidnes of þis lyf and regneþ ioifulli in heuene wiþ Crist; and þe toþer part is here ȝit in erþe, bisili and contynueli fiȝtinge dai and niȝt aȝens temptaciouns, | þe fend forsakinge and hatinge þe prosperite of f. 39
þis world, dispisinge and wiþstondinge her fleischli lustis, whiche oonli ben þe pilgrymes of Crist wandrynge towardis heuene bi stable feiþ, bi stidefast hope and bi parfit charite. For þese heuenli pilgrimes moun not neiþer þei wolen be lettid of her purpos bi þe reyne of ony doctrine discordinge from holi writt, neiþer bi þe floodis of ony temperal goodis and tribulaciouns, neiþer bi wyndis of ony pride or boost or manassynge of ony creature. For alle þei ben sadli groundid

888 bisinesse . . . maner] maner . . . besinesse A 892 forþi þat . . . and (893)] to A 896 purpos] power A euer] *om.* P 898 I clepid] was A 904 euere] euery A charite] perfecta caritate VP 906 wickidnes] wretchednesse A, miseriam VP 907 bisili and] *om.* VP 908 þe[1]] of þe A 909 dispisinge and] desistens V 910 oonli] *om.* P stable] stedfast A, stabilem et veram VP 911 stidefast] groundid A 912 purpos] goode purpos A reyne] reason A 913 doctrine] doctours A 914 goodis and] *om.* AVP tribulaciouns] tribulacioun AVP wyndis] the winde AVP 915 or manassynge] criminacionis P

vpon þe corner-stoon Crist, heerynge his word and louynge it, bisiinge hem feiþfulli and contynuelli in alle her wittis to do þeraftir.'

And þe Archebischop seide to hise clerkis, 'Se ȝe not how his herte f. 39v is endurid, and how it is traueilid wiþ þe deuel, occupiynge him þus | bisili and redili to alegge suche sentencis to maynteyne wiþ hise errours and eresies? Sertis, þus he wole occupie vs here al dai if we wolen suffre him.'

And oon of þe Archebischopis clerkis seide þanne to him, 'Ser, he seide riȝt now þat þis certificacioun þat cam to ȝou from Schrouesbirie is vntruli forgid aȝens him. Þerfore, ser, appose ȝe him now here in alle þe poyntis which ben certified aȝens him, and so we schulen heere of his owne mouþ his answeringis and wittnesse hem.'

And þe Archebischop took þanne þe certificacioun in his hond and he lokide þerevpon a while, and so þanne he seide to me 'Lo, here it is certified and witnessid aȝens þee bi worþi men and feiþful of Schrouesbirie þat þou prechedist þere opinli in seint Chaddis chirche f. 40 þat þe sacra|ment of þe auter was material breed after þe consecracioun. What seist þou? Was þis truli prechid?'

And I seide 'Ser, I telle ȝou truli, I touchide no þing þere of þe sacrament of þe auter, no but in þis wise as I wol wiþ Goddis grace schewe ⌜here⌝ to ȝou. As I stood þere in þe pulpitte, bisiinge me to teche þe heestis of God, oon knyllide a sacringe belle, and herfor myche peple turned awei fersli and wiþ greet noyse runnen frowardis me. And I, seynge þis, seide to hem þus "Goode men, ȝou were better to stoonden here stille and to heere Goddis word! For, certis, þe vertu and þe mede of þe moost holi sacrament of þe auter stondiþ myche moore in þe bileue þereof þat ȝe owen to haue in ȝoure soulis þan it f. 40v doiþ in þe outward siȝt þerof. And þerfore ȝou were better to stonde | stille quyetefulli and to heeren Goddis worde, siþ þoruȝ heeringe þerof men comen to veri bileue." And oþer wise, ⌜ser⌝, I am certeyne I spak not þere of þe worschipful sacrament of þe auter.'

And þe Archebischop seide to me, 'I trowe þee not, whateuere þou seist, siþe so worschipful men haue witnessid aȝens þee. But siþ þou denyest þat þou seidest not þus þere, what seist þou now? Dwelliþ þer after þe consecracioun of þe oost material breed or nai?'

916 corner-stoon] suer stone A 919 it] he A 920 and redili] *om.* A to maynteyne] ad manutenendum et defendendum VP 923 archebischopis] *om.* A 930 and witnessid] *om.* A 933 truli] *om.* P 936 pulpitte] publico P 937 heestis] commaundement A 938 fersli] hastely A, frequenter V 939 better] *om.* V 942 soulis] soule AVP 946 worschipful] woorthy A 947 trowe] beleue AVP, trowide R 950 of] in A

And I seide, 'Ser, I knowe nowhere in holi writt where þis terme "material breed" is writun. And þerfor, ser, whanne I speke of þis mater I vse not to speke of material breed.'

And þe Archebischop seide to me, 'How techist þou men to bileue in þis sacrament?'

And I seide,'Ser, as I bileue mysilf so I teche oþere men.'| f. 41

And he seide to me, 'Telle out playnli þi bileue þereof.'

And I seide wiþ my forseide protestacioun, 'Ser, I bileue þat þe ni3t bifore þat Crist Iesu wolde suffre wilfulli passioun for mankynde on þe morwe, after hee took breed in his holi and worschipful hondis and, "liftynge vp his i3en he dide þankynges to God his fadir, and blessid breed and brake it, and he 3af to hise dissciplis, seiinge to hem 'Takiþ þis and etiþ of þis alle; þis is my bodi.'" And þat þis is and owiþ to be alle mennes bileue, as Mathew, Mark, Luk and Poul witnessen. Oþir bileue, ser, siþ I bileue þat þis suffisiþ in þis mater, haue I noon, neiþir wole haue ne teche; but in þis bileue þoru3 Goddis grace I purpose to lyue and die, knowlechinge, as I beleue and teche oþer to beleue, þat þe worschipful sacrament of þe auter | is verri Cristis fleisch and his f. 41$^v$ blood in forme of breed and wyne.'

And þe Archebischop seide to me, 'It is soþ þat þis sacrament is Cristis bodi in fourme of breed, but not in substaunce of breed; but þou and þi sect techen it to be in substaunce of breed. þinke þee þis true techinge?'

And I seide, 'Ser, neiþer I ne ony oþer of þe sect þat 3e dampnen techiþ ony oþir wise þan I haue toold to 3ou, neiþir bileueþ oþer wiise to my knowynge. But naþeles ser, I axe of 3ou for charite þat 3e telle here pleynli how we schulen vndirstoonde þis tixte of þe apostil Poul þat seiþ þus "þis þing fele 3e in 3ou or vndirstonde þat is [in] Crist Iesu whiche whanne he was in fourme of God." Ser, wheþir Poul clepiþ not here "þe fourme | of God" þe substaunce o[r] þe kynde of f. 42 God? And also, sir, seiþ not þe churche in þe houres of þe moost blessid Virgyne acordingli herto, where it is writen þus "þou Autour of helþe, haue mynde þat sum tyme þou tokist of þe vnwemmid

958 forseide] *om.* A *margin* nota R 960 *margin* sacrament of þe auter mathew 26 c$^o$ m$^r$ þe 14 c$^o$ luk 22 c$^o$ poul in cor. þe 10 c$^o$ and þe 1 c$^o$ R 962 breed] *om.* VP 963 alle] all you A 968 verri] the sacramente of A 971 Cristis] very Christis A but$^2$ . . . breed (972)] *om.* A 977 we] ye A *margin* poul R 978 seiþ] dixit P or vndirstonde] *om.* AVP in$^2$] AVP, *om.* R 980 or] AVP, of R 982 *box in margin for reference not supplied* R

Virgyne þe fourme of oure bodi"—wheþer þe "fourme of oure bodi" be not clepid here þe kynde of oure bodi?'

And þe Archebischop seide to me, 'Woldist þou make me to declare þese tixtis to þi purpos? Siþ þe chirche haþ [now] determyned þat þere dwelliþ no substaunce of breed aftir þe consecracioun of þe sacrament of þe auter, bileuest þou not to þis ordinaunce of holi chirche?'

And I seide, 'Ser, whateuer prelatis han ordeyned in þe chirche
f. 42v anentis þis mater and oþer, oure bileue stondiþ euere hool. | And I haue not lerned þat þe ordinaunce of men bineþe þe bileue schal be putt into bileue.'

And þe Archebischop seide to me, 'If þou hast not lerned þis biforehonde, lerne now and knowe þat þou art out of bileue if in þis mater and oþere þou bileuest not as holi chirche bileueþ. What seyn doctouris tretinge ⌜in⌝ þis mater?'

And I seide, 'Sir, seynt Poul, þat was a greet doctour of holi chirche, spekinge to þe peple and techinge to hem þe riȝt bileue of þis moost worþi sacrament, clepiþ it "breed þat we breken". And also in þe canoun of þe masse after þe consecracioun þis moost worþi sacrament is clepid "holi breed". And euery preest in þis lond, aftir þat he haþ reseyued þis blessid sacrament, seiþ in þis wise "þat þing þat we haue taken wiþ oure mouþ, take we wiþ clene and pure
f. 43 mynde"—þat is, [as] I vndir|stonde, we praien God þat we moun resceyue [þoruȝ] veri bileue þis holi sacrament worþili. And, sir, seynt Austyn seiþ "þat þing þat is seen is breed, but þat þing þat mannes feiþ axiþ or desiriþ to be enformed of is verri Cristis bodi." And also Fulgens an autetike doctour seiþ "As it were an errour to seie þat Crist was no but o substaunce, þat is very man and not veri God, eiþer to seie þat Crist was veri God and not veri man, so it is, þis doctour seiþ, an errour to seie þat þe sacrament of þe auter is no but oo

984 wheþer] tell me for charyte therfore whether A 987 þese tixtis] this texte A now] nowe A, nunc VP, *om.* R 988 of[2]] in A 992 anentis . . . oþer] *om.* A 993 lerned] herde A bineþe] circa VP bileue] fidem uel capi ut fides VP 997 mater] sacrament A 999 *margin* poul seiþ to cor. þe 10 c° þe breed which we breken is þe part taking of þe bodi of þe lord And in þe 11 c° he clepiþ it breed þriis R 1000 hem] þe peple *canc.* hem R 1001 worþi] holy A 1004 blessid] *om.* A 1005 take] we praye god that we maye take A, domine . . . capiamus VP clene and pure] pura VP 1006 as] AVP, *om.* R 1007 þoruȝ] AVP, *om.* R 1008 breed] panis . . . et calix quod oculi renuncciant VP 1009 or desiriþ] *om.* AVP bodi] corpus . . . et calix sanguis eius VP 1010 autetike] ententyfe A 1011 very] vnus P veri] vnus P 1012 veri[1,2]] vnus P

substaunce." And also, sir, acordingli herto in þe secrete of þe masse in þe mydis þereof on Cristinmasse dai it is writun þus *Sicut homo genitus idem refulsit Deus, sic hec terena substancia nobis conferat quod diuinum est*, which sentence, ser, wiþ þe secrete also of þe fourþe *feri quatuor temporum* | (f. 43v) *Septembris* I preie ȝou, ser, þat ȝe wol declare here opinli in Ynglische.'

And þe Archebischop seide to me, 'I perceyue wel inowȝ where aboute þou art, and how þe deuel blyndiþ þee þat þou maist not vndirstonde þe ordenaunce of holi chirche, neiþer consente to obeie þerto. But I comaunde to þee now answere to me schortli. Bileuest þou aftir þe sacringe of þis forseid sacrament þere dwelliþ substaunce of breed or nay?'

And I seide, 'Ser, as I vndirstonde, it is al oon to graunte, eiþer bileue, þat þere dwelliþ no substaunce of breed and to graunte, or to bileue, þat þis moost worþi sacrament of Cristis owne bodi is an accident wiþouten soget. But, ser, forþi þat ȝoure axinge passiþ myn vndirstondinge, I dar neiþer denye it ne | (f. 44) graunte it, for it is scolemater aboute whiche I neuer bisied me for to knowe in. And þerfor I committe þis terme *accidentem sine subiecto* to þo clerkis which deliten hem so in curious and so sotil sofestrie, þat þei mouen ofte so defficult materis and straunge, and waden and wandren so in hem fro argument into argument wiþ *pro* and *contra* to þe tyme þat þei witen not ofte where þei ben neiþer vndirstonden clerli hemsilf. But þe schame þat þese prowde sofestris haue to ȝelden hem to men and bifore men makiþ hem ofte folis and to ben concludid schamefulli bifore God.'

And þe Archebischop seide to me, 'I purpose not to oblische þe to þe sotil argumentis of clerkis, siþ þou art vnable herto, but I purpose to make þee to obeie | (f. 44v) þe to þe determynacioun of holi chirche.'

And I seide, 'Ser, bi open euydence and bi greet witnesse a þousand ȝeer after þe incarnacioun of Crist, þe determynacioun which I haue confessid heere bifore to ȝou was accept of al holi chirche as sufficient of saluacioun of alle hem þat wollen bileue it feiþfulli and worchen þeraftir charitabli. But, ser, þe determynacioun of þis mater which

1014 substaunce] substaaunce, *2nd* a *canc.* R 1015 sicut . . . genitus (1016)] *om.* A 1016 hec] *om.* A 1018 temporum] temporum//temporum R opinli] *om.* VP 1022 to obeie] *om.* A 1027 no] *om.* A 1029 ȝoure] is ȝoure R 1033 mouen] determine A 1035 ofte] *om.* A 1036 clerli] *om.* A 1037 men[1]] omnibus P 1038 bifore] et peccant coram VP 1044 confessid] rehersed A 1045 wollen] wolde AV

was brouȝt in siþ þe fend was losid bi frere Tomas Alquyne, specialli clepinge þe moost worschipful sacrament of Cristis bodi an accident wiþouten soget, which terme, siþ I knowe not þat Goddis lawe appreueþ it, in þis mater I dar not graunte. But vttirli I denye to make þis freris sentence or ony oþer sich my bileue, do wiþ me, God, what f. 45 þou wolt!' |

And þe Archebischop seide to me, 'Wel, wel, þou schalt seie oþir wise or þat I leue þee!

2 *questio*

'But what seist þou to þis secunde point þat is recordid aȝens þee of worþi men of Schrouesbirie, seiinge þat þou prechedist þere openli þat ymagis owen not to be worschipid in ony wise?'

And I seide, 'Ser, I prechid neuer þus, neiþer þoruȝ Goddis grace I wol in ony tyme consente to þenke ne to seie þus, neiþer priuyli ne apeertli. For, lo, þe Lord witnessiþ bi Moisees þat alle þingis whiche he made weren riȝt goode, and so þanne þei weren and ȝit ben and schulen ben goode and worschipful in her kynde. And þerfore to þe eende þat God made hem þei ben alle preisable and worschipful; and f. 45ᵛ speciali man, þat was maade aftir þe image and lickenesse of God, | is ful worschipful in his kynde—ȝhe, þis holi ymage þat is man God worschipid. And herfore euery man schulde worschipe oþer in kynde, and also for heuenli vertues þat man vsiþ charitabli. Also I seie þat tree, stoon, gold, siluer or ony oþer mater þat ymagis ben maad of, alle þe creaturis ben worschipful in her kynde and to þe eende þat God made hem fore. But þe keruynge, þe ȝetynge, neiþer þe peyntynge of ymagerie wiþ mannus hond, al be it þat þis ⌜doinge⌝ be accept of men of hiȝeste astaat and dignite, and ordeyned of hem to be a kalender to lewde men þat neiþer kunnen, ne wolen be leerned to knowe God bi his word, ne bi his creaturis, neiþer bi his wondirful and diuerse worchyngis, ȝit þis ymagerie owiþ not to be worschipid in þis foorme f. 46 ne in liknesse of mannes crafte, al be it þat euery | mater þat peyntours peynten wiþ, siþ it is Goddis creature, owiþ to be worschipid in þe kynde, and to þe eende þat God made it, and ordeyned it to serue man.'

And þe Archebischop seide to me, 'I graunte wel þat no liif owiþ to

1047 Alquyne] agayn A 1055 2 questio] *om.* AVP 1061 alle] the A 1062 goode] bona Gen.3 VP 1065 maade] ma *canc.* maade R 1067 worschipid] worshippeth AVP 1069 tree stoon] woode tynne A 1070 worschipful] venerabiles et honorabiles VP 1075 neiþer] ut ipsas fecit nec VP

do worschip to ony siche ymage for itsilf. But a crucifix owiþ to be worschipid for þe passioun of Crist þat is peyntid þereinne, and is brouȝt þereþoruȝ into manus mynde. And þus þe ymage of þe blessid virgyne Marie, Cristis modir, and oþer ymagis of seyntis owen to ben worschipid. For, lo, erþeli kyngis and oþer lordis, which vsen to senden her lettris enselid wiþ her armes or wiþ her priuy sygnetis to men þat ben wiþ hem, ben worschipid of þese men; [for whanne þese men] resceyuen her lordis lettris, in which þei seen and knowen her willis and þe heestis of | f. 46v her lordis, in worschip of her lordis þei don of her cappis or her hoodis to her lettris. Whi not þanne, siþ in ymagis maad wiþ mannes hond we moun rede and knowe manye dyuerse doingis of God and hise seintis, schulen we not worschipen her ymagis?'

And I seide, 'Ser, wiþ my forseide protestacioun I seie þat þis worldli vsage of temperal lordis þat ȝe speken now of, whiche in caas may be don wiþouten synne and also left, is no symylitude to worschipe ymagis maad bi mannes hond, siþ Moyses seiþ in Deut.iiii.c°, and Dauiþ seiþ in þe Ps. 96, and þe Wise Man seiþ in þe 14.15 c°, and also Baruk þe profete seiþ in þe 6°, and oþer dyuerse seintis of þe bible forboden so pleynli þe worschipynge of alle siche ymagis.'

And þe | f. 47 Archebischop seide to me, 'Lewid losel, in þe olde lawe, bifore þat Crist toke mankynde, was no liknesse of ony persone of þe Trinyte neiþer schewid to man ne knowen of dedli man, but now siþ Crist ⌜bi⌝cam man it is leful to haue ymagis to schewe his manhood. Ȝhe, þouȝ many men, which ben riȝt greete clerkis and oþer, also holden it errour to peynte þe Trinyte, I seie it is wel don to make and to peynte þe Trinyte in ymagis. For it is a greete moovynge of deuocioun to men to haue and to bihoolde þe Trinyte and oþer ymagis of seintis koruen, ȝoten or peyntid. For biȝonde þe see ben þe beste ymage makers and

1082 ymage] ymages A itsilf] themselfe A 1084 ymage] ymages A 1085 virgyne] trinite and of virgyn A oþer . . . seyntis] ymagines aliorum sanctorum VP 1087 sygnetis] signet A 1088 for whanne þese men] for whan thes men A, quia cum isti VP, *om.* R 1091 or her hoodis] *om.* AVP 1093 doingis] thinges A 1095 þis worldli vsage] these worldly vsages A 1097 and also left] *om.* A symylitude] probabilis similitudo VP 1099 96] 96 10.12 R *margin* Moises in det° 4 c° dauit in þe Ps 96°.10 12 þe wise man seiþ in þe 14 and 15 c° baruk þe 6 c° R seiþ[1] . . . 6° (1100)] Dauid Salomon Baruch AVP 1100 dyuerse] *om.* A 1101 forboden] forbidde AVP 1103 losel] *om.* V 1105 dedli] *om.* A 1107 holden] helde A 1109 for . . . trinyte (1110)] *om.* P 1111 ymage . . . and] *om.* A and peyntours (1112)] *om.* VP

peyntours þat euer I siȝ. And, seris, I telle ȝou þis is her manere, and it is a good manere: whanne þat an ymage maker schal kerue, ȝete or
f. 47v peynte an ymage, | he schal go to a preest and schryue him as clene as if he schulde þanne die, and take penaunce, and make sum certeyn avow of fastynge or of preier or of pilgrimage doynge, prainge þe preest to praie speciali for him þat he mai haue grace to make a faier and a deuoute ymage.'

And I seide, 'Ser, I doute not þat if þese peyntours þat ȝe speken of or ony oþer peyntours vndirstonde [truli] þe textis of Moyses, of Dauiþ, and of þe Wise Man, and of þe profete Baruk, and of oþer seintis and doctours, þese poyntours schulen be moued for to schryue hem to God wiþ ful entere sorowe of hert, takinge vpon hem to do riȝt scharpe penaunce for þe synful and veyn craft of keruynge, ȝetynge or
f. 48 of peyntynge þat þei haden vsid, bihootinge to God | and holdynge couenant neuer to do so after, knowelechynge opinly bifore alle men her repreuable errynge. And also, ser, þo prestis þat schryuen, as ȝe seien, þo peyntours and enioynen hem to penaunce and to praien for her spede, bihotynge to helpe hem wiþ her preieris for to be curious in her synful craftis, synnen hereinne more greuousli þan þe peyntours. For þese prestis conforten hem, and ȝeuen hem counseil to do þat þing which of greet peyne,—ȝhe, vp peyne of Goddis curs,—þei schulden vtterli forbeden hem. For certis, ser, if þe woundirful worchinge of God, and þe holi lyuynge and techynge of Crist and of hise apostlis and profetis weren maade knowen to þe peple bi holi lyuynge, and trewe and bisie techynge of preestis, þese þingis weren
f. 48v sufficient bokis and kalenders to knowe God bi and | his seintis, wiþouten ony ymage maade wiþ mannes hond. But certis þe viciousnesse of preestis and her coueitise ben cheef cause of þis errour and of alle oþer viciousnesses þat rengnen among þe peple.'

And þe Archebischop seide to me, 'I holde þee a vicious preest and acursid, and alle hem þat ben of þi sect. For alle preestis of holi chirche, and alle ymagis þat mouen þe peple to deuocioun, þou and siche oþer bisien for to distroie. Losel, were it a faire þing to come into a chirche and se þerinne noon ymage?'

1114 an ymage] ony ymages A  1120 truli] truely A, vere VP, *om.* R  *boxes in margin for references not supplied* R  1121 þe profete] *om.* AVP  1123 entere] inwarde A  1124 and veyn] *om.* P  1125 and holdynge couenant] feithfully A  1127 errynge] earning A  1129 preieris] oracionem P  1138 ymage] ymages A  1139 viciousnesse] vicious lyuynge A  1140 viciousnesses] viciousnesse A

And I seide , 'Ser, þei þat comen to þe chirche for to preie deuoutli to þe lord God moun in her inward wittis be þe more feruent, þat alle her outward wittis ben schit fro alle vtward seeing and heeringe, and fro alle disturbaunce and lettyngis. And siþ Crist blessiþ hem þat seen him neuere | bodili and haue bileued feiþfulli into him, it sufficiþ f. 49 þanne to alle men þoruȝ heerynge and knowinge of Goddis worde, and in doinge þeraftir, for to bileuen into God þouȝ þei seeȝen neuere ymage maad wiþ mannes hond after ony persone of þe Trynytee eiþer of ony oþer seynt.'

And þe Archebischop seide to me wiþ a feruent spirit, 'I seie to þee, losel, þat it is riȝt wel doon to make and to haue an ymage of þe Trinyte! Ȝhe, what seist þou? Is it not a stiringe þing to ⌜bi⌝holde suche an ymage?'

And I seide, 'Ser, ȝe seide riȝt now þat in þe olde lawe, er þat Crist toke mankynde, noo lickenesse of ony persone of þe Trinyte was schewid to men; wherefore, ser, ȝe seide it was not þan leueful to haue ymages; but now ȝe seie, siþ Crist is bicome man, it is | leueful for to f. 49v make and to haue an ymage of þe Trynyte, and also of oþer seintis. But, ser, þis þing I wolde lerne of ȝou: siþ þe Fadir of heuene, ȝhe, and euery persone of þe Trinite was wiþouten biginnynge God almyȝti, and many holi profetis þat weren deedli men weren martrid violentli in þe olde lawe, and also manye men and wymmen diede þan holi confessours, whi was it not þanne as leeful and nessessarie as now to haue maad an image of þe Fadir of heuene, ⌜and⌝ to haue hadde oþer imagis of martrid profetis and of holi confessouris to haue ben kalenderis to lewid men, mouynge hem to deuocioun, as ȝe seien þat imagis now done?'

And þe Archebischop seide, 'Þe synagoge of Iewis hadde not autorite to appreue þese þingis, as þe chirche of Crist haþ | now.' f. 50

And I seide, 'Sir, seint Gregor was a greet man in þe new lawe and of greet dignyte and, as comoun lawe witnessiþ, he comendide greetli a bischop forþi þat he forbed vttirli þat imagis maad wiþ mannis honde schulden not ben worschipid.'

And þe Archebischop seide, 'Vngraciouse losel, þat sauerest no

1147 feruent] feruenciores in orando VP 1149 blessiþ] blessed A 1153 ymage] ymagis A 1166 violentli] *om.* VP 1169 maad] made and hadde A and . . . of[1] (1170)] et aliarum personarum trinitatis et VP 1170 martrid] martires A 1171 lewid] aduise A 1172 done] faciunt . . . et . . . valde bene VP 1178 not] *om.* A 1179 vngraciouse] *om.* P sauerest] fauerist A

more treuþe þan an hound! Siþ at þe roode at þe norþe dore at Londoun, and at Boxleye, at Walsyngam and in manye oþir dyuerse places in Yngelond ben manye greete and preysable myraclis done, schulden not þe ymagis of siche holi placis, at þe reuerence of God and of oure Ladi and of oþer seintis, ben more worschipid þan oþer ymagis where noo siche myraclis be done?'

And I seide, 'Sir, þer is no suche vertue in ony imagerie þat ony f. 50v ymage schulde | herfore be worschipid. Wherfore I am certeyne þat þer is no suche myracle don of God in ony place in erþe, bicause þat ony ymage maad wiþ mannys honde schulde be worschipid. And herfor, sere, as I prechide openli at Schrouesbirie and elliswhere, I seie now here bifore ȝou þat no liif schulde triste þat þere were ony vertu in suche ymagerie maad wiþ mannys honde; and herfore no liif schulde avowe to hem, neiþer seche hem, ne knele to hem, [ne bowe to hem, ne preye to hem, neiþer offren ony þinge to hem, ne kissen hem], ne encense hem. For, lo, þe moost worþi suche ymage maad at Goddis biddinge þe good king Ezechie distroiede worþili and þankfulli, forþi þat it was encensid. Forþi, sere, if men taken good hede to þe wrytynge and to þe loore of seint Austyn, and of seint Gregor, and of f. 51 Ioon Crisostem, and of oþere seintis and doctours, how þei | speken and writen of myraclis þat schulen be done now in þe laste ende of þis world, it is to drede lest for þe vnfeiþfulnesse of men and of wymmen þe fend haþ power for to worche manye of þese miraclis þat now be done in siche placis; for boþe men and wymmen deliten now more for to knowe and to here of myraclis þan þei done to heere Goddis word and to knowe it effectualli. Wherfore, into gret confusioun of alle hem þat þus done, Crist seiþ "þe generacioun of avowtereris sechiþ or coueitiþ toknes or miraclis and wondris." Naþeles, as dyuerse seintis

1180 roode] reddam siue crucifixum VP at[2]] in ecclesia sancti Pauli VP 1181 and at Boxleye] at our lady A Boxleye . . . Walsyngam] Walsyngeham . . . Boxlen V, Walsurgham . . . Roxle P 1182 Yngelond] istius regni VP 1183 placis] seyntis and placis A 1185 ymagis] placis and ymagis A 1187 ymage] ymagis A þat] *twice* R 1189 ymage] ymagis A 1192 vertu] uirtus spiritualis VP 1193 ne[2] . . . hem[4] (1194)] nor bow to them nor pray to them nor offer any thing to them nor kysse them A, nec oraret nec offeret illis nec inclinaret illis . . . nec oscularetur illas VP, *om.* R 1195 ymage] ymagis A maad] the brasen serpente by Moyses made A 1196 *margin* ezechie distriede þe ymage 4 boke of kingis 18 c° R 1197 men] omnes P 1198 *margin* seint austin gregor and crisostem R 1201 and of wymmen] *om.* VP 1203 placis] locis de quibus loquemini VP and wymmen] *om.* VP 1204 knowe . . . here] heare. . . .knowe AVP 1206 *margin* crist seiþ R Crist seiþ] dixit Christus Mt.12 VP sechiþ or coueitiþ] requireth A or coueitiþ] *om.* VP 1207 toknes . . . wondris] signum V, signa P

seien, now whanne þe feiþ of God is stablischid in cristindom, þe word of God suffisiþ to mannys saluacioun wiþouten siche miraclis. And þus also þe word of God suffisiþ to alle | men and wymmen f. 51v wiþouten ony siche ymage. But, good sire, siþ þe Fadir of heuene, þat is God in his godheede, is þe most vnknowen þing þat mai be and þe moost wondirful spirit, hauynge in it no schap or lickenesse of ony membre [of] ony dedeli creature, in what lickenesse þan or ymage mai God þe Fadir be schewid or peyntid?'

And þe Archebischop seide, 'As holi chirche haþ suffrid and ȝit suffriþ þis ymage of alle þe Trynyte and oþer ymagis to be peyntid and schewid suffisiþ to hem þat ben membris of holi chirche. But siþ þou art a roten membre, kitt aweie from holi chirche, þou sauerist not þe ordenaunce þerof. But siþ þe daie passiþ faste, leue we þis mater now.'

And þanne þe Archebischop seide to me, 'What seist þou now to þe þridde poynt | þat is certefied aȝens þee, preching at Schrouesbirie f. 52 opinli þat pilgrimage is vnleeful? And ouer þis þou seidist þere þat þo men and wymmen þat goen on pilgrimage to Cantirbirie, to Beuerleye, to Bridlyngtoun, to Walsyngam or to ony suche pilgrymage ben acursid and maad foolis spendi[n]ge her goodis in wast.'

3 [*questio*]

And I seide, 'Sere, bi þis certificacioun I am acusid to ȝou þat I schulde teche þat no pilgrimage is leeful. But, ser, I seide neuere þus, for I knowe þat þere is trewe pilgrimage and leeful and ful plesynge to God. And þerfore, ser, howeuere myn enemyes haue certified to ȝou of me, I toolde at Schrouesbirie of two manere of pilgrimagis, seiinge þat þer ben trewe pilgrimes and fals pilgrimes.'

And þe Archebischop seide to me, | 'Whom clepist þou trewe f. 52v pilgrimes?'

And I seide, 'Sere, wiþ my forseid protestacioun, I clepe hem trewe

1208 stablischid] publisshed A 1209 wiþouten ... suffisiþ (1210)] *om.* P 1211 ymage] ymagis A 1212 vnknowen] ignota in passibilis V, ignota possibilis P 1214 membre] membres A of] AVP, þat R 1217 ymage] ymagis A trynyte] diuinitatis V 1219 sauerist] fauerest A 1220 faste] *om.* A 1221 now] nunc ... et ad aliam transeamus VP, *om.* A 1222 and ... wast (1227)] *in red* R þe archebischop] he A now] *om.* A 1226 Bridlyngtoun] Karlington A pilgrymage] other placis A, loca VP 1227 spendinge] spendige R 1228 3 questio] 3 R, *om.* AVP 1231 trewe] vna P 1233 seiinge ... pilgrimes[2] (1234)] *om.* A

pilgrymes trauelynge toward þe blis of heuene whiche, in þe staat, degree or ordre þat God clepiþ hem to, bisien hem feiþfulli for to occupie alle her wittis, bodili and goostli, to knowe treweli and to kepe feiþfulli þe heestis of God, hatynge euere and fleynge alle þe seuene dedli synnes and euery braunche of hem, reulynge vertuousli, as it is seide bifore, alle her wittis, doynge discretli, wilfully and gladli alle þe workis of mercy, bodili and goostli, aftir her kunnynge and her power, ablynge hem to þe ȝiftis of þe Holi Goost, disposynge hem to resceyue into her soule and to holde þerinne þe eiȝte blessingis of Crist,
f. 53 bisiynge hem to knowe and to kepe þe seuene principal vertu|es. And so þanne þei schulen deserue herþoruȝ grace for to vsen þankfulli to God alle þe condiciouns of charite; and þanne þei schulen be mouyd wiþ þe good spirit of God for to examyne ofte and bisili her conscience, wiþ þat neiþer wilfulli ne witingli þei erren in ony article of bileue, hauynge contynuely, as freel kynde wole suffre, al her bisinesse to dreede and fle þe offence of God, and to loue ouer al þing and seche to done euer his plesynge wille. Of þese pilgrymes I seide whateuer good þouȝt þat þei ony tyme þenken, what vertues worde þat þei speken, and what fructuouse werk þat þei worchen, euery such þouȝt, word and werk is a stap noumbrid of God toward him into
f. 53v heuene. þese blessid pilgrymes of God, whan | þei heeren of seyntis or of vertuouse men or wymmen, þei bisien hem to knowe þe lyuynge of seyntis and of vertues men and wymmen, how þei forsoken wilfulli þe prosperite of þis lyf, how þei wiþstoden þe sugestiouns of þe fend, and how þei ref[r]eyneden her fleischli lustis, how discreet þei weren in [penaunce doynge, how pacient þei weren in] alle her aduersitees, how prudent þei weren in conselynge of men and of wymmen, mouynge hem to haten euere al synne and to fle it. and to schame euere greetli þerof, and to loue alle vertues and to drawe to hem, ymagynynge how mekeli Crist and his sueris bi ensaumple suffry[d]e[n] scornes and sclaundris, and how pacientli þei aboden

1238 toward . . . of] *on eras.*R 1241 euere] *om.* A 1243 discretli] districte P 1244 kunnynge . . . power] possibilitatem . . . cognicionem VP 1246 eiȝte] right A 1248 deserue] obteyne A 1252 freel kynde] frailte A 1254 euer] solicite et continue VP 1258 blessid] forsaid A whan] delyte sore whan A 1259 or wymmen] *om.* VP þei . . . wymmen (1260)] *om.* A 1261 sugestiouns] suggestion A 1262 refreyneden] reffeyneden R, restreined A, restrinxerunt VP weren] sunt V 1263 penaunce . . . in²] their penaunce doyng how pacient they wer in A, in faciendo suam penitenciam quomodo pacientes fuerunt in VP, *om.* R 1264 and of wymmen] *om.* VP 1265 it] them A 1267 ymagynynge] ymaginantes sepe et solicite VP mekeli] *om.* A 1268 suffryden] AVP, suffrynge R

and token þe wraþful manassynges of tirauntis, how | homely þei f. 54 weren and seruysable to pore men for to releue hem and conforte hem bodili [and gostli] aftir her kunnynge and her power, and how deuoute þei weren in preieris, how feruent in heuenli desiris, and how þei absentid hem fro spectaclis and fro veyn siȝtis and heeringe, and how stable of contenaunce þei weren, how herteli þei weileden and sorewiden for synne, how bisi þei weren to lette and to distroie alle vicis, and how laborouse and ioieful þei weren to sowe and to plante vertues. Þese heuenli condiciouns and suche oþer haue þo pilgrimes eiþer þei bisien hem to haue, whos pilgrimage God acceptiþ.

'And aȝenward,' I seide, 'as her werkis schewen, þe moost parte of hem, boþe men and wymmen, þat gon now on pilgrimage haue not þese forseide condiciouns, neiþer louen to bisien hem | feiþfulli to f. 54v haue hem. For, as I wel knowe, siþ I haue ful ofte assaied, examyne whoeuere wole and can twenti of þese pilgrimes, and þere schulen not be founden ofte þree men or wymmen among þese twenti þat knowen þriftili oon heest of God, neiþer þei cunnen seien þe Pater noster, neiþer þe Aue neiþer þe crede in ony manere langage. And, as I haue lerned and also I knowe sumdel bi experience of þese same pilgrimes, tellinge þe cause whi þat manye men and wymmen now gon hidir and þidir on pilgrymage, it is more for þe helþe of her bodies þan for þe helþe of her soulis, more for to haue richessis and prosperite of þis world þan for to be enrichid wiþ vertues in her soulis, more for to haue here worldli or fleischli frendschip þan for to haue frendschip of God or of hise seintis | in heuene—for whateuere þing man or womman f. 55 doiþ, neiþer þe frendschip of God ne of ony seint mai be hadde wiþouten kepynge of Goddis heestis.

'Forþi wiþ my protestacioun, I seie now as I seide in Schrouesbirie, þouȝ þei þat haue siche fleischli willis traueilen soore her bodies and spenden myche moneye to sechen and visiten þe bones eiþer ymagis, as þei seien þei don, of þat seint or of þat, siche pilgrymage is neiþir preisable ne þankful to God neiþer to ony seint of God, siþ in effecte

1269 wraþful manassynges] wrongfull manasyng A 1270 weren] veri amatores Christi fuerunt VP 1271 and gostli] and gostely A, et spiritualiter VP, *om.* R kunnynge ... power] power ... connyng AVP 1274 of ... bisi (1275)] *om.* A 1275 bisi] bisili R 1277 vertues] virtutes in singulis christianis VP 1278 acceptiþ] approbat ... et acceptat VP 1283 and can] *om.* AVP 1284 ofte] *om.* A among ... twenti] *om.* A 1286 aue] *om.* P in] redely in AV 1290 more ... soulis (1291)] *om.* V 1293 in heuene] *om.* VP 1296 forþi] forther A 1297 siche] *om.* A soore] fer A 1298 and visiten] *om.* VP

alle siche pilgrymes dispisen God and alle hise seyntis. For þe heestis of God þei wolen neiþer knowen ne kepe, neiþer þei wolen conforme hem to lyue vertuesly bi ensaumple of Crist and of hise seyntis. f. 55v Wherfor, ser, I haue prechid and tauȝte opinli and priuyli, and so | I purpose al my lyf tyme to do wiþ Goddis helpe, seiinge þat siche madde peple wasten blamfulli Goddis goodis in her veyne pilgrymageyng, spendynge þese goodis vpon vicious hosteleris and vpon tapsters, whiche ben ofte vnclene wymmen of her bodies, and at þe laste þo goodis, of þe whiche þei schulden do werkis of mercy aftir Goddis heeste to pore nedi men and wymmen, þese pore men goodis and her lyflode þese renners aboute offren to riche preestis whiche haue moche moore lyfelode þan þei neden. And þus þo goodis þei wasten wilfulli and spenden hem vniustli aȝens Goddis heeste vpon strangeris, wiþ þe whiche þei schulden helpe and releeuen aftir Goddis wille her pore and nedi neiȝebores at home. Ȝhe, and ouer þis f. 56 foli, ofte tymes dyuerse | men and wymmen of þese þat rennen þus madly hidir and þidir on pilgrimagynge, borow[e]n herto mennys goodis, ȝhe, and sumtyme þei stelen mennes goodis herto, and þei ȝelden hem neuere aȝen.

'Also, sire, I knowe wel þat whanne dyuerse men and wymmen wolen goen þus aftir her owne willis and fyndingis out on pilgrimageyngis, þei wolen ordeyne biforehonde to haue wiþ hem boþe men and wymmen þat kunnen wel synge rowtinge songis, and also summe of þese pilgrimes wolen haue wiþ hem baggepipis so þat in eche toun þat þei comen þoruȝ, what wiþ noyse of her syngynge, and wiþ þe soun of her pipinge, and wiþ þe gingelynge of her Cantirbirie bellis, and wiþ þe berkynge out of dogges aftir hem, þese maken more noyse þan if þe king came þere awey wiþ his clarioneris and manye oþer f. 56v mynystrals. And if þese men and wymmen ben a moneþe oute | in her pilgrymage, manye of hem an half ȝeere aftir schulen be greete iangelers, tale tellers and lyeris.'

And þe Archebischop seide to me, 'Lewid losel, þou seest not fer inowȝ in þis mateer, for þou considrist not þe grete traueile of

1301 seyntis] commaundmentis and seyntis A  1304 and priuyli] *om.* AVP  1306 pilgrymageyng] pilgrimagis A  1307 and vpon tapsters] et super capistrices uel propinatrites VP, *om.* A  1313 heeste] precepta P  1317 borowen] borowe A, mendicant P, borowynge R, *om.* V  1321 aftir ... willis] vane VP  1323 rowtinge] wanton A  1325 noyse] sonum et strepitum VP  1328 clarioneris] clarions A  1330 ȝeere] anni uel amplius VP  1331 tale tellers] nugigeruli loquaces VP

pilgrymes, and þerfore þou blamest þat þing þat is preisable. I seie to þee þat is riȝt wel don þat pilgrimes haue wiþ hem boþe syngeris and also baggepipes, þat, whanne oon of hem þat gon barefot smytiþ his too aȝens a stoon and hurtiþ him soore and makiþ him blede, it is wel done þat he or his felowe take þanne vp a songe, eiþer ellis take out of her bosum a baggepipe for to dryue awei wiþ siche myrþe þe hurt of his sore, for wiþ siche solace þe traueile and werinesse of pilgrymes is liȝtli and myrili brouȝt forþ.'

And I seide, 'Sere, seint Poul te|chiþ men to wepe wiþ men f. 57 wepinge.'

And þe Archebischop scornede me and seide, 'What ianglist þou aȝens mennys deuocioun? Whateuere þou and siche oþer seyen, I seie þat þe pilgrimage þat is now vsid is to hem þat done it a preparacioun and a good m⌜e⌝ene to come þe raþer to grace. But I holde þee vnable to knowe þis grace, for þou enforsist þee to lette þe deuocioun of þe peple, siþ bi autorite of holi writt men mowen lefulli haue and vse siche solace as þou repreuest. For Dauiþ in his laste psalme techiþ men to vsen dyuerse instrumentis of musik for to preise wiþ God.'

And I seide, 'Sere, bi þe sentence of dyuerse doctours expownynge þe salmes of Dauiþ, þe musyk and þe mynstralcie þat Dauiþ and oþer seyntis of þe olde lawe speken of owen not now to be taken neiþer | f. 57v vsid after þe letter. But þese instrumentis wiþ her musyk owen to be interpretid goostly, for alle þei figuren hiȝe vertues and grete, wiþ þe whiche vertues men schulden now plese God and preisen his name. For seint Poul seiþ "Alle siche þingis bifellen to vs to figure." And þerfore, sere, I vndirstonde þat [þe lettre of þis psalme of Dauiþ and of siche oþere psalmes and sentencis sleen hem þat taken hem now aftir þe lettre. This sentence I vndirstonde, sere,] Crist appreueþ himsilf, castynge out mynstrals or þat he wolde quyken þe dede damysel.'

1336 baggepipes] pipers A smytiþ] AVP, and smytiþ R 1339 myrþe] leticia uel solacio VP 1340 sore] felow A 1342 men wepinge] them þat wepe A 1344 scornede me and] *om.* A 1346 a preparacioun] praysable A 1351 vsen] haue A 1352 *margin* dauiþ in þe last Ps. and in M[t] crist cast oute myn[/terals in þe 9 c[o] R 1354 speken] spake A 1356 þei figuren] those figures are called A grete] grace A 1357 now] *om.* A 1358 *margin* Poul seiþ in þe (*gap*) R vs] them A 1359 þe . . . sere (1361)] the letter of this psalme of Dauid and of soche other psalmes and sentences dothe slee them that take them now letterally. This sentence I vnderstond syr A, litera illius psalmi Dauid et aliorum talium psalmorum sentencia eorum (et sentenciarum P) occidit eos qui nunc capiunt ea litteraliter. Istam sentenciam domine ut ego intelligo VP, *om.* R 1361 *margin* And crist seiþ in þe nynþe c. of m[t] castinge out mynstr[a]ls R

And þe Archebischop seide to me, 'Lewid losel, is it not leful to vs for to haue orgeynes in þe chirche for to herien wiþal God?'

And I seide, '3he, ser, bi mannes ordinaunce, but bi þe ordynaunce of God a good sermoun to þe peple vndirstondynge were þan moche more plesynge to God.'

And þe Archebischop seide þat orgeynes, goode and delitable f. 58 songe quykneden and scharpiden ofte more | mennys wittis þan schulde ony sermoun.

And I seide, 'Ser, lusti men and worldli louers delyten, coueiten and traueile to haue alle her wittis quykned and scharpid wiþ dyuerse sensyble solace. But alle þe feiþful louers and suers of Crist haue al her delite to heeren Goddis word, and to vndirstonden it truly, and to worchen þeraftir feiþfuli and continuelli. For, no doute, drede to offende God and loue to plesen him, in al þing and ouer al þing, quycken and scharpen so alle þe wittis of Cristis chosen peple, and ablen hem so to grace þat þei ioien gretli to wiþdrawen her i3en, her eeren and alle her oþer wittis and membris from al worldli delite and fro al fleischli solace. For as seint [Gregor] seiþ "I gesse no lyf may ioie wiþ þis world and regne in heuene wiþ Crist".'

And þe Archebischop, as he hadde ben disp[le]sid wiþ myn f. 58v answeringe, seide to hise clerkis, 'What | gesse 3e þat þis ydeote wol speke þere he haþ no drede, siþ he spekiþ þus now in my presence? Wel, wel, bi God þou schalt be ordeyned fore.'

And þanne þe Archebischop seide to me al angrili, 'What seist þou to þe fourþe poynt þat is sertefied a3ens þee, prechynge openli and boldeli in Schrouesbirie þat preestis haue noo titil to tyþis?'

þe 4 question of tiþe

And I seide, 'Ser, I nempnede þere no word of tiþis in my prechinge. But more þan a moneþ aftir þat I was þere arestid and in prisoun a man cam to me into prisoun, and he askide me what I seide of tiþis. And I seide to him, "Ser, in þis toun ben manye clerkis and preestis, of which summe ben clepid religeous men, þou3 manye of

1370 ofte] *om.* A 1374 solace] solaciis VP 1377 loue] to loue R and[2] . . . þing[2]] *om.* A 1379 her i3en] *om.* A 1381 Gregor] Gregorius VP, Iereom R, Jerome (as I thinke) A, *margin* Iereom R I gesse] *om.* AVP 1382 in heuene] *om.* A 1383 displesid] displeased A, displicuisset VP, dispisid R 1386 wel wel] *om.* P 1387 and . . . tiþe (1390)] *red* R and] þe 4 and R þe archebischop] he A 1390 þe . . . tiþe] *om.* AVP 1392 and] *om.* A 1393 and he askide] askynge A 1394 clerkis] -l- *altered from* -h- R

hem ben seculeris, þerfore aske ȝe of hem þis questioun." And þis man seide to me, "Oure preestis seyne þat alle men be so ob|lischid to f. 59 paien tiþis of alle þingis þat renewen hem, þat þei ben acursid þat wiþholden ony part wytingli of her tiþingis." And I seide, ser, to þat man, as wiþ my protestacioun I seie now here bifore ȝou, þat I hadde wondir þat ony preest dar seie men to be acursid wiþouten grounde of Goddis word. And þe man seide "Oure preestis seyne þat þei cursen þus men bi autorite of Goddis lawe." And I seide, "Ser, I knowe not where þis sentence of cursinge is autorisid now in þe bible. And þerfore, ser, I praie ȝou þat ȝe wole aske þe moost kunnyng clerke þat ȝe knowe in þis toun where þis sentence, cursinge hem þat tiþen not now, is iwriten in Goddis lawe. For if it were writen þere, I wolde riȝt gladli be lerned where." But schortli þis man wolde not go fro me to aske þis questioun of ony lyf, but | he requyride me þer, as I wolde f. 59v answere bifore God, þat I schulde telle to hym if in þis caas þe cursynge of preestis were lawefulli appreued of God.

'And anoon herwiþ cam into my mynde þe loore of seint Petir, techynge preestis specialli to halowe þe lord Crist in her hertis, beynge euermore redi in þat þing þat in hem is to answere þoruȝ feiþ and hope to hem þat asaien of hem resoun. And þis lessoun Petir techiþ men to vsen wiþ a meke spirit and wiþ drede of þe Lord. Wherefore, ser, I seide to þis man in þis wyse, "In þe olde lawe which eendid not fulli into þe tyme þat Crist roos vp aȝen from deeþ to liif, God comaundide tiþis to be ȝouen to Leuytis for þe greete bisynesse and bodeli traueile þat parteynede to her office. But to preestis, forþi þat her office was | myche more esi and liȝter þan was þe office of f. 60 Leuytis, God ordeyned þat preestis schulde take for her lyflode to don her office þe tiþe part of þo tyþis þat weren ȝouen to Leuytis. But now," I seide, "in þe newe lawe neiþer Crist ne ony of hise apostlis token tiþis of þe peple, neiþer comaundide þe peple to paie tiþis neiþer to preest ne to dekne. But Crist tauȝte þe peple to do almes, þat is werkis of mercy, to pore nedi men of þe surpluys of her temperal

1397 preestis] prelates A alle . . . so] we ar also A 1398 tiþis] oure tythes A hem] to vs and that A 1399 wiþholden] withdrawe A 1404 cursinge] cursing A, excommunicacionis VP, cursinges R 1405 þat[2] . . . in (1406)] of A 1406 where] that ye may knowe where A 1410 þat . . . hym] *om.* A 1411 lawefulli] VP, lawfulli and R, laufull and A 1415 asaien] aske A *margin* For to halowe þe lord crist in peter 3 c$^{o}$ R 1417 *margin* nota R 1418 from . . . liif] *om.* VP 1420 bodeli] dayly A 1425 comaundide] fecerunt P 1426 preest . . . dekne] priestes . . . deacons A

goodis, whiche þei weldiden more þan þei nediden resonabli to her necessarie lyuelode." And þus, ser, I seide not of tiþis but of pure almes of þe peple Crist lyuyde, and also hise apostlis, whanne þat þei weren so bisie in techinge þe word of God to þe peple þat þei myȝten f. 60$^{v}$ not traueilen oþir ⌜wise⌝ | for to geten her lyuelode. But after Cristis ascencioun and whanne þe apostlis hadden resceyued þe Holi Goost, þei traueiliden wiþ her hondis for to geten her lyflode, whanne þat þei myȝten þus done for her bisie prechinge. For þer bi ensaumple of himsilf seint Poul tauȝte alle þe preestis of Crist for to traueile wiþ her hondis, whan for bisie techinge of þe peple þei myȝten þus done. And þus alle þo preestis, whos preesthode Crist acceptide eiþer now acceptiþ eiþer wole accepte, diden in þe apostlis tyme [and] aftir her deseese and wolen done to þe worldis ende.

'But, as Cistrence telliþ, in þe þousand ȝeer of oure lord Iesu Crist two hundrid seuenti and oon pope Gregori þe [ny]nþe ordeynede first f. 61 tiþis to be ȝouun to preestis now in þe newe lawe. But seint Poul | in his tyme, whos traas or ensaumple alle þe prestis of God enforsiden hem bisili to suen, seeynge þe auerice þat was among þe peple, desyrynge to distroie þis foul synne þoruȝ þe grace of God and bi vertuous ensaumple of himsylf, Poul wroot and tauȝte alle preestis for to suen him as he suede Crist pacientli, wilfulli and gladli in hi[ȝe] pouerte. Wherfore Poul seiþ þus "þe Lord haþ ordeyned þat þei þat prechen þe gospel schullen lyue of þe gospel. But we," seiþ Poul, "þat is we þat coueiten and bisyen vs to be þe feiþful suers of Crist vsen not þis power." For lo, as Poul witnessiþ aftirward whanne he was ful pore and nedi, prechynge amonge þe peple, he was not chargiouse to hem, but wiþ his hondis he traueilide to gete not oonli his owne lyuelode f. 61$^{v}$ but also | for þe lyuelode of oþer pore and nedi creaturis. And siþ þe peple was neuere more couetous ne so auerouse, I gesse, as þei ben now, it were goode counseile þat alle prestis toke now good heede to þis heuenli lore of Poul, seuynge him hereinne in wilful pouerte, noþing chargynge þe peple for her bodili lyuelode. But forþi þat

1436 tauȝte] teacheth A   1437 hondis] hande A   1438 Crist] God A   acceptide eiþer] *om.* A   1439 and] AVP, *om.* R   1441 Cistrence] Cisterciensis A   1442 seuenti and oon] and aleuenth yere one A   nynþe] nonus P, tenþe RA, decimus V   1444 enforsiden] enforce AVP   1445 bisili] *om.* A   1446 bi] true A   1447 ensaumple] lyuynge and example A   Poul] *om.* A   1448 gladli] gaudenter et continue VP   hiȝe] hye A, alta V, his R, multa P   1449 *box in margin for reference not supplied* R   1451 we þat] VP, þat we R, that A   1453 chargiouse] curiosus V   1457 now$^{2}$] *om.* A

manye preestis contrarien now Poul in þis forseid lore, Poul biddiþ take heede to ⸢þo⸣ prestis þat suen him as he haþ ȝouun to hem ensaumple, as if Poule wolde seie þus to þe peple "Accepte [ȝ]e noon oþer prestis þan hem þat lyuen aftir þe fourme þat I haue tauȝte ȝou; for certis, in whateuere dignite or ordre þat ony preest is, if he conforme him not to sue Crist and hise apostlis in wilful pouerte and in oþer heuenli vertues, and specialli in trewe prechinge of Goddis word, þouȝ suche oon be | nempned a preest, he is no but a prest in f. 62 name, for þe werk and þe vertue of a very preest suche oon lackiþ." þis sentence appreueþ Austyn, Gregor, Crisostem and Grosthede pleynli.'

And þe Archebischop seide to me, 'þinke þe þis holsum lore and for to sowe opinli or priuyli amonge þe peple? Certis, þis lore contrarieþ pleynli þe ordynaunce of holi fadris, whiche haue ordeyned, grauntid and licencide prestis to ben in dyuerse degrees and statis to lyue bi tiþis and offryngis of þe peple and bi oþer dewetees.'

And I seide, 'Ser, if preestis weren in mesurable noumbre, and lyueden vertuously and tauȝten bisili and trewli þe word of God bi ensaumple of Crist and of hise apostlis, wiþouten tiþis and offryngis and oþer dewetees þat preestis now calengen and taken, þe peple wolde ⸢freli⸣ ȝeue hem sufficient lyflode.'

And a clerke seide to me, 'How wolt þou make | þis goode, þat þe f. 62v peple wole ȝeue freely to prestis her lyuelode, siþ now bi reddure of þe lawe vnneþis prestis mowen constreyne þe peple to ȝeue hem her lyuelode?'

And I seide, 'Ser, it is no wondir þouȝ þe peple grucche to ȝeuen to prestis þe lyuelode þat þei axen, for myche peple knowiþ now how prestis myȝten lyue, and how þat þei lyuen contrarie to Crist and to hise apostlis. And herfore þe peple is ful heuy to paie as þei done her temperal goodis [to parsones and to oþere vicaris and prestis, þat schulden be feiþful dispensouris of þe parischens goodis], takinge to

1462 accepte ȝe] accepte ye A, acceptetis VP, accepte he R 1468 werk . . . vertue] virtute . . . opere VP, worke A lackiþ] *om.* P 1473 contrarieþ] is not *canc.* contrarieþ R 1475 statis] *om.* A 1477 noumbre] mesure and numbre A 1480 taken] recipiunt iniuste VP 1483 reddure of] *om.* A 1490 to[1] . . . goodis (1491)] to persones and to other vicares and priestes whiche sholde be feithfull dispensatours of the pareshes goodes A, rectoribus et vicariis et aliis sacerdotibus qui per suam legem propriam (*om.* P) obligarunt se ipsos esse fideles dispensatores bonorum temporalium suorum parochianorum VP, *om.* R

hemsilf no but a scarse lyuelode of tiþis neiþer of offringis bi þe ordenaunce of þe comoun lawe. For whateuere þat prestis take of þe peple, be it tiþe or offrynge or ony oþer dewtee eiþer [sowde], þe prestis owe not to haue hereof no but a bare lyuelode, and to departe al þe remnant to pore men and wymmen speciali of þe parischen, in whiche f. 63 þei taken þese temperal goodis. But | þe mooste dele of þese prestis now wasten þese parischens goodis and spenden hem at her owne wille aftir þe world in her lustis, so þat in fewe places pore men haue deweli as þei schulden haue her sustynaunce, neiþer of tyþis, ne of offringis, ne of oþer large wagis and sowdis þat prestis taken of þe peple in dyuerse maners, ouer þat þei neden for nedeful sustynaunce of mete and hilynge. But þe pore and nedi peple ben forsaken and left of preestis to be susteyned of þe parischens, as if prestis token no þing of parischens for to releeue wiþ þe pore peple. And þus, sere, into greete charge of þe parischens þei paien her temparal goodis twyes, where oonys myȝte suffice, if prestis weren trewe spenders. And also þe parischens þat paie her temperal goodis, be þei tiþis or ellis, to preestis þat done not her office amonge hem iustli ben partyners of f. 63v euery | synne of þese prestis, forþi þat þei susteynen þese prestis folili in her synne wiþ her temperal goodis. If þese þingis ben wel considrid, what wondre is þan, sere, if parischens grucche aȝens suche spensers?'

And þanne þe Archebischop seide to me, 'þou þat schuldist be deemyd and rulid bi holi chirche, presumpteouseli þou demist holi chirch to haue errid in ordynaunce of tiþis and of oþer dewtees to be paide to preestis. [It schal be longe or þou þryue, losel, þat dispisist þi gostli modir. How darist þou speke þis, losel, among þe peple? Ben not tiþis ȝouen to preestis] for to lyue bi?'

And I seide, 'Sere, seint Poul seiþ þat tiþis weren [ȝouen] in þe olde lawe to Leuytis and to prestis þat camen of þe lynage of Leuy. But

1493 take] vendicant uel capiunt VP 1494 sowde] stipendium per suam ordinanciam propriam VP, seruyce A, *om.* R 1497 goodis] lyuynge A þese[2]] *om.* AVP 1498 þese] *om.* P 1501 wagis and] *om.* VP and sowdis] and foundacions A 1503 of . . . hilynge] *om.* VP *margin* nota R 1504 as if] volunt V 1507 prestis] sacerdotes sicut se ipsos obligarunt VP spenders] dispensatores temporalium que a secularibus receperunt VP 1508 ellis] offeringes A 1511 synne] peccatis VP if] sed V 1513 spensers] infideles dispensatores VP 1517 it . . . preestis (1519)] yt shall be long or thou thryue losell that thou despicest thy gostely mother. How darist thou speake this losell among the people Ar not tythes geuyn to priestis A, diu erit antequam vigeas loselle qui sic despicis matrem tuam spiritualem quomodo audes tu sic loqui in populo Nonne sunt decime date sacerdotibus VP, *om.* R 1520 ȝouen] AVP, *om.* R [oure prestis, he seiþ, camen not of þe lynage of Leuy, but] of þe lynage of Iuda, to which Iuda no tiþis weren bihoten for to ȝeue. And þerfore, Poul seiþ, siþ þe presthode is chaungid fro þe generacioun of Leuy to þe generacioun of Iuda, it is necessarie þat chaunginge be maad of þe lawe, so þat prestis lyuen now wiþ|outen tiþis and oþer f. 64 dewtees þat þei now cleymen, suynge Crist and hise apostlis in wilful pouert as þei haue ȝouun to hem ensaumple. For siþ Crist lyuede al þe tyme of his prechinge bi pure almes of þe peple, and bi ensaumple of him hise apostlis lyueden in þe same wise bi pure almes eiþer ellis bi þe traueile of her hondis, as it is seide aboue, euery preest þan whos presthode Crist appreueþ knowiþ wel and confessiþ in word and in werk þat a dissciple owiþ not to be aboue his maistir, but it suffisiþ to a dissiple to be as his maistir, symple, pore, and meke and pacient. And bi ensaumple speciali of his maistir Crist euery preest schulde rule him in al his lyuynge; and so aftir his cunnynge and his power a prest schulde bisie him to enforme and to rule whomeuere he schal mowe charitabli.'

And | þe Archebischo[p] seide to me [wiþ a grete spirit], 'Goddis f. 64v curse haue þou and myn for þis techinge! For þou woldist herebi make þe olde lawe more free and parfiȝt þan þe newe lawe. For þou seist þat it was leeful to Leuytis and to prestis to take tiþis in þe olde lawe, and so to ioien her priuylege, but to vs prestis now in þe newe lawe þou seist it is not leeful to take tiþis. And þus þou ȝeuest to Leuytis of þe olde lawe more fredam þan to prestis of þe newe lawe.'

And I seide, 'Ser, I merueile þat ȝe vndirstonde þis pleyne tixt of Poul þus. Ȝe witen wel, ser, þat þe Leuytis and prestis in þe olde lawe þat toke tiþis were not so free neiþir so perfiȝt as Crist and hise apostlis þat token noo tiþis. And, ser, þer is a doctour, as I vndirstonde it is seynt Ierom, þat seiþ þus "þoo prestis þat calengen now in þe newe lawe | tiþis seyen in effect þat Crist is not bicomen man, neiþer f. 65 he haþ suffrid ȝit deþ for mannes saluacioun." Wherfore þis doctour

1522 oure . . . but] our priest he saith came not of the lynage of Leui but A, nostri sacerdotes ut ipsi dicunt (ipse dicit P) non descenderunt de tribu Leui sed VP, *om.* R 1524 fro . . . Iuda (1525)] *om.* VP 1527 cleymen] vendicant iniuste VP 1528 as . . . ensaumple] *om.* VP 1529 prechinge] predicacionis quantum ad noticiam humanam VP 1530 bi[1] . . . almes] or A 1532 in[1] . . . werk (1533)] *om.* P 1534 pore] and pure A 1537 to rule] regendum per verbum Dei VP 1539 archebischop] archebischo R wiþ . . . spirit] A, cum magno spiritu VP, *om.* R 1543 priuylege] priuelegies A 1546 of Poul] *om.* V 1547 in þe olde lawe] *om.* VP 1550 *box in margin for reference not supplied* R 1552 saluacioun] loue A

seiþ þis sentence: "Siþ tiþis weren þe hyris and wagis lymyti[d] to Leuytis, and to prestis of þe olde lawe for þe beringe aboute of þe tabernacle, and for þe sleeynge and fleynge of bestis, and for þe brennynge of sacrifices, and for clensynge of þe temple, and for trumpinge to bateile bifore þe oost of Israel and for oþer dyuerse obseruaunces þat parteyneden to her office, þo prestis þat wolen now calengen or take tiþis, denye þei þat Crist is comen in fleische, and do þei prestis office of þe olde lawe for whiche tiþis weren grauntid. Or ellis," as þis doctour seiþ, "prestis take now tiþis wrongfulli."'

And þe Archebischop seide to hise clerkis, 'Herde ȝe euer losel f. 65v speke þus? Certis, þis is þe lore of hem alle, þat whereeuere þei | come, if þei mowen be suffridde, þei enforsen hem to enpungne þe freedam of holi chirche.'

And I seide, 'Sere, whi clepe ȝe þe takynge of tiþis "þe freedam of holi chirche", and siche oþer dewetees whiche preestis calengen now wrongfulli "þe freedam of holi chirche", siþ neiþer Crist, ne hise apostlis calengiden, ne toke no siche dewetees? Herfore þis takynge of prestis now is not clepid iustli "þe freedam of holi chirche", but alle siche ȝeuynge and takinge owen to be clepid and holden þe sclaundrouse couetise of men in þe chirche.'

And þe Archebischop seide to me, 'Whi, losel, wolt þou not and oþer þat ben confedrid wiþ þee sechen out of holy writt and of þe sentence of doctours as scharpe auctoritees aȝens lordis and knyȝtis and squyeris and aȝens oþer seculer men, as ȝe done aȝens preestis?'

f. 66 And I seide, 'Sere, whateuere men | or wymmen, lordis or ladies, or ony oþer þat ben present in oure prechynge specialli eiþer in oure comounynge, aftir oure kunnynge we tellen out to hem her office and her charge. But, sere, siþ Crissostem seiþ þat prestis ben as þe stomke of þe peple, it is ful nedeful in prechinge and also in comownynge to be moost bisie aboute þis presthode, siþ bi þe viciousenesse of prestis boþe lordis and comouns be moost synfull effect and led into þe werst ende. For þe couetise of prestis and þe pride and þe boost þat þei haue and maken of her dignyte and power disstroieþ not oonli þe vertu of presthode in prestis silf, but also ouer þis it terriþ God to take

1553 lymytid] AVP, lymytis R 1554 beringe aboute] formacione V 1556 sacrifices] sacrifice A clensynge] keping A 1558 now] *om.* A *margin* nota R 1559 calengen] mendicare V 1560 whiche] whome A 1566 þe[2] ... chirche (1567)] *om.* A 1569 þis takynge] thes takyngis A 1575 as] all A 1580 charge] charges A *margin* crissostem R 1581 ful] *om.* A 1583 synfull] -i *eras.* R 1584 ende for] and because that A 1586 vertu] vertues A

greet veniaunce, boþe vpon lordis and vpon comouns, whiche suffren þese prestis to lyuen as þei now done and wolen not bisien hem to amende þese prestis charitabli.'

And þe Archebischop seide to me, 'þou demest | euery preest to be f. 66v proude þat wole not go arayed as þou goist. By God, I deme hym to be more meke þat goiþ euery daie in a scarlet gowne þan þee in þat þreedbare blew gowne! Wherbi knowist þou a proud man?'

And I seide, 'Ser, a proud preest may be knowen whanne he denyeþ to sue Crist and hise apostlis in wilful pouert and in oþer vertues, and coueitiþ worldly worschip, and takiþ it gladly and gedriþ togidre, eiþer wiþ pletynge, manassynge, eiþir cursynge, eiþer wiþ flatring or wiþ symonie ony worldli goodis, and most if a preest bisie not him cheefli in himsilf, and siþ in alle oþer men and wymmen, aftir his kunnynge and his power to wiþstonde synne.'

And þe Archebischop seide to me, 'þou3 þou knowe a preest to haue alle þese vicis, 3he, þou3 þou se a preest lye now bi a womman knowyng hir fleischli, woldist þou herfore deme | þis preest f. 67 dampnable? And I seie to þee þat in þe turnynge aboute of an honde suche a synner mai be very repentaunt!'

And I seide, 'Sere, I wol not dampne ony liif for ony synne þat I knowe done or may be done lyuynge 3it þilke synner. But bi autorite of holy scripture he þat synneþ þus opinli as 3e schewen here is dampnable for doynge of siche synne, and most specialli a preest þat schulde be ensaumple to alle oþer, for to hate and flee synne. And, in how schort tyme þat euere 3e seie suche a synnere may be repentaunt, him owiþ not of hem þat knowen his synnyng to be demed verrili repentaunt wiþouten opin euydence of greet schame for his synne and herteli sorowe. For whoeuere it be, and specially what prest þat vsiþ pride, enuye, couetise, lecherie, symonye or ony oþer vice, and schewiþ not as open euydence | of repentaunce as he haþ 3eue yuel f. 67v ensaumple and occasioun of synnynge, if he contynue in ony sich synne as longe as he may, it is lickeli þat synne leue suche a man, and he not synne. And, as I vndirstonde, suche oon synneþ vnto þe deeþ, for whom no lyf owiþ for to praye, as seynt Ioon seiþ.'

1588 to[1] . . . prestis (1589)] *om.* A lyuen] viuere viciose VP 1595 pouert] voluntate P 1597 eiþir . . . eiþer[2]] or A flatring] adulacione ypocrisi VP 1602 lye] louely lye A 1607 lyuynge . . . synner] so that the synner leuyth his synne A 1608 is] excommunicatus est a Deo pro declinacione a mandatis eius et sic tunc est VP 1610 hate and flee] fugiendum et odiendum VP 1614 and . . . vsiþ] *om.* V 1615 vice] vices A 1620 *margin* seint Ioon R, I Johannis 5 *add* VP

And a clerke seide þanne to þe Archebischop, ‘Sere, þe lengir þat ȝe appose him, þe [worse he is; and þe more þat ȝe bisie ȝou to amende him, þe] more weyward he is. For he is of so schrewid a kynde þat he schameþ not oonly to haue himsilf a foule nest, but wiþouten schame he bisieþ him to make his nest foule.’

And þe Archebischop seide to þis clerk, ‘Suffre a while, for I am nyȝ at an ende wiþ him; for þer is oo poynt ȝit certefied aȝens him, and I wole heere what he seiþ þerto.’

And so þanne þe Archebischop seide to me, ‘Lo, it is here certefied f. 68 aȝens þee þat þou prechedist at | Schrouesbirie openly þat it is not leueful to swere in ony caas.’

5 question

And I seide, ‘Sere, I [prechide] neuer so opinli, neiþer I haue tauȝte in þis wyse priuyli in ony place. But, ser, as I prechid in Schrouesbirie, wiþ my protestacioun I seie to ȝou now here þat, bi autorite of þe gospel and of seint Iame, and bi witnesse of dyuerse seyntis and doctours, I haue prechid opinli and tauȝte in oo place and in oþir þat it is not leeful in ony caas for to sw[er]e bi ony creature. And I ouer þis, sere, I haue also prechid bi þe forseide autoritees þat no lyf schulde swere in ony caas, if wiþouten [ooþ on] ony wise he þat is chargid to swere miȝte excuse him to hem þat haue power to make him swere in leeful þingis and laweful; but if a man may not excuse him wiþouten f. 68$^{v}$ ooþ to hem þat haþ power to make him swere, | þanne he owiþ to swere oonly bi God, takynge him oonly þat is truþe for to witnesse þe truþe.’

And þanne a clerke askid of me if it were not leeful to a soget at þe biddyng of his prelate for to knele doun and touche þe holy gospel boke, and kisse it, seiynge “So helpe me God and holidoome!” ‘He schulde aftir his kunnynge and his power do al þing þat his prelate comaundide to him.’

1622 worse . . . þe (1623)] worse he is and the more that ye besy you to amende him the A, peior est et quanto magis nitimini ad eius correccionem tanto VP, *om.* R 1624 haue] be A foule] fouler A 1626 nyȝ] *om.* A 1629 and . . . question (1632)] *red* R þe archebischop] he A 1630 not] *om.* P 1632 5 question] *om.* AVP 1633 prechide] preachid A, predicaui VP, seide R 1634 priuyli] *om.* A 1636 *margin* M$^{r}$ 5 c$^{o}$ Ioon þe 5 c$^{o}$ ebreos 6 c$^{o}$ det$^{o}$ 6 c$^{o}$ R 1637 and tauȝte] *om.* A 1638 swere] swe, *altered by addition of* r *between* w *and* e *dh* R 1639 prechid] preachid and tauchte AVP 1640 ooþ on] othe in A, iuramento VP, *om.* R 1650 comaundide] commaundeth A, preciperet et mandaret VP

And I seide to him, 'Sere, ȝe speken here ful generalli or largeli. What if a prelate comaunde his suget to done vnlaweful þing? Schulde a suget obeie herto?'

And þe Archebischop seide to me, 'A suget owiþ not to suppose þat his prelate wolde bidde him do ony vnlaweful þing, for a suget owiþ to trowe þat his prelate wole bidde him do no þing, no but þat þing þat his prelate wolde answere fore bifore God þat it is leeful. And þanne, | f. 69 ⌜þouȝ þe heeste of þe prelate be vnleeful, þe suget haþ no peril to fulfille it, siþ he demiþ and tristiþ þat what þing his prelate biddiþ him do it is leeful to him for to do it.'

And I seide, 'Sere, I triste not herto. But, ser, to oure firste purpose. Sere, I seie to ȝou þat I was oones in a gentilmannys hous and þere weren þanne two clerkis, a maistir of dyuynytee and a lawyer, which lawyer was also cunnynge of dyuynytee. And amongis oþer þingis þese men spaken of ooþis. And þe lawyer seide at þe biddynge of his souereyne, which hadde power to charge him to swere, he schulde leye his hond v[p]on a book and heere his charge; and if his charge to his vndirstonding were vnleeful, he wolde anoon wiþdrawe his hond fro þe book; and if he perceyuede his charge to be leeful he wolde holde stille his hond vpon þe book, takynge þere oonli | f. 69ᵛ God to witnesse þat he wolde fulfille þat leeful charge aftir his power. And þe maistir of dyuynyte seide þanne to him þus, "Certis, he þat leyeþ his hond in þis wyse vpon a booke, and makiþ þus þere a biheeste to done þat þing þat he is comaundid, is oblischid þere þan bi book-ooþ to fulfille his charge, for no doute he þat chargiþ him to leye his hond þus vpon þe booke holdiþ þe touchynge of þe book [þe book-ooþ]. And þerfore he þat chargiþ a man to leye þus his hond vpon þe book and to kisse it, bihotynge in þis fourme to do þat þing or þat, wole seie and witnesse þat he þat touchiþ þus a book and kisse[þ] it haþ sworn vpon þat book. And alle oþere men also þat seein a man þus do, and also alle þei þat heeren hereof, wolen in þe same wyse seien and witnessen þat þis man haþ sworn vp|on a book." f. 70 Wherfore þe maistir of dyuynyte

1651 him] them A 1652 comaunde] commaunded A vnlaweful þing] illicitum ut mentiri super se ipso reuocando veritatem quam predixit uel promittere quod debet cessare a disciplina verbi Dei et non communicare illud caritatiue VP 1655 wolde] will A ony] an A 1656 þat þing] *twice* R 1657 his prelate wolde] he will A 1658 þouȝ] *margin corr.*R 1659 demiþ and tristiþ] thinketh and iudgeth A 1664 cunnynge] comuning A 1667 vpon] vnon R 1676 holdiþ . . . kisse it (1677)] towching the booke and swearing by it and kyssing it A þe book-ooþ] iuramentum per librum VP, *om.* R 1679 kisseþ] AVP, kisse R

seide it was not leeful to ony man neiþer to ȝeue ne to take siche charge vpon ony booke, for euery book is noþing ellis, no but dyuerse creaturis of whiche it is made. Þerfore to swere vpon a book or bi a book is to swere bi creaturis, and þis sweringe is euer vnleeful. Þis sentence witnessiþ ⌜Ie[r]om and⌝ Crisostom pleynli, blamynge him greetli þat bryngeþ forþ a book for to swere vpon, amonestynge clerkis þat in no wyse þei compellen ony lyf to swere wheþer þei gessen a man to swere trewe or fals.'

And þe Archebischop and his clerkis scorneden me and blameden me g[r]eeteli for þis seiinge; and þe Archebischop þreetide me and manassid me wiþ scharpe ponyschinge but I lefte þis opynyoun of f. 70v sweringe. And I seide, 'Sere, þis is not myn opynyoun but it is | þe opynyoun of Crist oure sauyoure, and of seynt Iame and of Crissostom and of oþere dyuerse seyntis and doctouris.'

And þanne þe Archebischop badde a clerke rede þis omelie of Crissostom, whiche omelie þis clerk helde in his honde writen in a rolle, whiche rolle þe Archebischop made to be taken fro my felowe at Cauntirbirie. And so þanne þis clerk redde þis omelie til þat he came to a clause where Crisostom seiþ þat it is synne to swere wele. And þan a clerke, Maluerne as I gesse, seide to þe Archebischop, 'Ser, I preie ȝou, witiþ of him how þat he vndirstondiþ Crisostom here seiynge it to be synne to swere wele.'

And so þe Archebischop askide me how I vndirstod here Crisostom. And certis I was sum deele agast to answere herto, for I hadde not f. 71 bisyed me to stodie aboute þe witt þerof. But, | liftynge vp my mynde to God, I preied him of grace. And anoon I þouȝte how Crist seide to hise disciplis 'Whanne for my name ȝe schulen be brouȝt before iugis, I schal ȝeue to ȝou mouþ and wisedom, þat alle ȝoure aduersaries schulen not aȝenseie.' And tristing feiþfulli to þe word of Crist, I seide, 'Sere, I knowe wel þat many men and wymmen haue now so swerynge in custum þat þei knowen not, neiþer wole knowe þat þei don yuel for to sweren as þei done. But þei gessen and seien þat þei

1683 to ony man] *om.* A 1684 ony] a A 1685 or . . . book (1686)] *om.* A bi] bi/bi R 1687 Ierom and Crisostom] Ieom and *added marginally to text* R, Chrisostome A, Crisostomus in Imperfecto Omelia 12 VP, *margin* Iereom and Crissostom on Mt 5 co R him] them A 1688 greetli] *om.* P 1692 greeteli] geeteli R þreetide me and] *om.* AVP 1693 manassid] iurabatur V scharpe ponyschinge] great punisshement and sharpe A 1700 omelie] rolle A 1707 but] but//But R 1708 *box in margin for reference not supplied* R 1709 disciplis] apostles A 1710 to ȝou] into your A and] *om.* A alle] *om.* AV 1711 Crist] God A

done wele for to sweren as þei done, þouȝ þei witen wele þat þei sweren vntreweli. For þei seien now þei mowen bi her swerynge, þouȝ it be fals, voyde blame or temperal harme whiche þei schulden haue if þei sworen not þus. Also, sere, manye men and wymmen now | f. 71v meynteynen strongli þat þei sweren wele, [þouȝ þei neden not to sweren but bi yuel custum,] whanne þat þing is sooþ þat þei sweren fore. Also ful many men and wymmen seien now þat it is wele idone to swere bi creaturis, whanne þei mowen not, as þei seyne, oþer wyse ben trowid. And also ful many men and wymmen now seyne þat it is wele idone to swere bi God and bi oure Ladi and bi oþer seyntis, and so for to haue hem in mynde. But siþ alle þese seyinges ben now excusaciouns in synne, me þinkiþ, ser, þat þis sentence of Crisostom mai be aleggid skilfulli aȝens alle sich swerers, witnessinge þat alle þese synnen greuousli, þouȝ þei d[em]e hemsilf to sweren in þis forseide wyse wele. For it is yuel don and gret synne for to swere truþe, whan in ony manere a man may excuse him wiþouten ooþ.'

And þe Archebischop | seide to me þat Crissostom myȝte be þus f. 72 vndirstonde.

And þanne a clerk seide to me, 'Wyliam, tarie my lord no lenger, but submytte þee now mekeli to þe ordynaunce of holi chirche and leie þin honde vpon a boke, touchinge þe holi gospels of God, bihotinge not oonli wiþ þi mouþ but also wiþ þin herte to stonde to my lordis ordynaunce.'

And I seide, 'Ser, haue I not tolde to ȝou now here how þat I herde a maistir of dyuynyte seie þat in suche a caas it was al oon to tuche a book and to swere bi a booke?'

And þe Archebischop seide, 'þere is no maistir of deuynyte in Yngelonde so greete þat, if he holde þis opynyoun bifore me þat ne I schal ponysche him as I schal do þee, but if þou swere as I schal charge þee.'

And I seide, 'Sere, is Crisostem an | autetike doctour?' f. 72v

And þe Archbischop seide, 'Ȝhis.'

And I seide, 'Sere, if Crisostem preue him worþi grete blame þat

1716 now] *om.* AVP 1718 sworen] sweare A now] *om.* A 1719 þouȝ . . . custum (1720)] quamuis non necessitentur iurare nisi per conswetudinem malam VP, *om.* RA 1722 bi . . . swere (1724)] *om.* VP oþer] ben oþer R 1724 and so] *om.* A 1725 now] but A 1726 in] and A 1727 skilfulli] wel A 1728 deme] iudicent VP, thinke A, done R 1733 Wyliam] wilt thou A, Villane Willelme V, vellem P 1735 gospels] gospell A 1745 autetike] ententyfe A

bringiþ forþ a book for to swere vpon, it mote nedis sue þat he is more to blame þat sweriþ vpon þat book.'

And þe Archebischop seide, 'If Crisostem mente acordingli to þe ordynaunce of holi chirche, we wolen accepte him; and if he mente contrarie to þis ordynaunce he owiþ not to be accept.'

And þanne seide a clerke to me, 'Is þe word of God and God himsilf equypolent, þat is of euene autorite?'

And I seide, '3his.'

And he seide to me, 'Whi wolt þou not swere bi þe holi gospel of God þat is Goddis word, siþ it is al oon to swere bi þe word of God and to swere bi God himsilf?'

And I seide, 'Ser, siþ I mai not now oþir wise be trowid no but bi f. 73 swerynge, | and I perseyue, as Austin seiþ, þat it is not spedeful þat 3e þat schule be my breþeren bileuen me not, þerfore I am redi [bi þe word of God, as þe Lord comaundide me bi his word] for to swere.'

And þe clerk seide to me, 'Leie þan þin hond vpon þe booke, touchinge þe holi gospels of God and take þi charge.'

And I seide, 'Ser, [I vndirstonde] þat þe holi gospels of God mown not be touchid wiþ mannes hond.'

And þe clerke seide þat I maddede and seide not sooþ. And I askid þis clerke wheþer it was moore to rede þe gospel or to touche þe gospel, and he seide it was moore to rede þe gospel. And I seide, 'Ser, bi autorite of seint Ierom, þe gospel is not þe gospel for redyng of þe lettre, but for þe bileue þat men haue in þe word of Crist—þat is þe gospel þat we bileue, not þe lettre þat we reden. Forþi þe lettre þat is touchid wiþ mannes honde is not þe gospel, but þe sentence þat is f. 73v verily | bileued in mannes herte þat is þe gospel. For, lo, seint Ierom seiþ þe gospel þat is ver[tu of] Goddis word is not in þe leues of a book but it is in þe roote of resoun, neiþer þe gospel, he seiþ, is in þe writynge aloone of lettres but þe gospel is in þe marw3 of þe sentence of scripturis. þis sentence appreueþ seint Poul, seiynge þus "þe

1751 and . . . accept (1752)] *om.* A 1753 is] AVP, it is R 1754 equypolent . . . autorite] equalis auctoritatis VP euene] one A 1755 and . . . 3his] *om.* P 1756 holi] *om.* A 1757 bi . . . swere (1758)] *om.* V 1758 to swere] *om.* A 1760 *margin* Austyn R 1761 bi . . . word[2] (1762)] by the worde of god (as the lorde commaunded me by his worde) A, per uerbum dei sicud dominus per verbum suum precepit VP, *om.* R 1764 gospels] gospell A 1765 I vndirstonde] AVP, *om.* R gospels] gospell A *margin* nota R 1770 *margin* Ierom R 1771 Crist] God A þe[3]] A, to þe R 1774 bileued] *om.* P *margin* Ierom R lo] so A 1775 vertu of] vertue of A, uirtus VP, verri R 1777 aloone] aboue A marw3] marking A, modulo V 1778 *margin* seint poul seiþ R

rewme of God is not in word but in vertue." And Dauiþ seiþ ["þe vois of þe Lord, þat is his word, is in vertue." And aftir Dauiþ seiþ] "þoruȝ þe word of þe Lord heuenes ben formed, and in þe spirit of his mouþ is al þe vertue of hem." And I praie ȝou, sere, notiþ wele how Dauiþ seiþ "In þe spirit of þe mouþ of þe Lord is al þe vertue of aungels and of men."'

And þe clerke seide to me, 'þou woldist make us alle madden wiþ þee! Seyne we not þat þe gospel[s] of Crist ben writen in þe masse book?'

And I seide, 'Sere, | þouȝ men vsen to seien þus, ȝit þis is vnperfit f. 74
speche: forwhi, þe pryncipal part of a þing is propirli al þilke þing. For, lo, a mannys soule, þat may not now here be seen ne touchid wiþ ony sencible þing, is propirli man; and al þe vertue of a tree is in þe roote þerof þat mai not be seen, for do aweye þe roote and a tree is distroied. And, sere, as ȝe seide to me riȝt now, God and his word ben of oon autorite. And, sere, seint Ierom witnessiþ þat Crist, veri God and veri man, is hid in þe lettre of his lawe; þus also, sere, is þe gospel hidde in þe lettre. For, sere, as it is ful lickli, many dyuerse men and wymmen here in erþe touchiden Crist and seen him and knewen his bodili persone, which neiþer touchiden, ne seeȝen, ne knewen goostli his godhede. Riȝt þus, sere, manye men now touche and seen, write[n] and | reden þe scripture of Cristis lawe, whiche neiþer touchen, ne f. 74v
seen, ne reden effectualli þe gospel. For, as þe godhede of Crist þat is þe vertue of God is knowen þoruȝ bileue, so is þe gospel þat is þe vertue of Cristis word.'

And þe clerke seide to me, 'þis is ful derk mater and vnsauery þat þou schewist heere to vs.'

And I seide, 'Sere, if ȝe þat ben maistris knowen not þis sentence pleynli, ȝe mowen soore dreden lest þe rewme of heuene be take awei fro ȝou, as it was from þe prynce[s] of prestis and from þe eldir men of þe Iewis.'

1779 þe . . . seiþ (1780)] The voice of y$^{e}$ lorde that is his worde is in vertue. And after dauid saith A, vox domini quod est verbum eius est in virtute et iterum dicit VP, *om.* R 1780 *margin* dauiþ R 1781 formed] opned *canc.* formed R 1785 alle] *om.* A 1786 gospels] AVP, gospel R of Crist] *om.* AP 1789 al þilke] the hooll A 1792 roote$^{1}$] radicem ab arbore VP 1794 *margin* Ierom R 1795 *margin* nota R 1799 writen] AVP, writer R 1800 scripture] scriptures A Cristis] Goddis A 1802 þoruȝ] solum per VP, by the vertue thorow A þe vertue of] *om.* A 1804 derk mater] mystie maters A 1807 *margin* þou hast hid þese þingis Mt. v c. R 1808 prynces] princes A, principibus VP, prynce R

And þanne anoþer clerk, as I gesse Maluerne, seide to me, 'þou knowist not þin equyu[oc]aciouns, for þe rewme of heuene haþ dyuerse vndirstondingis. What clepist þou in þis sentence þat þou schewist here þe rewme of heuenes?'

f. 75 And I | seide, '[Sere, bi good resoun and sentence of doctours] þe rewme of heuene is clepid þe vndirstondinge of Goddis word.'

And a clerk seide to me, 'From whom demyst þou þat þis vndirstondynge is taken awey?'

And I seide, 'Sere, bi autorite of Crist himsilf þe effectual vndirstondyng of Cristis word is taken awei from alle hem chefly whiche ben grete lettrid men, and presumen to vndirstonden hiȝe þingis and wolen b[en] holde wise men, and desiren maistirschipe and hiȝe staate and dignyte, but þei wolen not conforme hem to þe lyuynge and techynge of Crist and of hise apostlis.'

And þanne þe Archebischop seide, 'Wel, wel, þou wolt deme þi souereyns! Bi God, þe king doiþ not his deuer but if he suffre þee to be deemed!'

And þanne anoþer clerk seide to me, 'Whi on Fryday [þat] last was
f. 75v counseiledist [þou] a man of my lordis þat he schulde not schryue |
him to a man but oonli to God?'

And wiþ þis axynge I was astonyed, and anoon þanne I knew þat I was sotilly bitraied of a man þat cam to me into prisoun on þe Fryday bifore, comownynge wiþ me in þis mater of confessioun. And certis bi his wordis I gessid þat þis man cam þan to me of ful feruent and charitable desyre, but [now] I knowe þat he cam to tempte me and to acuse me—God forȝeue him if it be his wille þis treesoun, and I do wiþ al myn herte! And so þan, whanne I hadde þouȝt þus, I seide to þis clerk, 'Sere, I preie ȝou þat ȝe wolde fecche þat man hider, and alle þe wordis as niȝ as I can reporte hem which I spak to him on Fridaie in prisoun I wole reherse here now bifore ȝou alle and bifore him.'

1811 equyuocaciouns] equyuaciouns R þe] þe/þe R 1813 þe . . . heuenes] *om.* A 1814 sere bi . . . doctours] Sir by good reason and sentence of doctours A, domine per bonam rationem et sentenciam doctorum VP, *om.* R 1815 vndirstondinge] effectualis intelleccio VP 1818 Crist himsilf] Christimet sicut sequitur ex predicta sentencia Mathei VP 1821 ben holde] AVP, biholde R 1826 deemed] condempned A 1827 and . . . god (1829)] *in red* R þat] *om.* R 1828 þou] *om.* R 1834 now] nowe A, iam VP, *om.* R 1835 þis . . . and] *om.* A 1836 and . . . þan] *om.* A 1838 reporte] repete A

And as I gesse þe Archebischop seide þan to me, 'þei þat ben now | f. 76
here suffisen to reporte þee. How seidist þow to him?'

And I seide, 'Sere, þat man cam to me and axid ⌜of⌝ me dyuerse
þingis, and aftir his axynge I answeride to him as I vndirstoode þat
good was. And, as he schewide to me bi his wordis, he was heuy of his
beynge in court, and riȝt soreweful for his owne viciouse lyuynge and
also for þe viciousnesse of oþer men and speciali of prestis yuel
lyuynge. And herfore he seide to me wiþ a soroweful herte, as I
gesse[d] þat he purpose[de] fulli wiþinne schort tyme for to leue þe
court, and to bisie him to knowe Goddis lawe and to confourme al his
liif þerafter. And whanne he hadde seide to me þese wordis and mo
oþer which I wolde reherse if he were present, he preiede me to heere
his confessioun. And I seide to him, "Sere, whi | coueite ȝe to be f. 76v
confessid of me? Ȝe witen þat þe Archebischop puttiþ and holdiþ me
here as him þat is vnworþi to ȝeue or to take eny sacrament of holi
chirche." And he seide to me, "Broþer, I wote wel, and so witen many
oon mo, þat þou and suche oþer ben wrongfulli disesid; and herfore I
wole comoune wiþ þee þe more gladli." And I seide to him, "Certis, I
wote wel þat many men of þis courte, and specialy preestis of þis
houshold, wolden be ful yuel apaiede boþe wiþ ȝou and wiþ me, if þei
wisten þat ȝe weren confessid of me." And he seide þat he chargid not
her wraþþe for he hadde ful litil affeccioun in hem. And for, as me
þouȝte, he seide þese wordis and many | oþer of so good wille and of f. 77
hiȝe desir for to haue knowe and done þe plesynge wille of God, I
seide þanne to him, as wiþ my forseide protestacioun I seie to ȝou now
here, "Ser, I counseile ȝou for to absente ȝou fro al yuel companye,
and to drawe ȝou to hem þat louen and bisien hem to knowe and to
kepe þe heestis of God. And þanne þe good spirit of God wol moue
ȝou for to occupie bisili alle ȝoure wittis in gederynge togedere of alle
ȝoure synnes, as ferforþ as ȝe cunne biþinke ȝou, schamynge greetly of
hem, and sorowynge ofte hertli for hem—ȝhe, sere, þe Holi Goost
wole þanne putte into ȝoure herte a good wille and a feruent desir for
to take and holde a good purpos, to hate euere and to fle aftir ȝoure

1841 reporte þee] repete them A 1842 to me] *om.* AV and[2]] ad carcarem et VP 1844 bi his wordis] pro sua causa P 1845 beynge] lyuynge A and[2] . . . viciousnesse (1846)] *om.* V 1848 gessed . . . purposede] gessed . . . purposed A, estimaui . . . proposuit VP, gesse . . . purpose R 1852 whi . . . ȝe] wherfore come ye to me A 1853 puttiþ] posuit V 1859 and wiþ me] *om.* VP 1861 her wraþþe] therfore A 1862 and[1]] of *canc.* and R 1866 louen and bisien] diligunt VP 1870 ofte] *om.* A 1872 to hate] ad obediendum P

cunnynge and ȝoure power euery occasioun of synne. And so þanne f. 77v wisedam schal come to ȝou from aboue, | illumynynge wiþ dyuerse bemes of heuenly grace alle ȝoure wittis, enfourmynge ȝou how ȝe schulen triste stidefastli in þe mercy of þe Lord, knowlechinge to him al holy al ȝoure viciouse lyuynge, preienge to him euere ful deuoutli of charitable continuaunce, l[e]uynge wiþouten doute þat if ȝe perceyuere þus, bisiynge ȝou feiþfully to knowe and to kepe his heestis þat [h]e wole, for he oonly may, forȝeue ȝou alle ȝoure synnes."

'[And þis man seide þan to me "þouȝ God forȝeue men her synnes], ȝit moten men be asoylid of preestis, and do þe penaunce þat þei enioynen to hem."

'And I seide to him, "Sere, it is al oon to assoile men of synne and to forȝeue to men her synnes. Wherfore, siþ it perteyneþ oonly to God to forȝeue synne, þerfore Crist seiþ in Mathew þe 4 c° "Do ȝe penaunce for þe rewme of heuenes schal nyȝe", þus it suffisiþ in þis caas to f. 78 preestis for to counseile men and | wymmen for to leue here synne, confortynge hem þat bisien hem þus to done for to hope stidefastly in þe merci of God. And aȝenward preestis ouȝten to telle scharpli to custumable synners þat, if þei wolen not maken an ende of her synnes, but contynue in dyuerse synnes whilis þat þei mowen synne, alle suche deseruen peyne wiþouten eende. And herfore preestis schulden bisie hem euere to lyue wele and holyli, and to teche þe peple bisili and treweli þe word of God, schewinge to alle folkis in opin prechinge and in priuy counseylynge þat God oonly forȝeueþ synne. And þerfore þo preestis þat taken vpon hem to asoyle men of her synnes blasfemen God, siþ it parteyneþ oonly to þe lord God to assoyle men of alle her f. 78v synnes; for no doute a þousand ȝere aftir þat Crist was man noo | preest of Crist durste take vpon him to teche þe peple, neiþir priuyli ne apeert, þat þei moten nedis come to be asoylid of hem as prestis now done. But bi autorite of Cristis wordis preestis bounden endurid cus-

1873 euery] all A 1875 heuenly grace] grace and of heuenly desyre A 1877 al holy] onely A, integre et sepe VP ful] *om.* A 1878 continuance] counsell and continuance A leuynge] VP, lyuynge R, hoping A wiþouten doute] cum deuocione V, sine duracione P 1880 he] AVP, ȝe R 1881 and . . . synnes] And this man said than to me. Though god forgyue men their synnes A, et iste homo tunc dixit mihi quamuis deus remittat hominibus peccata ipsorum (eorum P) VP, *om.* R 1884 synne] synnes AVP 1886 þerfore . . . nyȝe (1887)] *underlined* R, *om.* AVP *margin* $m^1$ þe 4 c° and in þe 33 c° of ezechi R 1887 to preestis] *om.* A 1889 confortynge] and to comforte A 1891 synnes] synne A, peccato . . . volenter VP 1896 God] þe God R synne] omne peccatum VP 1902 done] faciunt . . . atque docent VP bounden] ligarunt hoc est ostenderunt VP

tumable synners to euerlastinge peynes, which no tyme of her lyuynge wolden bisyen hem feiþfully for to knowe þe heestis of God, neiþer kepen hem. And aȝenward alle þei þat wolen occupien [alle her wittis to hate and to flee alle occasioun of synne, dredynge ouer alle to offende God, and louynge forto plese hym] feiþfully, to þese men and wymmen þe prestis schewiden how þe lord God asoyliþ hem of alle her synnes. Þus Crist bihotiþ to conferme in heuene al þe byndinge and þe asoylynge þat prestis, bi autorite of his word, bynden men in synne þat ben endurid þerinne, and losen hem out of synne here vpon erþe þat ben veryly repentaunt."

'And þis man, heerynge þes wordis, seide þat he myȝte in his | con- f. 79
scien[c]e wele consente to þis sentence. But ⸢he seide⸣, "I[s] i[t] not nedeful to þe lewid peple þat cunnen not þus done to go schryuen hem to prestis?" And I seide, "Ser, if a man fele himsilf so distroublid wiþ ony synne þat he can not bi his owne witt voide þis synne, wiþouten counseile of hem þat ben hereinne wyser þan he, in suche a caas þe counseile of a good preest is ful nessessarie. And if good prestis failen, as þei done now comenli in suche a caas, seynt Austyn seiþ þat a man may leefully comoune and counseile wiþ a vertues seculer man. But, certis, þat man or womman is ouer-lewid and to beestly which cunne not brynge her owne synnes into her mynde, bisiynge hem nyȝt and dai for to haten and forsaken alle her synnes, doynge aseeþ for hem aftir her cunnynge and her power. And, sere, ful acor-
dingly to þis sentence, vpon mydlenten | Sundai two ȝere I gesse now f. 79v
ago I herde a monke of Feuersam, þat men clepiden Meredoun, preche at Cauntirbirie at þe cros wiþinne Cristis chirche abbeye, seyynge þus of confessioun: as, þoruȝ þe sugestioun of þe feend wiþouten counseile of ony oþer liif þan of h[e]msilf, manye men and wymmen ⸢also⸣ cunne ymagyne and fynde meenys inowe to cu[m]e to pride, to þefte, to lecherie and to oþer dyuerse vicis, in þe contrarie wyse, þis monke seide, siþ þe lord God is more redy to forȝeue synne, þan þe

1905 kepen] voluntarie obseruare VP alle[2] . . . hym (1907)] all their wittes to hate and to flie all occasion of synne dreding ouer all thing to offende god and loouyng for to please hym A, omnes sensus suos ad odiendum et fugiendum omnes occasiones peccati timentes super omnia offendere deum et diligentes maxime placere sibi VP, *om.* R 1907 feiþfully] continually AVP 1908 asoyliþ] propter istas predictas uirtutes absoluit VP 1909 bihotiþ] promysed A 1913 conscience] consciene R 1914 he seide] *above line corr.* R is it] AVP, it is R 1919 good] boni et sapientis VP 1922 ouer-lewid] ouerladen A 1927 of Feuersam] *gap* P Meredoun] Moredon AVP 1928 Cristis chirche] cchirche R 1930 hemsilf] AV, himsilf R, se P 1931 cume] come AVP, cunne R

fende is or may be of power to moue ony liif to synne, þanne whoeuere wolen schamen and sorowen [herteli] for her synnes, knowlechynge hem feiþfully to God, amendynge hem aftir her kunnynge and her power, wiþouten counseile of ony oþer liif þan of God and hemsilf, þoruȝ þe grace of God suche men and wymmen mowen fynde suffi-
f. 80 cient | meenes to cu[m]e to Goddis mercy, and so to ben clene assoylid of him of alle her synnes." þis sentence, sere, I seide to þat man of ȝouris and þese wordis as nyȝ as I can gesse.'

And þe Archebischop seide, 'Holi chirche appreueþ not þis lore!'

And I seide, 'Holi chirche, [of] whiche Crist is heede in heuene and in erþe, mote nedis appreue þis sentence! For, lo, herebi alle men and wymmen mowen, if þei wol, be tauȝt sufficientli for to knowe and to kepe þe heste[s] of God, and to hate and flee alle occasiouns of synne contynualli, and to loue and seche vertues bisily, and to bileeue into God stidefastly and triste to his mercy stidefastly, and so to cu[m]e into perfiȝt charite and to laste þereinne perseuerauntly; and more þing þe Lord axsiþ not of ony man heere now in þis liif. And, certis, siþ Crist Iesu diede vpon þe cros wilfully to make man fre, men in þe
f. 80v chirche now ben to bolde | and to bisie to make men þralle, byndinge hem vp peyne of endeles curs, as þei seien þei mouun, to manye obseruaunces and ordynaunces whiche neiþer þe lyuynge ne þe techinge of Crist ne of hise apostlis appreuen.'

And a clerk seide þan to me, 'þou schewist out pleynli here þi conseit, whiche þou hast lerned of hem þat [traueiliden and ȝit] traueilen to sowe cockil among wheet. But I counseile þee to go awei clene from al þis lore, and submytte þee loweli to my lord, and þou schalt fynde him ȝit to be to þee graciouse.'

And anoon þan anoþer clerk seide to me, 'How was þou so bolde at Poulis cros in London to stonde þere caproun-hardi, wiþ þi tepet aboute þin hed and to repreue in his sermoun þe worþi clerk Alkirtoun, drawynge awei þens alle hem þat þou myȝtist?—ȝhe, and þe same daie aftir noone þou, metynge þat worþi doctour in Watlynge
f. 81 strete, | clepidist him fals flaterer and ypocrite.'

1934 power] voluntate uel potestate VP 1935 herteli] hartely A, cordialiter VP, *om*. R 1936 kunnynge . . . power] power . . . connyng A 1937 hemsilf] hymself A 1939 cume] AVP, cunne R 1940 of him] *om*. A 1943 of whiche] AVP, whiche R 1946 hestes] AVP, heste R occasiouns] occasion A 1948 cume] AVP, cunne R 1952 now] *om*. A 1953 þei² . . . to] to doo A 1954 and ordynaunces] *om*. V 1957 conseit] disceite A traueileden . . . ȝit] laborauerunt et adhuc VP, *om*. RA 1958 among wheet] in fermitantem V 1962 caproun-hardi] harde A 1966 and ypocrite] *om*. V

And I seide, 'Sere, I gesse certeynly þat þere was no man ne womman þat hatide verily synne and louede vertues, heerynge þe sermoun [of þe clerk of Oxenford and also Alkirtouns sermoun], þat ne þei seiden eiþer myȝte iustly seien þat Alkirtoun repreuede þe clerk vntrewli, and sclaundride him wrongfully and vncharitabli, [as I seide to hym in Watlynge strete]. For no doute if þe lyuynge and techinge of Crist cheuely and of his apostlis be trewe, no liif þat loueþ God and his lawe wole blame ony sentence þat þe clerk prechide þan þere, siþ bi þe autorite of Goddis word and bi appreued seyntis and doctours and bi opin resoun þis clerk prouede clereli alle þingis þat he þere prechide.'

And a clerk of þe Archebischopis seide to me, 'His sermoun was fals as he is fals, and þat he schewiþ opinly siþ he dare not stonde forþ and defende his prechinge þat he prechid þan þere.'

And I seide, 'Sere, I gesse þat he purposeþ to stonde styfly þerbi, and ellis he sclaundriþ foule | himsilf and also many oþer þat haue gret f. 81v
trist þat he wol stonde bi þe truþe of þe gospel. For I woot wel þat his sermoun is writun boþe in Latyn and in Engelisch, and many men haue it and þei setten greet priys þerbi. And, ser, if ȝe were present wit þe Archebischop at Lamhithe, whanne þis clerke apperide and was at his answere bifore þe Archebischop, ȝe witen wel þat þis cle[r]k denyede not þere his sermoun, but two daies he meynteynede it bifore þe Archebischop and his clerkis.'

And þan eiþir þe Archebischop or oon of his clerkis, I noot whiche of hem, seide, 'þat harlot schal ȝit be met wiþ for þat sermoun! For no man but he and þou and siche oþere fals harlotis preisen ony siche prechynge.'

And þe Archebischop seide þan, 'Ȝoure cursid sect is bysie, and it ioieþ gretli, to contrarie and to distrie þe priuylege | and þe fredam of f. 82
holy chirche.'

And I seide, 'Ser, I knowe no m[e]n þat traueilen so bisily as þis sect doiþ þat ȝe deprauen to make reste and pees in holy chirche. For pride, couetyse and symonye, whiche disturblen moost holy chirche, þis sect hatiþ and fleeþ, and traueiliþ bysyli to moue alle oþer men to

1969 of[1] . . . sermoun[2]] of the clerke of Oxforde and also Alkertons sermonne A, clerici Oxoniensi (Oxonie P) et similiter sermonem Alkyrton VP, *om.* R 1971 as . . . strete (1972)] ut sibi plane dixi in Watlyngsarte (Watlingvsterwe P) VP, *om.* RA 1974 blame] nec posset rationabiliter culpare VP 1976 and . . . clereli] *om.* V 1979 as . . . fals[2]] *om.* A 1987 clerk] clek R 1997 men] AVP, man R 1998 deprauen] repreue A, dampnatis V

don in lik manere. And mekenesse, wilful pouert and charite, and free mynystrynge of euery sacrament þis sect loueþ and vsiþ, and is ful bisie to moue alle oþer folkis to do so; for þese vertues oonen alle þe membris of holi chirche to her hed Crist.'

And þan a clerk seide to þe Archebischop, 'Ser, it is forþ daies, and ȝe haue ferre for to ride tonyȝt. Þerfore, sere, make an ende wiþ him, for he wol noon make; but þe moore, sere, þat ȝe bisien ȝou for to drawe [him] towardis ȝou, þe more contumax [he] is maade and þe ferþer fro ȝou.'

f. 82v And þan Maluerne | seide to me, 'William, knele doun and preie my lord of grace, and leue alle þi fantasies and bicome a chyld of holi chirche.'

And I seide, 'Ser, I haue preied þe Archebischop ofte and ȝit I pree him, for þe loue of Crist, þat he wole leeue his indyngnacioun þat he haþ aȝens me, and þat he wole suffre me aftir my cunnynge [and power] for to do myn office of presthode, as I am chargid of God to don it. For I coueite not ellis, no but to serue my God to his plesynge in þe staate þat I stonde inne and haue take me to.'

And þe Archebischop seide to me, 'If of good herte þou wolt submytte þee now ⌜here⌝ mekely to be reulid fro þis tyme forþ by my counseile, obeiynge þee wilfully and lowely to myn ordynaunce, þou schalt fynde it moost profitable and best to þee for to do þus. Þerfore tarie þou me now no lenger; graunte to do þis þat I haue seide to þee f. 83 now here schortly, eiþir | denyen it vtterli.'

And I seide to þe Archebischop, 'Owen we, sere, to bileuen þat Iesu Crist was and is very God and verry man?'

And þe Archebischop seide, 'Ȝhe.'

And I seide, 'Sere, owen we to bileue þat al Cristis lyuynge and his techynge was trewe in euery poynt?'

And he seide, 'Ȝhe.'

And I seide, 'Sere, owen we to bileue þat þe lyuynge and þe techynge of þe apostlis of Crist and of alle þe prophetis ben trewe, whiche ben writun in þe bible for þe helþe and saluacioun of alle Goddis peple?'

2001 and[1]] vnto A 2002 euery sacrament] þe sacramentis A 2003 oonen] owe A 2008 him] AVP, *om.* R he] AVP, *om.* R 2015 haþ] sine causa habet VP and power] A, et potenciam VP, *om.* R 2020 here] *margin corr.* R to . . . þee (2021)] *om.* P 2021 wilfully and lowely] mekely and wilfully AV, velociter P 2026 is] est et semper erit VP 2031 and[2] . . . apostlis (2032)] of þe apostles and the teaching A 2033 alle] *om.* AVP

And he seide, 'Ȝhe.'

And I seide, 'Sere, owen alle cristen men and wymmen, aftir her kunnynge and her power, for to conforme alle her lyuynge to þe lyuynge and techynge of Crist specialy, and also to þe lyuynge and to þe techinge of hise apostlis and of hise profetis, in alle þingis þat ben plesynge to God and edificacioun of his chirche?'

And he seide, 'Ȝhe.'

And | I seide, 'Sere, owiþ þe doctrine, þe heestis eiþer þe counseil f. 83v
of ony liif to be accept eiþer obeied vnto, no but þis doctrine, þese heestis and þis counseil moun ben groundid in Cristis lyuynge and techinge speciali, eiþer in þe lyuynge and techinge of hise apostlis or of hise prophetis?'

And þe Archebischop seide to me, 'Oþer doctrine owiþ not to be accept, neiþer we owen to obeie to ony mannys heeste or counseile, [no but we mowen perseyue þat þis heeste or counseile] acordiþ wiþ þe lyuynge and techinge of Crist, and of hise apostlis and prophetis.'

And I seide, 'Ser, is not al þe lore, þe heest[is] and þe counseilis of holy chirche meenes and hel[e]ful remedies to knowe and to wiþstonde þe priuy suggestiouns and þe aperte temptaciouns of þe fend, and also hel[e]ful meenes and remedies to haten and fleen pride, and alle oþer dedly synnes and þe braunchis of hem, and souereyn meenes to purchace grace for to wiþstonde and ouercome alle fleisch|ly lustis and mouyngis?' f. 84

And þe Archebischop seide, 'Ȝhis.'

And I seide, 'Sere, whateuer þing ȝe or ony oþer liif biddiþ eiþer counseiliþ me to do acording to þis forseid lore, aftir my kunnynge and my power, þoruȝ þe helpe of God I wole mekeli of alle myn herte obeie þerto.'

And þe Archebischop seide to me, 'Submitte þee þan now here wilfulli and mekeli to þe ordenaunce of holi chirche whiche I schal schewe to þee.'

And I seide, 'Sere, acordingli as I haue rehersid to ȝou I wole be

2037 alle] *om.* V 2038 lyuynge and[1]] *om.* A lyuynge[2] . . . techinge (2039)] teaching . . . lyuynge A 2042 heestis] bidding AVP 2043 þese heestis] istud preceptum VP 2044 groundid] graunted and affermed A 2049 no . . . counseile] A, nisi ipse a quo obediencia petitur sciat clare percipere quod ista doctrina istud preceptum uel istud consilium VP, *om.* R 2050 lyuynge] bidding A 2051 heestis] AVP, heest R 2052 heleful] healfull A, viuencia VP, helpful R to[1] . . . remedies (2054)] *om.* VP 2054 heleful] A, helpful R haten and fleen] slee A pride . . . hem (2055)] vanam prosperitatem huius seculi VP 2064 wilfulli and mekeli] mekely and wilfully A

now redy to obeie ful gladli to Crist ⌜þe⌝ heed of al holi chirche, and to þe lore and to þe heestis and to þe counseilis of euery plesyng membre of him.'

And þan þe Archebischop, smytyng wiþ his fist fersli vpon a copbord, spake to me wiþ a grete spirit, seiynge, 'Bi Iesu, but if þou
f. 84v leeue suche | addiciouns, obeiynge þee now here wiþouten ony accepcioun to myn ordinaunce, or þat I go out of þis place I schal make þee as sikir as ony þeef þat is in Kent! And avise þee now what þou wolt do.'

And þan, as if he hadde ben angrid, þe Archebischop wente from þe copbord where he stood to a wyndowe. And þan Maluerne and anoþer clerk camen nerhond to me, and þei spaken to me manye wordis ful plesyngeli, and also oþer wise, manassynge me and counseilynge me ful bisili to submytte me, eiþer ellis, þei seiden, I schulde not ascape ponyschinge ouer mesure. For I schulde, þei seiden, be degratid, cursid and brent and so þanne dampned. 'But now,' þei seiden, 'þou maist exchewe alle þese myscheues, if þou wolt submitte þee mekeli
f. 85 and wilfully to þis worþi prelate þat haþ cure | of þi soule. And for þe pitee of Crist,' þei seiden, 'beþinke þee how greete clerkis þe bischop of Lyncoln, Herforde and Purueie weren and ȝit ben, and also Bowland, þat is a wel vndirstondynge man, which alle foure haue forsaken and reuokiden al þe lore and opynyouns þat þou and sich oþer holden! Wherfore, siþ ech of hem is myche wiser þan art þou, [for as þou confessidist er þis, þese men weren þin infourmeris and techeris,] we counseile þee for þe beste þat bi ensaumple of þese foure clerkis sue þou hem [now in þe weie of truþe as þou didest bifore in þe weie of errour], submittinge þee as þei diden.'

And oon of þe Archebischopis clerkis seide þan þere þat he hadde herde Nicol Herforde seie þat, siþ he forsoke and reuokide alle þe Lollers opynyouns, he haþ had gretter sauoure and more delite to

2067 now] nunc et semper si Deus uelit VP ful gladli] *om.* P 2072 addicioun] addiciouns // addiciouns R 2074 Kent] þe pryson of Lantern A 2076 þe archebischop] he A 2079 manassynge ... counseilynge] they manased ... counselled A 2080 ful bisili] *om.* VP 2081 be ... cursid (2082)] excommunicari degradari VP 2083 mekeli and wilfully] wilfully and mekely A 2086 Herforde] Nicolaus Herforde V, Nicolaus Efordie P 2087 Bowland] B A alle foure] also A 2089 holden] nunc tenetis VP 2090 for ... techeris (2091)] quia sicut ante confessus es isti viri fuerunt tui informatores et magistri VP, *om.* RA 2092 now ... errour (2093)] nunc in via ueritatis sicut prius fecisti in uia erroris VP, *om.* RA 2093 diden] omnes fecerunt ecclesie sancte ordinacionem VP 2094 and ... herde (2095)] quia audiui dixit vnus istorum clericorum VP 2096 Lollers] learning and Lolardes A sauoure] fauour A

holde aȝens hem þan euere he hadde to holde wiþ hem whilis þat he heeld wiþ hem. And þerfor Maluerne seide to me, 'I vndirtake, if | [f. 85v] þou wolt take to þee a preest, and schryue þee clene, and forsake alle siche opynyouns, and take þi penaunce of my lord here for þe holding and techynge of hem, wiþinne schort tyme þou schalt be greetly confortid in þis doynge.'

And I seide to þese clerkis þat þus bisili counseileden me to sue þese forseide men, 'Seres, if Philip of Repingtoun, Nicol Herforde, Ion Purueye and Robert Bowland, of whom ȝe counseilen me to take ensaumple, hadden þei forsaken beneficis of temperal profit and of worldly worschip, so þat þei hadden exchewid and alyened hem from alle occasiouns of couetise, and of fleischly lustis, and hadden taken hem to symple lyuynge and wilful pouerte, þei hadden hereinne ȝouun good ensaumple to me and to manye oþer for to haue sued hem. But now, siþ alle þese foure men haue | [f. 86] schamefulli and sclaundrousli don contrarie, consentynge to resceyuen and to haue and holden temperal beneficis, lyuynge now more worldli and fleischly þan þei diden biforehonde, confourmynge hem to þe maneres of þis world, I forsake hem hereinne and alle her sclaundrouse doynge. For I purpose wiþ þe helpe of God, in remissioun of alle my synnes and of my ful cursid lyuynge, to hate and fle priuyli and apeertli to sue þese [foure forseide] men [in þe brode weie of þis world in þe whiche now alle þei walken in sclaundre. And I purpose wiþ þe helpe of God in al þe tyme of my liif acording to my cunnynge to go] techinge and counseilinge whomeuere I may for to late and exchewe þe wei þat þei haue chosen to goon inne, which wol lede hem into þe worst ende, if in couenable tyme þei repenten hem not, verili forsakinge and reuokinge opinli þe sclaundre þat þei haue put and euery dai ȝit putten to Cristis chirche. For, certis, so opin blasfemye and sclaundre as þei haue spoken and don | [f. 86v] in her reuokinge and forsakinge of truþe owiþ not, neiþer may, priuyly be amendid deweli!

'Wherefore, seres, I preie ȝou þat ȝe bisien ȝou not for to moue me

2097 whilis . . . hem (2098)] *om.* VP 2104 Philip . . . Bowland (2105)] thes men A Herforde] erford P 2106 hadden] hadden þei R 2107 exchewid] absented A from . . . hem (2109)] *om.* V 2111 schamefulli and sclaundrousli] slaunderously and shamefully A 2117 foure forseide] quatuor predictos VP, *om.* RA 2118 in[1] . . . go (2120)] in lata uia huius mundi in qua nunc omnes illi ambulant scandalose Et cum dei adiutorio secundum scientie meum propono toto tempore uite mee VP, *om.* RA 2121 late] flye A, abhominari VP þei] isti predicti scandalisatores ueritatis VP 2122 lede] non dubito ducet VP

to sue þese men in reuokinge and forsakinge of treuþe, as þei haue do and ʒit done; whereinne bi open euydence þei terren God to grete wraþþe, and not oonli aʒens hemsilf, but also aʒens alle þilke þat fauouren hem eiþer counsenten to hem hereinne, eiþer comounen wiþ eny of hem, no but into her amendement. Forwhi [w]here biforehonde þese men weren pursued of enemyes of treuþe, now þei haue oblischid hem by ooþ for to sclaundren and pursuen Crist in his membris. Wherefore, as I triste stedefastly in þe goodnesse of God, þe worldly couetyse, þe lusty lyuynge, and þe slydinge fro treuþe of þese renegatis schulen ben to me and to manye oþer men and wymmen
f. 87 ensaumple | and euydence to stonde þe more styflier bi þe treuþe of Crist. For, certis, riʒt many men and wymmen marken and hideousen þe falsnesse and þe cowardise of þese forseide vntrewe men, how þat þei ben stranglid wiþ benefices and wiþdrawen from þe treuþe of Goddis word, forsakinge to suffre þerfore bodili persecucioun. For bi þis vnfeiþful doynge, and apostasie of hem specially þat ben greete lettrid men and haue knowlechide opinly þe treuþe, and now, eiþer for plesyng[e] or displesinge of tirauntis, haue take hire and temperal wagis to forsaken þe treuþe and to holde þeraʒens, sclaundringe and pursuynge hem þat coueiten to suen Crist in þe weie of riʒtwesnesse, manye men and wymmen herfore ben now moued; but many herafter þoruʒ þe grace of God schulen be moued herebi for to lerne þe treuþe
f. 87v of God, | and to don þeraftir, and to stonde boldeli þerbi.'

And þanne þe Archebischop seide to his clerkis, 'Bisie ʒou no lengir aboute him, for he and oþer such as he is ben confedrid so togidre þat þei wolen not swere to ben obedient and to submitte hem to prelatis of holi chirche. For now, siþ I stod here, his felowe sent me word þat he wol [swere and þat he counseilede him þat he schulde] not swere to me. And, losel, in þat þing þat in þee is þou hast bisied þee to lese þis ʒonge man—but blessid be God, þou schalt not haue þi

2129 treuþe] trewthe and sothefastenesse A 2130 done] faciunt in spiritualem lesionem plurimum personarum VP 2133 forwhi . . . biforehonde (2134)] for whereas A where] VP, here R 2134 of treuþe] *om.* A 2138 renegatis] quatuor predictorum renegatorum VP 2139 ensaumple] ensa/ensaumple *catchword* R 2140 marken] benedictus Deus vocant VP 2141 falsnesse] foulnesse A 2142 stranglid] ouercome and stopped A, suffocantur et strangulantur VP 2145 opinly] per ante palam VP 2146 plesynge] AVP, plesyngis R 2149 herafter] *om.* A 2150 lerne] discere diligenter VP 2151 don] facere fideliter VP þerbi] VP *add c.21 lines, see Appendix II* 2156 swere . . . schulde] uellet iurare et quod consuluit sibi quod V, not sweare and that he counselled hym that he sholde A, nollet iurare et quod consuluit sibi quod P, *om.* R

purpos of him! For he haþ forsaken al þi lore, submyttinge him to be buxom and obedient to þe ordynaunce of holi chirche. And he wepiþ ful bittirly, and cursiþ þee ful hertely for þe venymouse techinge which þou schewedist to him, conseilynge him to done þeraftir. And for þi fals counseilinge of him and of many | oþer þou hast grete cause f. 88 to be riȝt sory, for longe tyme þou hast bisied þee for to peruerte whomeuere þou myȝtist. And forþi as many deþis þou art worþi as þou hast ȝouun yuel counseilis! And þerfore, by Iesu, þou schalt go þidir where Nychol Herforde and Ioon Purueye weren herborwide. And I vndirtake, or þis dai eiȝte daies, þou schalt be riȝt glad for to don whateuer þing I bidde þee done. And, losel, I schal asaie if I can make þee þere as sorewful as it was told to me þat þou were glad of my laste goynge out of Yngelonde. Bi seint Tomas I schal turne þi ioie into sorewe!'

And I seide, 'Sere, þer mai no liif preue lawefulli þat I ioiede euere of þe manere of ȝoure outgoynge of þis londe. But, sere, to seie þe soþe, I was ioieful þat, whanne ȝe | weren gon, þe bischop of London, f. 88v [in] whos prison ȝe putten me and lafte me, fond in me no cause for to holden me no lengir in prisoun. But at þe preers of my freendis he delyuerede me to hem, axynge of me no manere of submittinge.'

And þan þe Archebischop seide to me, 'Wherfore þat I wente out of Yngelonde is vnknowe to þee. But b[e] þis þing wel knowe to þee: þat God, as I woot wel, haþ clepid me aȝen and brouȝt me into þis londe, for to distrie þee and þe fals sect þat þou art of. And, bi God, I schal pursue ȝou vnto Acle, so þat I schal not leue oo stap of ȝou in þis londe!'

And I ⌜seide⌝ to þe Archebischop, 'Sere, þe holi profete Ieremye seide to þe fals prophete Ananye "Whanne þe word, þat is þe prophecie of a profet, is knowen or fulfillid, þanne it schal be knowen þat þe Lord sente | þat prophete in treuþe."' f. 89

And þe Archebischop, as if he hadde not [ben] quyetid wiþ my seiinge, turnede him aweiward, and ȝede hidir and þidir, and seide, 'Bi God, I schal sette vpon þi schynes a peire of pillers þat þou schalt be gladde to chaunge þi vois!'

2159 lore] uitam ... doctrinam V 2160 ordynaunce of] *om.* P 2163 cause] *om.* P 2167 Herforde] erford P Ioon] tom A herborwide] herborwiden R 2176 in] *om.* R putten me and] *om.* A 2180 be] bi R 2181 into þis londe] ad Angliam VP 2182 sect] scet R 2183 vnto Acle] usque ad vngwem VP, so naroulye A 2185 *margin* Ieremye seide to þe fals prophet ananye R 2189 ben] *om.* R 2190 and ȝede] *om.* A 2191 pillers] prillorum VP, perlis A

þeese wordis and manye moo suche greet wordis weren þere spoken to me, manassynge me and alle oþer of þe same sect for to ben poniyschid and distryed vnto þe vtmest. And þanne þe Archebischop clepid to him a clerk and rowned wiþ him; and þat clerk went þan forþ, and soone he brouȝte in þidir þe constable of Saltwode castel. And þanne þe Archebischop rownede a good while wiþ him, and þanne þe constable wente forþ þens. And þan cam in to vs dyuerse seculers, and þei scorneden me on eche side, and þei manasseden me f. 89v gretli, and summe conseileden | þe Archebischop to brenne me anoon, and summe oþer counseileden to drenche me in þe see for it was nyȝhonde þere. And oo clerk, stondinge besides me knelide doun bifore þe Archebischop, preeynge him þat he wolde delyuere me to him for to seie matyns wiþ him, and he wolde vndirtake þat wiþinne þre daies I schulde not aȝenseie ony þing þat were comaundid me to do of my prelate. And þe Archebischop seide to him þat he wolde ordeyne for me himsilf. And þan þeraftir cam in þidir aȝen þe constable, and spak priuyl[y] to þe Archebischop. And þan þe Archebischop comaundide þe constable to lede me forþ ⌜þens⌝ wiþ him, and so he dide.

And so whanne we weren goon forþ þens, I was sent aftir aȝen. And whanne I cam inne aȝen bifore þe Archebischop, a clerke bad me f. 90 knele doun and axe grace and submitte me lowely, | and I schulde fynde it for þe best. And I seide þanne to þe Archebischop, 'Ser, as I haue seide to ȝou dyuerse tymes todaie, I wole wilfuli and lowely obeye and submitte me to be obedient and buxsum euer aftir my kunnyng and my power to God and to his lawe, and to euery membre of holy chirche as ferforþ as I can perseyue þat þese membris acorden wiþ her heed Crist, and wolen teche, reule me or chastise me bi autorite specially of Goddis lawe.'

And þe Archebischop seide, 'I wiste wel he wolde not wiþoute suche addiciouns submitte him.'

And þanne I was rebukid and scorned and manassid on ech side. And ȝit after þis dyuerse persoones crieden vpon me to knele doun to submytte me. But I stood stille and spak no word. And þanne þere

2193 wordis[1] . . . greet] and many mo wonderous and convicious A manye] manye oon R 2206 aȝenseie] resiste A 2209 priuyly] priuyl R 2212 I was] we wer A 2217 obedient . . . euer] ordenid euer A, obedientem V 2220 or] consulere mihi uel VP 2221 lawe] VP *add c.67 lines, see Appendix II* 2222 wolde not] uellet V

weren spoke of me and to me many greete | wordis; and I stood and f. 90v herde hem curse and manasse and scorne me, but I seide no þing.

And þanne a while þeraftir þe Archebischop seide to me, 'Wolt þou not submitte þee to þe ordynaunce of holy chirche?'

And I seide, 'Sere, I wol ful gladly submytte me as I haue schewid to ȝou.'

And þan þe Archebischop bad þe constable to haue me forþ þens anoon. And so þanne I was led forþ and brouȝt into a ful [vn]honest prisoun where I cam neuere bifore. But, þankid be God, whanne alle men weren gon forþ þenns from me, schittinge [faste] after hem þe prisoun dore, anoon þerafter I, beynge þereinne bi mysilf, bisiede me to þenke on God and to þanke him of his goodnesse. And I was þanne gretli confortid in alle my wittis, not oonly forþi þat I was þan de|lyuered for a tyme fro þe siȝt, fro þe heeringe, fro þe presence, fro f. 91 þe scornynge and fro þe manassinge of myn enemyes, but myche more I gladid in þe Lord forþi þoruȝ his grace he kepte me so boþe amonge þe flateryngis specialli, also amonge þe manassingis of myn aduersaries [þat] wiþouten heuynesse and agrigginge of my conscience I passid awei fro hem. For as a tree leyde vpon anoþer tree ouerthwert on crosse wyse, so weren þe Archebischop and hise þree clerkis alwei contrarie to me and I to hem. Now, goode God, for þi moost holy name and to þe preisyng of þi moost blessid name, oone vs togidre if it be þi wille bi autorite of þi word, þat is þoruȝ parfiȝt charite, and ellis not. And þat þus be, alle þat þis writinge reden or | heere preieþ f. 91v herteli to þe lord God, þat he for his grete goodnesse þat may not be told oute graunte to vs, and to alle oþere þat in þe same wyse and for þe same cause specialy or for ony oþer cause ben at distaunce, to ben oonyd in trewe feiþ, in stidefast hope and in parfiȝt charite. Amen, amen, amen.

2234 vnhonest] vnhoneste A, inhonestum VP, honest R 2236 faste] A, firmiter VP, *om.* R 2237 bisiede] I bisiede R 2243 flateryngis] flatering A, tribulaciones P manassingis] manasyng A 2244 þat] *om.* R 2246 þree] *om.* VP 2248 and . . . name[2]] *om.* VP 2249 þoruȝ] true A 2254 oonyd] vniri perseueranter VP, knette and made one A

# NOTES

## 1. THE SERMON OF WILLIAM TAYLOR

**Text** John 6:5–14, gospel for 25 Sunday after Trinity in the Sarum ritual.

**1** See, for instance, Augustine PL 38.725–8 and 35.1592–6, Bede PL 92.705–8, Hugh of St. Victor PL 175.758–9.

**6** Matt. 4:4, Luke 4:4.

**8** cf. John 6:51.

**10** Isa. 58:7.

**15** Luke 22:19.

**17** Mark 16:15 (cf. Matt. 28:19–20).

**18ff** For Lollard stress upon the pastoral duty of teaching cf. *SEWW* 2/146–54, *EWS* i.E15/6, ii.58/48, 110/19, *MC* 540. See further discussion in the note to Thorpe 707, and *PR* pp. 353–6.

**20** 1 Tim. 5:17.

**23** Heb. 13:17.

**25** Luke 10:7.

**26** The payment considered by Lollards proper for priests who preach is examined in *PR* pp. 341–6, esp. 345. Their opponents made considerable play of the apparent inconsistency with which Lollards denied the legitimacy of clerical endowment or of mendicancy, but allowed that curates had a right to expect the necessaries of life from those to whom they ministered. See *SEWW* no. 2/81, and cf. Netter's objections *Doct.* IV.120 (i.822–95).

**29–38** Accurately translated from Augustine PL 39.2287–8, which includes the citation of Isa. 58:1 and Ezek. 3:18.

**32** Isa. 58:1.

**34** Ezek. 3:18.

**38–62** Grosseteste Dict 90, printed Brown, *Fasc. Rerum Expet.* ii.265. The parallel is introduced by Grosseteste 'Primum et consideremus quam miserabilis est pastor, qui gregem non pascit pone aliquem cibi inopem . . .'

**43** The emendation brings the text into line with Grosseteste 'et si forte qui parvum cibi habet, illud stulte abjicit'.

**45** The preacher omits after *feede* Grosseteste's parallel question 'reus quoque arrogantis praesumptionis et negligentiae et stultae effusionis?'

**51** Isa.3:7, added by Taylor.

**58–61** The syntax as it stands in the manuscript is just possible. The emendation here is preferred on the basis of the Latin which has *implicando* parallel to *vacando*, translated *ȝyuyng entent*, and *obliviscuntur* as the main verb.

**62** John 3:31.

**66** Apoc. 12:15.

**70** Gen. 3:121.

**81–91** For this interpretation of Apoc. 12:15 see Egerton f. 118 and Titus f. 35, where it is attributed to Nicholas Gorham; the commentary from which it actually derives is conveniently printed in *Sancti Thomae Aquinatis Opera Omnia* xxiii (Parma, 1869), 325–511, here pp. 430–1, though the true authorship is unclear. See references given in Hudson (1985[2]), p. 308, and see R. E. Lerner's paper in the same volume, pp. 157–89, where it is argued that the originator was Hugh of St. Cher, possibly with assistants (p. 186 n.74 observes the probable link between Hugh and Peraldus, for whom see next note).

**83** *Parisience* here is Peraldus, and the text most frequently cited was his *Summa Virtutum et Vitiorum.* For Wyclif's use of it see J. Loserth 'Johann von Wiclif und Guilelmus Peraldus', *Sitzungsberichte der königlichen Akademie der Wissenschaft zu Wien, phil.-hist. Klasse* 180 (1917), 3–101, and summary in Workman i.342. In the edition of (1669), ii.123 under the heading *De auaritia* 'Mulier ista Ecclesia est, quam serpens antiquus temporalium abundantia quaerit submergere.'

**92** Matt. 4:8–10.

**114** John 6:15.

**117** Matt. 22:21, Mark 12:17, Luke 20:25.

**117ff** For reiteration of this point cf. Matthew 364/21, Egerton f. 55.

**121** 1 Pet. 5:3.

**125** 1 Pet. 2:18.

**128** 1 Tim. 6:12.

**134ff** For this view of the point at which the church lost its original purity cf. *SEWW* no. 17/62 and note, Egerton f. 44[v], and *PR* p. 335. All reflect Wyclif's view as expressed, for instance, in *De eccl.* pp. 299–328, *De pot. pap.* pp. 169–71.

**135** Acts 18:3.

**143** Rom. 2:29.

**144** Matt. 16:6, Mark 8:15, Luke 12:1.

**148** 1 Pet. 3:21.

**152–79** The whole of this section derives from Bernard *Sermones in Cantica* cap. 33 (ed. J. Leclercq, C. H. Talbot and H. M. Rochais (Rome, 1957–8), i.243/14–245/1, though not in the order in which it here appears: after an expanded version of lines 1536, the order in Bernard is here lines 162–7, 156–62 (then some lines, p. 244/918, not used), 167–79. The quotations from Luke 12:1 at 161 and from Isa. 38:17 at 168 are not marked as from the bible by underlining in Douce, and only the first is noted as such in Bernard. The gloss (169) 'þis is þe vois of þe chirche' and the final phrase of 179–80 are Taylor's gloss, and more explicitly link the criticism to the clergy than Bernard does.

**157** John 15:6; Ps. 54:13.

**160** *nedeful* translates *necessarii* 'clients', a sense not recorded in MED (though cf. MED *necessari(e* n. sense (e)).

**161** cf. Matt. 10:36.

**162** Luke 12:1.

**168** Isa. 38:17.

**172** Ps. 39:6.

**173** Jer. 30:12.

**175** cf. Jer. 6:14, 8:11.

**177** Isa. 1:2.

**183** 1 Esd. 3:12.

**186ff** For the comparison between the pristine state of the apostolic church and its contemporary decline see Egerton f. 44[v].

**191** Apoc. 12:15.

**197** Gen. 19:24–5.

**200** Matt. 24:15, Mark 13:14.

**202** The argument that the contemporary church had grown rich at the expense of the poor is developed further in lines 468ff and in other texts, Thorpe 1426ff; cf. Arnold iii.372/14, Matthew 233/19.

**211** Zech. 11:5.

**217** Apoc. 12:16.

**221** For Hildegard (1098–1179), abbess of Rupertsberg near Bingen, see *ODCC* p. 650, and P. Dronke, *Women Writers of the Middle Ages* (Cambridge, 1984), pp. 144–201 and references. Many of her writings were set out in the form of enigmatic prophecies, obscurely foreshadowing disasters to come because of the corrupt state of the world. Best known now is her *Scivias*, a collection of these prophecies in continuous form. The Lollards, however, more probably knew her works from a compilation known as *Speculum futurorum temporum seu Pentachronon*, drawn in part from the *Scivias* and in part from Hildegard's letters with some additions; see the analysis by J. B. Pitra, *Analecta Sacra* viii (Paris, 1882), 483–8. No modern edition of this text has been made, and it seems that a number of variant versions survive. The sentiments here alluded to may be found in *Liber Divinorum Operum*, PL 197.1018–19, a section incorporated into the *Pentachronon*. In addition short passages of prophecy attributed, many doubtless inaccurately, to Hildegard are often found in medieval manuscripts. The commonest is that described by Szittya (1986), p. 220 and n. 102, which is most readily available in translation in Foxe iii.87–8. For Wyclif's use of these prophecies see Szittya p. 220 n. 103. Other Lollard use of Hildegard may be found in *Floretum*, Harley 401 f. 250 under *prophecia*, Arnold iii.413/3, 421/27, Matthew 11/20 and the translation of a section in Columbia Univ. Plimpton MS Add.3, ff. 240–241.

**224** Phil. 3:20.

**229** Matt. 17:26; the story is used to the same end in Matthew p. 230/2.

**233** PL 35.2269–70; the chapter is in the modern edition no. 75.

**234** The idea that the clergy should return endowments in time of national emergency is found before Wyclif: see Gradon (1982), pp. 186–8; it is evidently a narrow line to pass from this conditional return of endowments to a more general disendowment as promoted in the Lollard Disendowment Bill (*SEWW* no. 27), and anticipated by earlier Wycliffite thinkers. See Aston (1984[2]), pp. 49–53 and *PR* pp. 334–41. It seems that the target here, *specialy þo þat ben deed to þe world*, are the monks.

**237** 1 Tim. 6:8.

**241** See PL 32.53.

**244** See above line 221. This passage is again in the *Pentachronon*, here drawn from the *Liber Divinorum Operum*, PL 197.1018.

**251** The reference anticipates Arundel's Constitutions of 1407 (Wilkins iii.314–19), in which ownership of vernacular scriptures was forbidden, unless the version were pre-Wycliffite and ownership were approved by the bishop, and which placed considerable restriction on preaching. But the charge is found in Wyclif; see, for instance, *Sermones* i.377/19.

**252** PG 56.881.

**253** Matt. 23:13.

**256** 2 Thess. 2:8.

**257** John 6:64.

**259** 1 John 2:18, 4:3, 2 John 7.

**259** PL 35.2002–3.

**260** If the number is correct, the sermon is PL 38.734–7; but, whilst the text is John 6:56–7, the substance does not include any such observation. Closer is Augustine *Tractatus in Johannem* 27.6–8 (PL 35.1618–19).

**261** Grosseteste sermon 34 in Thomson's numeration, BL MS Royal 7 E.ii, ff. 372$^{r}$b–375$^{v}$b especially ff. 372$^{v}$b–374$^{r}$a.

**263** The identification of *anticrist* in Wyclif varies (e.g. the pope *Sermones* ii.420/17, iii.59/35; each evil man *De pot. pap.* 331; the friars *Pol. Wks.* i.64), and in Lollard writings (e.g. pope *EWS* i.E11/69, E50/77, *MC* 38, 1019, Arnold iii.247/12, 342/30, 360/36; clergy Egerton f. 77). The more general definition here crystallizes the main objection to these diverse entities: their opposition to the word of Christ as declared in the Bible. Cf. Arnold iii.457/18 'whatever pope or oþer preste, in maner of lyvynge or techynge or lawis-makynge, contrarius Crist, is verrey anticriste', and Ps. Bod.f. 183/1, *ALD* 54/16, *Ros.* (ed. von Nolcken) 60/1 'antecrist is generaly a man lifyng blameabel or synfully aȝens Criste', Laud. misc. 200 ff. 25, 31v.

**268** Rom. 6:11.

**270** cf. Ps. 18:5.

**276** Matt. 17:11, Mark 9:12.

**280** John 1:21, 25.

**283** Pseudo-Chrysostom on Matthew 21:10, PG 56.839.

**284** *discrasyng*: MED gives only one example of the noun, and that in the literal medical sense of 'diseased condition of the body'. The transferred sense of *discrasie* is recorded in the Worcester MS sermons (ed. Grisdale (1939)), 15/195. MED records the sense of 'corrupt morally' for the verb *discrasen* in *EWS* iii.238/21 and it recurs in Titus f. 55.

**291–313** The sentiments are commonplace from the gospels onwards; but the vehemence here probably owed something to Grosseteste (see, for instance, sermons nos.14, 19, 31, some passages of which are quoted in *Gl.G.* (see *SEWW* no. 12/73, 81, 122)). The date of the sermon is 1406, but the Arundel Constitutions set out the following year laid down in its third section that the errors of the clergy must not be castigated before the laity. The *touȝ breed* of 313 anticipates the image of Num. 21:5 quoted in 320.

**293** John 12:35.

**294** Matt. 5:13, Mark 9:49, Luke 14:34.

**297** Matt. 5:14.

**302** Exod. 14:19; 2 Cor. 11:14.

**314** John 6:10.

**320** Num. 21:5.

**331** Ezek. 9:6.

**332** Matt. 21:12, Mark 11:15, Luke 19:45–7, John 2:14–16.

**334** Peraldus (see above 83), *Summa Vitiorum* (1669), ii.111 under the heading of *De auaritia*. Castigation of simony is too omnipresent to need exemplification; for characteristic outbursts cf. Arnold iii.150/15, 226/22.

**337** Acts 8:20–3.

**340** The omission of any discussion of the eucharist is interesting. Though Taylor plainly held a position of some standing in the Lollard movement, his views on this central issue are not entirely clear. The trial material later (see introduction pp. xviii–xxv) makes no mention of this topic. Since investigations of Lollardy usually include this if nothing else, presumably because of its centrality and the relative ease of eliciting heretical statements about it, the possibility arises that Taylor's views were not plainly unorthodox on this topic—or that he knew enough to disguise them.

**342** The Latinate participial construction is reminiscent of EV literalism, but here no question of translation is involved.

**344** Matt. 25:31–46.

**345** Luke 16:19–31.

**349–58** Cf. Augustine PL 39.1651–2 but not verbatim; the source is rather PL 38.962 (where the passage is discussed incidentally). Note the literalness of the translation: *vnmanheed* renders *inhumanitatem*, and the last sentence translates *Si hæc ergo poena est avarorum, quæ poena raptorum*? The same point, that Dives was not damned for extortion but for a failure to act mercifully, is made in *EWS* i.1/71.

**361** Luke 12:16–20.

**363–70** The translation of Luke 12:16–20 is close to that of LV (notably 367 *into ful manye ȝeeris*, 369 *þo þingis þat þou hast arayed*), but does not correspond precisely with any variants given by FM (364 *stroye*, EV *distrye*, LV *throwe doun*).

**372–7** cf. *PPl*. B.V.188–303.

**380–7** The condemnation is on two grounds: neglect of the gospel command to tend the flock with care only for immediate necessaries of life, and preoccupation with worldly matters and secular affairs. Both points appear in *Twelve Conclusions*, *SEWW* no. 3/62–72; for the second see *PR* p. 346, though Gower's *Mirour de l'Omme* 20245ff shows it not be an exclusively Wycliffite objection.

**389** Grosseteste sermon 31, in MS Royal 7 E.ii, f. 341$^{v}$a; the passage is frequently quoted in Wycliffite writings (e.g. *SEWW* no. 12/73–8).

**395** Gregory *Cura Pastoralis* iii.4, PL 77.54; the passage is quoted by Grosseteste in sermon 31 'tot mortibus digni sunt, quot ad subditos suos perditionis exempla transmittunt'.

**397** Grosseteste sermon 34: this seems not to be an exact quotation, but it reflects perfectly the sentiments of the sermon (see Royal 7 E.ii, ff. 372ra–375vb). The sense of *vikeri* is 'benefice held by a vicar', and not as Alford (1988), p. 163 where the person is in question.

**400** Exod. 34:29.

**401** Exod. 19:1–25.

**403** Exod. 24:14.

**405** Exod. 32:7.

**412** *mennys lawis*: the words in Wycliffite texts are not limited in meaning to evil human conventions, or even to civil law, but are extended to cover all traditions beyond holy writ. See Wyclif *De mand.* pp. 32–5, Arnold iii.222/35, *ALD* 75/16, Additional 24202 f. 39v, *Op. Ard.* f. 156v.

**418** *newe cheuyshaunce*: see MED *chevisaunce* 6(b) 'usury' and compare their first citation for this sense in *Liber Albus* 'Ordinatio contra Usurarios ... le quele contrat ... ils appellent "eschange" ou "chevisance" qe plus verroiement serroit appelle "meschaunce"'. For Wycliffite observations on usury see Arnold iii.154/3, Additional 24202 f. 59v, Ps. Bod. 288, f. 107/1. Cf. Alford (1988), p. 27.

**419–22** See *SEWW* 15/255–62 and note. It is fruitless to endeavour to trace precise lineage in the Lollard instances of this familiar trope, as Heyworth in his edition of *Jack Upland* tried to do (pp. 35–6). Despite the fact that Wyclif's *De mandatis* p. 117/10–19 has an example, this is not the direct source here. The trope is not peculiar to Wycliffite texts, as may be seen from Robbins *Hist.Poems* no. 57; K. Ashley, 'Renaming the Sins: A Homiletic Topos of Linguistic Instability in the Canterbury Tales', in *Sign, Sentence, Discourse: Language in Medieval Thought and Literature*, ed. J. N. Wasserman and L. Roney (Syracuse NY, 1989), pp. 272–93 gives some other examples. The ultimate source may be Gregory *Moralia* xxxii.45 (PL 76.662).

**426** Luke 6:35.

**429** Matt. 6:19–20.

**434** Prov. 11:24.

**443** Luke 12:20.

**448** Luke 12:20.

**451** Luke 14:13–14.

**451–9** The linking of *poore* (452) in the biblical text with the following three categories of the feeble, lame and blind (and the specification of *þre bodily mysesis* 455), instead of its separation as a distinct fourth group has been noted as characteristic of Lollard writings by Aston (1984[2]) p. 70 n. 22; to her references may be added this, and MSS BL Harley 2398, f. 92 and *Lollard Sermons* no. 15/315. In fact, as Wendy Scase has pointed out (1989), p. 63, the limitation to three groups derives from FitzRalph: see his sermons in MS

Bodley 144, ff. 102[v], 116, and the *Defensio Curatorum* in Trevisa's translation p. 88/3ff. A document in Sidney Sussex MS 64, f. 4 notes that the friars had observed FitzRalph's construction of Luke 14:13, 21 'ut asseruit, debuit construi et intelligi ... "voca pauperes debiles, pauperes claudos, pauperes cecos"'.

**468–72** The effect of the endowment of the clergy on the poor is a point often stressed in Wycliffite writings, though, as *Piers Plowman* shows (e.g. ABC.X.456, B.XI.179–80 moderated in C.XIII.100, BC.XIII.440, B.XIV.174), it is not an argument peculiar to them. For the idea of the clergy as trustees for the poor see M. Mollat, trans. A. Goldhammer, *The Poor in the Middle Ages* (New Haven and London, 1986), esp. pp. 112–13, and in Wycliffite circles cf. Matthew 451/6 and Scase (1989), pp. 99–108, and for this in relation to images see Aston (1988), pp. 124–8.

**476** See Exod. 1–14.

**481** cf. Trevisa's translation of FitzRalph's *Defensio Curatorum* p. 60/9ff.

**482** Luke 9:13.

**489** See lines 345–9 and 361ff

**499** The period of *þe lawe of kynde* is regarded as that between the fall and the giving of the Old Testament law through Moses, a period when the children of Israel worshipped God but without any prescriptive rules of behaviour. See Augustine PL 33.681, 37.1574.

**501** Deut. 15:7–11.

**504** Matt. 22:21, Mark 12:17, Luke 20:25.

**505** Luke 20:19–26, v. 25 quoted; John 21:3–14.

**508** Luke 10:7.

**514** 1 Cor.16:1; EV keeps the Latin *collectis*, glossing this *or gaderingis*, the gloss alone being kept in LV. This passage is discussed to similar conclusions in Egerton, f. 109, TCD 244, f. 218[v] and BL Harley 1203, f. 79; see also Woodford *Responsiones contra Wiclevum et Lollardos* (ed. E. Doyle, *Franciscan Studies* 43 (1983), 17–187 at p. 153/5 where he cites Wyclif (*De civ. dom*. iii.8–9) as arguing 'S. Paulus sic mendicavit pro sanctis fratribus suis in Ierusalem ... apostoli mendicaverunt pro eis et fecerunt collectas pro eisdem.' Wyclif's later view was implacably hostile to this. See further note to 544.

**518** Matt. 25:31–46.

**523** 1 Tim. 5:9–10.

**527** See *Legenda Aurea*, ed. Th. Graesse (Leipzig, 1850), pp. 779–80. Clement of Rome was probably the third bishop of Rome after Peter (see *ODCC*), but was often regarded, as probably here, as Peter's immediate successor.

**530** Rom. 8:23.

**537** Matt. 26:11, Mark 14:7, John 12:8.

**539** Pseudo-Chrysostom, PG 56.892.

**544** cf. Acts 11: 29–30, Rom. 15:26, 1 Cor. 16:1, Gal. 2:10. For the noun *quyletis* see MED *quilet* n. (though add the form unrecorded there *quilage*); the word, and its alternative *collect*, is characteristic of Wycliffite writings (see TCD 244, f. 218$^{v}$, BL Harley 1203, f. 79$^{v}$ and Egerton ff. 109–10).

**547** Bede *Ad Egbertum episcopum Eboracencem*, PL 94.662 in summary.

**550** cf. Lollard Disendowment Bill (*SEWW* no. 27/11–23), but also *PPl.* C.VI.65ff.

**551** Rom. 3:12; Ps.13:3.

**559ff** For similar sentiments cf. *LL* 42/19, Matthew 321/22, TCC B.14.50, f. 50.

**566** Matt. 24:2, Mark 13:2, Luke 21:6.

**567** For these views on the suitable *house of God* compare *PR* pp. 321–3 and references there given, especially *LL* 35/37–43/28.

**586** cf. Jerome on Matthew, PL 26.171–2.

**589** Mark 10:46, Luke 16:20, 18:35, John 9:8.

**602** Taylor gives here in brief a number of the objections to the mendicants recited at much greater length in many Lollard tracts; for some references see *PR* pp. 347–51. The association of *fablis*, amusing illustrative tales not derived from scripture, with the friars is found throughout Wycliffite writings: e.g. Arnold iii.274/30, 299/31, 376/14, Matthew 26/31, 50/33, *Op. Ard.*ff. 138$^{v}$, 156$^{v}$–157, *Jack Upland* 233, Sidney Sussex 74, f. 7$^{v}$.

**608** John 4:10. The same story is discussed in Egerton f. 107, with a somewhat different slant. Here the requests of Christ (616–46) are interpreted spiritually, whilst in 616 and at more length in Egerton the requests are taken (to a dispassionate observer perhaps sophistically) as commands and hence irrelevant as justification of begging. The same line is taken here with the story of Zacheus, lines 647ff.

**611** John 4:8.

**622** John 4:32.

**625** John 4:9.

**631** John 4:16–18.

**647–58** The story of Zacheus, Luke 19:1–8, is paraphrased; only 649–50 can be regarded as strictly translation.

**649** Luke 19:5.

**660** Luke 2:46.

**662** Matt. 5:17.

**663** Deut. 15:7–8.

**668** Matt. 5:17–48.

**670** Aelred *De Iesu Puero* I.6–7, *CCCM* i.254–5. For Aelred see *ODCC*; he was strongly influenced by Bernard, and wrote his first major work at Bernard's suggestion. The force of *or* implies Taylor's uncertainty about the authorship of the tract mentioned, and it was often cited under Bernard's name in the medieval period (for instance by Bonaventura in the works cited under 681–2). The same attribution of a sermon on this text to Bernard, and the allegation that Bernard there asserted *Christus mendicavit*, is found in Wyclif's *De civ. dom.* iii.8/20, 54/13 and, most usefully since a quotation is given, 102/19 (corresponding to *CCCM* i.254/159–64); this last is introduced 'beatus Bernhardus vel, ut alii dicunt, fuit abbas Alredus Bernhardi discipulus, super illud Luc. 2:42 *Cum factus esset*'.

**672–4** The distinction is between occasional begging forced by circumstance, *begging constreyned*, and regular begging as a permanent method of livelihood, *clamerous and customable begging*. That of the mendicants was, the Lollards claimed, of the latter type.

**674** The admission here is perhaps surprising: the knights are presumably returning from war, usually castigated by Wyclif and his followers, or from crusade, an activity even more reprehensible in their view. See *PR* pp. 367–70 and cf. Walter Brut in Hereford reg. Trefnant pp. 308ff.

**677** Luke 2:51.

**679** Matt. 13:55, Mark 6:3.

**681–2** The claim of the mendicants that this period of Christ's life justified their practice is found, for instance, in Bonaventura *Apologia Pauperum* cap. 7 (*Op. Omn.* VIII.274) and *Expositio super Regulam Fratrum Minorum* cap. 6 (*Op. Omn.* VIII.424).

**683** Luke 2:52.

**688** See FitzRalph's *Defensio Curatorum*, translated by Trevisa, p. 80/28ff. FitzRalph (c.1295–1360), archbishop of Armagh, was more frequently called by his personal name in Wycliffite writings, or designated 'saint Richard' (as Arnold iii.281/13, 412/22, 416/20, Matthew 128/26).

**690** *Opuscula Sancti Patris Francisci Assisiensis* (Quaracchi, 1949), *Regula* I, caps. 7–9, *Regula* II, caps. 4–6 (pp. 33–7, 67–9) and especially *Testamentum* (p. 79) 'Et ego manibus meis laborabam et volo laborare; et omnes alii fratres firmiter volo quod laborent de laboritio, quod pertinet ad honestatem. Qui nesciunt, discant, non propter cupiditatem recipiendi pretium laboris, sed propter exemplum et ad repellandam otiositatem. Et quando non daretur nobis pretium laboris, recurramus ad mensam Domini petendo eleemosynam ostiatim.' The appeal to the unglossed and rudimentary sense of the Franciscan Rule is found most obviously in the text preserved in three manuscripts (printed Matthew pp. 40–51), where a straightforward translation of the Rule is followed by a castigation of later relaxations and sophistications, and of contemporary fraternal practices.

**701–7** cf. *Op. Ard.* ff. 204ᵛ-206ᵛ where a debate, perhaps originating in a university determination, is found on whether 'Christo iure hereditario pertinebat regnum David temporale'; cf. Egerton f. 12ᵛ.

**702** Gen. 1:26.

**709** Gal. 6:10.

**710** Matt. 25:31–46.

**712** Ps. 89:4.

**715** Summary of Augustine PL 35.2320.

**717** Gen. 1:22–2:2.

**719** The belief that Christ was born in the sixth millennium of this world is found in Augustine *De Genesi contra Manicheos* I.23, PL 34.190–3, also PL 35.2320 (see note lines 715), and in many other places; see, for Augustine's view (and that of earlier writers), A. Luneau, *L'histoire du salut chez les pères de l'église* (Paris, 1964). Cf. J. A. Burrow, *The Ages of Man* (Oxford, 1988), pp. 79–92. The more particular view that 'Crist ... bouȝte man in þe eende of þe secunde hundrid of þe sixte þousand' (721–3) is to be found in Jerome's version of Eusebius's *Chronicon* (largely lost in its Greek original), PL 27. Here it appears that Christ was considered to have been born 2015 years from Abraham (col. 558); according to one computation, from Adam to the flood was 2242 years, and from the flood to Abraham was 1015 years (col. 105). This gives a date for the creation of 5272. Taylor here has rounded this down to 5200, giving 800 years of the sixth millennium plus 605 of the seventh (720). Hence the dating of 1405 complete years, and the dating of the sermon in 1406 (see introduction p. xiii).

**726** Matt. 24:6–7, Mark 13:8, Luke 21:11.

**729** The time of *þe lawe of innocence* was before the fall of man, when the *contrariouse lawes* were those of God and of the already corrupted Lucifer (Gen. 2:15–17, 3:1–6). For *þe lawe of kynde* see note to 499.

**733** For instance, the story of Lot (Gen. 19) or of the persecution of the Jewish people by the Egyptians (Gen. 39–Exod. 12).

**734** See, for example, the captivity of the Jews in Babylon (4 Kgs. 24–5), or the constant strife waged by the Philistines against the Jewish people (Judges 14–16, 1 Kgs. 4–7).

**736** For instance, Acts 4: 1–22, 5:17–40, 12:1–10, and by pagans Acts 16:19–27, 19:21–20:2.

**737ff** The wording in 738–9 *he þat pretendiþ himsilf moost parfiit cristen man* would most naturally refer to the pope, but the second part of the sentence seems rather to describe the persecution of a Lollard preacher. The more immediate instigator of such persecution was Arundel, archbishop of Canterbury. Presumably the pope is here regarded as the ultimate source of Arundel's power and therefore of his action.

**743ff** Despite Wycliffite anxiety for the education of the laity, there was an appreciation of the need for discrimination in teaching the unlearned in theological matters. See, for similar comments, the Latin sermons in Bodleian Laud misc. 200, f. 44.

**746** John 6:12.

**746–8** The concentration upon the gospel message over that of other parts of the bible is characteristic of Wyclif and his followers (e.g. Wyclif *De ver. sac. scrip*. i.77, *Serm*. i.218/9ff; Arnold iii.504/5, Matthew pp. 256/29. 260/25). By *historial* Taylor means to imply both the veracity of the gospel stories and also the need for their literal understanding.

**753** 2 Cor. 8:14.

## 2. THORPE'S TESTIMONY

**20** For Thorpe's arrest in Shrewsbury see below 624ff and notes.

**30ff** Whilst Thorpe's first observation (lines 19–28) is just credible, it is difficult to believe that Arundel's officials would have allowed Lollards access, in person or by letter, to Thorpe once he had been imprisoned in Saltwood. But, for a possible parallel, see introduction pp. xlvi–xlvii. The implication may even be (or may, at least, have been intended to have been understood to be) that there were secret sympathisers within Arundel's retinue or household.

**36–9** Presumably the danger apprehended is that, if the account were not an accurate record, Thorpe's writing would be used as the basis of yet another prosecution of him.

**50** Wisd. 5:15.

**130ff.** Lollard attitudes towards likely persecution are at first sight somewhat varied. The biblical text almost always quoted is Matt. 10:23. Perhaps the most coherent discussion of this is in sermon 66 (*EWS* ii.66). One clear directive emerges from this: that falsehood must not be admitted, even for the sake of avoiding death (and falsehood may be defined, from other parts of the cycle, as departure from the precepts of Christ and the apostles). Beyond this, it is admitted that flight may be justifiable rather than awaiting certain persecution. As here, the activity that is held to excite persecution most surely is preaching God's word (cf. *EWS* i.E48/14, ii.119/26, iii.157/84, Arnold iii.132/31, 293/21, Matthew 252/2, *LL* 100/3, CUL Ii.1.26 f. 63, Ps.Lambeth f. 182v/2,

Add.24202 f. 54$^{v}$, Harley 1203 f. 72$^{v}$, Laud misc. 200 f. 149, Bodley 806 f. 70$^{v}$). For the relation of precept to Lollard practice see *PR* pp. 158–64, 372–4.

**148** Phil. 3:20.

**154** Gen. 15:1.

**167–9** Lammas Day, the feast of St. Peter ad Vincula, falls on 1 August. In 1407 this was a Monday. The date here to which Thorpe refers is, therefore, Sunday 7 August.

**170** Saltwood Castle was in ecclesiastical hands, with some interruptions, from 1036, and was a residence of the archbishop of Canterbury from 1199; see the account of the Castle by E. Hasted, *The History and Topographical Survey of the County of Kent* (Canterbury, 1797–1801), viii.218–24, and J. Newman, *The Buildings of England: North East and East Kent* (Harmondsworth, 1969), pp. 437–9. The current guide to the ruins of the Castle (Derby, 1975) contains some excellent photographs, including one of a tower defending the inner bailey that is named 'Thorpe Tower'; but the date at which the name was given is uncertain, and it is not mentioned by Hasted (the details about Thorpe provided by the guide are unreliable). Much of the surviving building dates from the time of Arundel's predecessor, archbishop Courtenay.

**170** A brief survey of the career of Thomas Arundel in given in Emden *Oxford* i.51–3; a fuller account of his earlier life is given by M. Aston, *Thomas Arundel: a Study of Church Life in the Reign of Richard II* (Oxford, 1967), and more briefly of his later life in R. G. Davies, 'Thomas Arundel as Archbishop of Canterbury, 1396–1414', *JEH* 24 (1973), 9–21. It was during Arundel's tenure of the primacy of Canterbury, 1396–7 and 1399–1414, that the main legislation against the Lollards was enacted (especially 1401 *De heretico comburendo* and 1407 his *Constitutions*); for his instigation of this, and of the persecution of Lollardy, see McNiven (1987), passim and esp. pp. 63–78. As Thorpe recognized (2245ff), Arundel was implacably hostile to all of his ideas, and was one of the most, if not the most, persistent enemies of Lollardy. He was, as Thorpe states, chancellor at various points of his career, including 30 January 1407 to 31 January 1410.

**176** For John Malvern see Emden *Oxford* ii.1211; he held various benefices, including as Thorpe says that of rector of St. Dunstan's-in-the-East, London from March 1402 till his death in March 1422. He was also physician to Henry IV. He is recorded as present at the trials of the Lollards Walter Brut in 1393 (Hereford reg. Trefnant p. 360), and of John Badby in 1409 (Wilkins iii.326).

**181–2** For Thorpe's possible activities in the north see introduction pp. xlviii–l. There is no evidence in Arundel's own register for his period as archbishop of York (1388–96) that Thorpe was prosecuted there during those years.

**188** Rom. 12:18.

**198ff.** The creed that Thorpe recites is, with a few exceptions that will be discussed below, entirely orthodox. It was because of the possibility that Lollards might produce such an apparently innocuous expression of belief (cf. the group of Bristol men in 1417 who answered unexceptionably about the articles of the creed, the commandments, works of mercy and cardinal virtues in Bath and Wells reg. Bubwith op.134a, (no. 716, p. 285)) that lists of specially devised questions were later drawn up. See Hudson (1973), pp. 133–5.

**208** The implications of Thorpe's equation of *foorme* with *kynde* here are made plain in the discussion of the eucharist, lines 968ff.

**221** Mark 1:11, cf. Matt. 3:17.

**230** Matt. 4:17.

**234–43** The account of the institution of the eucharist here is neither clearly heterodox nor unequivocally orthodox; Thorpe is forced to expand his view later (lines 932ff). The stress here, lines 241–3, on the memorial aspect of the sacrament is greater than might be expected in an orthodox account as brief as this.

**276–99** The most clearly heretical section of Thorpe's creed relates to his beliefs about the church. It is clear even at this early stage that Thorpe is not concerned with the institution of the church, but is talking about the *congregatio predestinatorum* in Wycliffite terms. It is to this *chirche* that he is prepared to submit (292–5). For a more explicit description of this church see below lines 899–917.

**305** A *forbycause to the praysynge* agrees with VP *quia ad laudem*, suggesting that R omitted *to* and misread a spelling, possibly abbreviated, of *preysynge* as *perseyuynge*.

**313–16** Implicit in Thorpe's statement here is the view, elaborated more fully below and underlying many of his replies, that nothing not found in *þe olde lawe and þe newe* is necessary for salvation.

**325–32** Thorpe's apparent admission of authorities other than scripture is, of course, seriously limited by his reservation at the end of the sentence: that scripture remains the touchstone for the authority of *alle þe seintis and doctours*.

**332–9** Thorpe's views about oaths are more fully set out in the fifth question, 1633ff.

**340** The emendation seems necessary, and A's reading is preferred because it explains R's mistake. But the number in VP is in fact accurate (see lines 175–7).

**349–60** The form of oath that Arundel wished Thorpe to swear is similar to those found in abjurations, promising not only to abandon earlier erroneous opinions but also to dilate other heretics to the authorities. For later examples see Alnwick courtbook, Tanner pp. 58–9, and Hudson (1973), pp. 135–7.

**360–4** In other words, Thorpe will not receive a licence to preach until his relinquishing of Lollard opinions is clear. For Thorpe's views on licences see below lines 751ff.

**367** Dan. 13:22.

**374–6** Thorpe's trial was after the introduction of *De heretico comburendo* in 1401, by which the death penalty was introduced into England as a punishment for obdurate heretics. For the workings of this and ensuing acts see Chichele reg. i.cxxix–cxxxviii.

**379–84** The extent to which ecclesiastical persecution of Lollardy produced a genuine return to orthodoxy is, of course, impossible to gauge; even the obverse, the number of those executed under the terms of the 1401 act, is not known. Some indication of proportions may be gained from the sixty people whose investigation for heresy between 1428 and 1431 is recorded in the surviving courtbook of bishop Alnwick of Norwich: of these, fourteen denied the charges and purged themselves, one seems to have escaped punishment, and on the rest penalties, ranging from solemn penance and fasting to imprisonment, were imposed; none was executed, though two were possibly relapsed heretics. But three men, William White, John Waddon and Hugh Pye, all well known leaders among the group, had been executed before these investigations began and a fourth, William Caleys, was executed in 1430. See Tanner (1977), pp. 22–5. Some Lollard texts explicitly urged men to equivocate under pressure, and return later to their old views (see *PR* pp. 158–61).

**401** Exod. 11:10.

**408** *schauen*: in order to remove the clerical tonsure; cf. the later case of William Taylor in 1423 Chichele reg. iii.172–3, esp. 173 'in signum degradacionis et actualis deposicionis coronam et tonsuram clericalem in nostra presencia facimus abradi'.

**409** Smithfield was the site of several Lollard burnings, including that understood by Thorpe to be referred to here, that of William Sawtry (417); see Wilkins iii.260. The site was doubtless chosen to give maximum publicity to the event, and so deter other Lollard sympathisers (cf. Wilkins iii.248–9).

**417** For Sawtry see briefly McFarlane (1952), pp. 150–2, and McNiven (1987), pp. 81–93; the case is covered in Wilkins iii.256, and his views appear in *FZ* pp. 408–10. He was the first English heretic to be burnt at the stake. A minor cleric of the Norwich diocese, he was first convicted of heresy in 1399 and abjured before bishop Despenser. But in 1401 he was tried again before Arundel, having moved from Norfolk to London in the meantime. This time he stuck to his views, and as a relapsed heretic who remained obdurate was executed—by royal warrant, some weeks before *De heretico comburendo* became law.

**423** Thorpe's regret reflects the persistent Lollard view that the laity were more favourably inclined towards them than the clergy (cf. Arnold iii.165/25, 324/12, Matthew 79/20, Laud misc. 200, f. 47v). Even as late as Pecock, the Lollards were identified with *the lay partie* (*Repressor* i.5/3).

**476** Thorpe implied (454ff) that Wyclif's name had already spread widely before he went to Oxford; this would imply a date of about 1375 or later, and accord with the length of time Thorpe claims he had adhered to Wycliffite doctrine.

**484–7** Thorpe had been released by bishop Braybrook of London in 1397, as is mentioned 2175ff; he had apparently managed to escape without recantation or formal condemnation. As has been argued (introduction pp. xlix–l), the excommunication added to the record in Lydford's notebook must be regarded as inauthentic. Arundel at no point in these conversations described Thorpe as a relapse; this was crucial, both to suspect and to interrogator. As a relapse Thorpe would be liable to the penalty of perpetual imprisonment if he again recanted, and to execution if he did not (see Richardson (1936), pp. 1–28 and Chichele reg. i.cxxix–cxxxvii). Though the practice in 1407 was less clearly defined than it later became, it seems inconceivable that Arundel should not mention an earlier recantation if one had occurred (see Thorpe's comment 486–7).

**499–501** For a brief biography of Nicholas Hereford see Emden *Oxford* ii.913–15. He was at The Queen's College Oxford by 1369, took orders as a secular priest in 1370, but seems to have been resident in Oxford until at least 1375. By 1382 he was back in Oxford (if indeed he had ever left), and was invited by the chancellor Robert Rygge to give the Ascension day sermon that year. The sermon he gave in English in St. Frideswide's churchyard caused a considerable furore, since it advocated a number of Wycliffite views in outspoken terms; most notably Hereford called for the disendowment of the church by the king, or, failing his action, by the laity in general. A notarial account of the sermon, taken down in Latin by one Peter Stokes, a Carmelite in the employ of archbishop Courtenay, survives in MS Bodley 240, pp. 848–850. For an account of the events surrounding this sermon see Hudson (1986), pp. 67–74 and *PR* pp. 70–3, and for an edition of Stokes's text see Forde (1989), pp. 237–41. In June 1382 Hereford was forbidden by Courtenay to preach publicly, and was summoned with Philip Repingdon before the Blackfriars Council in London. After a first appearance, when the gravity of their situation became plain, Hereford fled to the continent and eventually to Rome, apparently in the naive hope of support from pope Urban VI. In Rome he was imprisoned, but managed to escape in a popular rising in 1385. On his return to England he seems to have resumed preaching in support of Wycliffism, until he was arrested in Nottingham in January 1387 and imprisoned, first in the town gaol and then in the castle; the transfer was made at the request of the warden, Sir William Neville, named by Walsingham as one of the Lollard knights (see *CCR 1385–9*, p. 208, McFarlane (1972), pp. 198–9, F. D. Logan,

*Excommunication and the Secular Arm in Medieval England* (Toronto, 1968), p. 193, and Hudson (1978), p. 59). In the same year Hereford was reported by Walsingham to have dissuaded a dying Lollard priest from oral confession; this occurred at Shenley manor in Hertfordshire, home of Sir John Montague, another of the Lollard knights (*Hist. Angl.* ii.159–60). Despite this persistence, and despite the apparent support from sympathisers among the gentry, Hereford abandoned his Wycliffism some time between late 1387 and January 1391, since at the latter date he became rector of St.Mary-in-the-Marsh, Kent (Lambeth reg. Courtenay f. 279v) and was said to be zealous 'in preaching privately and openly in opposition to false teachers subverting the catholic faith' (see *CPR 1391–6*, p. 8). Arundel's evidence (see line 2167 and note) that Hereford had been imprisoned by the archbishop of Canterbury is supported by Knighton, *Chron.* ii.174 for 1385, but Courtenay's register does not mention this. After his recantation he held a number of clerical offices, notably the treasurership of Hereford cathedral from 1397 to 1417; in 1393 he acted as assessor for bishop Trefnant of Hereford in the trial of Walter Brut (Hereford reg. Trefnant pp. 359, 394, 401). In November 1417 he gave up his positions as secular priest and entered the Carthusian house at Coventry where, at a date unknown, he died. For the association of Hereford's name with the EV translation of the bible in Bodleian MS Douce 369, and the implications drawn from that colophon by the critics, see *PR* pp. 241–2 and references there given.

John Purvey in the primary sources is a much less well attested figure, though he has appeared prominently in critical speculation from the eighteenth century onwards. I have discussed the evidence, and the development of the legend of Purvey, elsewhere (1981), pp. 85–110; only the main points of the former are repeated here. He was ordained in March 1378 in the Lincoln diocese (Lincoln reg. 12, Buckingham, f. 161). By 1387 he was known as a disseminator of Wycliffite doctrines (Worcester reg. Wakefield f. 128v (no. 832)), and was linked there and again in other documents of 1388–9 with Hereford and Aston (*CPR 1385–89*, pp. 448, 536, *CPR 1388–92*, p. 172). The first dated record of any investigation of his views comes in 1401, when he was tried for heresy before archbishop Arundel; on 6 March he recanted at St.Paul's Cross in London (Lambeth reg. Arundel ii.184–5, printed Wilkins iii.260–2). On 11 August 1401 he was admitted as rector of West Hythe, Kent, when he had to promise not to preach against the determinations of the church on peril of relapse. By October 1403 the living was vacant (Lambeth reg. Arundel i.278, 290v). After that the only possible near-contemporary record of Purvey is the appearance of a man of that name in enquiries following the Oldcastle revolt in 1414, a man evidently active both in Derbyshire and in London. Some amplification of this story is given by Henry Knighton, though his dates cannot in this regard be trusted. Knighton describes Purvey as *capellanus simplex*, lists twelve errors that he had preached in Bristol, and alleges that he was 'invincibilis discipulus, doctrinamque magistri sui Johannis Wyclyf per omnia et in omnibus executor pervalidus' (ii.178–80).

The *Fasciculi Zizaniorum* includes the list of errors abjured by Purvey in 1401, and immediately before this gives a collection of errors collected from a book by Purvey at an unspecified date by the Carmelite Richard Lavenham (pp. 400–7, 383–99 respectively). Netter in the 1420s quoted from two books he ascribed to Purvey, *De compendiis scripturarum, paternarum doctrinarum et canonum* (apparently a set of *distinctiones*) and *Libellus de oratione*; neither of these seem identifiable with anything that has survived. Netter also describes Purvey as *doctor eximius*, *glossator Wicleffi* and *librarius Lollardorum* (*Doct*. II.70, 73, VI.13, 17, 117 (i.619, 637, iii.110, 127, 732)). That Purvey was a Wycliffite of some prominence and persistence seems clear (he was amongst the heretics known to John Walcote, a shepherd of Hasleton, Glos., in 1425, Worcester reg. Morgan p. 169, though the acquaintance may have been prior to 1413 since Oldcastle is also mentioned), but the details of his career remain from this time very obscure. Thorpe's own references to Purvey (see also lines 541–54) do not clarify much. Bale attributed nineteen works to Purvey (*Catalogus* i.542); later historians of the Lollard movement have added many more and have wished to associate him with the LV translation, but with little or no conclusive evidence.

Robert Bowland: a clerk of this name appears in Arundel's register (Lambeth reg. Arundel ii.185$^{v}$–186, see Wilkins iii.262–3), immediately after the trials of Sawtry and Purvey in 1401, accused of immorality with a nun of Nuneaton; he is there said to have been rector of the church of St. Antoninus in London. The possibility that this may be the man mentioned here is perhaps increased by the fact that he chose Philip Repingdon, by then abbot of St. Mary's Leicester, as judge for his first trial. The story is also incorporated into Usk's *Chronicon* p. 57, with the further detail that Bowland was notorious for 'diversis criminibus, heresibus, et erroribus'. Later in 5 April 1410 a pardon was granted to Robert Bowelond clerk for all 'treasons, felonies, misprisions, trespasses, offences, contempts, extortions, oppressions, rebellions, insurrections, concealments, conspiracies, appeals and confederacies', but these are not explained (*CPR 1408–13* p. 184).

Philip Repingdon: together with Hereford, Repingdon was the most celebrated of Wyclif's early followers. For his biography see Emden *Oxford* iii.1565–7. He came to Oxford as an Augustinian canon of St. Mary's in the Meadows Leicester. He was probably somewhat younger than Hereford, since he was not yet a doctor when Rygge invited him to give the Corpus Christi Day sermon in Oxford in 1382 (*FZ* pp. 306–7). Before that he had preached Wyclif's views on the eucharist at Brackley (*FZ* pp. 296–7). Unfortunately there is no account of Repingdon's sermon comparable to that of Hereford's; all that is said is that he *excusans magistrum Johannem Wycclyff, in omnibus sibi favens* (*FZ* pp. 299–300, see my comments on this account *PR* p. 71 n. 68). Like Hereford, Repingdon was summoned before Courtenay and the Blackfriars Council; unlike Hereford, in October 1382 Repingdon submitted (Wilkins iii.169). Subsequently Repingdon became abbot of the house at

Leicester in 1394, chancellor of Oxford university from 1400 to at least February 1403, and then bishop of Lincoln in 1404; he resigned the see in 1419 and died in 1424. For his sermons see S. Forde, 'Writings of a Reformer. A Look at Sermon Studies and Bible Studies through Repyngdon's "Sermones super Evangelia dominicalia"' (Birmingham Ph.D. thesis, 1985), and for his episcopal register the edition by M. Archer, Lincoln Record Society 57, 58, 74 (1963–82).

**505–6** Only Purvey's recantation at St.Paul's Cross is recorded in the extant documentation (see above note on 499–501; Wilkins iii.262 from Lambeth reg. Arundel ii.184–5). Like Smithfield for burnings, the site was chosen for its publicity—an advantage also used by Wycliffites themselves, as in the case of Taylor's sermon.

**507** Thorpe's charge against Repingdon (echoed by Arundel 605–7) is repeated more forcefully at 2104ff; see the note at 601–7.

**508** The sincerity of those early Wycliffites who recanted is for the most part unascertainable. Thorpe hints at 545–8 that Purvey's orthodoxy may be in doubt; Bowland was certainly in trouble during Henry IV's reign (above 499–501 note), but its nature is uncertain.

**541** Bishops appear to have hoped that a benefice in proximity to one of their own residences would maintain former Wycliffites in their newfound orthodoxy: Purvey was given the benefice of West Hythe (above 499–501) in August 1401 following his recantation, as Hereford had been given St.Mary-in-the-Marsh by Courtenay in 1391; both were within six miles of Saltwood.

**557–61** Wyclif's personal reputation is accepted by Arundel (597–9), with the proviso of the unacceptability of his doctrine. For a survey see von Nolcken (1987), pp. 429–43.

**570** For John Aston see Emden *Oxford* i.67. Aston, since he was in Oxford by 1365, may have been slightly older than the previous group of four; certainly he disappears from the record after 1392, and from Thorpe's testimony here was dead by 1407. In May 1382 Aston had been one of the Oxford group preaching Wycliffite views in the area of Odiham (Winchester reg.Wykeham f. 194$^{v}$ (ii.337–8)), and about the same time seems to have preached at Bristol and Leicester (Knighton ii.176–8). Called to answer for his opinions at the Blackfriars Council, he prevaricated for a while, tried to rouse the Londoners in his support, but eventually recanted (*FZ* 290, 329–33; see the review of the case in Aston (1987), pp. 297–300, 328–30). Probably the next year, however, he denounced the Despenser crusade (Knighton ii.178, the dating in 1382 cannot be correct), was linked with Hereford and Purvey as a preacher of error and his writings were condemned with those of Hereford and Wyclif in 1387 (Wilkins iii.202–3).

**573** *dane Geffrey of Pikeringe*: not otherwise mentioned as a supporter of Wyclif. Emden *Oxford* iii.1532 gives the few details that are known about his career.

He was a Cistercian monk from Byland in Yorkshire. VP substitute *abbas* for expected *monachus* (*monke* R 574), information which must come from a text of English origin; Geoffrey became abbot in 1397.

**587** Matt. 23:2.

**597–9** With Arundel's admission here, albeit reported by Thorpe, compare the evidence collected by von Nolcken (1987), pp. 429–43, and Knighton ii.151 'In philosophia nulli reputabatur secundus, in scholasticis disciplinis incomparabilis. Hic maxime nitebatur aliorum ingenia subtilitate scientiae et profunditate ingenii sui transcendere, et ab opinionibus eorum variare.'

**601–7** Despite Arundel's comments here and Thorpe's at 2104ff, Repingdon does not seem to have been either particularly venal or particularly harsh to his former associates. His own will (text in Chichele reg. ii.285–7, comments by McFarlane (1972), pp. 217–18) and his sermons, where a man of scrupulous conscience and attention to pastoral concerns is revealed, point against the first. Though Repingdon's episcopal register records a number of investigations of heresy, there were apparently no burnings in his diocese during his episcopacy, despite the fact that his huge diocese covered the Lollard strongholds of Northampton and Leicester and the area of the former Lollard knight, Thomas Latimer. Robert Hoke, priest of Braybrooke, Thomas Drayton, and William Emayn, wandering Lollard, were amongst those who seem to have found Repingdon amazingly lenient (see *PR* pp. 164, 35). See the comments in M. Archer's introduction to her edition of Repingdon's Lincoln register, Lincoln Record Society 57 (1963), l–li.

**608–10** For a rare confirmation of such a claim see the opinion of John Belgrave of Leicester in 1413 (Lincoln Vj/O, f.10) that a modern bishop (i.e. Repingdon) now acted contrary to his teaching in former days, when he had been accustomed to travel around on foot preaching the gospel.

**626–7** St. Chad's church Shrewsbury was a secular college, founded some time after 779 and suppressed in 1547 (see Knowles and Hadcock (1971), p. 438), with a dean and at this time about ten prebendaries. In May 1395 twelve men were arrested at Shrewsbury in the course of the pursuit of three Oxford men suspected of Wycliffism (see *CPR 1391–6* p. 591, *CCR 1392–6* pp. 344–5 and for the principals in the case *PR* pp. 88–9). There may be a reference to later Lollard disturbances in Shrewsbury in the lament recorded in Snappe's *Formulary* pp. 131–2 where Lollards lament that Arundel 'sanguinem effudisti tam Shrovesbury quam alibi, sed principaliter apud Bristolliam'; the text is not dated, but Salter suggests perhaps 1411. The area was not far from that in which Swinderby, Brut and later Oldcastle operated. For the buildings of St. Chad's see D. H. S. Cranage, *An Architectural Account of the Churches of Shropshire* (Wellington, 1894–1912), pp. 899–912; most of the church collapsed in 1788 and the rest was pulled down, only the Lady Chapel remaining (the present St. Chad's church is a neo-classical building on a different site).

**694** Matt. 2:3.

**697** Luke 4:29.

**702** Exod. 8:23.

**704** The emendation is supported by AVP.

**707ff.** The five topics on which the men of Shrewsbury accused Thorpe did not include the issue of preaching. Implicitly, however, the question had been raised by Thorpe's activities in the town. In practical terms for the Lollards the question of preaching was a central one for them: if the claims of the hierarchy to be the sole authoriser of preaching were justifiable, then the Lollards could never hope to advance their cause. The question of licences was one that had consistently been raised by both sides: amongst the errors condemned by the Blackfriars Council in 1382 had been one that those who ceased to preach, or who ceased to hear the word of God preached, because of the excommunication of men were traitors to God, and a second that it was legitimate for deacon or priest to preach the word of God without licence from the pope or any bishop (*FZ* p. 280, nos. xiv–xv). Eight of the thirteen sections of Arundel's *Constitutions*, devised in the year of Thorpe's encounter, were concerned with preaching (Wilkins iii.314–19). It would seem from 626 *þoruȝ leue grauntid to him for to preche* that Thorpe had some licence for his activities in Shrewsbury, though this is denied by Arundel in 746–7. Preaching was regarded by the Lollards as the pre-eminent, if not the only duty of the clergy: see *PR* pp. 351–6, and for example *EWS* i.E15/6, ii.56/84, Arnold iii.144/11, 479/32, Matthew pp. 57/12, 189/27, 344/35, *Ros*. ff. 79ᵛ, 93, 102–4, *Op.Ard*. f. 165ᵛ, *ALD* p. 30/29, Laud misc. 200 ff. 12, 88, *SEWW* no. 2/25–6.

**742–6** Arundel seems here to deny Thorpe's claim in 626. The full rigours of the *Constitutions* were not in force at the time of Thorpe's preaching, but Thorpe may indeed have been acting in defiance of existing legislation. This provided that priests with a cure of souls could preach in their own parish, and might give permission to others to do so there (cf. the case of Drayton and Taylor, above pp. xix–xx). After 1407 all priests required a licence from the diocesan bishop to preach anywhere other than in the parish in which they were beneficed. Friars were usually licensed by the bishop to preach throughout a diocese or even a province. See Robert Basevorn in Th.-M. Charland, *Artes Praedicandi: contribution à l'histoire de la rhétorique au moyen âge* (Paris and Ottawa, 1936), pp. 241–2, Pagula *Summa Summarum* v.59 in MS Bodley 293, f.226; for friars B. Z. Kedar, 'Canon Law and Local Practice: the Case of Mendicant Preaching in Late Medieval England', *Bulletin of Medieval Canon Law* ns 2 (1972), 17–32.

**742** Rom. 10:15.

**747** Eph. 6:5, Col. 3:22, Tit. 2:9; cf. 1 Pet. 2:18.

**750** *trowantis* is, in its variant spellings but with initial *tr-*, a distinctively Lollard form of the commoner *tiraunt* (see here T126, *EWS* i.E28/75, E32/99, E42/44, ii.85/70, 110/17). Thorpe here, and again at 817, adds a gloss to make its sense absolutely clear.

**751ff** For Thorpe's arguments against the need for licenses to preach cf. *EWS* iii.208/20, Arnold iii.271/25, 333/1, *Op. Ard.* f. 165$^{v}$, Laud misc. 200, ff. 12, 189$^{v}$, Matthew pp. 57/25, 79/7. The jealousy of the friars' relative freedom to preach (760) is not peculiar to the Lollards (see the restrictions cited Owst (1926), pp. 72–3 and notes and cf. on FitzRalph, Walsh (1981), pp. 406ff), but was often voiced by them (see Arnold iii.370/14, 375/29, 382/20, Matthew p. 444/27, *Op. Ard.* f. 165$^{v}$, *Upland* 237).

**761–2** The dislike of material manifestation of what Lollards regarded as spiritual matters is found in their comments on indulgences and letters of fraternity; cf. Ps. Bod. 288 f.136/1, *ALD* p. 90/25.

**779–82** The agreement of A with VP makes it plain that R has omitted a section of the sentence by homeoteleuton; hence the emendation. What is less clear is the construction of the clause dependent on *schulen beren witnesse*. R's *þe truþe . . . þis her vnfeiþfulnes* as an apparent double subject is supported by VP *ueritas . . . ista eorum infidelitas*. A alters the second subject by adding *thorow* before it.

**791** 2 Cor. 3:1.

**795ff** Arundel in 747–50 had brought together Paul's instructions of Eph. 6:5 with Peter's of 1 Pet. 2:18. Thorpe takes the first part in 796, elaborating it by means of Heb. 13:17. He quotes 1 Pet. 2:18 overtly in 821–3, paraphrasing part of verse 20 as well. Lollard discussion of this latter quotation usually understood it as referring to secular lords; cf. *EWS* i.E25/62, Arnold iii.147/7 and Matthew p. 371/14.

**803** Heb. 13:7; VP are closer to the Vulgate.

**806** Heb. 13:17.

**823** 1 Pet. 2:18.

**826–9** Compare *Decr.* II C.11 q.3 c.97 quoting Augustine (Friedberg i.670). For Arundel's understanding of the Petrine commands cf. *Summa Confessorum* (Nuremburg, 1518) III tit.33 q.v., and the *Summa Summarum* (MS Bodley 293, f. 54$^{v}$–55$^{v}$, bk. I c.55); Aquinas considers them briefly in *ST* II.2 q.104. See also *Dives and Pauper* IV caps. 17/18–19/70 for a more detailed investigation of the question, with references to canon law and the commentators.

**830** 1 Kgs. 15:22.

**832** Prov. 17:15, cf. Prov. 24:24; Rom. 1:32.

**832** Thorpe's allusion to Gregory is too vague for certain identification. But his *Cura Pastoralis* ii.4 (PL 77.30) is a possible source of the allusion.

**835** *Decr.* II C.11 q.3 c.93 (Friedberg i.669).

**839ff** Arundel, of course, is correct in his conclusion. Both sides, orthodox and heretic, used scriptural, canonistic and patristic quotations to support their own case; the immense Lollard *Floretum*, with its thousands of citations and quotations, was matched by Netter's *Doctrinale* with its heavy reliance upon extensive quotation from the fathers.

**843** Rom. 10:15.

**846** Luke 10:1.

**848** Matt. 10:5; Mark 16:15.

**850** Luke 10:1.

**852** Apparently a reference to the section of Gregory alluded to above (832) and quoted at length in *Decr.* dist.43 c.1 (Friedberg i.154).

**855** *GO* on Ezech. 3:20 (iv.1106). The same point, though with reference to Grosseteste rather than Gregory, is made in *Glossed Gospels* on John 10:12 (printed *SEWW* no. 12/74–80).

**863** A reference to, though not quotation of, Isidore *Sentences* iii.34–8 (PL 83.706–9).

**869** John 18:37.

**875** cf. Gregory *De Cura Pastoralis* I.5, PL 77.10.

**877–80** Grosseteste sermon 14, printed Brown *Fasc.Rer.Exp.* ii.251, freely translated, with Grosseteste's plural changed to the singular; the passage is quoted with varying degrees of accuracy in *Glossed Gospels* on John 10:12 (*SEWW* no. 12/111–14), Arnold iii.278/17, 470/10, Matthew p. 145/9, TCD 245, f. 154[v], TCC O.1.29, f. 73 and Bodley 647, f. 68[v]. The quotation here expands Grosseteste's wording at 880.

**889–93** Again, Arundel is precisely accurate. Unfortunately, the nature of the *Sauter* confiscated from Thorpe is not clear. Presumably it is more likely to have been a glossed Psalter than simply a text of the biblical book, Latin or English. For Lollard revisions of Rolle's English Psalter commentary, of which Thorpe's book may well have been a copy, see *PR* pp. 259–64.

**898–917** The Shrewsbury accusations included nothing specifically on the church. But the issue of the nature of the church had been central to Wycliffite thought from Wyclif onwards; see Leff (1967), ii.516–45 and *PR* pp. 314–27. Thorpe's description here of his understanding is not overtly radical, but its implications (and even more what it does *not* say) are typically Lollard. Clearly, to Thorpe the church has nothing to do with the established organization and its officials, let alone with the material possessions of that body. The church consists of *heuenli pilgrimes*, that is of those making their way inexorably to heaven; implicitly, though not in explicitly contentious terms, Thorpe is describing the *congregatio predestinatorum*. Cf. *EWS* ii.84/89, iii.233/19, Arnold iii.101/38, 339/14, 395/9, Matthew p. 198/32, *LL* p. 23/3, *Op.Ard*. f. 173ᵛ, *ALD* p. 35/23, Ps.Bod. 288, ff. 132ᵛ/1, 158/2, Add. 24202, f. 8, Laud misc. 200, ff. 76, 199.

**906** A's reading *wretchednesse* is the easier equivalent of the Latin *miseriam*.

**909** cf. Heb. 11:13, 1 Pet. 2:11.

**913** cf. Matt. 7:25.

**915** cf. Matt. 7:25, Matt. 21:42, Mark 12:10, Luke 20:17, Acts 4:11, 1 Pet. 2:7.

**923** It was wise of the clerk to direct Arundel's attention to the list of five points, since the argument on the church was one where nuance and reservations were hard to define. Significantly, the lists of questions to be asked of Lollard suspects, devised probably by the jurist Brouns for Chichele in 1428, do not include any on this topic (see Hudson (1973), pp. 133–4).

**934ff** Thorpe's skill in answering Arundel is nowhere so clear as in this first question. The eucharist was the issue on which Wyclif's fortunes hinged: the support which he had received from many up to the point, probably in 1379, when he first openly preached against transubstantiation was lost by this move. For an analysis of the questions involved see *SEWW* text 1 and notes thereto, and *PR* pp. 281–90. Thorpe's opinions here cover the three statements of the 1382 condemnation recorded in *FZ* pp. 277–8: lines 970–85, 999–1019 deal with the first 'Quod substantia panis materialis et vini maneat post consecrationem in sacramento altaris', lines 1026–38, 1046–52 with the second 'quod accidentia non maneant sine subiecto post consecrationem in eodem sacramento', and 940–5 imply the third 'quod Christus non sit in sacramento altaris identice, vere, et realiter in propria praesentia corporali.' Arundel's question in 948–50 is precisely the first of these; he repeats it in 970–3 and a third time in 1023–5, but there receives an answer directed at the second.

**937** The *sacringe belle* was rung at the time of the elevation in the mass. For parallels to Thorpe's observation to the Shrewsbury people see much later in 1499 the view of John Whitehorne, rector of Letcombe Bassett (Berks.) 'whoosoeuer resceive devoutly Goddis word, he resceyvith the verrey body of Criste' (Lambeth reg. Morton i. f. 194).

**951–3** Thorpe here reverts to Wyclif's position: that only the evidence of the bible can form the basis of belief, and that anything outside that source cannot be required of a christian; cf. 1042–52.

**958** That is in lines 317–24.

**961** Matt. 26:26, Mark 14:22, Luke 22:19, 1 Cor. 10:16–17, 11:23–6.

**963–4** The texts, Matt. 26:26–9, Mark 14:22–5, Luke 22:19–20 and 1 Cor.

11:23–7, form the basis of Wyclif's various discussions of the eucharist and of those by his followers.

**970–3, 976–85** As Arundel recognizes, Thorpe's statements so far have been ambivalent, and the ambivalence hinges upon Thorpe's understanding of the words *in forme of*. Thorpe replies by using a biblical and a liturgical text where *in forme of* is used, Phil. 2:6 and the hymn 'Memento salutis Auctor, / Quod *nostri* quondam *corporis* / Ex illibata Virgine / Nascendo *formam* sumpseris' (*Breviarium ad Vsum Sarum*, ed. F. Procter and C. Wordsworth (Cambridge, 1879–86), ii.559), and the third verse of the hymn *Christe redemptor omnium*, sung at matins on Christmas Day (i.clxxi). He hopes thereby to drive Arundel into admitting the legitimacy of his meaning in the eucharistic context, implying his understanding of *in forme of* there as 'in the nature of'. With this use of verbal parallels compare the discussion of the meaning of *est* in the sacramental words found in the Lollard sermon cycle *EWS* i.30/47ff (see notes to this in *SEWW* no. 21B/33–55). The appeal to liturgical words over the eucharistic issue is found in Wyclif, for instance *De euch*. pp. 12/14, 13/15, 21, 15/5, 26/17; *De apos*. p. 126/26.

**977** Phil. 2:5–6.

**986–90** The church's teaching on the eucharist had been refined and clarified in the course of the twelfth and thirteenth centuries, and its position is reflected in *Decr. de Cons*. (Friedberg i.1293–1361). But many of the statements there, often taken out of context from much earlier writers, were themselves ambivalent, as Thorpe briefly indicates, and other Lollard texts at much greater length reveal.

**992–8** The question turns on the source of *bileue*: Thorpe regards everything ordained by men as *binepe pe bileue* and scripture only as *putt into bileue*, whilst Arundel regards those as *out of bileue* who do not accept what *holi chirche*, in his own understanding of that term, decrees. The matter is, in other words, that of authority, and of *scriptura sola*. With Thorpe's view cf. *LL* p. 31/28, *Op. Ard*. f. 178v. Arundel appears unwilling to pursue the implications of Thorpe's position, and turns to the question of patristic opinion—thus giving Thorpe the opportunity to support his view from bible, liturgy and the fathers, despite his previous statement that only the first has true authority.

**999** 1 Cor. 10:16–17, 11:23, 26, 28.

**1001** See Wickham Legg p. 223; the words are *panem sanctum*.

**1004–6** Wickham Legg p. 228 'quod ore sumpsimus domine pura mente capiamus'.

**1008** The quotation is attributed to Augustine in canon law, *De cons*. dist.2 c.58 (Friedberg i.1336); see sermon 272, PL 38.1246. The same passage is quoted both by Wyclif (*De euch*. 125/5), and by Lollard writers (*SEWW* no. 21A/23, *ALD* p. 46/5, Titus f. 42v).

**1010** cf. Titus ff. 70[r–v]. This may derive from PL 170.40–1, but is not exactly as printed there. The author referred to here under the title of *Fulgens* is in fact Rupert of Deutz, an identity which was apparently not perceived at Thorpe's time. The text *De divinis officiis* was, however, frequently quoted by Wyclif and by his followers, and its author was sought by Netter (see Hudson (1985[2]), pp. 309–12).

**1014–19** See Wickham Legg p. 28 quoted here in the original, and p. 197 'Deus qui de hiis terre fructibus tua sacramenta constare uoluisti presta quesumus, ut per hoc opem nobis et presentis uite conferas et eterne.' Thorpe's interpretation rests upon *terena substancia* in the first and *terre fructibus* in the second.

**1030–8** Thorpe's affected dispising of *scole-mater* is not uncommon in Lollard writing: see Matthew 428/16, *LL* p. 5/16, *EWS* i.30/76, ii.62/19, 94/44. Despite the dismissal, it is plain from the method used that Thorpe, like most of the other writers, was from an academic background. The rejection of discussion on accidents and subjects is again usual, see Arnold iii.443/24, 502/19, Matthew pp. 357/9, 465/25, *Upland* 393.

**1042–52** Wyclif, followed by Thorpe and others, often maintained that his view of the eucharist was that followed by the church for the first thousand years after Christ (see *De euch*. 47, *Opus Evan*. ii.143/35, *SEWW* no. 1/26, *VO* 263). Wyclif dealt with Aquinas's teaching on the eucharist at length in *De euch*. 5ff, but the Dominican is not mentioned frequently by Lollard authors (for one example see *SEWW* no. 3/44).

**1058ff** Without even the exception of the eucharist, images are the most common question on which, according to the episcopal registers, Lollards were detected. It seems possible that this should not be taken to imply that images formed the central issue in the Lollard creed, but rather that this issue was a simple one, easy for episcopal officers to investigate and hard for the suspect to evade, either by sophistical answers or by pleading ignorance of the meaning of the question. Whilst distinguishing between orthodox criticism of the religious orders, in for instance *Piers Plowman*, and heterodox, as in *Pierce the Ploughman's Crede*, requires (as the history of criticism of the former shows) a good deal of finesse, the matter of images could be reduced to a few simple questions, to which the only possible answers were 'yes' or 'no'. The issue of the honour to be shown to images was apparently under discussion in Oxford before Wyclif; Wyclif himself had little to say on the subject, and no charge concerning it appears in the 1382 condemnation. Amongst his early followers rejection of images seems to have developed quickly, though the extremity of their rejection varied. Thorpe's attitude here is relatively moderate: he rejects their legitimacy and their usefulness, but does not overtly advocate the destruction of existing images. For the issue see Aston (1984[1]), pp. 135–92, her revised version in (1988), pp. 96–159 and note especially the material, pp. 120–3, on

Robert Holcot's Wisdom commentary which, she suggests, may have maintained and encouraged this earlier interest, and *PR* pp. 301–9.

**1059–61** In the light of what follows, Thorpe's first statement may seem surprising. But, though he does not use the terms, Thorpe is thinking of the academic distinction between *latria* and *dulia* (defined in the *Rosarium* under *adoracio* respectively as 'reuerence dew to God alone' and 'luffe or reuerence dewe to a pure creature'). Thorpe is prepared to accord *dulia* to man (1065–8), and to lower objects in their nature as wood, stone etc. His objection to images is that these are not *pure creature*, but *mannes crafte*, and that they are accorded greater honour than the *dulia* accorded to their components (1071–80). For further Lollard discussion of these terms see *SEWW* no. 3/101, Egerton ff. $42^{r-v}$, Titus ff. $75^{r-v}$, and cf. Dymmok pp. 183–8 and Holcot (reported by Aston (1988), pp. 121–2).

**1061** Gen. 1:31.

**1065** Gen. 1:26–7.

**1073** The notion of images as *a kalender to lewde men* is perhaps the most frequently cited on both sides of the argument: see, for instance, *LL* p. 85/21, *SEWW* no. 16/21, *Dives and Pauper* I.vi.1–3, BL Royal 6 D.x, f. 275. It goes back at least to Gregory ep. 13, PL 77.1128. Aston (1988), p. 132 n. 21 argues that *kalender* here 'has the meaning of the most elementary horn-book type of instruction', but MED *calender* n. hardly supports this.

**1082** Thorpe does not answer the point about the crucifix, but the *Twelve Conclusions* (*SEWW* no. 3/105) provides a typical Lollard response 'if þe rode tre, naylis, and þe spere and þe coroune of God schulde ben so holiche worchipid, þanne were Iudas lippis, qwoso mythte hem gete, a wondir gret relyk', with which may be compared Dymmok's response pp. 188–91. Cf. Laud misc. 200, ff. 108, 111, and the discussion of Aston (1988), pp. 105, 107, 118 including quotation from Harley 2398, f. 82.

**1086–91** For Arundel's comparison with the honour shown to a lord's letters, compare the Lollard interest in the purport of the Lord's letters, the gospel, in CUL Ii.6.26, ff. $5^{v}$–6.

**1099** Deut. 4:15–19; Ps. 96:7; Wisd. 14:12–15:19. After the reference to Ps. 96, repeated in the marginal references, appear the numbers *10.12*: the meaning of this addition is unclear.

**1100** Baruch 6:4–72.

**1106–11, 1155–65** Lollards particularly objected to representations of the Trinity; see Wyclif *De mandatis* 156/21–8, Arnold iii.491/3, *SEWW* nos. 3/97 and note, 16/6, *Rosarium* under *ymago* (von Nolcken 99/36), BL Add.24202, f. 26. Answers were provided by, for instance, Dymmok pp. 199–200, Deverose in Merton 318, f. $118^{v}$, Netter *Doct.* VI.155 (iii.932–9); see Aston (1988), pp. 99–100, 144–5.

**1119ff** Thorpe takes the position that the arts of the carver, moulder or painter are in themselves sinful, not just that the honour paid by others to their products is wrong. Wyclif in *De statu innocencie* 498/20 observes the uselessness of such things before the fall. Cf. also *Upland* 41. Thomas Palmer alludes to a comparable position in his orthodox defence (found in Harley 31, ff. 182–94[v] incomplete and without ascription, but complete and with ascription in Assisi Biblioteca Communale 192, ff. 133–46; here in the first ff. 182[r–v] and in the second f. 134) 'Si ymagines facere vel aliquod sculptile sit generaliter contra preceptum prime tabule, sequitur tunc quod omnes tinctores, pictores, illuminatores librorum, monetarii, carpentarii, aurifabri et sculptores et breuiter omnes artifices qui solent facere et earum similitudines vel ymagines sculpendo, texendo vel pingendo peccarent mortaliter cum eorum artes sint illicite et per consequens destruende.'

**1133ff** Thorpe's attribution of the rise of images to the deterioration in the life and teaching of the clergy can be compared with Arnold iii.463/18.

**1150ff** John 20:29. Cf. Augustine quoted in *Rosarium* under *ymago* (von Nolcken 101/18, the source is PL 34.1049) 'Al wais þai deserue for to erre þat soȝt Criste and his apostilles noȝt in holy bokes bot in peynted wayles'; also Laud misc. 200, f. 201[v].

**1175** *Decr.* III *de cons.* dist.3 c.27 (Friedberg i.1360), quoting Gregory ep. 105, PL 77.1027–8.

**1180** *þe roode at þe norþe dore at Londoun* was in St. Paul's, and was an object of pilgrimage. It is also mentioned in other Lollard texts, *SEWW* no. 16/157, MS Bodley Eng.th.f.39, f.12[v]. It was removed during the night of 16–17 November 1547 (Aston (1988), p. 261 n. 22) but renewed in 1554 (ib. p. 288).

**1181** *Boxleye*, again a rood, at Boxley Abbey near Maidstone (see J. Cave-Browne, *The History of Boxley Parish* (Maidstone, 1892), pp. 46–51)) mentioned in *SEWW* no. 16/157; on the destruction of the rood see R. C. Finucane, *Miracles and Pilgrims: Popular Beliefs in Medieval England* (London, 1977), pp. 208–9, and Aston (1988), pp. 234–6.

*Walsyngam*: a village in Norfolk which had a famous image of the Virgin; cf. Knighton ii.183, Tanner (1977), p. 148, *SEWW* no. 16/158, *Piers Plowman* B.Prol.54 and Bennett's note, and B.V.230 where it was one of the resorts of Avarice.

**1192–5** A similar list of modes of showing honour is found in *De mandatis* 160/23–7.

**1196** The story of king Hezekiah (4 Kgs. 18:16), noted in the margin against 1196, is mentioned in *Rosarium* under *ydolatrie* (von Nolcken 97/5) and *37 Concs.* f. 16 (p. 25). For its use in later discussion of images see Aston (1988), pp. 208–9, 246, 295.

**1198–9** The references are not sufficiently detailed for certain identification, but possible examples are Augustine *Tract.in Joh*. 17, PL 35.1527–8, Gregory as above 1175, pseudo-Chrysostom on Matthew, PG 56.739.

**1206** Matt. 12:39.

**1216–20** For examples of the typical representations of the Trinity, with God the Father as an old man, see *Lexicon der Christlichen Ikonographie*, ed. E. Kirschbaum (Rome, 1968–), i.526–37 and plates 6–10, G. Schiller, trans. J. Seligman, *Iconography of Christian Art* (London, 1971–2), ii. plates 770–93, and Aston (1988), p. 100.

**1224ff** The questions of images and pilgrimages are obviously linked, and the two topics are often dealt with together, both by Lollards (as in *SEWW* no. 16) and by their opponents (as the sequence of texts in Merton Coll. 175 ff. 273v–81v and Merton Coll. 68, ff. 29–40 show). Thorpe's answer here starts in a fashion similar to his previous one, by distinguishing true from false pilgrimage. But he then concentrates on the abuses of contemporary pilgrimages and pilgrims.

**1225** *Cantirbirie*: the pilgrimage to the shrine of Thomas à Beket, the most popular in England. For Lollard attitudes to Beket see *SEWW* no. 3/110 and references in the note there; cf. Arnold iii.283/24.

**1226** *Beuerleye*: for the shrine of St. John there see G. Poulson, *Beverlac; or the Antiquities and History of the Town of Beverley* (London, 1829), i.25–30, ii.514, 592–4, and G. Oliver, *The History and Antiquities of the Town and Minster of Beverley* (Beverley, 1829), pp. 43–4, 60–2.

*Bridlyngtoun*: the pilgrimage was to the shrine of St.John of Bridlington, i.e. John de Thwerp, prior of the Augustinian house there from 1362–c.1375; he was canonized by Boniface IX on 24 September 1401, but honour had been shown to his shrine before that (see J. S. Purvis, 'St.John of Bridlington', *Journal of the Bridlington Augustinian Society* 2 (1924), 1–50, and Hughes (1988), pp. 97–100). The life is found in Capgrave's *Nova Legenda Angliæ* (ed. C. Horstmann, Oxford, 1901), ii.64–78.

*Walsyngam*: see above 1181.

**1230ff** For the notion of true christian life as pilgrimage see Heb. 11:13 and 1 Pet. 2:11. It is not surprising, therefore, to find this in many Lollard works, for instance *Rosarium* sub *pilgrimage* (von Nolcken 80/3) and Laud misc. 200 ff. 166v–8 derived from this.

**1237–78** Thorpe goes back to his definition of the church, lines 276–99 and 898–917. The passage gives an instructive, if unsurprising, picture of the ideal Lollard way of life.

**1246** Matt. 5:3–11.

**1282–6** Cf. *SEWW* no. 16/163.

**1286–1331** Cf. *SEWW* no. 16/128, Laud misc. 200, f. 167r–v, Bodley 806, f. 22, and implicitly the account of a pilgrimage and the motives of those undertaking it given by Chaucer in *The Canterbury Tales*.

**1305ff** Compare the view of Hawise Moone (Tanner (1977), p. 142) in 1430 'all pilgrimage goyng servyth of nothyng but oonly to yeve prestes good that be to riche and to make gay tapsters and proude ostelers'.

**1312–15** Thorpe's observation is closely allied to the common Lollard point that poor men are the true images of Christ; cf. *SEWW* no. 3/99, 16/110, *ALD* p. 88/28, *Plowman's Tale* 909, *Dives and Pauper* I.lii.1–75, *Piers Plowman* B.XI.180 and Salisbury reg. Chaundler (1418), f. 17[v] 'only quicke men ben Goddes ymagis and liknesse of the Trinite'. The source seems to be pseudo-Chrysostom, PG 56.867–8. Cf. for this point Laud misc. 200, ff. 113, 166[v]–7, *LL* p. 85/29, Bodley 806, f. 22. See Aston (1988), pp. 118–19, 124–32.

**1326** *Cantirbirie bellis*: small bells were attached by pilgrims to the bridles of their horses (cf. *CT* A.170 and see the note on this line in the Riverside ed.).

**1329–31** Cf. *SEWW* no. 16/139 and Chaucer *HF* 2122.

**1342** Rom. 12:15.

**1350** Ps. 150:3–5.

**1352** Cf. Augustine *Enarr. in Ps. 149* PL 37.1953 'quando Alleluia cantas, porrigas et panem esurienti, vestias nudum, suscipias peregrinum; non sola vox sonat, sed et manus consonat, quia verbis facta concordant'; and see, for instance, the material quoted in *GO* for Pss. 149–50 and note Lyra's comment on Ps. 149:3 'per ista instrumenta designatur spiritualis gaudij redundantia de mente interiori ad extra, secundum illud Ps. 83 *Cor meum et caro mea exultauerunt in Deum viuum*'.

**1355ff** Thorpe's objections to music, and particularly to the use of music in church services (1366ff), are characteristic of Lollardy and are often expressed in conjunction with views about images and pilgrimages (cf. *SEWW* no. 16/124). The basic objections are that use of singing or organs has no justification in the New Testament (here 1355–63), that time is taken from the more important matter of preaching (here 1366–8), and that music obscures the words of scripture (here 1374–82). For comparable discussions see Arnold iii.203/18, 479/27, Matthew pp. 6/8, 91/29, 169/16, 191/4, *LL* p. 57/15, Ps. Bod.288 ff. 96[v]b, 133[v]b; cf. *PR* pp. 322, 387.

**1358** 1 Cor. 10:11.

**1361** Matt. 9:23–5.

**1381** R has *Iereom*, A *Jerome (as I thinke)*, VP *Gregorius*. The quotation is in fact from Gregory, *Hom. in Evan.* 11, PL 76.1117 (the adverbs *hic* and *illic* are omitted in translation). Were it not for A's parenthetical addition, it would be easy to argue that here (as occasionally elsewhere, see pp. xxxix–xl) the Latin version retains the original reading and both English versions are corrupt. But A's addition leads to the suspicion that the original version may have been in error (or unclear), and that this was corrected by the scribe of the archetype of VP from his independent knowledge.

**1383** Though MED *despisen* gives senses possible here (2(a) 'treat with contempt, disregard', (b) 'scorn'), it does not parallel the use with *wiþ*. The emendation is supported by A's *displeased* and VP *displicuisset*.

**1387ff** Although the charge is overtly on tithes alone, the discussion extends more widely to cover the whole issue of clerical maintenance. Charges against Lollards regularly claimed that the sect disapproved entirely of tithes: cf. *SEWW* no. 2/7 and the question in the 1428 list (Hudson (1973), pp. 133, 135 question 15) 'an decime debent dari personis ecclesie, vel si sint pure elemosine et si parochiani possint propter peccata suorum prelatorum ad libitum suum eas auferre.' The 1382 condemnation (*FZ* 280–1) listed the error 'quod decimae sunt purae eleemosynae, et quod parochiani possunt propter peccata suorum curatorum eas detinere, et ad libitum aliis conferre', reflecting observations such as those in *De civ. dom.* i.317 and mentioned in *Sermones* iii.471/26. Trials of Lollards, when any view on tithes is given, usually simply oppose tithes; thus Salisbury reg.Ayscough ii.f. 52ᵛ (1440), f. 53ᵛ (1443), and the Norwich courtbook cases of 1428–31 (see Tanner's table p. 11). But when fuller discussion is found, more diversity of opinion is encountered. In the *16 Points*, *SEWW* no. 2/81, tithes are regarded as legitimate provided they are regarded as advance payments for offices to be performed (*for þat ende þat curatis do þer office as God haþ comanded hem*), and provided that the curate to whom they are paid is poor—a view that agrees with *De civ. dom.* i.323/24. Add. 24202, ff. 34–35ᵛ contains a tract solely devoted to the subject: there true men (in the Lollard sense) are urged to pay tithes to true priests (also in the Lollard sense), but to withhold them from sinning clerics; stress is also laid on the evils of using threats of, and actual, excommunication to obtain them. See *PR* pp. 341–5, and compare the discussion in *Dives and Pauper* VII.xiv.20–100.

**1392ff** Whether the enquiry was a genuine one, or, as seems more likely in view of lines 1827ff below, the work of an *agent provocateur* is not clear.

**1397–9** Cf. Arnold iii.311/1, Matthew pp. 145/2, 417/16, 453/26, Add. 24202 f. 34ᵛ, TCC O.1.29 f. 74ʳ⁻ᵛ.

**1412** 1 Pet. 3:15.

**1419** See Lev. 27:30–2, Num. 18:24–8.

**1423–9** Cf. Arnold iii.309/21, 311/16, Ps. Bod.288 f. 22ʳb, Add. 24202 f. 34ᵛ.

**1426** Luke 11:41.

**1432ff** For this argument see more fully Egerton ff. 109ᵛ–110.

**1435** Acts 18:3.

**1441** *Cistrence*: Ranulph Higden of Chester. See his *Polychronicon* vii, RS viii.204. Only P has the correct reading, RAV all having Gregory *þe tenþe*. The pope in question, as stated by Higden, was Gregory IX, but the same error appears in *Rosarium* under *dymes* (von Nolcken p. 63/25) attributed to the same source. For this error see J. Selden, *The Historie of Tithes* (London, 1618), p. 147, referred to in von Nolcken (1979), pp. 109–10 and Aston (1984$^2$), p. 77 n. 79.

**1449** 1 Cor. 9:14.

**1450** 1 Cor. 9:12.

**1453** 1 Cor. 4:11, 2 Cor. 11:9, 2 Thess. 3:8.

**1459–68** As is clear from the phrasing of 1462, this is a free paraphrase not a quotation of Acts 20:28–35.

**1469–70** Again, certain identification is impossible, but see, for instance, Augustine PL 42.502–3, Gregory PL 76.455, pseudo-Chrysostom PG 56.881–3 and Grosseteste sermon 31, MS Royal 7 E.ii, ff. 341$^r$b–343$^v$a.

**1472–6** For the provisions of canon law concerning tithes see John of Freiburg *Summa Confessorum* (Nuremburg, 1518), bk.I tit.xv; Pagula *Summa Summarum* MS Bodley 293 ff. 122$^v$b–125$^r$a (bk.III c.33).

**1477** For the view that the number of priests was excessive cf. Arnold iii.151/33, 346/6, 418/12. The point recurred in connection with tithes in the sixteenth century, see S. Brigden, 'Tithe Controversy in Reformation London", *JEH* 32 (1981), 285–301 at p. 291.

**1486–9** As the two texts mentioned in the note to 1387ff show, the invariable condition Lollards placed on the provision of material means of life to priests was that those priests should fulfil their obligations. The same point is made Arnold iii.310/15, 468/28, 517/5, Matthew pp. 146/22, 436/1, Add. 24202 ff. 34$^v$, 40$^v$, *37 Concs*. f. 9.

**1494** *sowde*, VP *stipendium*; see OED *sold* sb$^1$.

**1499–1507** The harm done to the genuine poor by the demands of the clergy for dues is found in Taylor 540ff; cf. *12 Concs*. in *SEWW* no. 3/73, Arnold iii.170/25, 319/25, 372/8, Matthew pp. 102/29, 173/19.

**1520** Heb. 7:9.

**1524** Heb. 7:12–14.

**1526** *so þat prestis lyuen*: the verb is subjunctive, 'so that priests should live . . .'

**1529** *pure almes*: the force of these words is crucial to Thorpe's argument. The words imply *unsolicited* gifts, and are hence contrasted to the tithes that Arundel claims the parishioner is legally obliged to hand over and also to the money and goods that the friars obtain by *clamerous begging*. Thorpe does not give his views on the latter, but cf. Taylor 602ff and 672ff. See that section and its notes for discussion of the gospel stories (notably John 4:10, Luke 19:5) in which Christ sought material support.

**1533** Matt. 10:25.

**1550** I have not been able to trace this quotation; cf. Jerome on Mt.23:25, PL 26.171 and on Mal. 3:8, PL 25.1569–71, where there are some similarities of sentiment but not the precise wording of the present passage.

**1565** Arundel's *freedam of holi chirche* is a translation of *libertas ecclesie* mentioned frequently in canon law, e.g. *Decr.*II C.12 q.2 cc.61–4 (Friedberg i.706–8) in the context of the material rights of the church. The terms *freedam/libertas* are used in the legal sense: see MED *fredom* n. 3b 'the total body of rights and privileges claimed by', here, the church, and note the quotation there from *Jacob's Well* 56/30 'þou schalt . . . payen trewly þi tythe . . . and ȝif þou do noȝt þus, þou depryuest holy cherch of his fredom and of his ryȝt.'

**1573–6** Arundel's charge is a fair one. Wyclif did not explore the implications of his views on dominion with regard to secular rulers. He and his followers certainly castigated abuses in secular life, but often presented these as the result of clerical domination or machinations (cf. *EWS* ii.88/92, iii.130/46, Arnold iii.131/25, 232/20, Matthew pp. 24/12, 94/12, 181/10, 236/31). The issue of secular dominion is discussed in conjunction, as here, with tithes in the text known as *Of Servants and Lords*, Matthew p. 229/1ff.

**1580** Pseudo-Chrysostom PG 56.839, quoted in *Floretum* under *sacerdos*.

**1586** The idea that the laity hold a special duty to correct the clergy, under pain of God's wrath, was characteristic of Wycliffite thought; see, for example, Hereford's 1382 sermon 133–8 (ed. Forde (1989)), *Lollard Sermons* p. 25/513ff.

**1593** *þreedbare blew gowne*, VP *toga blodia depilata*. For the colour of Lollard clothes see *PR* pp. 144–7.

**1606–7** Thorpe's observations here, though brief, touch on the issue of predestination and its relation to the visible life of the christian. Wyclif asserted that no human being could be certain of the final destination either of his own soul or of another's, but alongside this castigated various ranks, especially of the clergy, as *antichristus* or the followers of antichrist (see references given in *PR* pp. 314–17). The question of the value of the ministry of a notoriously ill-living priest (especially one guilty of sexual vice) was discussed in orthodox circles at the time: see the evidence in A. Minnis, 'Chaucer's Pardoner and the "Office of Preacher"', in *Intellectuals and Writers in Fourteenth-Century Europe*, ed. P. Boitani and A. Torti (Tübingen and Cambridge, 1986), pp. 88–119. As *Dives and Pauper* VII.xiv.55ff shows, the issue is connected with that of tithes.

**1620** 1 John 5:16.

**1630ff** The basis of Wyclif's and the Lollards' rejection of oaths was the biblical precepts of Exod. 20:7 and Matt. 5:33–7. Often in trials the rejection was expressed in uncompromising terms such as those reported by Arundel in 1630–1; cf. *SEWW* no. 5/64 *þat it is not leful to swere in ony caas*, Salisbury reg. Chaundler ii, f. 17ᵛ (1418), Bath and Wells reg. Stafford, op. 53b (no. 263), (1428). In many texts, however, a more complicated attitude is found, albeit one which would lead to this simplified summary. Wyclif *De mandatis* 201/29–

206/20 sets out some of the same arguments as those advanced by Thorpe here: that oaths by creatures are forbidden (Thorpe 1634–90); that objections that statements will not be believed without an oath (Thorpe 1718–23), that oaths recall God and his words (Thorpe 1723–5) and that swearing is merely a habit (Thorpe 1712–16) are all invalid justifications for what is in truth a sin. For further comments see *PR* pp. 371–4. Lollard views on swearing are found in Arnold iii.483/3, *LL* p. 87/10, *37 Concs.* f. 21$^{v}$; detailed parallels are cited below.

**1636** Matt. 5:33–7; James 5:12.

**1637–8** The prohibition on swearing by creatures appears in Wyclif *De mandatis* 202/5, *LL* p. 89/26, and *37 Concs.* f. 22. The last of these points out that the prohibition is incorporated in canon law as *Decretals* II tit.xxiv c.26 (Friedberg ii.369); cf. John of Freiburg (Nuremburg, 1518), bk.I tit.ix q.vi, Pagula *Summa Summarum* MS Bodley 293 ff. 86$^{v}$b–87$^{r}$a (where it is noted that *Decr.* II C.22 q.1 cc.7–8 (Friedberg i.863) records prohibition of oaths by creatures but allowance of those by God). See also *Dives and Pauper* II.vii.

**1648** The oath was a common one (see MED *hali-dom* n.); the second noun, though grammatically singular, often had the force of a collective.

**1651–60** The point is the same as that discussed before 795ff, and is the issue of the individual conscience against the command of the church. Again Thorpe asserts the responsibility of the individual to judge in every case, and hence the legitimacy of resistance to instructions from a superior. The issue, implicit in many Wycliffite tenets, became an overt point of discussion in principle at the Reformation period; see S. E. Ozment, *Mysticism and Dissent: Religious Ideology and Social Protest in the Sixteenth Century* (New Haven and London, 1973), esp. pp. 79ff. See also *Decr.* II C.22 q.5 c.8 (Friedberg i.884–5); Gratian's comment here makes it clear that he regarded the matter as a difficult case.

**1664–87** The question of responsibility for an oath known to be false is discussed in John of Freiburg bk.I tit.ix q.xxxii, Pagula MS Bodley 293 f. 88$^{r}$b. Richard Wyche was, by his own account (Matthew (1890), 534–5), urged by officials of bishop Skirlaw that he could take an oath that would satisfy the bishop but make mental reservations about its meaning that would appease his own conscience. The reasoning Wyche rejected.

**1687** A mentions only Chrysostom; the marginal note in R gives Jerome and his name is added above the line; VP only mentions Chrysostom but adds correctly the homily reference. The reference to Jerome is PL 26.40, but not exact 'sic et jurare permitterentur in Deum: non quod recte hoc facerent, sed quod melius esset Deo id exhibere quam daemonibus'; the passage is quoted in *Decr.* II C.22 q.1 c.8 (Friedberg i.863). The Chrysostom passage is the usual *Opus Imperfectum* cap. 12, PG 56.698; part of it is cited in *Decr.* II C.22 q.1 c.11 (Friedberg i.864), 'Si aliqua causa fuerit, modicum uidetur facere qui iurat per

Deum. Qui autem per euangelium, maius aliquid fecisse uidetur. Quibus dicendum est: Stulti, scripturae propter Deum sanctae sunt, non Deus propter scripturas.'

**1697–1701** The sermon is that referred to in the last note; the sentence PG 56.698 'nunc autem cum sciatis, quia et bene jurare peccatum est'. It seems likely that the clerk started reading, not at the beginning of the sermon as that is printed in the modern edition, but at the beginning of the paragraph which is headed in that edition *Contra clericos qui Evangelia porrigunt juraturis*. Whether the roll contained the whole homily or only a section is unclear. Unfortunately, it is not known who Thorpe's *felowe* was. He is referred to again at 2155–9, where he is also called *þis ȝonge man*. From the later passage it is clear that he was a disciple of Thorpe's, and it seems likely he was arrested with him. The habit of recording texts on rolls in found elsewhere in documents concerning Lollardy: see Chichele reg. iii.207 and Ely reg. Grey f. 133. It is recorded that Taylor at his trial in 1421 (above p. xxi) 'extraxit de sinu suo quasdam auctoritates et dicta doctorum in quadam papiri cedula scripta'. See *PR* pp. 201–2.

**1709** Luke 21:12–15.

**1718** Objections to excessive swearing are not, of course, peculiar to Lollard texts; cf. Chaucer *CT* C.629–59 and *Book of Vices and Virtues* (ed. W. N. Francis, EETS 217 (1942)), pp. 61–3, *Dives and Pauper* II.xi.

**1745–9** Thorpe is trying to put Arundel into the dilemma set out so clearly by the author of *ALD* p. 46/7 where, having quoted a string of patristic authorities in support of the Lollard doctrine of the eucharist, the author concludes 'And syn þer wordis are canoniȝed and approuid of holi kirk, oiþer behouiþ to graunt þer wordis, or to denay þe canoniȝing and aprouing of þe kirk.'

**1759–66** Thorpe, having been forced to it, is prepared to swear but not to place his hand on the gospel book; this is in line with his argument 1639–45 and 1661–90. P against 1760 gives a marginal reference to canon law, *Decr*. II C.22 q.1 c.14 (Friedberg i.864); this is a quotation from Augustine sermon 180 (PL 38.972–9) which corresponds in sentiment though not precise wording to the text here.

**1767–84** Thorpe's point is again that the book of the gospels is a material object, and as such subject to the prohibition on oaths by creatures. The quotation in 1770 alludes to Jerome, PL 26.322; that in 1775 quotes Jerome, PL 26.322.

**1778** 1 Cor. 4:20.

**1779** Ps. 28:4.

**1780** Ps. 32:6.

**1788–1803** Thorpe's argument is that the gospel consists not in words on the page or pages in a book, but in the effect on the true believer. Cf. *ALD* p. 90/25ff, *Floretum* under *euangelium*.

**1794** Jerome epistle *Ad Paulinam*, PL 22.543, which, as noted in the margin of P, forms the prologue to the Vulgate.

**1807** Matt. 21:43.

**1811** *equyuocaciouns*: cf. WB GP p. 56/9 'Also hooly scripture tellith ofte the thouȝtis of men, and ofte the wordis and deedis; and whanne the thouȝtis, and wordis, and deedis of men ben contrarie, oo gospeller tellith the thouȝtis, and another tellith the wrdis; and bi this *equiuocacoun, either diuerse speking*, thei ben acordid, ȝhe, whanne thei seemen contrarie in wordis.'

**1818** Matt. 21:43.

**1825–6** Arundel is here threatening Thorpe with execution. The process of condemnation provided for the clerical authorities to examine and judge the suspect, to degrade him if a cleric, but then to hand him over to the secular powers for burning. See Richardson (1936), pp. 22–3, Chichele reg. i.cxxx.

**1827** A further issue not involved in the Shrewsbury list is introduced here, that of oral confession and the power of the clergy to absolve. The 1382 condemnation listed as the fifth heresy (*FZ* 278) 'quod si homo fuerit debite contritus, omnis confessio exterior est sibi superflua vel inutilis'. For Lollard discussion of the issue see *PR* pp. 294–301. The use by Arundel of an *agent provocateur* is here established (cf. lines 1392ff above).

**1880** This was the central issue in Wycliffite teaching: that God alone could forgive sin. Cf. *EWS* i.47/42, iii.169/99, Ps. Lambeth f. 186/1, Bodley 806 f. 114ᵛ.

**1881–3** The attempt by the clerk to differentiate between *forȝeue* and *assoile* depends on a distinction between *dimittere* (as in Matt. 6:12) and *absoluere*, the first appropriate to God alone in regard to sin, the second to the priesthood; cf. *Rosarium* under *absolucion* (von Nolcken p. 55/1–3), where a distinction is made between *absolucion auctoritatiue* by God, and *absolucion denunciatiue* by the priest. But the two verbs in Latin, as in English, are often used as virtual synonyms: cf. Lombard *Sentences*, PL 192.885–9. The relatively radical attitude of Thorpe, as compared with the more moderate *Rosarium*, is clear in his rejection of the distinction. The use of *assoile* for the action of God as well as of the priest is clear in Lollard circles: see *EWS* i.7/50 'For oure byleue techeth us þat no viker assoyleþ here but in as myche as Crist assoyluþ hym furst whom he assoyluþ in vertw of Crist.'

**1886** Matt. 4:17; Eze. 18:30.

**1899–1902** The same claim is made for Lollard teaching on oral confession as was made previously for their views on the eucharist (above 1042–52). Again Thorpe's point is traditional, see Arnold iii.257/19, 462/14.

**1902** Matt. 16:19, 18:18, John 20:23.

**1902–12** Thorpe is less than clear or unequivocal on the status of priestly absolution. In the light of other Lollard statements, the crucial phrase seems to be *bi autorite of his* (i.e. Christ's) *word*. If the absolution of a priest, or its withholding, is in accord with God's judgment, God being the only one to know the state of a sinner's mind, then that absolution, albeit only a pronouncing of God's previously given judgment, is valid; if not, then it is blasphemy (1896–9). Cf. *EWS* iii.169/99, Matthew pp. 335/4, 481/16.

**1916–19** In Thorpe's view, the function of the priest is purely advisory and his help is only necessary (1896–9) to those spiritually impoverished.

**1920–2** Attributed to Augustine *De Poenitentia*, PL 40.1122, in canon law *Decr.* II *De Poen.* dist.6 c.1 (Friedberg i.1242) 'Tanta itaque uis confessionis est, ut, si deest sacerdos, confiteatur proximo.'

**1927** R gives the name as *Meredoun*, A as *Moredon*, V *Morden*, P *Mordoun*. The only monastic house at Faversham was Benedictine. I have not been able to identify this monk. A man of the name *Mertoun* is mentioned abusively in the *O-and-I* poem on the Blackfriars Council (*Pol. Poems* i.261/14); but the two cannot be identical, since he is said to have been a Franciscan friar. Christ Church Canterbury was also a Benedictine foundation.

**1958** *cockil among wheet*: the allusion to Matt. 13:25 is complicated by the pun on the synonym of the biblical *zizania* (itself used in the title of *Fasciculi Zizaniorum*), *lollia*; this was often associated with the name *Lollard*, cf. *FZ* 1–3, Chaucer *CT* B.1173–83.

**1962–4** *caproun-hardi*: A has simply *harde*, VP *capitose*. The noun *caproun* means a hooded cloak (see MED *caperoun* n.). The first element of the compound was evidently not understood by A, but VP's reading 'in a headstrong fashion' seems probable. The modern 'bold as brass', in the light of the following comment, seems a likely rendering. Arundel interprets Thorpe's refusal to uncover his head at Alkerton's sermon as a mark of disrespect to the preacher and his message.

**1963ff** For Alkerton and this episode see above pp. xiv–xvii; the *clerk of Oxenford* of 1969 is thus William Taylor.

**1965** *Watlynge Strete*: this is not the well-known road from London to Holyhead, but a street that led east from the south-east corner of the precints of St. Paul's in London, becoming Budge Row after about half a mile. See the map in Stow *Survey* ii.endsheet.

**2008** *contumax*: the clerk doubtless has in mind the technical, as well as the general, sense of the word, 'being guilty of contempt of court' (for this see Alford (1988), p. 36).

**2016** Thorpe's conception of what constitutes his *office of presthode* is described earlier 713ff.

**2042–6** Thorpe here, in deceptively simple terms, puts the Lollard claim of *scriptura sola* as the basis for christian life.

**2070–5** If the whole of the last conversation, from 2025 on, is improbable as an accurate record of the investigation, it is even more improbable that Arundel would have revealed by this outburst after Thorpe's last agreement that his own command lay outside the terms of that agreement. The *accepcioun* is, of course, Thorpe's refusal to admit the legitimacy of Arundel's authority in spiritual matters over him.

**2077–84** It would seem from lines 484–7 that this was the first time that a trial of Thorpe had approached judgment. But, unless Thorpe were to recant, condemnation could result in either perpetual imprisonment or, if Arundel judged him entirely obdurate, in burning. See *Rot. Parl.* iii.467 and Chichele reg. i.cxxx.

**2085–7** For these four see above lines 499–501. It is not entirely fair that Purvey should be mentioned here since, as 545–8 have revealed, his orthodoxy was by this date not without question.

**2095** For Hereford's energies in the orthodox cause see *CPR 1391–6*, p. 8 'his zeal in preaching privately and openly in opposition to false teachers subverting the catholic faith', and Trefnant reg. pp. 394–6.

**2104–51** With this outburst of Thorpe against his former fellows compare the letter of an anonymous Lollard upbraiding Hereford as a renegade (Hereford reg. Trefnant pp. 394–6 under 1393). For a list of the benefices held by Hereford see Emden *Oxford* ii.914; they were not by contemporary standards excessive in number at any one time, though they were quite frequently exchanged. Since Bowland's identity is not very clear, it is impossible to gauge the fairness of Thorpe's allegations concerning him. It is not clear that Repingdon (Emden *Oxford* iii.1566) held any livings either as a canon and later abbot of the Augustinian canons in Leicester or after 1404 as bishop of Lincoln.

**2115–20** The emendation from VP here is one of the more dubious cases, but, as RA stand, there appears to be a gap between the thought of 2115 *for . . . men* 2118 and the remainder.

**2144** *hem specially þat ben greete lettrid men*: Thorpe's mention is interesting recognition of the effect on the movement of the recantation of the academic group.

**2155–62** The agreement of A with VP leads to the inserted amendment in R; *he* of the omitted clause is, of course, Thorpe. There is a curious error in R (complicated by R's further omission), A and P at 2156: RA agree in reading *he wol not swere*, a reading reinforced by P *iste nollet iurare*. V reads *iste uellet iurare*. The negative of RAP is the *difficilior lectio*, but is contradicted by the rest of Arundel's speech.

**2167** From the conversation that follows this is clearly Saltwood prison;

though there is no direct surviving evidence that either Hereford or Purvey had been confined there, it is credible that this could have been the case. Purvey's incarceration would presumably have been prior to the Convocation in 1401 at which he abjured (see Hudson (1981), p. 87). There is no evidence that Hereford was imprisoned in 1382 when he refused to submit to Courtenay: he failed to appear, left the country and made his way to Rome (see Emden *Oxford* ii.914). After his return he was imprisoned in Nottingham in early 1387 (see above notes to line 499), but his whereabouts between the end of that year and December 1391 when he was defending orthodoxy are unknown. He may well have spent some time before his recantation in the prison of the archbishop of Canterbury, at that time still William Courtenay.

**2169–78** The reasons for Arundel's exile from late 1397 to July 1399 were political: he was impeached in September 1397 for having acted in derogation of Richard II's authority during the ascendancy of the Lords Appellant, 1386–8 (see Emden *Oxford* i.52, Aston (1967) pp. 336–73, McNiven (1987), pp. 64–7). See above pp. xlvii–l for evidence supporting the claim that Thorpe had been imprisoned by bishop Braybrooke of London.

**2183** Not recorded in Whiting. Acle is in east Norfolk.

**2185** Jer. 28:9.

**2191** *a peire of pillers*: the sense of the last word and of its translation VP *prillorum* is obscure. But compare MED *piler(e* 4, where a fifteenth-century gloss *torques*: *a pillyre* is quoted as a possible mistranslation. Cf. MED *pillori(e* n. and Alford (1988), pp. 115–16, though Arundel's mode of punishment cannot have been the same, as is shown by *vpon þi schynes*.

**2201–2** As explained in the note to 1825–6, it was not within Arundel's power to organize the burning of a heretic; this had to be done by the secular authorities. The second suggestion is one for the murder of Thorpe, on the assumption that by this date his friends would be in no position to make effective protest.

# APPENDIX I
# THE SERMON OF THE HORSEDOUN

[The fragmentary text is edited from the only manuscript in which it is known to survive, Bodleian MS Douce 53, ff. 30–32v; the same conventions and method of editing are used as in the foregoing texts. For knowledge of the sermon by the London heretic John Claydon see above pp. xii–xiii.

The Latin text provided is Matt. 7:17, part of the gospel for the 8th Sunday after Trinity (a sermon on the full gospel is *EWS* i.8). The basis of the surviving part of the sermon, however, are the words of Paul, Romans 8:12–17 mentioned in line 1, which formed the epistle for the same occasion (another Wycliffite sermon on this is *EWS* i.E38). The form of the sermon would seem, therefore, to have followed approximately the 'modern' form of sermon (for which see most usefully Ross (1960), pp. xliii–lv), where after the text a protheme preceded the exegesis of that text; within the protheme and the main body of the sermon subdivisions were common. The surviving portion of the present sermon does not reach the end of the protheme, but even within its brief span the characteristic subdivisions are found. The first section, lines 1–11, outlines the three main divisions: the sense in which men are debtors (2–4, Romans 8:12), secondly the sense in which they are sons of God (4–10, Romans 8:14), thirdly the sense in which men are heirs of God (10–11, Romans 8:17). The remainder of the fragment goes back to examine in more detail the first of these, explaining how, despite man's complete dependence upon God, he owes God *worshipe, loue and dreede* (17), and analysing these three in turn, *worshipe* lines 18–28, *loue and dreede* together in lines 29–56. The final lines begin an analysis of man's debt to his own soul (57–62). If the remainder of the sermon continued in this fashion, it must have been a work of some length; the second and third major points from Paul's address to Romans have still to be analysed, with the gospel exegesis promised by the text to follow. Claydon's high regard for *unum sermonem alias predicatum apud Horsaldowne*,[1] if this was indeed the sermon of which this fragment is part, might confirm that the work was more than just a brief discourse.]

[1] Chichele reg. iv.133.

Here eendiþ þis sermoun and bigynneþ þe sermoun of þe Horsedoun.

*Omnis arbor bona fructus bonos facit*. Mt vii.

f. 30v In þe epistle of þis | day þat seynt Poul wroot to þe Romayns we shul vndirstonde þre gloriouse lessouns to oure lernyng. First he techiþ us þat we ben dettouris; and in þis he meueþ us þat we shulde knowe what is oure dette and quyte it. Þe secunde tyme he techiþ us þat we ben þe sones of God; and in þis we haue chosun God almyȝty to be oure fadir, his sone Iesu Crist to be oure abbot, hooly chirche to be oure modir, hooly writt to be oure reule, and we ouresilf due obedienciaries, buxum and lowly, sworun vndir peyne of perpetuel dampnacioun or wynnyng of blisse wiþouten eende þurȝ þis goostly generacioun. Þe þridde tyme Poul seiþ þat we ben eyris of God, þat is aftir þe hope of euerlastinge liif in oure lord Iesu Crist.

As for þe firste of þe apostlis wordis in þis mater, clerkis seyen þat euery cristen creature is dettour to his God. But what mowen we quyte f. 31 to | oure God siþ al is his? What hast þou man þat þou hast not takun? And whanne þou hast takun it of God, wherto makist þou glorie as if it were þyn owne? But we ben Goddis kyndely dettouris to paye hym worshipe, loue and dreede, for þis he axiþ of us in al þe tyme of oure liif. And þus he seiþ bi þe profete Isaye *Gloriam meam alteri non dabo et laudem meam sculpti libet*, I shal not ȝyue my glorie to anoþir, neiþir my preysyng to no grauun þing þat is maad bi mannys craft. And in þis he forbediþ ony creature in heuene, in erþe or in helle, quyk or deed, to resceyue þat worship þat longiþ to him, eiþir bi title of his godheed or ellis bi title of his manheed. And, siþ oure kynde is knyt to God in Crist Iesu, þer may noon ymage grauun in tree, gold or siluer, neiþir wrouȝt in cley, stoon or metal take þat worship in which eche man f. 31v shulde ⟨wor⟩|shipe oþir moost; for þei wanten liif and vertu, þei ben but bookis for mennys profiit, as Austyn seiþ and Gregory boþe, to stire mennys hertis þe sunner to compunccioun.

But touching drede and loue also, þat is dewe dette to God, spekiþ Salomon (*Ecc. ultimo*) *Time Deum et mandata eius obserua; hoc est omnis hom[inis] gloria. Omnis homo est productus in mundum propter hoc: ut timeat Deum et mandata eius obseruet sine quo nichil est omnis homo*; drede God and

2 *margin* I Cor. iiij° 4 *margin* 2 18 *margin* xlij° 10 *margin* 3 31 hominis] homo 12 *margin* I 16 *margin* I

kepe his comaundementis, for vnto þis euery man is brouȝt forþ into þis world. And þat þe keping of Goddis comaundementis is his loue shewiþ Crist hymsilf in his gospel, and seiþ *Qui habet mandata mea et seruat ea, ipse est qui diligit me. Super quo Augustinus 'Habet in memoria, seruat in vita; habet in sermonibus, tenet in moribus; habet in operando, seruat persuerando.'* Crist seiþ | 'He þat haþ my comaundementis and kepiþ hem he it is þat loueþ f. 32 me.' Seint Austyn seiþ 'He þat haþ hem in mynde and kepiþ hem in liif; he þat haþ hem in wordis and kepiþ hem in maneris; he þat haþ hem in worchyng and kepiþ hem aylastynge.' Loue and drede ben two ȝatis of liif. For who may plese God but he þat loueþ to do his wille, and drediþ for to greue or to offende hym? How shulde þis world be rulid if God were not riȝtwiis? And how shulden men lyue in erþe if God were not merciful? But God is riȝtwiis in mercy and merciful in riȝtwiisnesse; for riȝtwiisnes wiþoute mercy is but crueltee, and mercy wiþouten riȝtwiisnesse is but fatuytee. Þanne for drede of Goddis riȝtwiisnesse forsake we synne, or ellis he wole riȝtwiisly ponyshe us, and haue we hope of Goddis mercy in doynge verry | penaunce þat williþ mercy to hem þat turnen to hym, for loue þat he haþ to mankynde bi vertu of his incar- f. 32v nacioun and his blessid passioun. But drede liiþ aboue and dryueþ awey presumpcioun, and loue holdiþ us up fro disperacioun; and bitwixe þese twey ⟨ȝatis⟩ is an opyn hiȝe weye and entree to oure saluacioun. And þerfore seiþ þe prophete *Beneplacitum est Domino super timentes eum* ⟨. . .⟩ *et in* ⟨*eis qui*⟩ *sperant super misericordia eius*: ⟨. . .⟩ it is plesid to þe Lord on hem þat dreden hym and in hem þat trusten on his mercy.

Þe secunde tyme we ben dettouris kyndely to oure spiriit, þe which is oure soule, in two þingis: oon is compassioun, as þe Wise Man seiþ 'Haue ruþe of þin owne soule bifore al þing plesynge God.' And þis dette we payen, folewynge þe comunycacioun of hooly lyueris in norishynge oure soule wiþ Goddis word, now in preiynge, now in redinge, now in heerynge, now in talkinge . . .

33 brouȝt] br *canc.*/brouȝt 35 *margin* Jon xiii[ 43 world] wo *canc.*// world 55 et] *word of three letters illegible before this* it] *word of about four letters illegible before this* 57 *margin* 2 62 in talkinge] *catchwords*

## Notes

**1** Romans 8:12–17; the wording *þis day* establishes the occasion of the sermon.

**3** Romans 8:12.

**5** Romans 8:14.

**6** The idea of Christ as *abbot* is not original to the Wycliffites, though it is developed by them in their polemic against human abbots and the superfluity of rules or orders established outside the overt commands of scripture (e.g. Wyclif *De civ. dom.* ii.165/38). Cf. *EWS* i.30/24 (where Vulgate *quia prior me erat* of John 1:30 is translated *for he was my priour*), 31/67, E32/16 (where Vulgate *quia me priorem vobis odio habuit* of John 15:18 is translated *wete ȝee þat it hatede me ȝoure priour*), ii.62/21. The admission of *hooly chirche* as *oure modir* marks the preacher as less extreme than, for instance, those Lollard commentaries on the ten commandments that do not extend the precept to honour parents to the spiritual parenthood of the church (as, for example, that in Arnold iii.86), or severely criticise the uncritical honour granted to this (as, for example, the unprinted commentary found in York Minster XVI.L.12, ff. $14^{v}$–$15^{v}$ and Harvard Eng.738, ff. 15–16).

**10** Romans 8:17.

**12** See, for example, *GO* on Romans 8:12, or William of St. Thierry PL 180.630–1.

**14** 1 Cor. 4:7.

**18** Isa. 42:8.

**20–8** For the basis of this rejection of images see Thorpe 1058ff and notes. Again here the technical terms are avoided, but *þat worship þat longiþ to him* is *latria*. The view of images as *bookis for mennys profiit* is a medieval commonplace (see note on Thorpe 1073). The frequent Lollard view of men, or often more specifically *poor men*, as the more proper recipient of honour than images (see note on Thorpe 1312–15) is reinforced here by the reference line 23 to the Pauline language of Col. 1:3–20.

**27** Augustine, cf. *De Consensu Evangelistarum* i.10 (PL 34.1049) and Gregory epistola 13 (PL 77.1128).

**30** Eccles. 12:13; the translation is not that of WB.

**35** John 14:21; the rendering is the same as that of WB.

**36** Augustine *Tractatus in Iohannem* 75.5 (PL 35.1830). The translation would be more accurate without the *and* between the two verbs in each clause (39–41).

**47** *fatuytee*: MED does not record the word; OED records it first from Bale and then in the 17th century.

**54** Ps. 146:11; not as WB.

**59** Ecclus. 30:24; not precisely as WB.

# APPENDIX II
# ADDITIONAL MATERIAL IN VP IN THORPE'S TESTIMONY

[The two Hussite manuscripts of Thorpe's text in general present a version of the material which is remarkably faithful to the version found in R, and in numerous readings may be preferred to it (see chapter 2.b above). But they make two substantial additions to the text as that appears in either R or A; it has been argued above (p. xxxviii) that these additions are not original to the text. For the sake of completeness, however, they are transcribed here. The text is printed from V, with only significant variants from P recorded in brackets after the word(s) in question; where V appears to be wrong, it has been corrected from P, and the rejected reading likewise is recorded in brackets.]

a. After *þerbi* 2151 VP add:
Quia manifesta falsitas negancium ueritatem Christi mouet non solum fideles sed eciam frequenter infideles sic timere et verecundari (P scandalisari) scandalosam negacionem uerbi Dei quod nituntur sic diligere ueritatem quam isti infideles relinquunt quod tunc (P sunt) per hoc conuersi ad ueritatem et facti eiusdem fortes amatores. Et sic qui per ante fuit impius et iniustus est, Dei gracia, deditus et tractus ueritati in loco ipsius qui ad tempus se iustum finxit. Quia, quamuis ita sit quod mundi amatores et carnales viatores per hoc sic tegantur (P cecantur) et indisponuntur (P disponuntur) in singulis suis sensibus ad cognoscendum effectualiter veritatem verbi Dei quod fortificant se resistere ueritati aperta, tyrranides et grandis malicia istorum inimicorum Christi continue plures et plures contra se commouent (V commouet) et accendunt. Quia magna tribulacione et forti persecucione tirranorum in tempore apostolorum discipuli Christi fuerunt continue acrescentes et iugiter (P ingenter) multiplicati; et sic continue fuit et erit et potissime in fine mundi, hic (P hoc est) in tempore antichristi quod nunc sine dubio est, nunc crudeliter inceptum in magnam confusionem (P *om.*) sui et omnium obediencium et sibi consenciencium. et in maximam gloriam Christi et suorum sequencium fidelium. Quia ecce Crisostomus, asimilans

ueritatem Christi (P Dei) redolentibus speciebus, dicit quod hec quanto species (P *adds* plus) territur tanto melius et remocius dat odorem. Sic quanto crudelius ueritas que est uera fides persequitur et tirranice opprimitur, tanto melius et distancius eius noticia declaratur.

b. After *lawe* 2221 VP add:
Quapropter, domine, dico (P *adds* nunc) vobis ex quo confirmastis istam sentenciam, dicendo hic iam nunc quod nemo tenetur obedire aliter alicui superiori quam hic recitaui vobis, admiror, domine, quare contra (V *om.*) concessum vestrum proprium (P *om.*) wltis petere a me aliquem submissionem nisi ostendatis mihi clare per auctoritatem verbi Dei quod ista submissio uel obediencia est licita et a Deo precepta. Et eciam, domine, ex quo (V usquo) absque ficcione aliqua dixi vobis plane meam fidem et meum sensum de quolibet puncto de quo opposuistis michi, et, benedictus (P *adds* ⌜sit⌝) Deus (P *adds* ⌜quod⌝) non per aliquam sufficientem auctoritatem inprobastis aliquem articulum fidei mee, nec aliquam responsionem mearum, admiror quare nitimini ut faciatis (P facitis) ad habendum me obedientem vestre ordinacioni ex quo non habetis nec, ut in Domino confido, aliquo tempore me conuincetis legitime per aliquam auctoritatem verbi Dei recte intellectam, nec in errorem nec heresi contra veram viam (P fidem). Et dum sic sto, sic in Deo confido semper stabo, inconuictus uel de heresi uel errore, non debetis, domine, iudicare me inobedientem nec contrarium vestre ordinacioni nec alicui legitime regule uel regimini (V regiminis) alicuius rationabilis creature. Quapropter, sicut supra scribitur plane in principio huius capitoli, quam sentenciam hic coram quatuor ex clericis vestris concessistis esse veram, iam sum paratus et semper propono esse paratus submittere me vobis, et cuilibet superiori, et aliter non cum Dei adiutorio dum uita mea et sensus mei simul durant. Quia pro certo, domine, usque ad finem uite mee propono plene ad laudem nominis Dei in predicacione mea si debeam (P *om.* si debeam) permitti sic facere et in mea communicacione priuata et aperta et in mea scriptura publicare (V publice) et referre illam altam ueritatem quam hic confirmastis plane et recte in confusionem omnium illorum qui in opere uel sermone nituntur negare aliquem punctum predicte confirmacionis. Quia, cum adiutorio Iesu Christi, ista predicta sentencia quam vos, domine, rationabiliter confirmastis, concedendo (V concedo) quemlibet punctum eiusdem esse verum erit mihi et multis aliis, per graciam Dei, baculus fortis ad sustinendum nos et

clarum speculum ad nos intuendum et secura uia ad ambulandum in ea et scutum securissime defensionis contra omnes illos qui nituntur petere aliquem aliam obedienciam quam potest fundari in eadem. Et, domine, non reputo vos ita inprouisum quando habetis bonam memoriam quomodo recitaui vobis istam predictam sentenciam, et quomodo concessistis et confirmastis quemlibet punctum eiusdem. Et ideo, ut cogitto in corde meo, ostendo (P ostendi) vobis oretenus ex quo absque auctoritate istius uere predicte sentencie et confirmate hic palam a vobis vos nitimini sic solicite ad faciendum me submittere (V *adds* me) vobis. Iudico quod tota solicitudo vestra circa (V *om.*) istud non est aliud nisi ad temptandam meam instabilitatem, quia si sine auctoritate istius (P illius) predicte sentencie uere approbate a vobis in quolibet puncto eius submittam me vobis, domine, uel alicui creature, in vestra noticia possetis me iuste culpare duobus modis: primo ideo quia allego vobis, domine, istam sentenciam habendo plenam confidentiam et veram fidem quod nec ego nec alius viuens tenetur obedire alicui creature nisi per auctoritatem (V auctoritates) illius uere predicte sentencie. Sed ex quo per ullam (P nullam) auctoritatem istius (P illius) sentencie vos probatis me esse obligatum ad obediendum vestre ordinancie, iudico ut predixi quod sollicitatis (V solicitans) vos ad temptandum meam instabilitatem. Secundo, domine, quia sine auctoritate illius predicte sentencie vere confirmate palam a vobis hic nitimini trahere et flectere me a meo proposito ad vestram voluntatem, iudico quod si consentirem vobis secundum vestram peticionem quod uelletis sicut (V sed) racionabiliter possetis reprehendere me tamquam despectorem vestre recte confirmacionis. Et ideo, domine, estimans quod uelitis bene preuideri de ista vera (P mea) sentencia, et eciam quod wltis memorari quomodo hic palam confirmastis quemlibet punctum eiusdem, propono adhuc expectare vestram voluntatem quocumque wltis acceptari (P acceptare) me per vnam uiam uel per aliam, estimans quod cum deliberacione per mocionem Sancti Spiritus et per vestrum proprium consilium tempore futuro omnibus malis consiliatoriis ammotis vos wltis bene preuideri (P *adds* tam dista sentencia) et de verba aperta (P vestra apta) et iusta confirmacione. Ideo, domine, ne Deum offendam et fortificem aliquem inimicum ueritatis nec discam fortem (P *gap instead of* discam fortem) aliquem amicum Christi, per graciam Spiritus Sancti propono plene per auctoritatem istius predicte uere (P *om.*) sentencie et confirmate palam a vobis habere eam semper meam defensionem et proteccionem contra omnes illos qui cupiunt aliquem obedienciam sine auctoritate illius plane ostensam (P ostensa) et quod debeam sic facere ueritas istius sentencie specialiter, et (V *om.*) vos, domine, qui confirmastis eam hic palam, eritis auctores mei quia cum adiutorio Dei sine auctoritate istius sentencie plane edocte ad meum intellectum numquam propono (P propone) obedire volenter nec scienter alicui creature.

# APPENDIX III
# ADDITIONAL MATERIAL IN THE [1530] PRINT OF THORPE'S TESTIMONY

## A. PREFATORY MATTER

[The significance of this material for the date and possible instigation of the print has been discussed above pp. xxx–xxxvii.]

[Title-page]: The examinacion of Master William Thorpe preste accused of heresye before Thomas Arundell/ Archebishop of Canturbury/ the yere of ower Lorde. M.CCCC. and seuen.

¶ The examinacion of the honorable knight syr Jhoñ Oldcastell Lorde Cobham/ burnt bi the said Archebisshop/ in the fyrste yere of Kynge Henry the fyfth.

¶ Be no more ashamed to heare it/ then ye were and be/ to do it.

[sig. A.1v] ¶ Vnto the Christen Reader.

Grace and peace in oure lorde Jesu Christe. Reade here with iudgemente goode reader the examinacion of the blssed man of god/ and there thou shalt easelye perceyue wherfore oure holy chirch ([1]as the most onholy sorte of all the people wilbe called) make all their examinacions in darkenes/ all the laye people cleane excluded from their councels. For yf their lies had ben openly confuted and also that the accused of heresye myghte as well haue ben admytted to reason their articles with councell/ whether they were heresye or no as the accused of treason agenst the king/ is admytted to his councell to confute his cause and articles whether they be treason or not/ they shulde neuer haue murthered nor prisoned so many good christen men as they haue done. For their cloked lyes coulde neuer haue contynued so long in the lighte/ as they haue done in corners. They good men when they/ come in the pulpet and preache agenst the treuth/ crye: Yf their lernynge were goode and trew/ they wold neuer go in corners. but speke it openly. Where vnto I answere that besyde

[1] ( *reversed*

that Christe and his apostles were compelled (for because of the furyousnes of their fathers the bishoppes and preastes) whiche onely that tyme also wolde [sig.A.2] be called holy chyrche) often tymes for to walke secretly/ and absent themself and geue place to their malice. yet we haue daylye examples off more then one or two/ that haue not spared nor feared for to speake and also preache opnlye the trouthe whiche haue ben taken of them prysoned and brent/ besyde other that for feare of deathe haue abiured and caryed fagottes.

Of whos articles and examinacion there ys no leye man that can shewe a worde. Who can tell wherfore (not many yeres paste) there were seuen burnt in conuentrye on one daye. Who can tell wherfore that good preaste and holye martyr Syr Thomas hitton was brente/ now thys yere/ at maydstone yn Kent. I am sure no man. For this is their caste euer when they haue put to deathe or punyshed any man/ after their secrete examynacyon/ to slaunder hym of soche thynges as he neuer thought. As they maye do well Inough: seynge there is no man to contrarye them. Wherfore I exhorte the good brother/ whosoeuer thou be that redest thys treatyse/ marke hit well and consyder it seryouslye/ and there thou shalt fynde not onelye what the chyrche ys/ theyre doctryne of the Sacramente/ the worshyppynge off ymagyes/ pylgremage/ confessyon/ Swerynge and payinge of tythes. But also thou mayst se what stronge and substancyall argumentes off scripture and doctoures/ and what clerkely reasons/ my lorde/ the [sig.A.2v] hedde and prymate of the holye chyrche in England (as he wilbe taken) bryngeth agenst this pore/ folysh/ symple/ and madde losell/ knave/ and heretike as he calleth hym. And also the verye cause wherfore all their examynacions are made in darkenes. And the lorde of all lyght shall lighten the with the candle of his grace/ for to se the trewth. Amen.

¶This I haue corrected and put forth in the english that now is vsed in Englande/ for ower sothern men/ nothynge therto addynge ne yet therfrom mynysshyng. And I entende hereafter with the helpe of God to put it forthe in his owne olde english/ which shal well serue/ I doute not/ bothe for the northern men and the faythfull brothern of scotlande.

## Notes

**35** For the seven burned in Coventry in 1519 see Foxe iv.557–8; an eighth was burned two years later in 1521. The earlier history of these Lollards appears in the Lichfield courtbook of 1511–12, Lichfield Episcopal Archives MS B.C.13, on which see J. Fines, 'Heresy Trials in the Diocese of Coventry and Lichfield, 1511–12', *JEH* 14 (1963), 160–74.

**36** Sir Thomas More states in his *Confutation of Tyndale's Answer* (CW 8, p. 11/24 and cf. p. 13/28) that the heretics have 'in theyr calendar . . . a new saynt / syr Thomas Hitton the heretyke that was burned in Kent . . . Hym haue they set in on saynt Mathy is euen, be the name of saynt Thomas the martyr.' The *Confutation* was probably written in late 1531, and the whole published in 1532–3 (p. 1419), and the *calendar* seems to refer to the *Ortulus anime* (1530). Hitton was burned at Maidstone in late February 1530. Most of what we know of Hitton derives from More's hostile account in the *Confutation* pp. 13/22–17/16.

**54–9** Presumably this rather obscure comment acknowledges that the language of the print is modernized to a large extent from the manuscript exemplar. If the *olde english* of that exemplar were similar to the language of R, it would hardly have helped a sixteenth-century audience in the north of England or Scotland; but see above p. lix–lx for slight hints that the exemplar of the print was in a more northerly dialect. For the Lollard heresy in the north and Scotland see Thomson pp. 192–210, *PR* pp. 126–7 and references there given. Foxe's material on the trial for heresy and burning of Patrick Hamilton in St. Andrew's in 1527, together with Firth's translation of his work, *Patrick's Places*, follows straight on from the case of the Coventry heretics mentioned in line 35 (iv.558–80).

## B. THE TESTAMENTE OF WILLIAM THORPE

[This epilogue appears only in A, and in the sixteenth-century texts that derive from it.[1] The absence from VP, the two Latin manuscripts, may not be significant: they also lack the *prolog*, concerning whose authenticity there seems no room for doubt. It has been argued above (pp. xxxii–xxxiii) that R is unlikely ever to have contained it, though formal proof is not available.

Quite apart from the manuscript evidence and the possibility that

[1] Whether Bale included it in his addition to the manuscript of *Fasciculi Zizaniorum* is impossible to ascertain, since the text of the trial itself now ends incomplete. It appears in all Foxe's versions of Thorpe (see above pp. xxxii–xxxiii).

Thorpe left England not long after his meeting with Arundel (above pp. lii–liii), there are other internal difficulties in accepting the *Testamente* as part of the original text. The colophon in A, the sole authority for it, gives a date of 1460 to it. Thorpe's trial before Arundel is dated by him as having occurred in 1407; since that trial ends with neither verdict nor indication of future procedure, it is credible (despite the colophon in R 161–2, see above p. lii) that the account was written that same or the following year and quite certain that it was written within at most ten years of the event it records. The *Testamente* cannot therefore have been part of it, unless its own colophon is incorrect; it must have been added to it after 1460.

The question still remains, however, of whether the *Testamente* could be a later writing of Thorpe's, appended to the earlier either by the [1530] printer or by a late fifteenth-century scribe whose manuscript was his exemplar. But there is first a problem to be faced in that the only connection of the *Testamente* with Thorpe is furnished by the colophon: if that is unreliable, then the rest could be the writing of any fifteenth-century Lollard. The implications for Thorpe's life of accepting the 1460 date are difficult. If Thorpe's statements in his main text are reliable (and the reasons for accepting this have been set out in the introduction), he must have been in Oxford by 1381–2 at the very latest; he is unlikely at that time to have been less than fifteen to seventeen years old and probably (given his comments in lines 440–59) twenty or more.[1] It would seem likely therefore that Thorpe must have been born at the latest in 1365. He would thus have been 95 in 1460, an improbable age at that period, and one that might well have excited remark within the *Testamente* or in an authentic colophon. Even if Thorpe's claims to have known Wyclif, and early followers such as Repingdon before their defection, are dismissed as exaggerated, acceptance of a date of 1460 for a work by him is not easy. Using only evidence outside the autobiographical account of the trial, Thorpe must have been at least 25 by 1382–6 when he was in trouble, as a *capellanus ... pretensus*, with Braybrooke (above pp. xlviii–xlix); the objection to Thorpe is nowhere there said to include his being under age for ordination. It seems fair to assume that the date in the colophon cannot be accepted.

Even if the colophon is unreliable, its date perhaps deriving from a

[1] For the usual age at which boys reached Oxford see A. B. Cobban, *The Medieval English Universities: Oxford and Cambridge to c.1500* (Aldershot, 1988), pp. 351–3.

misunderstanding of a scribe's dating of his copy as if it were the date of the text copied, could the *Testamente* notwithstanding be a work of Thorpe written after the main text here but substantially earlier than 1460? The main beliefs declared in the *Testamente* are condemnations of the ecclesiastical hierarchy of the day and of the practices of most of the lower clergy; to the faults of the priesthood the writer attributes all the ills of the present, including morrain and pestilence. These opinions are not out of line with those which Thorpe put forward in his trial—but nor are they out of line with the views of most Lollards or Lutherans from the 1380s to the 1530s. The only individualising detail, and that of a fairly vague sort, is the declared willingness of the author to undergo physical torment in defence of his beliefs. There seems nothing in the ideas or in the phrasing distinctive enough to link the *Testamente* certainly with Thorpe's longer work. It was observed above that there is a generic similarity between the methods of argument and alleged submission in the document Thorpe wrote in answer to Braybroke's charges and those in his later account of his own trial before Arundel.[1] The same sort of parallel cannot be made in regard to the *Testamente*. In this, apart from one reference to canon law, only biblical citation is used and little coherent argument; there is no profession, however hedged about, of willingness to submit to authority. Any argument from language is faced with the difficulty that the sixteenth-century edition or its exemplar manifestly modernized fifteenth-century idiom in the trial; absence of earlier Lollard language or presence of apparently later vocabulary cannot therfore decide the issue of the *Testamente*'s antiquity. So far as the evidence is worth, it may be said that the *Testamente* contains a few typical Lollard idioms, but also contains a few words, notably *lounderers* and *cokir noses*, which from the evidence of MED and OED are very uncommon in the Middle English period.[2] A misunderstanding of the typical Lollard *strong beggars*, i.e. friars, is seen where at line 123 the printer has given *straunge beggers*. But this does not help towards the attribution of the *Testamente*.

The *Testamente* is included here in an appendix because of the uncertainty of its origin. My own view is that any connection with Thorpe is probably mistaken, and derives from the occurrence of the text without author's name in a manuscript, following Thorpe's 1407

[1] See above p. xlviii.

[2] Lines 109 and 112; neither word is recorded by MED, whilst in the OED this text is the only evidence for the second and one of only two (the other being Wyntoun's *Chronicle*) for the first word.

trial account, from which it was copied or printed with erroneous connection to the foregoing material.]

(sig. G.6) Thus endeth the examynacion of Master Wyllyam Thorpe. And here after foloweth hys testamente.

Mathew an apostle of Christe and his gospeler witnessith truly in the holy gospell the moste holy lyuynge and the moste holsome teaching of christe. He rehersith how that Christe likeneth them that heare his wordis and kepe them/ to a wyse man that bildeth his house vpon a stone/ that is a stable and a sadde grounde. This house is mannis soule in whome Christe deliteth to dwell/ if it be grounded that is stablisshed feithfully in his lyuyng and in his trewe teaching/ adourned or made fayre with diuerse vertues/ which Christe vsed and taucht without ony medlyng of ony errour/ as ar chefely the condicions of charite. This forsaid stone is Christe vpon which euery feithfull soule must be bylded/ syns vpon none other grounde than vpon Christis lyuyng and his teaching no body may make eny byldyng or housyng/ wherein Christe will come and dwell This sentence witnesseth seynt Paul to the corinthians shewing to them that no body may sett ony other grounde than is sett/ þt is Christis lyuyng and his teaching. And because þt all men and women sholde gyue all their besynesse here in (sig.G.6v) this lyfe to bylde them vertuously vpon this sure foundacion: seynt Paul knouleging the feruent desyre and the goode will of the people of Ephesy wrote to them comfortably sayng: Now ye ar not straungeris/ gestis/ nor yet comelingis but ye ar the citezyns and of the housholde of god/ byldyd aboue vpon the foundament of the apostles and prophetis. In which foundament euery byldyng that is byldyd or made thorow the grace of god/ it encreaseth or growith into an holy temple: that is/ euery body/ that is grounded or bylded feithfully in the teaching and lyuyng of Christe is there thorow made the holy temple of god. This is the stable grounde and stedfaste stone Christe/ which is the sure corner stone faste ioynyng and holdyng myghtely togither two wallis. For thorow Christe Jesu meane or middill persone of the trinite/ the father of heuen is pituous or mercifully ioynyd and made one togither to mankynde. And thorow dreade to offende god/ and feruent looue to please hym/ men be vnseparably made one to god and defended surely vnder his proteccion. Also this forsaid stone Christe was figured by the square stones of which the temple of god was made. For as a square stone/

wher soeuer it is caste or layde/ it abydeth and lieth stabely: so Christe and euery feithfull membre of his chirche by example of hym abydeth and dwellith stabely in true faithe/ and in all other heuenly vertues in all aduersites that they suffer in this valley (sig.G.7) of tearis. For lo/ whan thes forsaid square stones wer hewen and wroughte for to be layde in the wallis or pillers of goddis temple none noyse or stroke of the workemen was harde. Certein this silence in workyng of this stone figureth Christe chefely and his feithfull membres/ which by example of hym haue ben and yet ar/ and euer to the worldis ende shall be so meke and pacient in euery aduersite that no sounde nor yet ony grudging shall ony tyme be perceiued in them Neuerthelesse this chefe and most worshipfull cornerstone whiche onely is grounde of all vertues proude beggers repreuyd: but this despite and reprefe Christe sufferid moste mekely in his owne person for to gyue example of all mekenesse and pacience to all his feithfull folowers. Certeyn this worlde is now so full of proude beggers which ar namyd priestis: but the very office of workyng of priesthode/ which Christe approuyth trewe and acceptith/ is farre fro the multitude of priestis that now reigne in this worlde. For fro the hyest prieste to the lowest/ all (as who say) studie/ that is they ymagine and trauell besely/ how they may please this worlde and their flessch. This sentence and many soch other dependeth vpon them if it be well considered/ other god the father of heuen hath deceiuyd all mankynde by the liuyng specially and teaching of Jesu Christe/ and by the liuyng and teaching of his apostles and prophetis: or els all the popys þt haue ben/ syns I hadde ony knowlege or discretion/ (sig.G.7v) with all the college of Cardinallis Archebishopis and bisshopis/ Monkys chanons and friers with all the contagious flocke of the comunaltie of priesthode whych haue all my lyfe tyme and mekell lenger reigned and yet reigne and encrease dampnably fro synne into synne/ haue bene and yet be proude/ obstinate heretikes/ couetous symoners and defoulyd aduulterers in þe ministring of the sacramentis/ and specially yn ministryng of the sacrament of the altare. For as their workys shewe wherto Christe biddeth vs take hede/ the hyest priestis and prelatis of this priesthode chalenge and occupie vnlefully temporall lordeshippes. And for temporall fauour and mende they sell and gyue benefices to vnworthy and vnable persones/ ye thes symoners sell synne sufferyng men and women in euery degre and estate to lye and continew fro yeare to yeare in diuerse vices sclaunderously. And thus by euill example of hye priestis in the chirche/ lower priestis vnder them ar not onely suffered/ but they ar maynteined to sell full dere to þ$^{e}$ people for temporall mede all þ$^{e}$ sacramentis. And thus all this forsaid priesthode is blowen so hye and borne vp in pride and vayn glorie of their estate and dignite/ and so blindid with worldly couetousnesse þ$^{t}$ they disdeyne to folow Christe in very mekenesse and wilfull pouerte lyuyng holily/ and preaching goddis worde treuly frely and contineually/ takyng their lyuelode at the fre will of þ$^{e}$ people of their pure almose/ where and whan they suffyse not for their trewe and besy (sig.G.8) preaching to gett their sustenaunce with their handis. To this trew sentence grounded on Christis owne liuyng and teaching of his apostles/ thes forsaid worldly and fleschly priestis will not consente effectually. But as their werkys and also their wordis shewe/ boldeli and vnshamefastly thes forsaid named priestis and prelatis couett/ and enforse them mightely and besely þ$^{t}$ all holy scripture wer expoundid and drawne accordingly to their maners and to their vngroundid vsagis and fyndyngis. For they will not (syns they holde it but foly and madnesse) comforme their maners to the pure and symple liuyng of Christe and his apostles/ nor they will not folow frely their learnyng. Wherfore all the emperours and kynges/ and all other lordis and ladies/ and all the comon people in euery degre and state/ which haue before tyme knowen or myght haue knowen/ and also all they that now yet knowe or myght knowe this forsaid witnesse of priesthode/ and wolde not nor yet will enforce them after their connyng and power to withstonde charitably the forsaid enemyes and traitours of Christe and of his chirche all thes stryue with Antechriste ageinst Jesu And they shall beare the indignacion of god almightie withouten ende/ if in conuenient tyme they amende them not/ and repente them verely doyng therfore dew moornyng and sorow after their connyng and power. For thorow presumptuousnes and necligence of priestis and prelatis (not of the chirche of Christe/ but occupiyng their pre(sig.G.8v)lacy vndewly in the chirche and also by flateryng and false couetousnes of other diuerse namyd priestis) lousengers and lounderers ar wrongfull made and named heremites/ and haue leue to defraude poore and nedy creatures of their lyuelode/ and to lyue by their false winnyng and begging in slouthe and in other diuerse vyces. And also of thes prelates thes cokir noses ar suffered to lyue in pride and hypocresy / and to defoull themself both bodely and gostely. Also by the sufferyng and counsell of thes forsaid prelatis and of other priestis/ ar made vayne both brotherhodis and susterhodis full of pride and enuye/ which ar full contrarie to the brotherhode of

Christe/ syns they ar cause of mekill dissension/ and they multiplie and susteyne it vncharitably: for in lusty eatyng and drinkyng vnmesurably and out of tyme they exercyse themself. Also this vayne confederacye of brotherhodis/ is permitted to be of one clothyng and to holde togither. And in all thes vngrounded and vnlefull doynges/ priestis ar parteners and[1] greate meddelers and counsellers And ouer this viciousnes/ heremitis and pardoners/ ankers and straunge beggers ar licensed and admitted of prelatis and priestis for to begyle the people with flateringis and leasingis sclaunderously ageinst all goode reason and trewe beleue/ and so to encrease diuerse vices in themself and also among all them that accepte them or consente to them. And thus the viciousnes of thes forsaid named priestis and prelatis haue ben long tyme/ and yet is/ and shall be (sig.H.i) cause of warres both within þe realme and without. And in the same wise thes vnable priestes haue bene/ and yet are/ and shall be chefe cause of pestilence of men/ and moren of beestes/ and of barenesse of the erthe/ and of all other mischefes/ to the tyme þt lordes and comons able them thorow grace for to knowe and to kepe the commaundementes of god/ enforsyng them than feithfully and charitably by one assente for to redresse and make one this forsaid priesthode to the wilfull/ pore/ meke/ and innocent lyuyng and teaching specially of Christe and his apostles. Therfore all they that knowe or myght knowe the viciousnes that reigneth now cursedly in thes priestes and in their learning/ yf they suffyse not to vnderstond this contagious viciousnes: let them praye to the lorde hartely for the health of his chirche/ absteyning them prudently fro thes endured enemies of Christe and of his people/ and frome all their sacramentes/ syns to them all that knowe them or maye knowe they are but fleschely deades and false: as seynt Cipriane witnesseth in the first question of decrees/ and in the firste cause. Ca. Si quis inquit. For as this seynte and great doctours witnesse there/ that not onely vicious priestes. but also all they that fauoure them or consente to them in theire viciousnes shall togither perisshe with them yf they amende them not dewly: as all they perished that consented to Dathan and Abijron. For nothing wer more confusyon to thes forsaide vicious priestes/ than to eschewe them prudently in all their vnlefull sa(sig.H.iv)cramentes/ while they continew in their synfull lyuyng slaunderously/ as they haue longe tyme done and yet do. And no dody (*sic*) nede to be afraide (though

[1] and] and/and

dethe did folow by one wise or other) for to dye out of this worlde without takyng of ony sacrament of these forsaid christes enemies/ syns christe will not faile for to ministre himselfe all lefull and healfull sacramentes and necessarye at all tyme/ and specially at the ende/ to all them that are in trewe feyth/ in stedfaste hope/ and in perfyte charite. But yet some mad foolis saye for to eschewe slaunder/ they will be shriuen ones in the yeare and comuned of theire proper priestes/ though they knowe them defouled with slaunderous vices. No doute but all thei that thus do or consente priuely or apertly to soch doynge ar culpable of great synne/ syns seynt Paul witnesseth that not only they that do euyll are worthy of dethe and dampnacion: but also they that consente to euyll doars. Also (as their slaunderouse workes witnesse) thes forsaid vicious priestes despyce and caste from them heuenly connyng that is gyuen of the holy goste. Wherfore the lorde throweth all soche despisers frome hym that they vse nor do ony priesthode to hym. No doute than all they that wittingly or wilfully take or consente þt any other bodye sholde take/ ony sacrament of ony soche named prieste/ synneth openly and dampnably ageynst all the trinite and ar vnable to ony sacrament of healthe. And that this forsayde sentence is all togither trewe/ into re(sig.H.2)mission of all my synfull lyuyng trustinge stedfastly in the mercy of god I offer to him my soule. And to proue also this forsaid sentence trewe with the helpe of god I purpose fully for to suffer mekely and gladly my moste wretched body to be tormented/ where god will and of whome he will/ how he will/ and whan he will/ and as longe as he will/ and what temporall peyne he will and dethe/ to the praising of his name and to the edificacion of his churche. And I that am moste vnworthy and wretched caytyf shall now thorow the speciall grace of god make to him plesaunte sacrifice with my moste synfull and vnworthy body. I beseche hartly all folke that rede or heare this ende of my purposed testament/ that thorowe the grace of god they dispose verely and vertuously all their wittes/ and able in like maner all theire membres for to vnderstonde truely and to kepe feythfully charitably and continually all the commaundementes of god/ and so than to pray deuoutly to all the blessed trinyte/ that I maye haue grace with wisdome and prudence frome aboue/ to ende my lyfe here in this forsaid truethe and for this cause/ in true feith and stedfaste hope and in perfite charite. AMEN.

(sig.H.2v) Here endeth sir William Thorpis testament on the friday after the rode daye and the twentye daye of September/ In the yeare of our lorde a thousand foure hundred and sixtie. And on the sonday nexte after the feste of seynt Peter that we call Lammesse daye in the yeare of our lorde a thousand/ foure hundrth and seuen/ the said sir William was accused of thes poyntes before writen in this booke before Thomas of Arundell Archebishoppe of Canterbury as it is sayde before. And so was it than betwixt the day of his accusing and the daye that this was wryten three and fiftye yeare and as mekill more as fro the Lammesse to the wodemesse. Beholde the ende.

¶The strengeth of euery tale is in the ende.

¶ Here folowethe the Examinacion of the Lorde Cobham.

## Notes

**5** Matt. 7:24.

**16** 1 Cor. 3:11.

**22** Eph. 2:19–21.

**35** Cf. Eze. 43:13–17, 3 Kgs. 6:2–6.

**40** 3 Kgs. 6:7.

**46** Eph. 2:20; cf. Matt. 21:42.

**145** *Decr*. II C.1 q.1 c.70 (Friedberg i.382) from a letter of Cyprian.

**150** Num. 16:12–35.

**165** Rom. 1:32.

**202** *wodemesse*: Holy Rood Day (see line 194). OED does not include the word.

# GLOSSARY

The Glossary is a select one, intended to provide a guide for readers accustomed to Chaucerian English. Line references prefixed with T refer to the Taylor sermon, whilst those without any prefixed letter refer to the Thorpe text; those prefixed by H refer to the sermon of the Horsedoun in appendix I. The actual forms found in the two texts are entered, not hypothetical infinitives etc. The commonest spelling is treated as the head word; variant spellings or forms that are not easily referable to a head word are entered in their alphabetical place with a cross reference. Where the infinitive of a verb is found, other parts of the verb are only given in the case of strong verbs or in weak verbs where any difficulty may arise; where the verbal forms do not include the infinitive, a full list of forms is included. Normal abbreviations for grammatical terms are used.

Words are only glossed if their meaning departs from that of modern English, or if their form within the texts is likely to cause difficulties of recognition; thus, when one Middle English sense of a word here coincides with modern English, but another does not, only the second is regularly included here. Hence the material under each head-word is not necessarily a full inventory of either paradigms or senses in the texts (e.g. a full repertory of the verb *be* is not given). Phrases likely to cause difficulty are entered under the word within them that departs from its normal sense.

Throughout *i/y* variation is included under *i*; *ȝ* follows *g*, *þ* follows *t*. The scribes normally use *v* initially, *u* medially for both the consonant and the vowel: in the glossary these are sorted into modern usage.

**abeggid**, *adv. go* . . . ~ go begging T481
**abiect**, *adj.* wretched T569
**able**, *adj.* ~ *for to* qualified to 753
**ablen**, *v.* ~ *refl...to*, prepare self to 60, 85, 101 etc.; **ablynge** *pres. p.* preparing 95, 1245
**ablyndid**, *v. pa. p.* misled T610
**aboden**, *pl. pa. ind.* suffered 1268
**aboundaunce**, *sb.* plentifulness T164
**accepcioun**, *sb.* condition 2073
**accepte(n**, *v.* accept, approve 568, 721, 1278 etc.
**acordinge**, *adj. moost* ~ *lore to* teaching most in accordance with 565
**acordingli**, *adv.* in agreement 570, 833, 982 etc.; ~ *as* in the same fashion as 2066
**acordiþ**, *3 sg. pres. ind.* (**acorden** *pl. pres. ind.*, **acordinge** *pres. p.*) agree 342, 363, 895 etc.; ~ *to* agree with T261, 327, is suitable for 386
**acumbre**, *v.* ~ *in/wiþ* encumber with, embroil in T65, T88, T130 etc.
**admitte**, *v.* admit, approve 326, 745
**affeccioun**, *sb.* ~ *in hem* inclination towards them 1861
**affiaunce**, *sb.* trust 488
**afore**, *adv.* previously T636
**aftir**, *prep.* according to T711, 1536
**aftir-comers**, *sb.pl.* successors 239
**agast**, *v. pa. p.* frightened 413, perplexed 1706
**agrigginge**, *sb.* burdening 2244
**aȝenbeie**, *v.* redeem 158
**aȝens**, *prep.* against T74, 77 etc., with regard to T628
**aȝenseie**, *v.* contradict, deny 139, 1711, refuse 2206
**aȝenstonde**, *v.* oppose 139
**aȝenward**, *adv.* on the contrary, to the contrary 673, 779, 1279 etc., again 1890
**aylastynge**, *adv.* everlastingly H41
**aking**, *sb.* aching T287
**al**, *adv.* ~ *oon* the same thing 1026
**alegge** *v.* (**aleyde** *sg. pa. ind.*, **aleggid** *pa. p.*) adduce as proof T464, 920, 1727
**aleggeaunces**, *sb.pl.* citations of authorities 839
**alyened**, *v.pa. p.* removed 2107
**almesdede**, *sb.* giving of alms T342
**aloone**, *adv.* only 1777
**also**, *adv.* just as T408

**altogidre**, *adv*. completely 421
**amendement**, *sb*. amendment T167, betterment 2133, ~ *of* remedy for T214
**amonestynge**, *v. pres. p*. urging 1688
**and**, *cj*. if T610
**anentis**, *prep*. concerning 992
**angrid**, *v. pa. p*. annoyed 2076
**angwysschis**, *sb.pl*. ~ *ben to me* griefs beset me 367
**anoon**, *adv*. immediately T81, T559, 407 etc., quickly 618
**answere**, *sb*. *at his* ~ on trial 1987
**apaiede**, **apay(e)d**, *pa. p. adj*. satisfied T238, T374, 1859
**apeert**, *adv*. openly 1901
**apeertli**, *adv*. openly 112, 352, 638 etc.
**apelour**, *sb*. accuser 371
**aperte**, *adj*. open, plain 2053
**ap(p)osynge**, *sb*. questioning 26, 34, 109
**apostasie**, *sb*. apostasy, abandonment of faith 2144
**appetiit**, *sb*. desire, longing T110, T319
**appose**, *v*. question 136, 161, 925 etc.
**appropren**, *v*. appropriate T595
**ap(p)reue**, *v*. approve, authorise 599, 791 etc., prove 717
**araye**, *v*. ~ *hem* arrange for them T611; **arayed** *pa. p*. clothed T201, 1591, prepared T369, T448, T622
**areren**, *v. pres. pl. ind*. raise up T202
**asaie**, *v*. try, test 64, 2169; **asaien** *pres. pl. ind*. find out by examination 1415; **assaied** *pa. p*. investigated 1282
**ascape**, *v*. escape responsibility T496
**aschamed**, *pa. p. adj*. ashamed 636
**aseeþ**, *sb*. satisfaction, atonement 1925
**as(s)oile**, *v*. absolve 438, 1882, 1884 etc.
**asoylynge**, *sb*. absolution 1910
**aspie**, *sb*. spy 371
**astonyed**, *pa. p. adj*. astonished, perplexed 104, 1830
**aswagiþ**, *v. 3sg. pres. ind*. alleviate T286
**at**, *prep*. in 1183
**audience**, *sb*. hearing 196
**autetike**, *adj*. authoritative 1010, 1745
**au(c)tour**, *sb*. author 982, originator 598; *pl*. teachers T324
**auarous(e**, *adj*. avaricious T357, 1456
**auaunce**, *v*. advance T547; **avaunsid** *pa. p*. promoted, given a benefice 544
**avise**, *v. imp.sg*. ~ *þee* take heed for yourself 2074; *I am not avisid* I am not aware T499, T667
**auoutrie**, *sb*. adultery, hence moral adultery T194, T631, T638
**avow**, *sb*. vow 1116
**avowe**, *v*. make vow 1193
**avowtereris**, *sb.pl*. adulterers 1206
**aweyward**, *adv*. in the opposite direction T304, 2190
**axe**, *v*. ask, demand, require T27, T38, 40 etc.
**axinge**, *sb*. request, question 1029, 1830, 1843

**bad(de**, *v. 3sg. pa. ind*. ordered 1697, 2213, 2233
**bailyes**, *sb. gen. sg. and pl*. king's officer in town 619, 644
**bareyn**, *adj*. unproductive T538
**beestly**, *adj*. brutish 1922
**ben**, *v. pl. pres. ind*. are T204, T211; **be** *pa. p*. been T543, T545
**bernes**, *sb. pl*. barns T364, T373, T441
**beþinke**, **biþinke**, *v*. (**biþouȝt** *pa. p.*) *with refl*. recollect 1869, consider 2085, *art þou* ~ have you decided? 435
**better**, *comp. adj*. *ȝou were* ~ it would be better for you 939, 943
**betwexe**, **bitwixe**, *prep*. between 251, 702
**bi**, *prep*. with T438, through 238, ~ *placis* in various places T726
**bie**, **bigge**, *v*. buy T613, T642, redeem T722
**bifel(le(n**, *v. pt. ind. and sj*. turned out, happened 21, 24, 1358
**biggeris**, *sb. pl*. buyers T334
**bigylid**, *pa. p. adj*. misled, deluded T700
**bihalue**, *sb*. *on Goddis* ~ for God's sake 33, *on her* ~ for their sake 636
**biheeste**, *sb*. pledge 1673, *lond of* ~ promised land T302
**biho(o)lde**, *v*. (**biheeld** *sg. pt.ind.*) behold 415, 1110, 1157
**bihotiþ**, *v. 3sg. pres. ind*., **bihotinge** *pres. p*., **behiȝt(e** *pt.ind*., **bihoten** *pa. p*. promise T343, T517, 191 etc.
**bihoued**, *v. 3sg. pret.ind*. *me* . . . ~ it was necessary for me 427
**bildyng**, *sb*. building T560, T564, T566
**bile(e)ue**, *sb*. faith T624, 164, 378 etc.
**bilyȝe**, *v*. slander T643
**bilongiþ**, *v. 3sg. pres. ind*. pertains T118, ~ *not us* it is not right for us T447
**bimadden**, *v. pl. pres. ind*. enrage T604

**bynden**, *v.* (**bounden** *pl. pret.ind.*, **bounden** *pa. p.*) bind 248, oblige T40, T42, condemn 1902, refuse to absolve 1910
**bynding(e**, *sb.* condemnation (i.e. refusal to give absolution) T249, 1909
**bineþe**, *prep.* subordinate to 993
**bineþ(e)forþ**, *adv.* below 2, 19, 167
**birie**, *v.* (**biried** *pa. p.*) bury T349, T489, 266 etc.
**bisi**, *adj.* assiduous T20
**biside**, *prep.* against T587
**bisie(n**, *v.* endeavour 1144, *with refl.pron.* exert self T248, 36, 40, 57 etc.
**bisily**, *adv.* eagerly T29
**bisinesse**, *sb.* eagerness 183, 735
**bisottid**, *v. pa. p.* besotted, made foolish T111
**bitakun**, *v. pa. p and pa. p.adj.* entrusted T210, T470
**biþinke, biþouȝt** *see* **beþinke**
**bitide**, *v.* (**betidde, bitidde** *pa. ind. and pa. p.*) happen, occur T37, T251, T439 etc.; *it ~ þee* it should happen to you T449; *~ of* become of T346, T370
**blame**, *sb.* blame, condemnation 510, 1717, 1747
**blame**, *v.* condemn, blame, reproach T198, T527, 865 etc., *is to ~* is to be condemned 827, 1749
**blamfulli**, *adv.* reprehensibly 1306
**blew**, *adj.* russet 1593 (*see note*)
**blyndelyngis**, *adv.* blindfold 536
**boistous**, *adj.* ignorant T743
**boncheef**, *sb.* good fortune, *for ~ or myscheef* for good or ill 396
**bood**, *v. 3sg. pa. ind.* waited T721
**book-ooþ**, *sb.* oath sworn on bible 1674, 1676
**boond**, *sb.* obligation, legal constraint T45, **bo(o)ndis** *pl.* limits, bounds 509, 756
**bostinge**, *sb.* boasting 820
**bradder**, *adv. comp.* more widely T166
**brake**, *v. 3sg. pa. ind.* broke 962
**brenne**, *v.* burn T360, 417, 2082 etc.
**brennynge**, *sb.* burning 1556
**brouȝt**, *v. pa. p.* *~ forþ* despatched 1341
**but**, *cj.* unless 75, 755; *~ if* unless T386, 549
**bux(s)um, buxom** *adj.* submissive, humble 323, 329, 330 etc.
**caas**, *sb.* situation T371, 1631, 1638; *in ~* perhaps 1096
**calengen**, *v. pl. pres. ind.*, **calengiden** *pl. pa. ind.* demand, claim 1480, 1550, 1559 etc.
**can** see **cunne**
**caproun-hardi**, *adj.* bold as brass 1962 (*see note*)
**cece**, *v.* come to an end T719, stop T32
**certeyn**, *adv.* indeed T63, T188
**certificacioun**, *sb.* official notification 924, 928, 1229
**certificat**, *sb.* official notification 618
**certified, sertefied**, *v. pa. p.* reported officially 637, 926, 930 etc.
**certis, sertis**, *adv.* indeed T181, T423, 90 etc.
**chanoun**, *sb.* canon (i.e. Augustinian canon) 573, 602, 605
**charge**, *sb.* responsibility T575, 456, 1580, importance T18, T342, burden 1506, command 1667, 1669, 1671 etc., obligation 1764
**charge**, *v.* command 191, 1666, 1744 etc., burden 1459, impose responsibility upon T511, regard as important T17, T143, T146, 1860 etc.
**chargeous(e**, *adj.* burdensome T593, 1453
**cheere**, *sb.* *heuy ~* gloomy countenance 448
**che(e)f(f)li**, *adv.* especially, primarily 11, 284, 533 etc.
**cheritable**, *adj.* benevolent 44
**cheritabli**, *adv.* in charity 65
**chese**, *v.* (**chees** *sg. pa. ind.*) choose 382, 578, 594
**cheuely**, *adv.* especially 1973
**cheuyshaunce**, *sb.* profit T422, *newe ~* new profit, as euphemism for usury T418, T423
**chynche**, *sb.* niggard T447, T450, T489
**circumcidid**, *v. pa. p.* circumcised 215
**citeseyns**, *sb. pl.* inhabitants T242
**clamerous**, *adj.* clamarous, insistent T589, T673
**clarioneris**, *sb.pl.* trumpeters 1328
**clause**, *sb.* section 1701
**clene**, *adv.* fully 1939, 1959, 2099
**clepe**, *v.* call T260, T638, 168 etc., summon 2181
**clerk**, *sb.* ecclesiastic T380, T448 etc.
**cleuen**, *v. pl. pres. ind.* adhere T255

**closen**, *v. pl. pres. ind.* shut up T253
**closet**, *sb.* private chamber 173, 175
**closing**, *sb.* shutting up (of city) T250, T251
**cockil**, *sb.* cockle (trans. Vulg. *zizania*, prob. darnel) 1958
**colect**, *sb.* collection T514 (cf. **quyletis**)
**colour**, *sb.* guise, pretext T493
**coloure**, *v.* make falsely acceptable T607, T659
**colourid**, *pa. p. adj.* disguised T425
**comente, comyntee**, *sb.* citizens T239, T510, community T571, 10
**comyn, comoun** common T530, 472; ~ *lawe* common law of the church, i.e. canon law 852, 1176, 1493
**comyne, comoune, comowne** *v.* communicate, converse 561, 577 etc., partake T61, study T740
**comynge**, *v. pres. p. to* ~ to come T15, T213, T445; ~ *þe truþe* when truth has come T666
**comynyng, comunyng, comownynge**, *sb.* conversation T626, T630, 1579 etc.
**comouns**, *sb.pl.* common people 645, 1583, 1587
**comounte, comunte(e**, *sb.* community T222, 644, 692 etc.
**competent**, *adj.* adequate T605
**competently**, *adv.* adequately T415
**compilid**, *pa. p. adj.* ~ *togidere* put together 337
**comun**, *v. pa. p.* come T281
**concludid**, *v. 3sg. pa. ind. and pa. p.* refuted 228, 1038
**condicioun**, *sb. in* ~ in mode of behaviour T281
**confederacie**, *sb.* alliance, gang (derogatory) T263
**confed(e)ren**, *v. pl. pres. ind.* ~ *to hem* make accomplices with themselves T475; **confedrid** *pa. p.* allied, come into a conspiracy 1574, 2153
**conferme**, *v.* conform 569
**conforte**, *v.* inspire 425, encourage 1131, 1889, comfort 2101, strengthen 2239
**conne** *see* **cunne**
**conseit**, *sb.* opinion 1957
**conseyue**, *v.* understand T38
**consenten**, *v.* submit 384
**consentynge**, *sb.* consent 801
**constable**, *sb.* warden of castle 2197, 2199, 2209 etc.
**conteyne**, *v.* ~ *hem* keep themselves T292
**contenaunce**, *sb.* bearing 1274
**contrarie**, *adj.* opposite T308, opposed 583, 1488 etc.
**contrarie**, *adv.* contrariwise 1752, 2112
**contrarie**, *v.* oppose 1995, act contrary to 703, contradict 363, 589, 1460 etc.
**contrarious(e**, *adj.* opposing T731, ~ *to* rebellious against T113
**contumax**, *adj.* disobedient, contumacious 2008
**copbord, cupbord**, *sb.* sideboard 621, 2071, 2077
**costlew**, *adj.* extravagant T564, T568
**coueite**, *v.* wish, desire 92, 290, 305 etc.
**couenable**, *adj.* appropriate 76, 206, 2122
**couenant**, *sb.* promise 1126
**coue(i)tise**, *sb.* avarice, avariciousness, greed T131, T421, T498 etc.
**crepiþ**, *v. 3sg. pres. ind.* creeps T165
**culuer**, *sb.* dove 220
**cumbrid**, *v. pa. p.* overwhelmed T91, 403
**cunne, conne**, *v.* (**can, kan** *1,3 sg. pres. ind.*, **can, cunne(n, kunnen** *pl. pres. ind.*, **cowde** *sg. pa. ind.*, **kouden** *pl. pa. ind.*) know, know how to T52, T57, 489 etc.
**cunnynge**, *adj.* ~ *of* skilful in 1664
**cunnynge, kunnyng(e**, *sb.* understanding 1536, ability 9, 1873, 1925, 2015, knowledge T58, T60, T752 etc., learning 560
**cupbord**, *see* **copbord**
**curat**, *sb.* priest T24, T390
**cure**, *sb.* spiritual care T211, 2084, benefice T386, T387; *haþ a vikery in* ~ has in his responsibility a benefice as vicar T398
**curious**, *adj.* elaborate 1033, ingenious 1129
**curiously**, *adv.* ingeniously T744
**curiouste**, *sb.* idle interest T565
**curs(e**, *sb.* curse, cursing 482, 685, 1132 etc., damnation 1953
**curse**, *v.* curse, excommunicate 481, 1402 etc., damn 397
**cursid**, *pa. p. adj.* dampned 366, dampnable 1994, 2116
**cursinge**, *sb.* excommunication 1404, 1597; ~ *of* excommunication by 1411
**custum**, *sb.* habit 1720; *so swerynge in* ~ such a habit of swearing 1713

**custumable**, *adj*. habitual T140, T583, 687 etc.

**daies**, *sb.pl. or þis dai eiȝte* ~ before a week is out 2168
**dampne**, *v*. condemn T356, T385, 600 etc.
**dampnyng**, *sb*. condemnation T350, T354
**dane**, *sb*. lord (as title of a scholar) 573
**dar(e** *v. 1 and 3sg. and pl. pres. ind.*, **dur** *pl. pres. ind.*, **durste** *3sg. pa. ind.* dare 614, 759, 762 etc.
**daunger**, *sb*. hardship T439
**decre**, *sb*. ruling 408; **decrees** *pl*. papal laws 835
**dede**, *sb*. fact 21
**de(e)dli**, *adj*. mortal, human 301, 1105, 1166 etc., deadly, mortal 1242, 2055
**defame**, *v*. accuse 487
**defaute**, *sb*. lack T165, T289, T340 etc., insufficiency T247, T577; *in his* ~ through his deficiency 857
**defoulid**, *pa. p. adj*. corrupted T144, T179
**defouliden**, *pa. p. haue* ~ have corrupted 504
**degratid**, *pa. p. adj*. degraded 2081
**del(e**, *sb*. part 1497
**dele**, *v*. (**delyden** *pl. pa. ind.*) divide T324, T483
**delectacioun**, *sb*. delight T72
**delitable**, *adj*. pleasing 1369
**delyueraunce**, *sb*. relinquishing, surrender T225
**delyuere**, *inf*. hand over, deliver, release T220, T236, 2178 etc.
**de(e)me**, *v*. adjudge, consider T447, 195, 397 etc., judge T724, condemn 1824
**denye**, *v*. refuse 1050, 1594
**departe**, *v*. divide 422, distribute T434, 1495, separate 554
**deprauen**, *v. pl. pres. ind*. denigrate 1998
**depryuyng**, *sb*. handicap T457
**dereworþe**, *adj*. precious 158
**deseese**, *sb*. death 1440
**determyned**, *v. pa. p*. pronounced judgment 987
**dette**, *sb*. obligation 714, 731, 735
**deuely**, *adj*. dismal T742
**deuer**, *sb*. duty 1825
**deuysioun**, *sb*. division 702
**dew(e)li**, *adv*. properly 193, 1500, 2127, in proper form 790
**dew(e)tee**, *sb*. fee 543, 1476, 1494 etc.
**dicte**, *sb*. saying (title given to writings of Grosseteste, on similar subjects to sermons but with shorter expositions) T39
**diligence**, *sb*. *do ... his* ~ exert himself T386
**discordinge**, *v. pres. p*. diverging 913
**discrasyng**, *sb*. disharmony T284
**dise(e)se**, *v*. (**disesid** *pa. p.*) harm 373, 380, 1856
**disesi**, *adj*. disagreeable 442
**dispensouris**, *sb. pl*. distributors 1491
**dispiteous**, *adj*. pitiless 256
†**displesaunce**, *sb*. displeasure 882
**dispose**, *v*. dispense T245; **disposynge** *pres. p.* preparing 1245; **disposid** *pa. p.* prepared 723
**disposicioun**, *sb*. administration T470
**dissencide**, *v. 3sg. pa. ind*. descended 221
**disseuered**, *pa. p. adj*. separated T79
**distaunce**, *sb*. *at* ~ in disagreement 2253
**distrie**, *v*. eradicate 1995, 2182
**distroublers**, *sb.pl*. disturbers 356
**distroublid**, *pa. p.adj*. troubled 1916
**disturblen**, *v. pl. pres. ind*. trouble 1999
**dyuynyte(e, deuynyte**, *sb*. theology 574, 1663, 1664 etc.
**do(o)m(e**, *sb*. judgment 374, 670, last judgment T36, T75, T80
**don**, *v. pl. pres. ind.* ~ *of* take off 1090; **dide** *3sg. pa. ind. þat he* ~ *to* to whom he performed T509; **idone** *pa. p.* done, performed 1721, 1724
**doute**, *v. 1sg. pres. ind.* ~ *me* doubt T371
**drede**, *v*. *it is to* ~ it is to be feared 1201
**drenche**, *v*. drown 2202
**drye**, *adj*. *wexe* ~ become dry, i.e. ineffectual T157
**drowen**, *v. pl. pa. ind. ... to* joined with 561; **drawun** *pa. p.* ~ *of* carried away by T69, T84, T226
**dukis**, *sb. pl*. leaders T322
**dur, durste** *see* **dar**
**dwelliþ**, *v. 3sg. pres. ind*. remains 988, 1024, 1027

**eche**, *v*. ~ *to* increase 303
**edefien**, *v*. strengthen 496, benefit 867
**eelde**, *adj*. ~ *testament* old testament T585
**eernis**, *sb*. foretaste 525
**e(e)nde**, *sb*. purpose 1064, fulfilment T665, *to þis* ~ for this purpose T470

**effect**, *pa. p. adj.* infected 1583
**effect(e**, *sb.* effect T617, *in* ~ in fact T211, T443, 1300 etc.
**effect(u)al(l)i**, *adv.* satisfactorily 678, 683, 1205 etc.
**effectual**, *adj.* valid 1818
**eiþir**, *cj.* or 15, 310
**ellis**, *adv.* otherwise T312, T319, 1508 etc.
**enaunter**, *cj.* lest perchance 38
**enauntir**, *adv.* perchance T449
**encense**, *v.* burn incense before 1195, 1197
**endured**, *pa. p. adj.* hardened 919, 1902, 1911, *hard* ~ strongly hardened 402
**enfecte**, *v.* infect 184
**enfeffen**, *v.* put upon as a legal obligation 385
**enformacioun**, *sb.* instruction 474, 556
**enfo(u)rme**, *v.*, instruct T741, T752, 1009 etc.
**enforsist**, *v. 2sg. pres. ind*, **enforsen** *pl. pres. ind.* **enforsinge** *pres. p.*, **enforsed** *sg. pa. ind.*, **enforcid** *pa. p.* strive T273, *with refl.* exert self 11, 47, 54 etc.
**englaymed**, *v. pa. p.* befouled 116
**enhaunce**, *v. imp. sg.*, **enhauncid** *pa. p.* raise up T33, T178, 115 etc.
**eny** *see* **ony**
**enioyede**, *v. 3sg. pa. ind.* ~ *himsilf* rejoiced T620
**enke**, *sb.* ink 762
**enpungne**, *v.* oppose 1564; **enpugned** *pa. p.* challenged 46
**ensaumple**, *sb.* example T127, T131, 284 etc.; *in* ~ *of* as an example to T98; *at þe* ~ from the example T105, T240, *bi* ~ from the example 513
**ensaumplynge**, *v. pres. p.* giving a model to T506
**enselid**, *v. pa. p.* sealed 1087
**entent**, *sb.* purpose 315, T629; *taken* ~, *ȝyue* ~ pay attention T29, T59, T228; *in* ~ *to* for the purpose of 334, 439
**entere**, *adj.* sincere 1123
**enuenym**, *v.* poison 187, 505, 521
**equypolent**, *adj.* of equal authority 1754
**equyuocaciouns**, *sb. pl.* ambiguities 1811 (*see note*)
**er**, *cj.* before 553, 1159
**erlis**, *sb.* foretaste 84
**esy**, *adj.* untroubled 429, light 1421
**euen**, *sb.* eve 604
**euencristen**, *adj. as sb. pl.* fellow christians 3
**euene**, *adj.* equal 201, 204, 1754
**euene**, *adv.* directly 90; ~ *to* in accordance with T237
**euydent**, *adj.* clear T725
**examyned**, *v. pa. p.* appraised T415
**exchewe**, *v.* avoid 2083, 2121; **exchewid** *pa. p.* shunned 2107
**execucioun**, *sb.* execution T706, *doen* ~ *of* put into effect T265
**expowne**, *v.* expound T55, 1352

**fablis**, *sb.* idle tales T603, 612
**faile**, *v.* fail 120, be lacking 1920
**fatte**, *adj.* rich, well-endowed T110
**fatuytee**, *sb.* stupidity, a worthless thing H47
**faute**, *sb.* lack T445
**fauoure**, *v.* give assent to, look with favour on 354, 2132
**feynen**, *v. pl. pres. ind.* dissimulate 589
**feyned**, *pa. p. adj.* pretended T288
**feynyng(e**, *sb.* pretence 110, 508, 515
**fe(e)le**, *adj.* many 446, 578
**felle**, *adj.* cruel 254
**felle**, *sb.* skin 251
**felowis**, *sb.pl.* companions T243
**fer**, *adj.* distant T669
**fer(re**, *adv.* far T196, T481, 1332 etc.
**ferede**, *v.3sg. pa. ind.* terrified 658
**ferforþ**, *adv. as* ~ *as* as far as 1869, 2219; *so* ~ to such an extent T110; *so* ~ *þat* to such an extent that T60
**fersli**, *adv.* roughly 938, 2070
**ferþer, ferþir, firþer**, *comp. adv.* further, more distant 48, 2009; ~ *not* no further 331
**ferþeryng**, *v. pres. p.* assisting 114
**ferþermore**, *adv.* furthermore T614, T647
**feruent**, *adj.* enthusiastic, ardent T77, T139, 133 etc., alert 1147
**feruently**, *adv.* ardently T192
**feste**, *sb.* festival 167
**figure**, *sb. to* ~ as a symbol 1358; **figuris** *pl.* symbols T665, T666
**figuriþ**, *v. 3sg. pres. ind.*, **figuren** *pl. pres. ind.* symbolise T335, 1356
**filþehede**, *sb.* defilement T195
**fynde**, *v.* provide livelihood for T467, T470; **fond** *3sg. pa. ind.* found 2176; **founden** *pa. p.* discovered 1284

**fyndyng**, *sb.* provision of maintenance T575; *pl.* devices 1321
**first**, *adv.* primarily T552
**fleynge**, *sb.* flaying 1555
**fleynge**, *v. pres. p.* fleeing T68
**flood**, *sb.* river 219
**foli**, *adj.* foolish 405
**folily**, *adv.* foolishly T44, 1510
**fool**, *adj.* foolish T89, T408
**for**, *cj.* in order that T12
**for**, *prep.* ~ *to now* up to the present T541
**forbeden**, *v.* (**forbed** *3sg. pa. ind.*, **forboden** *pl. pa. ind.*, **forbodun** *pa. p.*) forbid T501, 1101, 1133 etc.
**foorme** *see* **fourme**
**formed**, *v.pa. p.* created 1781
**forme-don**, *adj.* previously done 74
**forsoþe**, *adv.* truly, indeed T24, T178, T319 etc.
**forswering**, *sb.* perjury T194
**fortraueilid**, *pa. p. adj.* worn out with toil T550
**forþ**, *adv.* ~ *daies* well on in the day 2005
**forþi**, *adv.* therefore 189, 295, 395 etc.
**forþi ( . . . ) þat** *cj.* because 2, 84, 259 etc.
**forþward**, *adv.* onward T686
**fouchesaaf**, *v.* agree 454
**fourme, foorme**, *sb.* kind, fashion 239, 984; manner 1463, 1678; *in ~ of brede* having assumed the form of bread 236, 969, 971 etc. (*see note to* 970); *in ~ of God* in the form of God 979
**fre(e)dam, fredom**, *sb.* liberty T101, 54, 55 etc.; ~ *of labour* ability to toil T515
**free**, *adj.* at liberty 1548, 1951; uninhibited 2001
**freeliche**, *adv.* eagerly T606
**fro**, *prep.* from T158, T220, 398 etc.
**frowardis**, *prep.* away from 938
**fru(c)tuous(e**, *adj.* profitable 530, 1256
**ful**, *adv.* very T139, T184, 446 etc.
**fulfille**, *v.* satisfy T110; fill T373; **fulfillid** *pa. p.* completed T80
**fullid**, *v. pa. p.* baptised 219

**gadere** *see* **ged(e)re(n**
**gaderingis** *see* **gederinge**
**gat(e(n** *see* **gete(n**
**ged(e)re(n, gadere**, *v.* gather, collect T363, T365, 1596 etc.
**gederinge**, *sb.* collecting 1868; ~ *togidre* collecting together, i.e. congregation 286, 289; **gaderingis** *pl.* collections (of money) T544
**generacioun**, *sb.* race, progeny 1524, descent H10
**gesse(n**, *v.* consider, think 127, 376, 381 etc.
**gete(n**, *v.* (**gat** *3sg. pa. ind.*, **gaten** *pl. pa. ind.*, **geten, gotun** *pa. p.*) obtain T377, T380, 1432 etc.
**getyng**, *sb.* acquiring T497
**gileful**, *adj.* fraudulent T375
**gilis**, *sb. pl.* wiles T277
**gladid**, *v. 1sg. pa. ind.* rejoiced 2242
**glose**, *sb.* gloss T623, 855, sophistical interpretation T695
**glose**, *v.* gloze over, falsify T388
**godward**, *sb. to ~* towards God T552
**goostli**, *adj.* spiritual T22, T61, 1240 etc.
**go(o)stli**, *adv.* spiritually, in spirit 376, 495, 861 etc., allegorically 1356
**gotun** *see* **gete(n**
**gouernaunce**, *sb.* authority 293, 297, 317
**graunte**, *v.* allow 647, 745, 754 etc., agree, assent to 1026, 1027, 1030 etc., give 2252; **grauntid** *pa. p.* given T132, 626, 1560
**grauun**, *v. pa. p.* and *pa. p. adj.* carved H20, H24
**gree**, *sb.* position T431
**ground(e**, *sb.* ~ *of* foundation in T685, 1401
**groundid**, *v. pa. p.* founded 915, ~ *in* justified from 2044
**growun**, *v. pa. p.* accrued T365
**grucche**, *v. pl. pres. ind.* complain 1512, ~ *to ȝeuen* complain about giving 1486; **grucchiden** *pl. pa. ind.* found fault T654
**grucchyng(e**, *sb.* complaint T543, 87, 118 etc.

**ȝaf(f, ȝauen** *see* **ȝeue(n**
**ȝede**, *v. 3sg. pa. ind.* went T654, T677, 2190
**ȝelden**, *v.* give T117, T504, repay 1319; ~ *hem* submit 1037
**ȝerde**, *sb.* rod 82, 118
**ȝete**, *v.* cast in metal 1113
**ȝetynge**, *sb.* casting of metal 1071, 1124
**ȝeue(n, ȝyue**, *v.* (**ȝaf(f** *1 and 3sg. and pl. pa. ind.*, **ȝauen** *pl. pa. ind.*, **ȝeue, ȝoue(n, ȝouun** *pa. p.*) give, grant T25, T36, 9 etc.; ~ *to telle out þe truþe* give up telling the truth 593
**ȝeuynge, ȝyuyng**, *sb.* giving T549, 1571
**ȝhe**, *adv.* yes, indeed T57, T413, 197 etc.

**ȝhis, ȝis**, *adv*. yes 847, 1746, 1755 etc.
**ȝistirday**, *sb*. yesterday T713
**ȝit**, *adv*. yet, still T43, T56, 259 etc.
**ȝyue, ȝyuyng** *see* **ȝeue(n, ȝeuynge**
**ȝoten**, *pa. p. adj*. cast in metal 1111
**ȝoue(n, ȝouun** *see* **ȝeue(n**

**habiite**, *sb*. clothing, guise T602
**habundaunce**, *sb*. plenty T82
**half**, *sb*. side 269
**halowe**, *v*. honour 1413
**halp**, *v. 3sg. pa. ind*. helped T218
**han**, *v. pl. pres. ind*., **hast** *2sg. pres. ind*., **haþ** 3sg. pres. ind. have T55, T178, 353 etc.
**hap**, *sb*. chance T458; *in* ~, *up* ~ perhaps T427, T721, 104
**harlot**, *sb*. wretch 552, 1991, 1992
**hastynge** *v. pres. p*. hastening (i. e. in haste) T649
**he(e)de**, *sb*. heed, notice T181, T205, 1197
**he(e)d(e**, *sb*. head, chief 1943, 1963, 2067 etc.; **heed money** poll tax (see Matt. 17:27) T230
**heedlyngis**, *adv*. headlong 701
**heepynge**, *v. pres. p*., **hepid** *pa. p*. gather T492, T494
**heerde**, *sb*. shepherd T46, T47
**heeringe**, *sb*. hearing 801, 1148, 1151 etc.
**heest(e**, *sb*. commandment T53, T266, 6 etc.
**hei** *see* **hiȝ(e**
**heiȝþe**, *sb*. height, peak 700
**he(e)lþe**, *sb*. salvation T49, T54, 99 etc.
**hem**, *pron. pl. obj. and refl*. them, themselves T14, T17, T23 etc.
**her**, *pron. pl. poss*. their T108, T112, 6 etc.
**herbifore**, *adv*. before this T199, 364
**herborwide**, *v. pa. p*. lodged 2167
**he(e)ren**, *v*. hear T209, T545, 30 etc.
**herien**, *v*. praise 1365
**hert(e)li, hertily**, *adj*. eager T378, heartfelt 655, 1614
**herteli**, *adj*. eagerly 23, sincerely 1935
**herþoruȝ**, *adv*. through it, through this 98, 107, 413 etc.
**heuy**, *adj*. unwilling 1489, ~ *of* tired with 1844, ~ *towardis* annoyed with 441
**hideousen**, *pl. pres. ind*. feel horror for 2140
**hiȝ(e, hei**, *adj*. high T93, 3, 130 etc., great T104
**hiȝte**, *v. 3sg. pa. ind*. promised 271
**hilyng(e**, *sb*. covering, i.e. clothing T238, 1503
**hir**, *pron. fem. sg. obj. and poss*. her T244, T528, 213 etc.
**hire**, *sb*. payment 1553, 2146
**historial**, *adj*. authentic T747
**holde**, *v*. (**heeld** *3sg. pa. ind*., **holden, hooldun** *pa. p*.) keep 70, 586, 606 etc.; consider 420, 1141, 1347 etc.; maintain 606, 1742, 2089; oblige T741; ~ *hem* consider themselves T237, T373; ~ *aȝens* argue against 2097; ~ *to do* obliged to do 876
**holding**, *sb*. maintaining 2100
**holidoome**, *sb*. relic 1648 (*see note*)
**holy**, *adv*. completely 1877
**holsum**, *adj*. wholesome 634, 1471
**hom(e)ly**, *adj*. familiar T629, 577, 1269
**honestee**, *sb*. uprightness T419, honour T420
**hool**, *adj*. complete 289, 992
**hope**, *v*. believe T267, 1889, expect T426, trust 142, 282, 737; *it is to* ~ it is to be believed T221
**hosteleris**, *sb.pl*. innkeepers 1307
**housho(o)ld**, *sb*. *of* ~ within the community T161, T171
**how þat**, *cj*. however 733
**hurtynge**, *sb*. injury 493
**husbondderie**, *sb*. agricultural produce T572

**iangelers**, *sb.pl*. boasters 1331
**ianglist**, *2sg. pres. ind*. ~ . . . *aȝens* raise objections against 1344
**idone** *see* **don**
**iewise**, *sb*. judicial sentence 648, 649
**iȝen**, *sb.pl*. eyes T186, T712, 961 etc.
**ymagerie**, *sb*. representation, piece of sculpture or picture 1072, 1076, 1186 etc.
**in**, *prep*. on 630
**inconueniient**, *sb*. offence 321, 398; *pl*. offences T542, T580
**indifferent**, *adj*. impartial T489
**infect**, *pa. p. adj*. ~ *wiþ* corrupted by T144
**†infourmeris**, *sb.pl*. instructors 2090
**ingrowun**, *adj*. internal T173
**ynnere**, *comp. adv*. further in T167
**inpugne**, *v. 1sg. pres.ind*. criticize T673
**interlynarie**, *adj*. interlinear 855
**into**, *prep*. in 274, 1152, 1947, during T367,

to 389, 483, 689 etc., until 1418, for 7, 869, 2133
**inwardli**, *adv.* earnestly 415
**ioie**, *sb.* mirth T209, 2171
**ioie(n**, *v.* delight, rejoice 1379, 1382, 1995 etc., enjoy 1543
**ioieful**, *adj.* glad 1276, 2175
**ioifulli**, *adv.* joyfully 906
**iornay**, *sb.* enterprise 459
**yuel(e, yule**, *adj.* evil T296, T584, 787 etc.
**iwriten** *see* **write**

**kalender**, *sb.* reminder 1073, 1137, 1171
**kerue**, *v.* carve 1113
**keruynge**, *sb.* carving 1071, 1124
**kynde**, *sb.* nature T750, 980, 1066 etc., bodily form 208; *lawe of* ~ natural law, i.e. that form of law available before the law of Moses T499, T732
**kyndely**, *adj.* natural T421, H16
**kitt**, *v. pa. p.* cut 1219
**knyllide**, *v. 3sg. pa. ind.* rang 937
**knowynge**, *sb.* knowledge 331
**know(e)leche, -lich**, *v.* acknowledge, confess 145, 295, 592 etc., profess 664
**knowleching(e** *sb.* confession 130, 146
**koruen**, *pa. p. adj.* carved 1110
**kunnen, kouden** *see* **cunne**
**kunnynge** *see* **cunnynge**

**laborouse**, *adj.* diligent 1276
**lad**, *v. pa. p.* led 536
**lafte, laft** *see* **leue**
**lammasse**, *sb.* Lammas (i.e. 1 August) 168
**large**, *adj.* comprehensive 758, substantial 1501
**largeli**, *adv.* extravagantly 1651
**lasse**, *comp. adv.* less T419, T564
**last**, *cj.* lest 550
**late**, *v.* leave 2121
**le(e)ful, leueful**, *adj.* lawful 631, 837, 1106 etc.
**le(e)f(f)ully**, *adv.* lawfully T675, 1349
**leenyng**, *sb.* loan T427
**leeue**, *v.* believe T488, trust T708; *me leeueþ* it is believed T217
**leyen**, *v. pl. pres. ind.* ~ *for hem* cite as an excuse for themselves T326
**lenger(e, lengir**, *comp. adv.* longer T575, 1621, 1733 etc.
**lerid**, *pa. p. adj. as sb.* learned men (i.e. the clergy) T152
**le(e)rned**, *v. pa. p.* instructed 501, 503, 713 etc.
**lese**, *v.* forsake 77, destroy 2158
**lesynge**, *sb.* falsification T103
**lete**, *v.sg. /pl. pres.sj.* let T698, T708; **letiþ** *imp. pl.* let T753
**leten**, *v.pl. pa. ind.* considered 453
**lette**, *v.* impede, prevent from 187, 705, 885 etc.
**lettyngis**, *sb.pl.* impediments 1149
**lettrid**, *pa. p. adj.* learned 1820, 2145
**lettrure**, *sb.* learning T605
**leue**, *sb.* permission 458, 626
**leue**, *v.* (**lefte, lafte** *3sg. pa. ind.*, **leeft, laft** *pa. p.*) leave, abandon 357, 1054, 1220 etc.; remain 175; **leuyng** *þe world* not caring for worldly things T90
**leueful** *see* **le(e)ful**
**lewid, lewde**, *adj.* ignorant 406, 741 etc.; lay, secular T152, 1074, 1171 etc.
**licence**, *sb.* permission 454; *lettre of* ~ letter of formal permission 755 (*see note to* 742)
**licencide, licensid**, *v. pa. p.* authorised 747 (*see note to* 742), 1474
**lic(k)li**, *adj.* probable 493, 524, 667 etc.
**li(i)f**, *sb. no* ~ nobody 1191; *ony* ~ anybody 1409, 1606, 1934
**lyf(e)lode, liiflood**, *sb.* necessities of life 1311, 1312, 1422 etc., food T238, T246, T381
**ligge**, *v.* (**liiþ** *3sg. pres.ind.*) lie T307, T348, H52
**liȝtli**, *adv.* (**liȝtloker** *comp.*) readily T425, T708, quickly 1341, perhaps T723
**liȝtned**, *v. pa. p.* enlightened T207, 97
**liking**, *sb.* pleasure T73
**lymyte(n**, *v.* assign 757, 760, appoint T657
**list**, *v. 3sg. pres. ind.* (**lust** *3sg. pa. ind.*) *ȝou* ~ it pleases you 844; *him* ~ it pleased him T621
**lyuynge**, *v. pres. p.* ~ *ȝit þilke synner* while that sinner is still alive 1607
**lyuynge**, *sb.* life 1903
**longiþ**, *v. 3sg. pres.ind.* pertains T281, belongs T504
**loof**, *sb.* (**lo(o)uys** *pl.*) loaf T40, T55, T482
**loone**, *sb.* loan T426, T431, T433
**lo(o)re**, *sb.* teaching, doctrine T557, 363, 475 etc., instruction 439
**losel**, *sb.* wretch, rascal 406, 519, 538 etc.

**losen**, *v. pl. pres.ind.* (**losid** *pa. p.*) loose 1047, 1911
**losid**, *v.pa. p.* praised 460
**loþide**, *v. 3sg. pa. ind.* hated T591
**lowe**, *adv.* abjectly T100
**lust** *v. see* **list**
**lusty**, *adj.* enjoyable T443, 2137, energetic 1372
**lustily**, *adv.* eagerly T326
**lustis**, *sb.pl.* pleasures T60, T321, 90 etc.

**madden**, *v.* go mad 1785, be out of one's mind 1767
**maynteyne**, *v.* defend 890
**maistirschipe**, *sb.* lordship 1821
**maistirful**, *adj.* overbearing 820
**maistirfully**, *adv.* authoritatively T657
**maistri**, *sb.* mastery T273
**manasse**, *v.* threaten 447, 1693, 2079 etc.
**manassynge**, *sb.* threat 413, 658, 820 etc.
**maner**, *sb.* kind; *þre ~ breed* three kinds of bread T3; *of a ~ . . . curiouste* out of a kind of idle interest T565
**manheede**, *sb.* humanity 226
**mankynde**, *sb.* human form 1104, 1160
**marchaundise**, *sb.* trade T231, T572, trading T179
**marken**, *v. pl. pres.ind.* point out 2140
**marwȝ**, *sb.* marrow (i.e. centre) 1777
**material**, *adj. ~ breed* physical substance of bread, i.e. ordinary bread 629, 932, 950 etc. (*see note to* 934ff)
**mawmetrer**, *sb.* idolator T119, T732
**me**, *impers. pron.* a man, *~ leeueþ* it is believed T216
**me**, *refl. pron.* myself 40, 43 etc.
**me(e)de**, *sb.* pay T26, reward T432, 156 etc., spiritual value 941
**medicyn**, *sb.* spiritual remedy T286
**medlid**, *v. pa. p.* mixed T204
**meene**, *adj.* intermediary T694
**meene**, *sb.* intermediary T120, method T377, T440, 1347 etc.
**meene**, *v. þat is to ~* that is to be understood T321, T431
**meyne(e**, *sb.* household T16, T442, T474
**meynteynen**, *v. pl. pres.ind.* (**meynteynede** *3sg. pa. ind.*) argue 1719, defend 1988
**mesurable**, *adj.* just T126, moderate 1477
**mesurably**, *adv.* in moderation T416
**mesure**, *sb. ouer ~* immeasurably 477, in abundance 2081; *pl.* measures (of weight, length etc.) T376
**mete**, *sb.* food T42, T50, 225 etc.
**meuyng**, *sb.* persuasion T689
**myche, moche**, *adj.* much T540 etc., a great number of 172, a great deal of 438, 526, 609 etc.
**myche, moche**, *adv.* greatly 102, 391, 561, much T129, T234, 489 etc.
**mydis**, *sb.* middle 1015
**mynde**, *sb.* mind 1006, 1707, remembrance 70, 1084, 1412 etc.; *haue ~* remember T186, 803, 983
**myndeful**, *adj. be ȝe ~* remember 804
**myndefulnesse**, *sb. into ~* in remembrance 242
**mynystracioun**, *sb.* dispensation T22
**mysbileue**, *sb.* lack of faith 304
**myscheef**, *sb.* affliction T174, T214, 396; *pl.* misfortunes 2083
**myse(e)se**, *sb.* pain T206, distress T207, T355; *pl.* disabilities T456, T460
**mo(o**, *comp. adj.* more (in number) 1850, 1856, 2193; *as sb.* T728, 502
**moche**, *adj. and adv. see* **myche**
**moeblis**, *sb.pl.* personal possessions, movable goods T485
**moneþ(e**, *sb.* month 211, 1329, 1392
**moost**, *adv.* especially T21
**moral**, *adj.* ethical, moral T49, T54
**moralizen**, *v. pl. pres.ind.* expound the moral significance of T1
**more**, *comp. adj. as sb.* greater men T244
**mote**, *v. 3sg. pres.ind.* (**moten** *pl. pres.ind.*, **moste(n** *pres. ind.*) must T315, T649, 67 etc.
**mouable**, *adj.* movable T465
**mo(o)uynge**, *sb.* persuasion 44, inspiration 736, 1109; *pl.* inclinations 2057
**mow(e**, *v.* (**moun, mow(e)n** *pl. pres. ind.*) be able to, may T36, T50, 113 etc.
**musist**, *v. 3sg. pres. ind.* (**musynge** *pres.p.*) hesitate about 432, ponder 368

**nakid**, *adj.* barren T300
**named**, *v. pa. p.* reputed 455, 461, 559 etc.
**namely**, *adv.* especially, in particular T350, T683
**naþeles, neþeles**, *adv.* notwithstanding T98, T199, 18 etc.
**ne**, *adv.* not, *þat ~ þei wolen* that they will not 144; *I doute not . . . þat ~* I have no doubt but that 667; *þere is no . . . þat . . .*

~ *I schal* there is no . . . whom I shall not 1742; *þere was no . . . þat ~ þei* there was no . . . but that they 1970
**ne**, *cj.* nor T52, T231, 5 etc.
**nec(g)ligence**, *sb.* neglect T27, T343
**nede**, *adv.* of necessity 427
**nedeful**, *adj. as sb.* clients (*trans. Lat. necessarii, see note*) T160
**nedis**, *adv.* necessarily 1748, 1901, 1944
**nediþ**, *v. 3sg. pres. ind.* (**nede(n** *pl. pres. ind.*, **nedide(n** *pa. ind.*) be necessary (*usually with refl. pron.*) T133, T509, T513 etc., need 793, 794, 1428 etc; *pa.* forced T589, was compelled T655.
**neiȝiþ**, *v. 3sg. pres. ind.* (**neiȝide** *3sg. pa. ind.*, **neiȝed** *pa. p.*) approach 226, 230; ~ *to* comes to, takes up 852
**neiþer . . . neiþer** *cj.* neither . . . nor 676, 682
**nempnede**, *v. 1sg. pa. ind.* (**nempned** *pa. p.*) mentioned 1391, reputed 1467
**nerhond**, *adv.* ~ *to* close up to 2078
**neþeles** *see* **naþeles**
**nyȝ**, *adj.* ~ *kyn* close kindred T727
**nyȝ**, *adv.* nearly 1626, accurately 1838, 1941, closely 539
**nyȝ**, *prep.* near 37
**nyȝe**, *v.* come near 1887
**nyȝhonde**, *adv.* close at hand 2203
**noblete(e**, *sb.* splendour, worthiness T187, T189
**no but**, *adv.* only 85, 199, 541 etc.
**no but**, *cj.* unless 680
**no but**, *prep.* except 175, 290, 722
**noyous**, *adj.* offensive 387
**noot**, *v. 1sg. pres. ind.* do not know 1990
**noþing**, *adv* in no way 1459
**notiþ**, *v. pl. imp.* take note 1782
**nouȝt**, *pron.* nothing T188
**nownpower**, *sb. at* ~ impotent T468, T669

**o**, **oon**, *num.* one 369, *in* ~ together 42, 363; *al* ~ the same thing 1026, 1739
**obedienciaries**, *sb.pl.* people who practice obedience to a superior, subjects H8
**oblesche(n, oblische(n**, *v.* bind by a vow 348, 755, 759 etc., pledge 110
**ocupacioun**, *sb.* position T409
**oc(c)upie**, *v.* occupy T100, T744 etc.; busy 94, 531, 1240, 1905 etc.; possess T410; ~ *vs* take up our time 921; ~ *me/him* concern myself/himself 43, 919
**of**, *prep.* out of T565, for 1045, concerning 1585
**offence**, *sb.* offending 1253
**office**, *sb. of* ~ by virtue of their position or office T14, T316
**omelie** , *sb.* homily 1697, 1698, 1700
**ony, eny** *adj.* any T214, T500, 25, 1854 etc.
**oone**, *v. 3sg. pres.sj.* (**oonen** *pl. pres. ind.*, **ooned, oonyd** *pa. p.*) unite 325, 2003, 2254 etc.
**oones, oonys**, *adv.* once 1507, 1662
**oost**, *sb.*[1] host, multitude T301, 1557
**oost**, *sb.*[2] host, the bread consecrated at the eucharist 950
**ooþ**, *sb.* oath 756, 1640, 1643 etc.
**openly**, *adv.* plainly T38
**opynyouns**, *sb. pl.* rumours T726
**or**, *prep.* before 2168
**ordeyne**, *v.* arrange T245, T502, 206 etc., establish 859
**ordenaunce, ordynaunce**, *sb.* commandment T541, T576, 193 etc., determination, decree 293, 989 etc., provision T484
**orrible**, *adj.* fearful T419
**or þat**, *cj.* before 449, 1054, 1362 etc.
**oþerwise**, *adv.* in any other fashion T567
**ouȝt**, *pron.* anything T58
**oute**, *adv. told* ~ revealed fully 2252
**outgoynge**, *sb.* ~ *of* departure from 2174
**ouer**, *adv.* excessively 388
**ouer**, *prep.* beyond T601, T659, 35 etc., above 1906
**ouerchargid**, *v. pa. p.* overburdened T526
**ouerledyng**, *sb.* oppression T375
**ouer-lewid**, *adj.* excessively ignorant 1922
**ouerthwert**, *adv.* transversely 2245
**owiþ**, *v. 3sg. pres.ind.* (**owen** *pl. pres. ind.*) ought 59, 71, 188 etc.; *me owiþ/him owiþ* I/he ought 341, 1612
**owhere**, *adv.* anywhere 580

**paie(n**, *v.* render as due T232, T573, 1398 etc.
**payinge**, *sb.* payment T230
**paynym(y)s**, *sb.pl.* heathen people T176, T734, T736
**parchemyne**, *sb.* parchment 762

**parfi(ȝ)t**, *adj.* perfect 911, 2254
**parischen**, *sb.* community of parish 1496; *pl.* parishioners 1498, 1504, 1505 etc.
**parseyue**, *v. 1sg. pres. ind.* perceive 405
**parteyneþ, perteyneþ**, *v. 3sg. pres. ind.* (**parteynede(n** *pa. ind.*) belong 1420, 1558, 1898, belongs as a legal right 1885
**partie**, *sb.* part T225, T261, 468 etc.
**partyner**, *sb.* sharer 856, 1509
**partynge**, *v. pres. part.* sharing T510
**passe**, *v.* pass 50, 1313, surpass 464, 756, 1029 etc.
**passing**, *adj.* surpassing, preeminent T19, T27, 149 etc.
**passing**, *adv.* preeminently 559
**patroun**, *sb.* founder, protector T339
**peese**, *v.* pacify T239
**peire**, *sb.* pair 2191
**perbrekinge**, *sb.* breaking asunder 213
**perceyuere**, *v. pl. pres. ind.* (**perseyuered** *pa. p.*) persevere 527, 1878
**perceueerauntli, perseuerauntli**, *adv.* steadfastly 117, 665, 1949
**peril**, *sb.* ~ *to fulfille* danger in fulfilling 1658
**persoun**, *sb.* (**persoones** *pl.*) parson, clerk T327, 176, 177
**pike**, *v.* pick 889
**pillers**, *sb. pl. a peire of* ~ a pair of manacles 2191 (*see note*)
**pistle**, *sb.* epistle T127, T147, T256
**pitee**, *sb.* mercy T452, T516; *for* ~ a matter of grief 56; *for þe* ~ *of Crist* for the sake of Christ 2085
**piteousli**, *adv.* mercifully 65
**pleyneþ**, *v. 3sg. pres. ind.* complains T152, T578
**plente(e**, *sb.* sufficiency T40, fullness T107
**plenteuous**, *adj.* plentiful T298, T362
**plenteuously**, *adv.* plentifully T40
**plesaunce**, *sb.* pleasure 882
**plesid**, *v. pa. p. it is* ~ *to þe Lord on* the Lord is pleased with H55
**plesyng**, *adj.* acceptable 2068; *done þe* ~ *wille of God* perform the will of God acceptably 1863
**plesynge**, *sb.* pleasure 2017, 2146
**pletynge**, *sb.* pleading, carrying on a law suit 1597
**pluralitee**, *sb.* simultaneous tenure of more than one benefice T382
**poynt**, *sb.* limit 512
**poyntours**, *sb.pl.* painters 1122
**pollicie**, *sb.* procedure T541, T577, T580
**postle**, *sb.* apostle T267
**pouert**, *sb.* poverty T460, 528, 1528 etc.
**power**, *sb.* right 1452
**pree**, *v. 1sg. pres. ind.* (**preeynge** *pres.p.*) pray, petition 2013, 2204
**preers**, *sb. pl.* petitions 2177
**preisable**, *adj.* praiseworthy 1064, 1182, 1300 etc.
**prelacie**, *sb.* office of being a prelate 720
**prelat(e**, *sb.* bishop 1647, 1649; ecclesiastical dignitory (usually derogatory in Wycliffite writings) 10, 420, 719 etc.
**presentiþ**, *v. 3sg. pres. ind.* stand in, act as a representative 845
**prestly**, *adj.* sacerdotal T65, suitable for a priest 740
**presume**, *v.* proceed on the assumption of right 746, pretend arrogantly T579, 4, 709 etc.
**presumynge**, *sb.* presumption 795
**pretendiþ**, *v. 3sg. pres. ind.* ~ *himsilf* sets himself up to be T738
**preue**, *v.* prove 841, 1747, 2173
**pri(y)s**, *sb.* value 61, 1985
**prysonyng**, *sb.* imprisonment T458
**priuy**, *adj.* secret 1896, 2053, private 173, 1087
**priuyli**, *adv.* secretly 112, 352, 638 etc.
**proces(se**, *sb.* argument T11, T535, narrative T733
**proctours**, *sb. pl.* agents 761
**procure**, *v. 3sg. pres. sj.* obtain (means of subsistence) T512
**profite**, *sb.* prophet 830
**profite**, *v.* do good T396, 101, 147; ~ *in* do good to T337
**puple**, *sb.* people, esp. lay people T12, T15, T20 etc.
**purpos(e**, *sb.* aim, desire T84, T248, 186 etc., intention T535, 722, 884 etc., issue T276, will 2159, subject of discourse 1661
**purpose**, *v.* intend T2, 582, 715 etc., plot 122
**pursue(n**, *v.* persecute T154, T739, 88 etc.
**pursuyng**, *sb.* persecution 59, 128
**puruyaunce**, *sb.* provision T445, T462, T516
**putten**, *v.* impute 2124; ~ *vp* disclose 358, 372, 378; ~ *upon* allege against T608,

T708; ~ *þis caas* supposes this situation T39

**quenche**, *v*. extinguish T272
**quyetefulli**, *adv*. quietly 944
**quyetid**, *v. pa. p*. satisfied 2189
**quyk**, *adj*. living T269
**quyletis**, *sb. pl*. collections T544 (*see note*)
**quyte**, *v*. repay H4, H13; ~ *me to* avenged myself on 553

**radde**, *v. 3sg. pa. ind*. (**rad** *pa. p.*) read 623, 632
**raþere**, *comp. adj*. earlier T187, T189
**raþer(e**, *comp. adv*. more readily T120, T197, 381 etc., sooner 1347
**raueyne**, *sb*. robbery T359, T435
**raueynour**, *sb*. plunderer, robber T351, T358
**recheles**, *adj*. negligent T57, T390
**rechelesly**, *adv*. carelessly T212
**reckiþ**, *v. 3sg. pres. ind*. (**recken** *pl. pres. ind.*, **reckinge** *pres.p.*) care T412; ~ *of* care about T86, T209, T266 etc.
**reddure**, *sb*. rigour 1483
**refourme**, *v*. convert T407
†**refreyneden**, *v. pl. pa. ind*. suppressed 1262
**reherse**, *v*. repeat 353, 1839
**reioycen**, *v. pl. pres. ind*. (**reioisid** *pa. p.*) gladden 660; ~ *hem* have delight T111
**rekenyng**, *sb*. account (for something entrusted to charge) T25, T37
**relapis**, *sb*. relapsed heretic 487 (*see note*)
**relifs**, *sb. pl*. remnants T746
**religious, religeous**, *adj*. religious, i.e. one bound by formal vows to a religious order T469, 1395
**renegatis**, *sb. pl*. apostates 2138
**renewen**, *pl. pres. ind*. ~ *hem* reproduce themselves, bear fruit 1398
**rennen**, *v. pl. pres. ind*. (**runnen** *pl. pa. ind.*) run 938, 1316
**renners**, *sb. pl*. runners 1311
**repareilid**, *v. pa. p*. restored T563
**repreef**, *sb*. (**repreues** *pl.*) reproof 233, 480
**repreuable**, *adj*. reprehensible 1127
**repreue**, *v*. reprove T197, T326, 1350 etc.
**repreuer**, *sb*. reprover T198
**reuli**, *adj*. disciplined 559
**reuerence**, *sb*. honour 1183
**reuokinge**, *sb*. recantation 506
**reward**, *sb*. *in* ~ *of* in comparison with T187
**rewardyng(e** , *sb*. rewarding T454, *þe laste* ~ the last recompense, i.e. judgment T399
**rewme**, *sb*. realm, kingdom T235, T546, 230 etc.
**richessis**, *sb.pl*. riches T372, 1290
**riȝt**, *adv*. truly 520
**riȝtful**, *adj*. upright T119
**rison**, *v. pl. pa. ind*. rose 699
**roode**, *sb*. cross 1180
**rootid**, *pa. p. adj*. endemic T165, established T196
**rowned(e**, *v. 3sg. pa. ind*. whispered 2196, 2198
**rowtinge**, *pa. p. adj*. roaring 1323
**runnen** *see* **rennen**
**ruþe**, *sb*. compassion H59

**sacringe**, *adj*. ~ *belle* bell rung at elevation of the host 937
**sacringe**, *sb*. consecration 1024
**sad**, *adj*. trustworthy 520
**sadli**, *adv*. steadfastly 915
**sauerist**, *v. 2sg. pres. ind*., **sauouriden** *pl. pa. ind*. have pleasure from, consider valuable 562, 1179, 1219
**sauour(e**, *sb*. pleasure T60, satisfaction 2096
**scabbe**, *sb*. scab, disease T165
**schame**, *v*. be ashamed of 1265, 1624, 1869
**scharpiden**, *pl. pa. ind*. sharpened 1370
**scharplier**, *comp. adv*. more harshly 606
**schaue**, *v*. ~ *ȝoure beerdis ful nyȝ* would go to any lengths 539; **schauen**, *pa. p*. shaved (i.e. be degraded from priestly office, *see note*) 408
**schit**, *adj*. closed 1148
**schittinge**, *v. pres. p*. shutting 2236
**schrewid**, *adj*. evil-disposed, wicked 183, 1623
**schryue**, *v*. ~ *him/hem* make his/their confession(s 1114, 1122, 1828 etc.; hear confession 1127
**sclaundre**, *sb*. disgrace 503, 597, 2119 etc.; *pl*. malicious accusations 1268
**sclaundre(n**, *v*. defame T604, 515, 1982 etc., accuse 382, 478, 1971; **sclaundrid** *pa.p*. ~ *wiþ* accused of 351
**sclaundres, sclaundrou(u)s(e**, *adj*. wicked, scandalous 505, 591, 687 etc.

**sclaundrousli**, *adv*. scandalously 2111
**scole-mater**, *sb*. academic question 1030
**scorne**, *v*. scorn, mock 248, 382, 1344 etc.
**scornes**, *sb. pl.* mockery 1268
**scornynge**, *sb*. mockery 2241
**seche**, *v*. seek 279, 290, 1193 etc.
**seculerly**, *adv*. in secular fashion T231
**seculers**, *sb. pl.* lay people 2200
**see**, *v*. (**seest** *2sg. pres. ind.*, **see(i)n** *pl. pres. ind.*, **seeȝen** *pl.pres. sj.*, **seynge**, *pres. p.*, **siȝ** *1 & 3 sg. pa. ind.*, **siȝen, seen, seeȝen** *pl. pa. ind.*, **seyn, seen** *pa. p.*) see T75, T89, 453 etc.
**seie**, *v*. (**seist** *2sg. pres. ind.*, **seiþ** *3sg. pres. ind.*, **seie(n, seyn(e** *pl. pres. ind.*, **seiinge**, *pres. p.*) say T17, T20, 35 etc.; **seid(e** *pa. p.* reputed 668, 673
**seiing(e**, *sb*. speech, word, utterance T724, 1692, 1725
**seintuarie**, *sb*. sanctuary T331
**seme**, *v. 3sg. pres. sj.* appear T581
**sensyble, sencible**, *adj*. physical 1374, 1791
**sentence**, *sb*. account, statement 2, 18, 29 etc.
**sequestre**, *v*. separate 186
**ser(e**, *sb*. sir 325, 332, 370 etc.
**serimonyes**, *sb. pl.* cerimonies T665
**sertefied** *see* **certified**
**sertis** *see* **certis**
**seruysable**, *adj*. willing to do service 1270
**seuynge** *see* **sue**
**shenden**, *v. pl. pres. ind.* destroy T336
**shewinge**, *v. pres. p.* ~ *hemsilf* putting themselves forwards T100
**shynyngly**, *adv*. brilliantly T201, richly T347
**shrift**, *sb*. confession T286
**shul(en**, *v. pl. pres. ind.* shall (often with implication of inevitability) T368, T370, T495 etc.
**sich(e**, *adj. & dem. pron.* such T44, T45, 103 etc.; ~ *oþer* others of a similar kind 841, 888, 1144 etc.
**sygnetis**, *sb. pl.* small seals (usually made with a signet ring) 1087
**sikir**, *adj*. safe 2074
**sikirly**, *adv*. safely T303
**silf**, *pron. in prestis* ~ in priests themselves 1586
**silleris**, *sb. pl.* sellers T334
**symylitude**, *sb*. *no* ~ *to* not comparable to 1097
**symonyentis**, *sb. pl.* simoniacs T335
**synfull**, *adv*. sinfully 1583
**siþ**, *adv*. afterwards 809, 1599
**siþ(e**, *cj*. since 62, 746, 786 etc.
**siþ(þ)en**, *cj*. since, because T350, T712, 694 etc.
**skile**, *sb*. reason T704
**skilfulli**, *adv*. reasonably 1727
**sleen**, *v. pres. ind. pl.* kill 1360
**slydinge**, *sb*. decline 2137
**sliȝte**, *sb*. cunning T417
**so**, *adv*. such 948; ~ *manye* . . . *how manye* as many . . . as T395
**sofestrie**, *sb*. sophistry 1033
**sofestris**, *sb. pl.* sophists 1037
**soget(t**, *pa. p. adj*. subordinated T56, T409
**sondir**, *adj*. various 41
**sooþ**, *sb*. truth 1767
**sooþfast**, *adj*. true 200
**so(o)þ**, *adj*. true 970, 1720
**soudeouris**, *sb. pl.* soldiers T413
**soun**, *sb*. sound 1326
**sourdow**, *sb*. leaven T144, T163
**souereyn**, *sb*. superior 747, 748, 749 etc.
**sowde**, *sb*. payment †1494 (*see note*), 1501
**sowneþ**, *v. 3sg. pres. ind.* (**sownen** *pl. pres. ind.*, **sowneden** *pl. pa. ind.*) imply 524, 669; *to þat* ~ agrees with that T221
**sped**, *v. pa. p.* carried out T628
**spede**, *sb*. success 1129
**spedeful**, *adj*. profitable 1760
**spedy**, *adj*. profitable T581, T743
**spedily**, *adv*. quickly T89
**spenders**, *sb. pl.* stewards 1507
**spensers**, *sb. pl.* stewards 1513
**spirit**, *sb*. *wiþ a grete* ~ with great vehemence 2071
**spoylide**, *3sg. pret. ind.* (**spuylid** *pa. p.*) robbed T361, T674
**staat**, *sb*. (**statis** *pl.*) estate (material and/or spiritual) T108, T181, 332 etc.
**stablischid**, *v. pa. p.* made secure 414, 653, 1208
**stap**, *sb*. step 1257, trace 2183
**stide**, *sb*. place T100, T135
**stid(e)fast**, *adj*. firm, steadfast T285, 140, 911 etc.
**stidefastli**, *adv*. firmly, steadfastly 282, 663, 737 etc.

**stiede**, *v. 3sg. pa. ind.* ascended 268
**styfly**, *adv.* (**styflier** *comp.*) resolutely 1981, 2139
**stike**, *v.* pierce 263
**stomke**, *sb.* stomach 1580
**stonde**, *v.* stand T182, 142, 664 etc.; ~ *to* obey 192, 407, 1736; *stondynge oure feiþ* according to our faith T491
**storie**, *sb.* history T533
**stranglid**, *v. pa. p.* choked 2142
**strecche**, *v.* extend 49; ~ *forþ her lyues* expend their lives 513
**streitly**, *adv.* strictly T40, T501
**stroye**, *v.* (**stried** pa. p.) destroy T364, T430
**substaunce**, *sb.* material T588
**sue**, *v.* (**suynge, seuynge** *pres.p.*, **su(e)de(n** *pa. ind.*) follow T113, T218, 408 etc., imitate 111, 678, 1595 etc., follow as a consequence T583, 707, 1748
**suer(i)s**, *sb. pl.* disciples, followers T493, 123, 711 etc.
**suffre**, *v.* allow 922, 1216, 1217 etc., endure 451, 1626
**suynge**, *adj.* pertaining T432
**suynge**, *sb.* imitation 807
**sumdel**, *adv.* to some extent 52, 379, 1287
**sumnour**, *sb.* summoner 371
**sumtyme**, *adv.* once T167
**sunder**, *adj.* diverse 23
**suppose**, *v.* think T687, 1654

**take**, *v.* (**toke(n** *pa. ind. & sj.*) give 458, 623; ~ *in* caught in T645; **tanne** *pa.p.* engaged 468
**tapsters**, *sb. pl.* barmaids 1308
**tarie**, *v.* delay T74, 611, 1733 etc.
**tariinge**, *sb.* delay 61
**temparal, temperal**, *adj.* worldly 235, 795, 914 etc.
**temperaltees, temporaltees**, *sb. pl.* temporal possessions T110, T227, T548 etc.
**tepet**, *sb.* short cape 1962
**terme**, *sb.* length 151, expression 951, 1032, 1049; *pl.* limits 510, 756, 758 etc.
**terriþ**, *v. 3sg. pres. ind.* (**terren** *pl. pres. ind.*) provoke 685, 854, 1586 etc.
**tirauntrie**, *sb.* tyranny T154, 16, 535
**tiþe**, *ord. num.* tenth 1423
**titil, title**, *sb.* legal right T507, T615, 631 etc.
**tixt(e**, *sb.* text 977, 987, 1546
**to**, *adv.* too T82, 758, 1952
**to**, *num.* two 799
**to**, *prep.* ~ *my knowynge* wittingly 331; ~ *þe tyme* until 361, 462
**tobawme**, *v.* daub, cover 249
**togidere**, *adv.* together T204, T569, 337 etc.
**touchide**, *v. 1sg. pret. ind.* mentioned 934
**touchinge**, *prep.* concerning 601, 751
**touȝ**, *adj.* substantial T313
**traas**, *sb.* path 1444
**traue(i)le**, *sb.* labour, exertion T479, 1333, 1340 etc.
**traue(i)le(n**, *v.* toil, labour T382, T528, 112 etc., journey 181, 1238; *traueilid wiþ* put to work by 919
**tretinge**, *v. pres. p.* ~ *in* dealing with 998
**trewa(u)ntis, trowantis**, *sb. pl.* tyrants T126, 750, 817 etc.
**trist**, *sb.* faith 1983
**triste(n**, *v.* trust, believe 391, 663, 736 etc., ~ *to* have faith in 489, 770, 1711
**tristili**, *adv.* confidently 142
**trowantis** *see* **trewa(u)ntis**
**trowe**, *v.* believe T416, 947, 1656 etc.
**trumpe**, *sb.* trumpet T33
**trumpinge**, *sb.* sounding of trumpet 1557
**trwe**, *adj.* true 669
**turnyng**, *sb.* conversion T288, T308, T621 etc., ~ *aboute* turn 1604
**twey**, *num.* two T483
**twyes**, *adv.* twice 1506

**þankful**, *adj.* pleasing 1300
**þankfulli**, *adv.* worthily 740, 1196, 1248
**þankynges**, *sb. pl.* thanks 961
**þanne**, *adv.* then T11, T138, 428 etc.
**þat**, *cj.* in that T363
**þenke**, *v.* (**þouȝte** *3sg. pa. ind.*, **þouȝt** *pa. p.*) think T104, 1060, 1255 etc.
**þen(ni)s**, *adv.* thence 174, 1964, 2199 etc.
**þeraȝen(s**, *adv.* against it 339, 2147
**þere**, *cj.* where 1385
**þes(e, þees(e**, *dem. pl.* these 323, 357, 1913 etc.
**þidir**, *adv.* thither T365, 174, 1289 etc.
**þilke**, *dem. adj. & pron.* that same, those same T670, 1607, 1789 etc.
**þinkiþ**, *v. 3sg. pres. ind.* (**þouȝte** *3sg. pa. ind.*, **þouȝt** *pa.p.*) *with indirect obj. (usually pron.)* it seems to 422, 442, 449 etc.; **þinke þe** (*3sg. pres. sj.*) would this seem to you? 1471

**þo(o**, *dem. adj. & pron. pl.* those T20, T245, 58 etc.
**þresten**, *v. pl. pa. ind.* thrust 699
**þreetide**, *3sg. pa. ind.* (**þretynge**, *v. pres. p.*) threaten 447, 1692
**þridde, þriide**, *ord. num.* third T5, T341, 92 etc.
**þrifte**, *sb. bi my* ~ as I may prosper 655
**þriftili**, *adv.* properly, soundly 1285
**þritti**, *card. num.* thirty 219, 476
**þroop**, *sb.* village T300, T310

**vnable**, *adj.* incompetent 1040
**vnabliþ**, *v. 3pl. pres. ind.* disables T456
**vnauysi**, *adj.* rash T272
**vnbynding**, *sb.* unbinding (i.e. absolution) T249
**vncurable**, *adj.* incurable T173
**vndirnommyn**, *v. pa. p.* rebuked 591
**vndirstondynge**, *adj.* intelligent 2087
**vndirstondingis**, *sb. pl.* meanings 1812
**vndisposiþ**, *v. 3sg. pres. ind.* . . . *to* makes it difficult for . . . to T459
**vndon**, *v. pa. p.* ruined 498
**vngroundid**, *pa. p. adj.* unfounded in scripture T607
**vngroundly**, *adv.* unjustifiably, in a manner not justifiable from scripture T708
†**vnhonest**, *adj.* disreputable 2234
**vnknowe**, *v. pa. p.* unknown 2180
**vnkunnyng(e**, *adj.* ignorant T408, 865
**vnkunnyngnesse**, *sb.* ignorance T444
**vnleeful**, *adj.* unlawful T376, T440, 366 etc.
**vnlettrid**, *pa. p. adj. as sb.* illiterate, i.e. laymen T491
**vnmanheed**, *sb.* inhumane behaviour T356
**vnmesurable**, *adj.* immeasurable T195
**vnmoeblis**, *sb. pl.* unmovable possessions T485
**vnneþe**, *adv.* scarcely T36, T39, T86
**vnneþis**, *adv.* scarcely 1484
**vnordynat**, *adj.* inordinate T111
**vnpacience**, *sb.* impatience 83
**vnpayed**, *pa. p. adj.* unsatisfied T544
**vnperfit**, *adj.* imperfect 1788
**vnpiteous**, *adj.* merciless 379
**vnquyetid**, *v. pa. p.* troubled 477
**vnreligiously**, *adv.* impiously T552
**vnsauery**, *adj.* offensive 1804
**vnschamefast**, *adj.* shameless 125, 688
**vnsufficient**, *adj.* insufficient T526
**vnsuffrable**, *adj.* intolerable T581
**vntruþe**, *sb.* falseness 479
**vntrwe**, *adj.* false 184
**vnþankful**, *adj.* unpleasing 877
**vnwarned**, *pa. p. adj.* unexpected 109
**vnwarned**, *adv.* unexpectedly 135, 475
**vnwemmid**, *pa. p. adj.* immaculate 983
**vnwitnessid**, *v. pa. p.* without a witness 776
**vp**, *prep.* upon 2102; **up hap** perhaps T721
**vplondish**, *adj.* rustic, remote T300, T309
**vpstiinge**, *sb.* ascension 270
**vse(n**, *v.* practise T678, 240, 586 etc.; ~ *for to constreynen* habitually force 383; *I ~ not to speke* I am not in the habit of speaking 953; ~ *to senden* habitually send 1086; ~ *to seien* habitually say 1788
**vtmest**, *superl. adj. as sb. vnto þe* ~ completely 2195
**vttirli**, *adv.* completely T116, 491, 1050 etc.
**vtward**, *adj.* external 1148

**veniaunce**, *sb.* vengeance T420, 13, 1587
**veri, verry**, *adj.* truthful, true T48, T137, 695 etc.
**very**, *adv.* truly 1605
**verified**, *v. pa. p.* proved true T725
**verili, verrili**, *adv.* truly 301, 679, 1612 etc.
**vertues**, *adj.* virtuous 96, 130, 455 etc.
**viker**, *sb.* vicar, deputy T388, T404
**vikery**, *sb.* benefice held by a vicar T398 (*see note*)
**vilþe**, *sb.* filth 67, 69
**vitaylis**, *sb. pl.* food T298, T300, T482 etc.
**voyde**, *v.* avoid 1717, clear away 1917
**vomed**, *v. pa. p.* ~ *out* cast out 550

**waden**, *v. pl. pres. ind.* wade about (i.e. get out of their depth) 1034
**waken**, *v. pl. pres. ind.* watch T24, 808, 810
**wandrynge**, *v. pres. p.* progressing 910
**wanten**, *v. pl. pres. ind.* lack H26
**wantyng**, *sb.* lack T461
**war**, *adj.* watchful T135, T345
**warde**, *sb.* safekeeping 186
**weeneþ**, *v. 3sg. pres. ind.* (**weenen** *pl. pres. ind.*, **wenynge** *pres. p.*) think T388, T674, T700

**weilen**, *v. pl. pres. ind.* (**weileden** *pl. pa. ind.*) lament T207, 1274
**wel**, *adv.* very T20
**welde**, *v.* possess 150, 1428
**wem**, *sb.* blemish 213
**werk**, *sb.* act 1256
**werne**, *v.* deny T746
**werst**, *superl. adj.* worst 1583
**weten** *see* **wite**
**wexe**, *v.* (**wexide** *3sg. pa. ind.*, **woxun** *pa. p.*) grow T157, T172, T684
**whan(ne**, *cj.* when T13, T46, 19 etc.
**wher, wheþir**, *cj.* whether, *interrogative cj. introducing a question* T214, T399, 979 etc.
**where aboute**, *rel.* ~ *þou art* what you are up to 1020
**wilful**, *adj.* voluntary T224, T672, 131 etc.
**wilful**, *adv.* voluntarily 246
**wilful(l)i**, *adv.* voluntarily 62, 76, 79 etc.
**wilis**, *sb. pl.* tricks T374
**wille**, *sb. of* ~ in disposition (Vulg. *ex animo*) T122
**willid**, *pa. p. adj.* disposed T229
**willynge**, *v. pres. p.* desiring T424
**wilneþ**, *v. 3sg. pres. ind.* (**willnynge**, *pres. p.*) desire 290, 469
**wise**, *sb.* manner, fashion T1, T117, 25 etc.
**wit**, *prep. see* **wiþ**
**wite**, *v.* (**wot(e, woot** *1 & 3sg. pres. ind.*, **witen, weten** *pl. pres. ind.*, **wite**, *1sg. pres. sj.*, **witiþ**, *imp. pl.*, **wiste(n** *pa. ind.*) know T72, T87, 584 etc.; learn 1703
**wiþ, wit**, *prep.* with 1985, in regard to T511
**wiþstonde**, *v. pa. p.* frustrated 185
**wiþ þat**, *cj.* lest 1251
**wiþ þat**, *prep. phrase* besides, as well as that T466
**witingli**, *adv.* knowingly T414, 1251, 1399
**witt**, *sb.* intelligence 1917, meaning 1707, method of comprehension T695; *pl.* mental faculties T744, 36, 43 etc., senses 1148
**wlatiþ**, *v. 3sg. pres. ind.* ~ *on* is disgusted by T320
**wol(e**, *v. 1 & 3sg. pres. ind.* (**wolt** *2sg. pres. ind.*, **wol(l)e(n** *pl. pres. ind.*, **wold(e(n** *pa. ind.*) wish T481, will 50, 64 etc.
**wondir**, *sb.* surprise 542
**wondrid**, *v. pa. p.* thought strange 693
**wone**, *sb.* habit T196
**worche(n**, *v.* act 777, 1045, 1376, perform 1202, 1256
**worchinge**, *sb.* action 1076, 1134, acting 802
**worþ**, *v. 3sg. pres. sj. wo* ~ may evil befall 535
**write**, *v.* (**iwriten** *pa. p.*) write 1407
**wrooþ**, *adj.* angry T66, T70, 617 etc.

# INDEX OF PROPER NAMES

Coverage and abbreviations are those used in the Glossary. The index includes those names found in the two main texts and in the Sermon of the Horsedoun. It does not include the author names of biblical books, nor the recipients of New Testament epistles; this information can be found in the scriptural index. The names are indexed under the form(s) found in the texts, and modern equivalents are only given in cases of obscurity in medieval spelling. The notes to the texts provide further information about some of the people and places named, and these are indicated by *n.* following the line number.

# INDEX OF BIBLICAL QUOTATIONS

Coverage and abbreviations are those found in the Glossary. The index includes those found in the two main texts and in the Sermon of the Horsedoun.

# BIBLIOGRAPHY

Abbreviations are explained in the list on pp. viii–x. The spelling of manuscript or edition of primary sources is retained, but modern punctuation and capitalization has been supplied (and sometimes modified in the case of older editions). References to patristic texts, for the sake of simplicity, are given to the PL and PG volumes unless the text here requires scrutiny of more recent editions.

## 1. PRIMARY UNPRINTED SOURCES

### *a. Manuscripts*

Foliation or pagination, as used in the manuscript, is followed, and supplied where absent, but not corrected when wrong; numbers without indication are recto. The following list indicates only the content of the manuscript that has been used here.


Brno, University Library Mk 28: *Opus Arduum* (Wycliffite Latin commentary on the Apocalypse)

Cambridge, Trinity College O.1.29: English anthology, some texts Wycliffite

Cambridge, University Library Ii.6.26: English texts on biblical translation

Cambridge, Mass., Harvard University Library Eng.738: English Wycliffite tract on the ten commandments

Dublin, Trinity College 245: English Wycliffite tracts

Trinity College 775: transcripts by Archbishop Ussher

London, British Library Additional 24202: English Wycliffite tracts

Cotton Titus D.i: *Thirty-Seven Conclusions*

Cotton Titus D.v: English Wycliffite tract

Egerton 2820: English Wycliffite tract

Harley 1203: two English Wycliffite texts

Harley 2398: English anthology, some texts Wycliffite

Royal 18 C.xxvi: Wycliffite revision of Rolle's English Psalter commentary

London, Lambeth Palace 34: Wycliffite revision of Rolle's English Psalter commentary

Oxford, Bodleian Library,

Bodley 288: Wycliffite revision of Rolle's English Psalter commentary

Bodley 647: English Wycliffite material

Bodley 806: English sermons, of Wycliffite colouring

Bodley 877: Wycliffite revision of Rolle's English Psalter commentary

Douce 53: Taylor's sermon and *Sermoun of þe Horsedoun*

Laud misc.200: Latin Wycliffite sermons
Rawlinson C.208: Thorpe's testimony
Prague, Metropolitan Chapter Library D.49: Hussite miscellany
Metropolitan Chapter Library O.29: miscellany, including Latin version of Thorpe's testimony
Vienna, Österreichische Nationalbibliothek 3936: miscellany, including Latin version of Thorpe's testimony

*b. Episcopal Registers*

With the two exceptions noted below, all material is cited from manuscripts in the form diocese (or for Canterbury, Lambeth), bishop's name, folio, page or opening). A full guide to the registers is to be found in:

D. M. Smith, *Guide to Bishops' Register of England and Wales* (London, 1981).

The two registers most frequently cited have been printed:

*The Register of Henry Chichele*, ed. E. F. Jacob (4 vols., CYS and Oxford, 1938–47).
*Registrum Johannis Trefnant*, ed. W. W. Capes (CYS, 1916).

## 2. PRIMARY PRINTED SOURCES

References are by line in the case of verse, by page, column or item number, followed (where given) by line number after an oblique stroke (ignoring all headings). Only opening line numbers are usually given.

*An Apology for Lollard Doctrines*, ed. J. H. Todd (CS, 1842).
Arnold, T. (ed.), *Select English Works of John Wyclif* (3 vols., Oxford, 1869–71).
Bale, John, *Illustrium maioris Britanniae Scriptorum ... Summarium* (Ipswich, 1548).
Bale, John, *Scriptorum Illustrium maioris Brytannie ... Catalogus* (2 vols., Basel, 1557–9).
*The Holy Bible ... made from the Latin Vulgate by John Wycliffe and his Followers*, ed. J. Forshall and F. Madden (4 vols., Oxford, 1850; repr. New York, 1982).
Bonaventura, *Opera Omnia*, ed. Collegium Sanctae Bonaventurae (Rome, 1882–1902).
Brown, E., *Fasciculus Rerum Expetendarum* (2 vols., London, 1690).
*Calendar of Close Rolls* (London, 1902– ).
*Calendar of Entries in the Papal Registers relating to Great Britain and Ireland: Papal Letters* (London, 1893– ).
*Calendar of Patent Rolls* (London, 1901– ).

*The Riverside Chaucer*, ed. L. D. Benson *et al.* (Boston, 1987).

*Dives and Pauper*, ed. P. H. Barnum (2 vols., EETS 275, 280, 1976–80)—cited by commandment and chapter number.

Dymmok, Roger, *Liber contra duodecim errores et hereses Lollardorum*, ed. H. S. Cronin (Wyclif Society, London, 1922).

*English Wycliffite Sermons*, ed. A. Hudson and P. Gradon (3 vols. continuing, Oxford, 1983– )—sermons cited by number in continuous sequence.

*Fasciculi Zizaniorum*, ed. W. W. Shirley (RS 1858).

*The Acts and Monuments of John Foxe*, ed. S. R. Cattley and J. Pratt (8 vols. in 16, London, 1853–70)—cited save where details require the use of the 1563 and 1570 editions.

John of Friburg, *Summa Confessorum* (Nuremburg, 1517).

Friedberg, E. (ed.), *Corpus Iuris Canonici* (2 vols., Leipzig, 1879–81; repr. Graz, 1959).

*The Complete Works of John Gower*, ed. G. C. Macaulay (4 vols., Oxford, 1899–1902; vols. 2–3 were also issued as EETS ES 81–2, 1900–1).

'Nicholas Hereford's Ascension Day Sermon, 1382', ed. S. Forde, *Medieval Studies* 51 (1989), 205–41.

*Jack Upland, Friar Daw's Reply and Upland's Rejoinder*, ed. P. L. Heyworth (London, 1968).

Langland, William, *Piers the Plowman and Richard the Redeless*, ed. W. W. Skeat (2 vols., London, 1886).

Langland *Piers Plowman: the Prologue and Passus I-VII of the B Text*, ed. J. A. W. Bennett (Oxford, 1972).

*The Lanterne of Liȝt*, ed. L. M. Swinburn (EETS 151, 1917).

*Lollard Sermons*, ed. G. Cigman (EETS 294, 1989)—from BL MS Additional 41321, Bodleian Library MS Rawlinson C.751 and John Rylands Library MS Eng 412.

*John Lydford's Book*, ed. D. M. Owen (Devon and Cornwall Record Society 19, Historical Manuscripts Commission Joint Publications 22, 1974).

Matthew, F. D. (ed.), *The English Works of Wyclif hitherto unprinted* (EETS 74, 1880, revd. edn., 1902).

*The Complete Works of St Thomas More*, ed. L. L. Martz, R. S. Sylvester, C. H. Miller *et al.* (New Haven and London, 1963– ).

*Mum and the Sothsegger*, ed. M. Day and R. Steele (EETS 199, 1936).

Netter of Walden, Thomas, *Doctrinale Antiquitatum Fidei Catholicae Ecclesiae*, ed. B. Blanciotti (3 vols., Venice, 1757–9; repr. Farnborough, 1967)—quoted by book and chapter number, followed in brackets by volume and column number.

*Heresy Trials in the Diocese of Norwich, 1428–31*, ed. N. P. Tanner (CS 4th series 20, 1977).

Pecock, Reginald, *The Repressor of over much blaming of the Clergy*, ed. C. Babington (2 vols., RS 1860).

Peraldus, William, *Summae Virtutum ac Vitiorum* (2 vols., Paris, 1668–9).

*Pierce the Ploughman's Crede*, ed. W. W. Skeat (EETS 30, 1867).

*Piers Plowman* see Langland.

*Political Poems and Songs . . . from the Accession of Edward III to that of Richard III*, ed. T. Wright (2 vols., RS, 1859–61).

Pollard, A. W. (ed.), *Fifteenth-Century Prose and Verse* (Westminster, 1903).

*Polychronicon Ranulphi Higden Monachi Cestrensis*, ed. C. Babington and J. R. Lumby (9 vols., RS, 1865–86).

*Praier and complaynte of the ploweman*, in *Harleian Miscellany* (8 vols., London, 1744–6), vi.84–106.

Robbins, R. H. (ed.), *Historical Poems of the XIVth and XVth Centuries* (New York, 1959).

*Rosarium Theologie* see von Nolcken.

Ross, W. O. (ed.), *Middle English Sermons* (EETS 209, 1940).

*Rotuli Parliamentorum* (7 vols., London, 1832).

*St Albans Chronicle* see Walsingham.

*The Sarum Missal*, ed. J. Wickham Legg (Oxford, 1916).

*Selections from English Wycliffite Writings*, ed. A. Hudson (Cambridge, 1978).

*Snappe's Formulary and other Records*, ed. H. E. Salter (Oxford Historical Society 80, 1924).

Stow, John, *A Survey of London*, ed. C. L. Kingsford (2 vols., Oxford, 1908).

Strype, John, *Ecclesiastical Memorials . . . under King Henry VIII, King of England, King Edward VI and Queen Mary I* (2 vols., Oxford, repr. 1822).

Tanner, see *Norwich*.

[*Thirty-Seven Conclusions of the Lollards* =] *Remonstrance against Romish Corruptions*, ed. J. Forshall (London, 1851)—text quoted from BL Cotton Titus D.i but with page references to Forshall's edition.

Trevisa, *Dialogus inter Militem et Clericum, Sermon by FitzRalph and þe Bygynnyng of þe World*, ed. A. J. Perry (EETS 167, 1925).

Usk, Adam of, *Chronicon . . . 1377–1421*, ed. E. M. Thompson (2nd ed. London, 1904).

von Nolcken, C. (ed.), *The Middle English Translation of the 'Rosarium Theologie'* (Heidelberg Middle English Texts 10, 1979).

Walsingham, Thomas, *Chronicon Anglie*, ed. E. M. Thompson (RS, 1874).

Walsingham, Thomas, *Historia Anglicana*, ed. H. T. Riley (2 vols., RS, 1863–4).

Walsingham, Thomas, *St Alban's Chronicle 1406–1420*, ed. V. H. Galbraith (Oxford, 1937).

Wickham Legg, see *Sarum Missal*.

Wilkins, D. (ed.), *Concilia Magnae Britanniae et Hiberniae* (4 vols., London, 1737).

*Three Middle English Sermons from the Worcester Chapter Manuscript F.10*, ed. D. M. Grisdale (Leeds Texts and Monographs 5, 1939).

'The Trial of Richard Wyche', ed. F. D. Matthew, *EHR* 5 (1890), 530–44.

Wyclif, John, *Latin Works*: all those used here were edited for the Wyclif Society between 1883 and 1921.

## 3. SECONDARY SOURCES

The normal form of reference to printed secondary materials is by author's surname, followed in brackets by date of publication, and usually by page numbers. Where an author issued more than one publication in the same year, superior numbers follow the date in brackets. In a number of cases several articles by the same author have been reprinted in a single volume; references are to the pagination of that reprint volume, but the date given is that of the article's original publication; details of original places of publication are given here following those of the collection.

Alford, J. A., *'Piers Plowman': A Glossary of Legal Diction* (Woodbridge, 1988).

Aston, M., *Thomas Arundel: A Study of Church Life in the Reign of Richard II* (Oxford, 1967).

Aston, M., *Lollards and Reformers: Images and Literacy in Late Medieval Religion* (London, 1984[1])—including, together with two new papers, the following reprinted papers used here: 'Lollardy and Literacy', *History* 62 (1977), 347–71; 'Lollardy and the Reformation: Survival or Revival?', *History* 49 (1964), 149–70; 'John Wycliffe's Reformation Reputation', *PP* 30 (1965), 23–51.

Aston, M., '"Caims's Castles": Poverty, Politics, and Disendowment', in *The Church, Politics and Patronage in the Fifteenth Century*, ed. R. B. Dobson (Gloucester, 1984[2]), pp. 45–81.

Aston, M., 'Wyclif and the Vernacular', *SCH* Subsidia 5 (1987), 281–330.

Aston, M., *England's Iconoclasts: I. Laws against Images* (Oxford, 1988).

Brigden, S., *London and the Reformation* (Oxford, 1989).

Crompton, J., '*Fasciculi Zizaniorum*', *JEH* 12 (1961), 35–45, 155–66.

Crompton, J., 'Leicestershire Lollards', *Transactions of the Leicestershire Archaeological and Historical Society* 44 (1968–9), 11–44.

Davies, R. G., 'Thomas Arundel as Archbishop of Canterbury, 1396–1414', *JEH* 24 (1973), 9–21.

Emden, A. B., *An Oxford Hall in Medieval Times* (Oxford, 1927, revd. edn. 1968).

Emden, A. B., *A Biographical Register of the University of Oxford to A.D. 1500* (3 vols., Oxford, 1957–9).

Emden, A. B., *A Biographical Register of the University of Cambridge to 1500* (Cambridge, 1963).

Fairfield, L. P., 'John Bale and the Development of Protestant Hagiography', *JEH* 24 (1973), 145–60.

Fairfield, L. P., *John Bale, Mythmaker for the English Reformation* (West Lafayette, 1976).

Gradon, P. 'Langland and the Ideology of Dissent', *Proceedings of the British Academy* 66 (1980), 179–205.

Hudson, A., *Lollards and their Books* (London, 1985[1])—includes the following reprinted papers cited here: 'A Neglected Wycliffite Text', *JEH* 29 (1978),

257–79; 'John Purvey: A Reconsideration of the Evidence for his Life and Writings', *Viator* 12 (1981), 355–80; 'The Examination of Lollards', *BIHR* 46 (1973), 145–59; 'Lollardy: the English Heresy?', *SCH* 18 (1982), 355–80.

Hudson, A., 'A Wycliffite Scholar of the Early Fifteenth Century', *SCH* Subsidia 4 (1985[2]), 301–15.

Hudson, A., 'Wycliffism in Oxford 1381–1411', in *Wyclif in his Times*, ed. A. Kenny (Oxford, 1986), pp. 67–84.

Hudson, A., *The Premature Reformation: Wycliffite Texts and Lollard History* (Oxford, 1988).

Hughes, J., *Pastors and Visionaries: Religion and Secular Life in Late Medieval Yorkshire* (Woodbridge, 1988).

Jacob, E. F., *The Fifteenth Century* (Oxford, 1961).

Kightly, C., 'The Early Lollards: A Survey of Popular Lollard Activity in England, 1382–1428' (unpubd. D. Phil. thesis, York, 1975).

Knowles, D., and Hadcock, R. N., *Medieval Religious Houses: England and Wales* (London, 1971).

Leff, G., *Heresy in the Later Middle Ages* (2 vols., Manchester, 1967).

McFarlane, K. B., *John Wycliffe and the Beginnings of English Nonconformity* (London, 1952).

McFarlane, K. B., *Lancastrian Kings and Lollard Knights* (Oxford, 1972).

McNiven, P., *Heresy and Politics in the Reign of Henry IV* (Woodbridge, 1987).

Mozley, J. F., *William Tyndale* (London, 1937).

Mozley, J. F., *John Foxe and his Book* (London, 1940).

Owst, G. R., *Preaching in Medieval England* (Cambridge, 1926).

Richardson, H. G., 'Heresy and the Lay Power under Richard II', *EHR* 51 (1936), 1–28.

Russell-Smith, J., 'Walter Hilton and a Tract in Defence of the Veneration of Images', *Dominican Studies* 7 (1954), 180–214.

Scase, W., *'Piers Plowman' and the New Anticlericalism* (Cambridge, 1989).

Snape, M. G., 'Some Evidence of Lollard Activity in the Diocese of Durham in the early fifteenth century', *Archaeologia Aeliana* 4th series 39 (1961), 355–61.

Szittya, P. R., *The Antifraternal Tradition in Medieval Literature* (Princeton, 1986).

Thomson, J. A. F., *The Later Lollards 1414–1520* (London, 1965).

Thomson, W. R., *The Latin Writings of John Wyclyf* (Toronto, 1983).

von Nolcken, C., 'Another Kind of Saint: A Lollard Perception of John Wyclif', *SCH Subsidia* 5 (1987), 429–43.

Walsh, K., *A Fourteenth-Century Scholar and Primate: Richard FitzRalph in Oxford, Avignon, and Armagh* (Oxford, 1981).

Whiting, B. J. and H. W., *Proverbs, Sentences and Proverbial Phrases . . . before 1500* (Cambridge Mass. and London, 1968).

Workman, H. B., *John Wyclif: a Study of the English Medieval Church* (2 vols., Oxford, 1926).